ARMS CONTROL AND DISARMAMENT AGREEMENTS

Typology of Agreements, p. xlvi

Notes, pp. xlvii-xlix

LS has 1990 ed.

1984

ARMS CONTROL AND DISARMAMENT AGREEMENTS

United States Arms Control and Disarmament Agency

With a New Introduction by
Dan Caldwell

Transaction Books
New Brunswick (U.S.A.) and London (U.K.)

New material this edition copyright © 1984 by Transaction, Inc., New Brunswick, New Jersey 08903.

Previous editions published by the United States Arms Control and Disarmament Agency, 1972, 1975, 1977, 1980, 1982.

Library of Congress Catalog Number: 83-18269
ISBN: 0-87855-948-5 (paper)
Printed in the United States of America

Library of Congress Cataloging in Publication Data
Main entry under title:

Arms control and disarmament agreements.

   Reprint. Originally published: 1982 ed.
Washington, D.C.: U.S. Arms Control and Disarmament Agency, 1982.
   Includes bibliography references.
   1. Atomic weapons and disarmament. 2. Arms control.
I. United States. Arms Control and Disarmament Agency.
[JX1974.7.A6724 1984]   341.7'33'0265   83-18269
ISBN 0-87855-948-5 (pbk.)

Contents

LATIN AMERICAN NUCLEAR-FREE ZONE TREATY 2/14/67
Treaty for the Prohibition of Nuclear Weapons in Latin America

NON-PROLIFERATION TREATY 7/1/68
(NPT) Treaty on the Non-Proliferation of Nuclear Weapons

SEABED ARMS CONTROL TREATY 2/11/71
Treaty on the Prohibition of the Emplacement of Nuclear
Weapons and Other Weapons of Mass Destruction on the
Seabed and the Ocean Floor and in the Subsoil Thereof

"ACCIDENTS MEASURES" AGREEMENT 9/30/71
Agreement on Measures To Reduce the Risk of Outbreak of
Nuclear War Between the United States of America and the
Union of Soviet Socialist Republics

"HOT LINE" MODERNIZATION AGREEMENT 9/30/71
Agreement Between the United States of America and the
Union of Soviet Socialist Republics on Measures To Improve
the USA-USSR Direct Communication Link (With Annex,
Supplementing and Modifying the Memorandum of
Understanding With Annex, of June 20, 1963)

CONTENTS

BIOLOGICAL WEAPONS CONVENTION 4/10/72
Convention on the Prohibition of the Development, Production
and Stockpiling of Bacteriological (Biological) and Toxin
Weapons and on Their Destruction

STRATEGIC ARMS LIMITATION TALKS (SALT I)

ABM TREATY 5/26/72
Treaty Between the United States of America and the Union
of Soviet Socialist Republics on the Limitation of Anti-
Ballistic Missile Systems

INTERIM AGREEMENT 5/26/72
Interim Agreement Between the United States of America
and the Union of Soviet Socialist Republics on Certain
Measures With Respect to the Limitation of Strategic
Offensive Arms

PREVENTION OF NUCLEAR WAR AGREEMENT 6/22/73
Agreement Between the United States of America and the
Union of Soviet Socialist Republics on the Prevention of
Nuclear War

CONTENTS

STRATEGIC ARMS LIMITATION TALKS (SALT II)

Treaty Between the United States of America and the Union of
Soviet Socialist Republics on the Limitation of Strategic
Offensive Arms   6/18/79

NUCLEAR MATERIAL CONVENTION   3/3/80
Convention on the Physical Protection of Nuclear Material

Introduction to the Transaction Edition

Dan Caldwell

A new weapon had been invented that many believed threatened to destroy the world.[1] There was great concern that Armageddon was rapidly approaching; so much concern, in fact, that the pope called an international conference to discuss the possible means of controlling the awesome new weapon. This new threat to the world was not a nuclear weapon, nerve gas, anthrax, or the charged-particle beam — it was the crossbow. The papal conference was called by Pope Innocent II in 1139.

Invariably, this example brings a smile to peoples' faces when they encounter it for the first time. How could people be so naive to believe that a weapon as unsophisticated as the crossbow could threaten massive destruction? The crossbow was, of course, a marked technological improvement over the long bow and was capable of inflicting many more casualties per unit of time. Indeed, it would theoretically be possible for millions of people to die from the arrows of crossbows; of course, such a slaughter would require years and years.

Today the death of millions and the destruction of society as we know it would require only 30 minutes — the flight time for an intercontinental ballistic missile between the United States and the Soviet Union. It is the relatively short period of time in which death and destruction can be wrought that distinguishes the nuclear era from those that preceded it.

But the contemporary concern over weapons is not a new phenomenon; people have been concerned about war and the threat of its destructive potential for centuries. The Old Testament prophets hoped for the day when swords would be beaten into ploughshares. In this essay, I first examine the ways in which twentieth-century statesmen have sought to control and limit weapons through internationally negotiated, formal agreements. So that the reader of these agreements may gain a better understanding of the substance and process of arms control and disarmament, I next briefly describe the historical setting of the agreements. Finally, I present a typology of the agreements in this volume, so that the similarities and differences between the agreements become clearer.

Although the terms *arms control* and *disarmament* are often used synonymously, this is not the case. Arms control refers to the limitation of numbers and/or quality of certain types of weapons. Disarmament refers to the eradication of certain types or even all weapons. Thus, disarmament is a far more comprehensive goal than the objective of arms control. In an essay on the objectives of arms control, Thomas Schelling and Morton Halperin identified three goals: (1) reducing the risk of war, (2) reducing destructiveness should war occur, and (3) reducing the cost of providing for military defense. In this essay, I will review attempts to achieve both arms control and disarmament. The reader should keep in mind the difference between these two endeavors.

Although there were several exceptions (the Napoleonic Wars and the Civil War), by and large the wars conducted prior to the twentieth century were limited in both their scope and methods employed. Statesmen during this period favored limitations to preserve the existing international order. Casualties in the wars of the eighteenth and nineteenth centuries were counted in the thousands rather than the millions. When World War I broke out, most expected a short-lived, small conflict. What occurred, however, was a prolonged, bloody affair costing the lives of more than 10 million people.

There have been four revolutions in warfare during this century. The improved technologies including machine guns, tanks, submarines, and poison gas used in World War I marked the first revolution. The losses inflicted by these new weapons during the war were staggering. During 1915 alone, the French suffered 1.4 million casualties. At the battle of Verdun during 10 months in 1916, Germany lost 336,000 men.[2]

Following the end of World War I, there was great public pressure to create institutions and international agreements that would make a repetition of the war impossible. The League of Nations was a new organization for managing power in international relations. It was hamstrung from the start, however, by the unwillingness of the United States to join.

In 1921, the United States took the initiative to convene a conference in Washington, D.C., to discuss possible limitations on naval armaments. Secretary of State Charles Evans Hughes made a dramatic proposal to reduce the U.S. battleship fleet as well as those of the other major powers. Within a matter of months, the negotiators reached an agreement to stop construction of capital ships (i.e. battleships and heavy cruisers), to place a freeze on the building of naval fortifications and bases in the Pacific, and to limit their total capital ship tonnage to the following limits: for the United States and Great Britain, 500,000 tons each; for Japan, 300,000 tons; and for France and Italy, 175,000 tons each. This agreement required that the signatories actually reduce their capital ships, and a total of 68 capital ships were scrapped. A second naval arms-control conference was held in London in 1930 that resulted in several minor controls to other categories of ships. In 1934, Japan announced its intention to withdraw from the 1922 treaty and within several years all of the major powers had embarked upon substantial naval construction programs.

The Washington Naval Treaty was probably the most significant attempt to control major weapons prior to the Strategic Arms Limitation Agreements of 1972. Indeed, several analysts have compared the two negotiations.[3] The Washington Naval Treaty limited the growth of capital ships in the naval arsenals of the major powers for over a decade and in that sense was a success. But several classes of ships were not controlled by the treaty, including submarines and aircraft carriers. These loopholes contributed to the demise of the treaty. but the fundamental cause of the failure of the treaty was due to the accession to power by expansionist-oriented, fascist governments in Germany, Italy, and Japan.

There are several valuable lessons to be learned from the Washington Naval Treaty. First, arms-control is a reflection of overall political relations rather than a cause of international peace. Second, diplomacy must keep pace with the development of new weapons or past diplomatic accomplishments will be nullified by technologial advancement. Third, each party to an arms-control agreement must feel that it has a stake in the agreement, otherwise it will abrogate the agreement as Japan did.

There were several other attempts during the period between World Wars I and II to achieve arms control and disarmament. The United States introduced a protocol in 1925 to prohibit the use of poison gas and bacteriological weapons. Although the Geneva Protocol was signed by the United States in 1925, it was not ratified until 1975. (For the history and text of this agreement, see pages 9-18.) In 1928, the Kellogg-Briand Pact, in which the signatories renounced the use of aggressive war, was signed. The agreement made no provision for sanctions. After World War II, the Kellogg-Briand Pact was the basis on which former Nazis were tried by the United States at Nuremberg.

An international disarmament conference was held under the sponsorship of the League of Nations in 1932. By this time, however, there was no consensus among the great-power states as to what weapons should be limited. Consequently, no agreement was reached. In January 1933, Adolf Hitler became chancellor of Germany. Soon after coming to power, Hitler ordered the withdrawal of Germany from the disarmament conference and the League of Nations. Two years later, Hitler announced that Germany would no longer abide by the clauses of the Versailles Treaty that prohibited Germany from rearming. A second London Naval Conference was held in 1935, but the interest in limiting naval weapons had significantly decreased as a result of Japan's abrogation of the 1922 Washington Naval Treaty in 1934. By the late 1930s, Germany, Italy, Japan, the United States, and Great Britain had all embarked on significant military construction programs. And on September 1, 1939, Germany attacked Poland thereby initiating World War II.

Statesmen during the interwar years failed in their attempts to outlaw war and achieve disarmament. They did achieve some success, however, in limiting the strategic weapons of that day, capital ships, for a 10-year period. In addition, they negotiated a ban on the use of poison gas and biological weapons. Significantly, Italy's use of poison gas in its attack on Ethiopia in 1935-36 was the only use of poison gas following the signing of the Geneva Convention. The arms-control agreements of the interwar period proved to be inadequate restraints on the power of the xenophobic ideologies that developed in the 1930s.

World War II catalyzed the second and third revolutions in warfare during the twentieth century. Shortly before and during the course of the war, the warring states developed large air forces, aircraft carriers, the strategic bombing of civilian targets, and Germany pioneered the use of rockets in warfare. These technological developments coupled with the intensity with which World War II was fought made it even more costly than the first World War; an estimated 50 million people were killed from September 1939 through August 1945.

The explosion of the atomic bombs on Hiroshima and Nagasaki marked the third revolution in warfare during the twentieth century. These bombs literally ended the war and marked the beginning of a new period of history: the nuclear era. Few people, even the scientists who had invented the atomic bombs, knew what the implications of the new weapons were. However, in 1946 a group of professors from Princeton published a book on the impact of the new weapons on world politics. One of the contributors to the volume pointed out, "To speak of it [the atomic bomb] as just another weapon was highly misleading. It was a revolutionary development which altered the basic character of war itself."[4]

In a fundamental sense, the debate over nuclear weapons since their initial use in 1945 has been over the question of whether they have, in fact, "altered the basic character of war itself," or whether they are simply more destructive variants of the weapons that have preceded them. Proponents of the latter view point out that more people were killed in the fire bombing raids on Dresden and Tokyo than were killed in Hiroshima and Nagasaki. This view underrates the much greater power of nuclear weapons today, however. If the United States or the Soviet Union were to use only one percent of the nuclear weapons in their arsenals, the resulting deaths and destruction would far exceed that of any previous international conflict. The third revolution in warfare during this century — the nuclear revolution — therefore marked a change quantitatively and qualitatively different from any that had preceded it.

Both the United States and the Soviet Union presented proposals at the United Nations in 1946 to attempt to put "the nuclear genie" back in its bottle. The U.S. representative to the United Nations, Bernard Baruch, presented the American plan to the U.N. Atomic Energy Commission in June 1946. The Baruch Plan called for the cessation of the manufacture of nuclear bombs, the disposal of existing U.S. bombs, and the creation of an international agency that would be given all information concerning the production of nuclear energy. This proposal would not be implemented, however, until both a means of verification and a system of sanctions for violators were agreed upon.

The Soviet Union responded with a proposal of its own, the Gromyko Plan, which called for two treaties. The first would prohibit the manufacture and use of nuclear weapons and would require the destruction of all stockpiled atomic weapons within three months of the entry into force of the treaty. The second treaty, which was to be negotiated within six months from the conclusion of the first, would establish sanctions for violators of the agreement. These sanctions would be administered by the UN Security Council and would be subject to the veto rights of permanent members.

The Baruch and Gromyko plans failed for two basic reasons: the Soviet Union did not want to foreclose its option of developing nuclear weapons and the United States wanted to have confidence that any agreement would be verifiable. The Soviet Union was unwilling to accept on-site verification within the Soviet Union, which precluded effective verification throughout the late 1940s and the 1950s. This in turn precluded any substantive progress in achieving arms control and disarmament.

In August 1949, the Soviet Union detonated its first nuclear explosion, becoming the second member of the "nuclear club." In January 1952, the UN General Assembly established the UN Disarmament Commission to investigate the possibility of negotiating the control of nuclear and conventional weapons. No real progress was made in this forum and following the death of Joseph Stalin in 1953 and the election of President Dwight D. Eisenhower, in 1954 the United Nations created a new forum, the Subcommittee on Disarmament. From 1954 through 1957, the United States, the Soviet Union, Great Britain, France, and Canada met to discuss a number of substantive proposals. Although these negotiations were significant in some respects, they failed to produce any formal agreements and the Soviet Union withdrew from the talks in 1957.[5]

In August 1957 the Soviet Union tested the first intercontinental ballistic missile (ICBM) and the following October launched the first earth-orbiting satellite, *Sputnik*. At the same time, the United States was also developing similar systems. The development and deployment of the ICBM marked the fourth revolution in modern warfare. Prior to the development of ICBMs, the geographic location of the United States shielded it from attack. The flight time of an ICBM going from the Soviet Union to the United States or vice versa is 30 minutes. Thus, ICBMs made the United States vulnerable to attack as never before in its history. During the 1960 presidential campaign, John F. Kennedy called attention to the "missile gap" that he felt existed between the United States and the Soviet Union, and emphasized the need for the United States to "catch up with" the Soviets. As a result, when he was inaugurated, President Kennedy called for the United States to build up its conventional and nuclear forces.

This was not the result that Nikita Khrushchev had intended. Indeed, through his boasting about Soviet military strength, Khrushchev had hoped to gain political leverage vis-à-vis the United States. By 1961, however, he was faced with an embarrassing situation: a missile gap favoring the United States. President Kennedy and his advisors recognized this fact following the deployment of the first reconnaissance satellite in early 1961.

As of October 1962, the military forces of the United States and Soviet Union were as follows:[6]

	U.S.	U.S.S.R.
ICBM launchers	229	44
SLBM launchers	144	97
Strategic bombers	1,300	155
MR/IRBM launchers	105	750

As one can see from this table, the United States had a significant superiority in the number of strategic intercontinental nuclear weapons (i.e. the first three categories of weapons yielded an advantage of 1,673 to 296), while the Soviet Union had a substantial lead in medium- and intermediate-range ballistic missiles (750 to 105). These MR/IRBMs had been designed and deployed for possible use in a European conflict and could not be used against the United States if deployed in the Soviet Union because of their limited range. However, if deployed in Cuba, they could easily reach most of the continental United States. Thus, by clandestinely deploying MR/ICBMs in Cuba, the Soviet Union could move substantially closer to the achievement of nuclear parity with the United States. The temptation for a "quick fix" of Soviet strategic inferiority was too great to resist, and during the summer of 1962 the Soviet Union began its secret deployment of MR/IRBMs to Cuba.

The United States discovered the Soviet missiles in mid-October. The Kennedy administration felt that the missiles had to be removed. The resulting crisis was the most serious of the post–World War II period. Once the Soviet Union agreed to remove its missiles, the crisis was resolved, but the probability of a Soviet-American war (as estimated by President Kennedy once the crisis was over) had been between one out of three and even.

Following the Cuban missile crisis, Kennedy and Khrushchev moved to lessen the risk of nuclear war by concluding the Hot Line Agreement and the Limited Nuclear Test Ban Treaty in 1963. These agreements, along with the Antarctica Treaty of 1959, were the initial building blocks of the contemporary arms-control regime.

In the following pages, I will briefly describe the contemporary arms-control agreements according to their principal purpose. The typology of arms-control agreements presented here complements the chronological description of the agreements that is presented in the introduction to this volume as well as the narrative sections that precede each of the agreements. Hopefully the presentation that follows will better enable readers to understand the similarities and differences between the agreements contained in this book.

Nuclear-Weapon-Free Areas

In 1957, scientists from around the world cooperated in a number of studies of the earth as a part of the International Geophysical Year. Some of these studies concerned Antarctica, and the scientists involved concluded that Antarctica should be off limits for military deployments. Upon the initiative of the United States, an international conference on Antarctica was called that resulted in a 1959 treaty that prohibited the testing and deployment of conventional and nuclear weapons and the disposal of radioactive waste in Antarctica. In addition, the signatories of the agreement agreed to suspend their territorial claims to Antarctica for a 30-year period. This treaty was the first post–World War II arms-control agreement and set a precedent for prohibiting the deployment of nuclear weapons to certain areas.[7]

Just as the village green was regarded in the past as the common property of the village, outer space and the oceans are similarly regarded today. In an attempt to avoid an arms race in space, the UN General Assembly unanimously adopted a resolution in 1963 urging all states to refrain from deploying nuclear weapons in outer space. This resolution constituted the basis of the Outer Space Treaty that was signed in 1967. The Seabed Arms Control Treaty signed in the same year prohibited the deployment of nuclear weapons and other "weapons of mass destruction" (such as biological weapons) on the seabed. These two agreements are attempts to assure that the global commons of the contemporary era will remain demilitarized. The Outer Space Treaty, however, is threatened by proposals to deploy nuclear weapons in space.

During the Cuban missile crisis, a number of Latin American leaders became concerned that their countries would suffer great harm should war between the United States and the Soviet Union occur. Their fear, of course, was justified. Following the resolution of the crisis, Bolivia, Brazil, Chile, Ecuador, and Mexico announced that they were prepared to renounce the manufacture, storage, deployment, and testing of nuclear weapons on their territory.[8] The UN General Assembly supported this statement and in 1967 the Treaty of Tlatelolco was signed calling for the creation of a nuclear-free zone throughout Latin America. Two "protocols" (or additional agreements) accompany the treaty and are explained fully on pages 61-63.

Nuclear Testing Restrictions

Several events in the 1950s and early 1960s called public attention to atmospheric nuclear testing and its effects on humans and the environment. In 1954, fallout from an American 15-megaton hydrogen bomb test conducted in the South Pacific contaminated a Japanese fishing boat, *The Lucky Dragon*. Indian Prime Minister Nehru and the British Parliament requested that the United States cease testing. Scientists in the 1950s detected an increasing incidence of radioactive isotopes in the bone marrow of children due to the ingestion of these isotopes through milk. If this trend continued, many doctors and scientists believed that the incidence of leukemia and other forms of cancer would increase. Furthermore, many believed that the major source of these isotopes, such as strontium 90, came from nuclear tests conducted in the atmosphere. Consequently, many in the scientific community, as well as ordinary citizens, called for the cessation of nuclear testing in the atmosphere. In the 1956 presidential election, Adlai Stevenson called for a nuclear test ban and within a year the pope, the German Bundestag, and the British Labour party made similar appeals to the United States and the Soviet Union.

The test-ban issue was discussed at the UN Disarmament Subcommittee negotiations, but, as noted previously, these negotiations ended with no agreements being reached. In 1958, the United States and the Soviet Union agreed to conduct a series of meetings of experts to discuss various arms-control issues, including a nuclear test ban. Although there were a number of technical and political differences between the Soviet and American experts, they nevertheless agreed to open negotiations among the three powers that possessed nuclear weapons at that time: the United States, the Soviet Union, and the United Kingdom. Following the opening of these negotiations in Geneva in November 1958, the three negotiating states observed a moratorium on nuclear testing until September 1961 when the Soviet Union tested an enormous weapon with an estimated yield equal to the destructive power of 58 million tons of TNT.

There was great concern over the Soviet decision to resume testing. In addition, France exploded its first nuclear weapon in 1960. Many people feared that as more and more states developed nuclear weapons the problem of atmospheric nuclear pollution would grow increasingly serious. The Cuban missile crisis made clear that nuclear war was not just a hypothetical possibility; it really could happen. Following the crisis, President Kennedy warned in a commencement address at American University in June 1963: "Today should total war ever break out . . . no matter how — our two countries would become the primary targets. . . . All we have built, all we have worked for, would be destroyed in the first 24 hours." Kennedy went on to speak of the need for a new approach in Soviet-American relations, and he proposed a treaty to outlaw nuclear tests. According to Kennedy, "The conclusion of such a treaty . . . would check the arms race in one of its most dangerous areas. . . . It would increase our security — it would decrease the prospects of war."[9]

The Soviets broadcast President Kennedy's speech in its entirety and, in July, Khrushchev indicated that the Soviet Union would be willing to engage in negotiations to limit nuclear testing. During the summer of 1963, American, Soviet, and British representatives met and by August they had drafted and agreed upon the Limited Test Ban Treaty, which prohibited nuclear tests in the atmosphere, outer space, and under water. This treaty was important for three principal reasons. First, at the very least it was a significant "clean air act" that resulted in a substantial reduction of atmospheric nuclear pollution.[10] Second, and more important, the Limited Test Ban Treaty was a first step toward controlling the testing of nuclear weapons. Third, the treaty, along with the "hot line" agreement, constituted the cornerstone of modern arms control.

Despite its value, however, the Limited Test Ban Treaty did not stop nuclear testing. France and the People's Republic of China have continued to test in the atmosphere, and the United States, the Soviet Union, and the United Kingdom have conducted extensive testing underground. Ever since the signing of the Limited Test Ban Treaty (LTBT), world leaders have cited a comprehensive test-ban treaty as their goal. For instance, in the preamble of the LTBT the signatories promise "to achieve the discontinuance of all test explosions of nuclear weapons for all time." And in Article VI of the Nonproliferation Treaty, the signatories promise "to pursue negotiations in good faith on effective measures relating to cessation of the nuclear arms race at an early date."

Every American President since Eisenhower has publicly stated that it was the goal of the United States to conclude a comprehensive test ban treaty (CTBT). Despite this goal, however, progress toward the achievement of a CTBT has been slow and incremental. Three major obstacles have precluded an agreement to date. First, the verification of a CTBT has been a contentious issue ever since it was initially discussed in the mid-1950s. Scientists and statesmen have discussed the requirements for "adequate verification." Some have argued that on-site inspection is required, while others have contended that seismographic devices placed within the countries are capable of providing adequate verification. Second, nuclear weapons developers in both the United States and the Soviet Union have opposed the conclusion of a comprehensive test ban since this would make their jobs more difficult. Third, leaders of the developing states that do not possess nuclear weapons contend that the United States and the Soviet Union have lacked the political will to conclude a CTBT. This criticism of the superpowers was particularly evident at the 1980 review conference of the Nonproliferation Treaty.

Despite the failure to conclude a CTBT, incremental progress in further limiting nuclear testing has been made. In 1974, President Richard Nixon and General Secretary Leonid Brezhnev signed the Threshold Test Ban Treaty (TTBT), which prohibits any nuclear test with a yield greater than 150,000 tons (150 kilotons) of TNT. Although the treaty did not call for on-site inspections, in a protocol to the treaty the United States and the Soviet Union agreed to exchange technical data concerning the geophysical characteristics and the location of test sites. At the time it was signed, the Threshold Test Ban Treaty was criticized by many as having set the threshold (150 kilotons) too high since almost all experts agree that modern seismographic devices could detect an underground explosion of five kilotons or even smaller. The TTBT was not submitted to the Senate for advice and consent to ratification until July 1976.

For years scientists in both the United States and the Soviet Union considered various means of utilizing nuclear explosions for peaceful purposes. For example, Soviet scientists have considered using a series of nuclear explosions to divert the flow of the Irtysh River, which now flows north into the Kara Sea. However, the practical problems of using nuclear explosions for such purposes were made clear by a U.S. government–sponsored research project, Project Ploughshare, and neither the United States nor the Soviet Union has immediate plans to use peaceful nuclear explosions.

Article III of the Threshold Test Ban Treaty stipulated that the provisions of the TTBT do not apply to peaceful nuclear explosions (PNE) and called on the United States and the Soviet Union to negotiate a limit on PNEs. In October 1974, these negotiations opened and resulted in the drafting and signing of the Peaceful Nuclear Explosions Treaty (PNET) in April 1976. The treaty, its accompanying protocol, and agreed statement call for the United States and the Soviet Union to not carry out any peaceful nuclear explosion greater than 150 kilotons (the same threshold called for in the TTBT). The agreement also specifies verification procedures (including certain limited provisions for on-site inspection). In addition, the treaty calls for the establishment of a Joint Consultative Commission (similar to the Standing Consultative Commission established by the Antiballistic Missile Treaty of 1972 discussed below). The purpose of this commission is to consider any questions of compliance or other questions that arise as the agreement is implemented.

The Peaceful Nuclear Explosions Treaty was submitted to the Senate with the TTBT in July 1976; however, to date the Senate has not taken action on either treaty. As a result, the status of both treaties is in question and the joint Consultative Commission has not been established.

During the first half of 1983, the Reagan administration considered charging the Soviet Union with violating the Threshold Test Ban Treaty. Since the United States has not ratified either the TTBT or the PNET, however, there was no established, effective mechanism for dealing with the administration's allegations. Had these two treaties been ratified, the United States would now be in a better position to raise questions and to determine whether or not the Soviet Union has complied with the two treaties limiting nuclear testing.

In addition, it is possible that if these treaties had been ratified, additional progress toward the conclusion of a comprehensive test ban treaty would have been made. In fact, substantial progress toward a CTBT was made in the late 1970s.[11] Following the 1980 presidential election and his inauguration, however, President Reagan decided not to resume the CTBT negotiations.

For the past two decades, the United States, Soviet Union, and a number of other states have sought to limit nuclear testing as a part of the contemporary arms-control regime. One international treaty — the Limited Test Ban Treaty — has been signed by well over 100 nations. The United States and the Soviet Union have negotiated and signed two other agreements — the Threshold Test Ban Treaty and the Peaceful Nuclear Explosions Treaty — but the goal of achieving a comprehensive test ban treaty remains elusive.

Crisis Management and Crisis Prevention

Soon after World War II, it became clear that the United States and the Soviet Union were going to be competitors, rather than collaborators, in the post-1945 international system. However, even during the height of the Cold War, Soviet and American leaders recognized that there were limits to the competition between their two countries. Leaders of both states realized that threats against the homeland of the other power threatened dangerous escalation and, consequently, neither state threatened the homeland of the other. In addition, leaders of both countries avoided direct confrontations between the military forces of the other power. The most serious crises since 1945 were precisely those in which these rules for avoiding crisis escalation were violated. Historians and political scientists generally agree that the three most serious crises were the Berlin crises of 1948 and 1961 and the Cuban missile crisis of 1962.

The United States and the Soviet Union generally communicated by deed rather than by word during the Cold War. Both countries used military forces, deployments, and maneuvers to send signals to the other side. Actions usually do speak louder than words, although they do not always convey as clear a meaning. For instance, during the Cuban missle crisis, a U.S. Air Force plane strayed off course and headed toward the Soviet Union. Soviet leaders could have plausibly interpreted this to be the vanguard of an American attack. Fortunately, Khrushchev recognized the incident for what it was and did not order a retaliatory attack. In his letter to President Kennedy of October 28, 1962, Khrushchev wrote:

> [A dangerous incident] occurred on October 28, when your reconnaissance aircraft invaded the northern area of the Soviet Union, in the area of the Chukotski Peninsula, and flew over our territory. One asks, Mr. President, how should we regard this. What is this — a provocation? Your aircraft violates our frontier, and this happens at a time as troubled as the one through which we are now passing, when everything has been put in battle readiness. For an intruding U.S. aircraft can easily be taken as a bomber with nuclear weapons, and that can push us toward the fatal step.[12]

Following their brush with nuclear war, Kennedy and Khrushchev decided that it would be good for American and Soviet leaders to have a means of communicating with one another quickly, accurately, and secretly. Consequently, the two countries negotiated and signed in June 1963 a "Memorandum of Understanding," which provided that the two states would establish a wire telegraph circuit a well as a radiotelegraph circuit between Moscow and Washington, D.C. The "hot line" was first used during the Arab-Israeli war of June 1967, when Israeli forces mistakenly attacked and sank a U.S. Navy ship, the U.S.S. *Liberty*. President Lyndon Johnson ordered American aircraft to the area to search for survivors and notified Soviet leaders of his action via the hot line so that there would be no misunderstanding.[13] The hot line has been used subsequently during the following crises: the Indo-Pakistani war of December 1971,[14] the Middle East war of October 1973, and following the Soviet invasion of Afghanistan in December 1979.

The hot line proved its worth during the 1960s, and even though it was not used extensively, it provided the means to clarify ambiguous and/or threatening events. But the hot line was vulnerable to accidental interruption as well as to sabotage and direct attack. Six incidents during the mid-1960s made this vulnerability clear. In 1964, a thief cut out a 20-foot section of the cable near Helsinki. In the same year, the communications link was put out of operation when a power station was damaged by a thunderstorm in southern Finland. In 1965, a fire in Rosedale, Maryland, cut the circuit, and later the same year a farmer in Finland ploughed through the cable. In 1966, a Finnish postal strike made the circuit inoperable for several hours, and several months later a Soviet freighter in Denmark severed the cable when it ran aground.[15] In these cases the United States and the Soviet Union could still communicate via the radio backup channel; nevertheless, these incidents underscored the need for a less vulnerable communications systems.

On September 30, 1971, the United States and the Soviet Union agreed to update the hot line with a satellite communications system consisting of two independent channels: one American, one Soviet. This system became operational in January 1978. The wire telegraph circuit was retained as the backup to the satellite circuit. Even with the new satellite link and the telegraph backup, however, it is a disturbing fact that the hot line is extremely vulnerable in the event of a nuclear exchange. Former Secretary of Defense Donald Rumsfeld noted in 1977 that "the system is not designed to survive a direct attack."[16] But this is precisely the time that a means of direct communication would most be needed.

Soviet and American leaders recognized the need to develop procedures to lessen the probability of accidental nuclear war. At the same time that the Hot Line Modernization Agreement was signed, the Accidents Measures Agreement was also signed. This agreement called for the United States and the Soviet Union to notify each other (1) immediately in the event of an accidental, unauthorized, or any other unexplained incident involving a possible detonation of a nuclear weapon which could create a risk of outbreak of nuclear war, (2) in the event of detection of unidentified objects, and (3) in the event of a planned missile launch beyond the territory of the launching party in the direction of the other party. The agreement calls for notification via the hot line. While this agreement did not call for the reduction of the arsenals of the United States or the Soviet Union, it provides an important means of building confidence, increasing crisis stability, and thereby decreasing the danger of crisis escalation.

At the 1972 Moscow summit meeting, President Nixon and General Secretary Brezhnev signed a number of agreements, the most impor-

tant of which were undoubtedly the two strategic arms limitation agreements. Another agreement, the Basic Principles of Relations between
the United States and the Soviet Union, was signed at the summit and
called for the two countries to "do their utmost to avoid military confrontations and to prevent the outbreak of nuclear war."[17] The two parties agreed to "do everything in their power so that conflicts or situations
will not arise which would serve to increase international tensions."[18]
According to Henry Kissinger at the time that the Basic Principles agreement was signed, it marked a new era of restraint and creativity in
Soviet-American relations.

A year after the Moscow summit, Leonid Brezhnev visited the United
States. At this meeting, Brezhnev and Nixon signed a second crisis
prevention agreement, the Agreement on the Prevention of Nuclear War.
The United States and the Soviet Union agreed to "act in such a manner
as to prevent the development of situations capable of causing a dangerous exacerbation of relations" (Article I) and to "refrain from the
threat or use of force against the other party, against the allies of the
other party and against other countries, which may endanger international peace and security" (Article 2).[19] This agreement contained an
even stronger obligation by the two states to consult with one another
directly if situations developed anywhere in the world that increased the
risk of nuclear war. In his memoirs, Henry Kissinger recounts the history
behind the drafting of the Agreement on the Prevention of Nuclear War
and notes that the original Soviet draft of the agreement had called for
joint U.S.-Soviet intervention in a conflict that threatened world peace,
which was, in essence, a call for a superpower condominium. The United
States would not accept this proposal and after further negotiations the
agreement, according to Kissinger, "evolved into an elaboration of the
'Basic Principles of U.S.-Soviet Relations' signed in Moscow the previous year."[20]

In additon to these crisis prevention agreements, the United States
and the Soviet Union signed several others that called for the reduction
of the risk of crisis escalation. The Incidents at Sea agreement, designed
to reduce the risk of confrontations between the United States and
Soviet navies, was signed at the Moscow summit. And the final agreement signed by 35 states, including the United States and the Soviet
Union, at the Conference on Security and Cooperation in Europe meeting in Helsinki called for the signatories to notify one another of major
military operations involving more than 25,000 troops. Such limited,
tension-reducing measures such as these can help to build confidence
and facilitate more substantial agreements.

By the late 1970s, the viability of the Basic Principles and the Agreement on the Prevention of Nuclear War had been called into question by

both the United States and the Soviet Union. American leaders felt that Soviet actions in the October War, Angola, and Afghanistan were inconsistent with the provision of the two detente agreements. For their part, the Soviets believed that American opposition to Salvador Allende in Chile and the attempt by the United States to exclude the Soviet Union from the Middle East were inconsistent with the agreements. The basic problem with the agreements is that they were couched in general terms that were nonoperational. Those agreements that called for specific Soviet and American actions, for example the Incidents at Sea Agreement, were adhered to; Soviet and American naval officers have met regularly since 1972 to discuss the means to reduce the risk of dangerous confrontations between their respective navies.

In a detailed study of Soviet-American crisis prevention, Alexander George and his collaborators conclude that "crisis prevention may well be considered the orphan of strategic studies," and that the United States and the Soviet Union should make a greater effort to develop a more exact and differentiated conceptualization of cooperation and that as part of this effort the Basic Principles and Agreement on the Prevention of Nuclear War should be systematically reviewed and evaluated.[21]

The United States and the Soviet Union developed a number of implicit norms and rules for managing crises during the Cold War period. These were not sufficient, however, to prevent the development of several very serious crises, most notably the Cuban missile crisis of 1962. Following the resolution of that crisis, the two superpowers moved to reduce the danger of nuclear war by providing for a direct communications link between Washington and Moscow. The hot line provided the technical means to prevent crises. Nixon and Brezhnev sought to codify several rules for preventing crises in the Basic Principles and the Agreement on the Prevention of Nuclear War, but these proved to be too vague and general to be effective. Nevertheless, crisis prevention remains an important goal for the superpowers.

Nonprofileration Agreements

The spread of nuclear weapons became a major concern of many leaders during the 1950s and 1960s. In the late 1950s, a number of states presented resolutions calling for nonproliferation. In 1960, France tested its first nuclear device, an event that heightened public concern. In 1963, President Kennedy noted that it was possible that 10 states would develop nuclear weapons by 1970, perhaps 15 or 20 by 1975. Kennedy regarded the possibility that a future president would have to face a world of 15 to 20 nuclear powers as "the greatest possible danger."[22] The "nuclear club" was further expanded in 1964 with the first Chinese nuclear explosion.

The French and Chinese detonations dramatized the potential dangers of nuclear proliferation and represented direct threats to the Soviet Union, but Soviet policymakers refused to discuss nonproliferation as long as the United States was considering a plan called the Multilateral Force (MLF) to equip naval vessels in Europe with nuclear weapons and to man these ships with crew members drawn from North Atlantic Treaty Organization (NATO) countries. Proponents of this plan argued that it was a means of advancing European integration while simultaneously avoiding proliferation. Opponents of the proposal in the West contended that the MLF clouded the issues of NATO defense and precluded serious arms control. Soviet leaders were particularly critical of the plan since they felt that the United States was simply attempting to provide West Germany with nuclear weapons. In 1965, however, the United States abandoned the MLF proposal, opening the way for negotiations on the problem of nuclear proliferation.

As a result of discussions at meetings of the Eighteen Nation Disarmament Committee from 1965 to 1967 and informal meetings between Secretary of State Dean Rusk and Foreign Minister Andrei Gromyko in 1967, the United States and the Soviet Union were able to agree on the text of a draft nonproliferation treaty. The non-nuclear weapons states were particularly concerned about three issues: safeguards, balanced obligations, and security assurances (see pages 85-87). In regard to the second issue — balanced obligations — the non-nuclear weapons states believed that their renunciation of nuclear weapons should be accompanied by a commitment by the nuclear weapons states to seek a reduction in their nuclear arsenals. This concern resulted in the addition of Article VI to the treaty calling for parties to the treaty "to pursue negotiations in good faith on effective measures relating to cessation of the nuclear arms race at an early date."

On July 1, 1968, the Nonproliferation Treaty (NPT) was opened for signature, and 62 states, including the United States and Soviet Union, signed. The treaty contained provisions for the nontransfer of nuclear weapons by signatories possessing nuclear weapons and for the continued nonacquisition of nuclear weapons by the other signatories. West Germany was therefore effectively prevented from acquiring nuclear weapons under its independent control, a matter of utmost importance to the Soviet Union. The treaty contained international safeguards to guarantee that material from peaceful nuclear programs was not diverted into weapons production. The nuclear states also promised to assist with the development of peaceful uses of nuclear energy in the non-nuclear weapons states. In essence the NPT resulted in a quid pro quo: the non-nuclear weapons states promised to forego the acquisition of nuclear weapons in exchange for a promise by the nuclear states to assist the non-nuclear states with their peaceful nuclear programs and to seek an end to the arms race.

As noted above, a number of non-nuclear weapon states were concerned that the same safeguard standards called for in the NPT be applied to both non-nuclear weapon states as well as those states possessing nuclear weapons. In response to this concern, President Johnson announced in 1967 that the United States would permit the International Atomic Energy Agency (IAEA) to apply all of its safeguards to all nuclear activities in the United States with the exception of those relating to national security. Following the entry into force of the NPT, the IAEA established a Safeguards Committee to develop safeguards procedures. In 1977, the United States and IAEA signed an agreement for the application of safeguards to the United States (see pages 201-231). Since the entry into force of the agreement, the IAEA has made several inspections of U.S. nuclear facilities.

The explicit objective of the NPT was to halt completely the spread of nuclear weapons. With the spread of technology and knowledge, however, that goal has proved to be impossible to achieve, as indicated by the test of a "peaceful nuclear device" by India in May 1974. Most experts believe that Israel has secretly produced a limited number of assembled or nearly assembled nuclear weapons.[23] In addition to these 2 states, there are about 20 non-nuclear weapon states that by the mid-1980s will have nuclear reactors capable of producing enough plutonium to produce nuclear weapons. These states include a number that are in crisis-prone areas of the world and 5 that are not signatories to the NPT — Argentina, Brazil, Pakistan, South Africa, and Spain.[24]

Since the proliferation of nuclear weapons has proved impossible to halt completely, the emphasis since the mid-1970s has been to attempt to slow the pace of proliferation. The Indian explosion of May 1974 served as a reminder that proliferation was still a problem, despite the existence of the NPT. One month after the Indian explosion, the Nuclear Exporters' Committee adopted a "trigger list" that specified those items (e.g. heavy water, reprocessing plants, and enrichment equipment) whose export would "trigger" IAEA safeguards.[25]

The United States felt that a more comprehensive trigger list and more stringent safeguards were needed, and in late 1974 moved to organize a meeting of the exporters of nuclear materials and equipment: Canada, France, West Germany, Japan, the United Kingdom, the United States, and the Soviet Union. This group began meeting in London and became known as the London Suppliers Group. In January 1976, the group endorsed a uniform set of guidelines for nuclear exports. This agreement is not, however, a formal treaty; rather, it is simply a multilateral statement of national policy. Essentially the guidelines call for any state importing nuclear technology to: (1) agree not to use the transferred material, equipment, or technology for the production of nuclear explosions, (2) accept international safeguards, (3) provide adequate security for nuclear materials and facilities to prevent theft and sabotage, and (4) agree not to retransfer materials, equipment, or technology unless the original supplier approves the retransfer. The London Suppliers Group provided an effective means of concluding limited but important restraints among the major exporters of nuclear materials and equipment. Some non-nuclear states, however, viewed the group as a conspiracy of the nuclear "haves" versus the nuclear "have-nots." While maintaining informal contact, the group has not met formally since 1978.

As the number of states with nuclear facilities has grown, so too has concern about the protection of nuclear material. At present there are over 240 commercial nuclear power reactors in operation in 22 countries.[26] All of these, of course, require nuclear fuel in order to operate and a number of these produce plutonium as a byproduct. It takes approximately 10 pounds of plutonium and a basic knowledge of nuclear physics to produce an atomic bomb. A 1982 U.S. intelligence report estimated that 31 countries, many of which are engaged in long-standing regional disputes, will have the ability to produce nuclear weapons by the year 2000.[27]

The International Atomic Energy Agency has long been concerned about the protection of nuclear material. Were terrorists or irresponsible international leaders to gain possession of nuclear materials, they could be used for blackmail, extortion, or to unleash enormous devastation.

The explosion of a nuclear device by India in May 1974 caused renewed concern about the dangers of proliferation and in 1974 the United States proposed the Convention on the Physical Protection of Nuclear Material. This proposal was taken up and endorsed by the 1975 NPT review conference. Negotiations ensued and the convention was signed in October 1979.

The purpose of the convention is to promote the physical protection of nuclear material both within states and while such material is being transported. This agreement is a significant addition to the two other nonproliferation agreements contained in this volume.

While there was hope at one time to halt all nuclear proliferation (this was, in fact, the objective of the NPT), that goal seems next to impossible to achieve, given the diffusion and pace of technological developments worldwide. In the 1980s, statesmen and international institutions increasingly turned their attention to slowing the pace of proliferation. In approaching this task, the establishment of laws within states, such as the United States' Nuclear Nonproliferation Act of 1978, and the development of ad hoc organizations such as the London Suppliers Group have been important adjuncts to the formal agreements contained in this volume.

Disarmament

As noted in the introduction to this article, "arms control" refers to the quantitative and/or qualitative limitation of weapons while "disarmament" refers to the elimination of certain types or all weapons. According to these definitions, all of the agreements discussed thus far are arms-control, rather than disarmament, agreements. However, one agreement contained in this volume — the Biological Weapons Convention — calls for the elimination of certain weapons.

Soon after entering office, President Nixon renounced the first use of chemical weapons and in addition stated that the United States unconditionally renounced all forms of biological warfare. Chemical weapons are produced by inorganic subelements whereas biological weapons, such as anthrax, are produced by biological processes. Toxins act like chemical agents but are produced by biological processes. In 1970, President Nixon indicated that the United States would extend its ban to toxins as well as the two other categories of chemical-biological weapons.

Nixon's unilateral decision to disarm the United States' biological weapons capability was not simply a magnanimous or idealistic gesture on his part. Indeed, during World War I poison gas was used extensively with devastating results. Part of the reason that it was so destructive was that its effects often could not be controlled; a shift in wind, for instance, could make the attacking party the victim of its own attack. Chemical and biological weapons do not observe boundaries. Nixon and his advisors reasoned that if biological weapons were ever used by the United States, the ultimate result could be as devastating for the United States as for the state or states we were attacking. This reasoning, coupled with the inherent horror associated with biological weapons, led to the unilateral American decision to eliminate biological weapons from the U.S. arsenal.

Discussion of an international convention prohibiting biological weapons took place at the Conference of the Committee on Disarmament (CCD), and in 1971 the United States and the Soviet Union presented identical texts of an agreement. The UN General Assembly urged acceptance of the convention, and it was opened for signature in April 1972. Within a short time, over 100 states signed the convention.

In April 1979, an epidemic of anthrax, a deadly disease that could be used as a biological weapon, broke out in Sverdlovsk, a city of 1.2 million people 850 miles to the east of Moscow.[28] Estimates of the number of fatalities during the epidemic range from 20 to 1,000. If the Soviet government were secretly producing anthrax, it would be in violation of the Biological Weapons Convention. The U.S. government commissioned a group of experts to assess the available evidence in order to determine whether the Soviets had violated the agreement. The group concluded that the Soviets had probably violated the treaty by producing anthrax and that Moscow had certainly failed to carry out its treaty obligations by refusing to provide information to clarify this situation.

In addition to the Sverdlovsk incident, American officials also became concerned about reports that the Soviet Union was using chemical weapons in Afghanistan and supplying Vietnam with these weapons.[29] Witnesses have described Soviet and Vietnamese planes dropping "yellow rain," and samples containing trichothecene mycotoxins — a chemical warfare agent — have been found on the border of Thailand and Cambodia. The use of such weapons (but not the manufacture) is prohibited by the 1925 Geneva Protocol. But the evidence remains somewhat ambiguous, and in May 1983 a leading American expert on chemical-biological warfare concluded that "yellow rain" could, in fact, be simply the excrement of bees. [30] Nevertheless, the Sverdlovsk and yellow rain cases have raised serious questions concerning Soviet compliance with the Biological Weapons Convention and the Geneva Protocol.

Environmental Protection

In a sense, any agreement to control nuclear arms or other weapons of mass destruction, such as biological or chemical weapons, are environmental protection agreements. If these weapons were ever extensively employed, their effects on the world's environment would be substantial. Scientists do not know what the exact physical effects of a general nuclear war would be; most agree however, that the world's physical environment would be profoundly affected. Three agreements have been explicitly concerned with environmental protection: the Antarctica Treaty, the Limited Test Ban Treaty, and the Environmental Modification Convention.

As previously discussed, the Antarctica Treaty prohibited the deposit of nuclear waste and the deployment of conventional and nuclear weapons to Antarctica. The Limited Test Ban Treaty, which prohibits nuclear testing in the atmosphere, resulted in a significant decrease in atmospheric pollution caused by radioactive isotopes such as strontium 90. Both of these treaties thus accomplish, among other things, the preservation and protection of the physical environment.

If a state were able to control certain physical phenomena such as earthquakes or rainfall, it would have a powerful weapon at its disposal.

Of course, all of the consequences of meddling with nature would be difficult, if not impossible, to predict. The unintended results of tinkering with the environment could be both significant and negative for the state seeking to modify the environment for its own purpose. If there is a principal law of ecology, it is that an action taken to influence an ecological system can often have substantial and unforeseen results.

In July 1972, the United States renounced the use of environmental modification techniques for military purposes. The House of Representatives and the Senate passed resolutions in 1973 urging that an international agreement prohibiting environmental modification be negotiated. In 1974 and 1975 the United States and the Soviet Union held discussions on this subject, and in August 1975 the Soviet and American representatives to the Conference of the Committee on Disarmament (CCD) presented identical drafts of a convention prohibitiing military or other hostile uses of environmental modification techniques. This draft agreement was discussed extensively in the CCD throughout 1976, and in December 1976 the UN General Assembly urged acceptance of the convention by its members. In May 1977, the agreement was signed by 34 states including the United States and the Soviet Union.

The convention prohibits the use of environmental modification techniques designed to cause physical phenomena such as earthquakes, tidal waves, and/or changes in weather patterns, climate, ocean currents, the ozone layer, or the ionosphere. The agreement calls for the establishment of a "Consultative Committee of Experts" to meet on an ad hoc basis to discuss any questions concerning compliance with the agreement.

The most important objective of arms control and disarmament is to reduce the risk of nuclear war, for if such a war ever occurred, human society and the world's physical environment would be significantly harmed if not destroyed. A secondary objective of arms control and disarmament is to protect the natural environment. Arms-control agreements to date have contributed in a limited way toward the achievement of that objective.

Strategic Nuclear Arms Limitations

The negotiations between the United States and the Soviet Union to limit strategic nuclear weapons have been the most important of the post–World War II era. These negotiations can be divided into three phases: SALT I (an acronym that stands for Strategic Arms Limitation Talks), which lasted from November 1969 to May 1972; SALT II, which lasted from November 1972 until June 1979; and START, the Strategic Arms Reductions Talks conducted by the Reagan administration. In this section, a brief history and summary of the major issues for each of these periods will be presented.

SALT I

During the mid-1960s, President Johnson made several overtures to the Soviet Union to begin negotiations to limit strategic nuclear weapons. Soviet leaders, however, were uninterested for several reasons. First, the Soviet Union had far fewer strategic weapons than the United States. In 1965, the arsenals of the two sides contained the following weapons:[31]

	U.S.	U.S.S.R.
ICBMs	854	224
SLBMs	496	107
Long-range bombers	630	160
Total	1980	491

As is readily apparent from this table, the United States had a four to one advantage in strategic weapons in 1965. If the Soviet Union had agreed to a freeze in weapons as President Johnson had proposed in 1964, the Soviet Union would have been frozen into a position of inferiority. Second, the Soviets were unwilling to accept on-site inspection, also called for in Johnson's proposal, and there were no commonly accepted means of verification. Third, Soviet leaders did not want to begin negotiations to limit nuclear weapons until they received firm assurance that West Germany would not develop nuclear weapons of its own.

Several developments occurred that made strategic arms negotiations more attractive to the Soviet leadership. In early 1967, President Johnson requested authorization to begin deployment of an antiballistic missile (ABM) system and stated that he would deploy the new missile defense system unless the Soviets indicated a genuine willingness to open negotiations to limit strategic nuclear arms. Within several months, Premier Kosygin expressed an interest in beginning the negotiations. As noted above, in July 1968 the Nonproliferation Treaty was signed by 62 states. West Germany accepted the NPT in principle in 1968 and formally signed it in November 1969. Finally, throughout the 1960s, both the United States and the Soviet Union developed and deployed sophisticated satellites and electronic equipment to gather intelligence data. Thus, by 1968 the time was right to begin the negotiations to limit strategic nuclear weapons.

On August 19, 1968, the Soviet ambassador to the United States, Anatoly Dobrynin, announced that his government had agreed to meet the following month to arrange a schedule for the negotiations. However, the next day Soviet military forces invaded Czechoslovakia, and in protest to the invasion the United States postponed the negotiations indefinitely. It is interesting to note in retrospect that Soviet leaders were willing to open the negotiations despite the involvement of over half a million American troops in Vietnam in 1968.

In January 1969, Richard Nixon was inaugurated, and he and his national security affairs advisor, Henry Kissinger, decided that they needed to conduct a major review of U.S. military doctrine and programs before opening negotiations. Thus, it was not until November 17, 1969, that the SALT I negotiations began in Helsinki, Finland. Meeting alternately in Helsinki and Vienna, the Soviet and American delegations held seven formal negotiating sessions over the next 30 months.

The United States SALT I delegation was headed by the director of the Arms Control and Disarmament Agency (ACDA), Gerard Smith, and consisted of representatives from the major departments and agencies with responsibilities in the foreign policy field, including the Departments of State and Defense, the Joint Chiefs of Staff, ACDA, the Central Intelligence Agency, and the National Security Council. President Nixon, often via Dr. Kissinger, issued instructions to the American delegation, which would then present the U.S. position to the Soviet delegation. Unknown to almost everyone, including Ambassador Smith and the rest of the American delegation, were "back-channel" negotiations being conducted in Washington by Kissinger and Soviet Ambassador Dobrynin.[32]

The Soviet delegation was headed by Deputy Foreign Minister V. S. Semenov and consisted of 24 officials, of whom one-third were military officers, one-third foreign ministry personnel, and the remaining one-third assumed to be from the Soviet intelligence agency, the Committee on State Security (KGB).[33] During the negotiations, the Soviet delegation strictly adhered to positions developed prior to interdelegation meetings and appeared to be uncomfortable with informal discussions that the American delegation occasionally proposed. The civilian members of the Soviet delegation, including Semenov, seemed uninformed about the military capabilities of both American and Soviet weapons systems, and at one point in the negotiations following a detailed discussion of a particular weapon, one of the military members of the Soviet delegation asked Ambassador Smith to restrict discussion of military systems to Soviet military officers.[34]

The major topics of discussion at the SALT I negotiations were the limitation of defensive (ABM) and offensive (ICBM and SLBM) missile systems. These negotiations touched upon important issues such as inspection and verification, and could not be conducted in isolation from other major defense and military issues. The Soviet Union, for instance, repeatedly expressed a desire to discuss American nuclear forces stationed in Europe, what the Soviets termed "forward-based systems" (FBS), and the U.S. negotiators were just as insistent that these systems not be discussed due to the negative impact that such negotiations would have on the NATO alliance. Eventually, the Soviet Union agreed to drop the FBS issue if the United States would drop its demand that the number of large Soviet ICBMs (SS-9, SS-18) be reduced.

Although both the Soviet and American governments attributed a great deal of importance to the negotiations, SALT could not be conducted without consideration of the broader context of U.S.-Soviet relations. At the end of March 1972, North Vietnam, with military equipment supplied by the Soviet Union and China, unleashed a major offensive against South Vietnam. The situation worsened for South Vietnam throughout April and became critical in May. Even though a summit meeting between President Nixon and Secretary Brezhnev was scheduled for late May, Nixon ordered the bombing of Hanoi and the mining of Haiphong and other North Vietnamese ports in order to prevent the defeat of South Vietnam. Most American experts on the Soviet Union, including Zbigniew Brzezinski, Richard Pipes, and Adam Ulam, predicted that the Soviets would cancel the summit meeting to protest American actions. However, the meeting was not cancelled and a number of agreements calling for economic, scientific, and technical cooperation were signed. The most significant achievements of the Moscow summit were the two SALT I agreements: the ABM Treaty and the Interim Agreement on Offensive Missiles.

In the ABM Treaty, the United States and the Soviet Union agreed not to deploy more than two ABM sites, one at the national capital and the other at a site at least 1,300 kilometers from the first site. Each side was limited to no more than 100 interceptor missiles and launchers. To assure compliance, the treaty called for "national technical means of verification," an official euphemism for satellite reconnaissance and the monitoring of electronic signals. The signatories promised neither to interfere with satellite verification procedures nor to deliberately conceal any ABM components. Restrictions were also placed on ABM radars, and the deployment of new ABM systems relying on new technologies, such as lasers, was proscribed. The treaty called for the establishment of an organization, the Standing Consultative Commission, in order to oversee the implementation of the treaty and to consider any questions from either party concerning compliance. The treaty is of unlimited duration although periodic reviews were scheduled for every five years.

Either party has the right to withdraw from the treaty on six months' notice. The ABM Treaty was a truly remarkable agreement since each side in essence agreed not to defend itself against an attack from the other side.

The Interim Agreement placed a quantitative limit on both international ballistic missiles and submarine-launched ballistic missiles (SLBMs). The United States was limited to 1,054 ICBMs, the Soviets to 1,618. Each side had the right under the agreement to deploy SLBMs in exchange for the dismantling of ICBMs. This was the so-called one-way freedom to mix (from land-based to sea-based forces) provision of the agreement. If all older ICBMs were dismantled, the United States could build up to 710 SLBMs on 44 submarines, and the Soviet Union could build up to 950 SLBMs on 62 submarines. The Interim Agreement had a duration of five years (1972-77), and both states stated that they intended to replace it with a permanent agreement. In summary, the agreement placed quantitative limitations on Soviet and American missile launchers without restricting qualitative improvements such as multiple independently targeted reentry vehicles (MIRV).

Because the ABM agreement was a treaty, the Nixon administration was required by the Constitution to submit it to the Senate for advice and consent. The Senate approved the treaty relatively quickly and near unanimously by a vote of 88-2. Although it was not a treaty, the Interim Agreement also had to be submitted to the Congress for approval according to the terms of the 1961 law that established the Arms Control and Disarmament Agency. There was considerable debate about whether the Soviet Union was granted superiority over the United States by the Interim Agreement. Critics pointed out that the agreement allowed the Soviet Union 50 percent more ICBMs (1,618 to 1,054) and a 4-1 superiority over the United States in deliverable payload if only missiles (and not bombers) were counted. Supporters of the agreement argued that the United States had four times as many bombers as the Soviets and that if bombers were counted, the two superpowers had approximately equal deliverable payloads. In addition, since the United States began deploying MIRVs on its missiles in 1970, it had a substantially greater number of warheads on its missiles.

Because of his concern over what he perceived to be the deficiencies of the Interim Agreement and perhaps also for personal political reasons (he was actively seeking the 1972 Democratic presidential nomination), Senator Henry Jackson (Wash.) introduced an amendment to the agreement which stipulated that any future arms-control agreement should "not limit the U.S. to levels of intercontinental strategic forces inferior to the limits for the Soviet Union." The Senate accepted the Jackson Amendment 56-35 and then approved the Interim Agreement 88-2. From that time on, American negotiators had to keep the Jackson Amendment in mind since it was unlikely that any agreement that did not conform to the provisions of the Jackson Amendment would be approved by Congress.

At the time they were signed, Henry Kissinger contended that the SALT I agreements were "without precedent in the nuclear age; indeed, in all relevant modern history," and that "nothing this administration had done has seemed to it more important for the future of the world than to make an important first step in the limitation of strategic arms." President Nixon stated that neither side won or lost by the agreement; rather, "both sides won, and the whole world won."[35] Thus, to Nixon and Kissinger the signing of the SALT I agreements marked a mutual step by the United States and the Soviet Union toward increased strategic stability and a significant improvement in Soviet-American relations.

There were others within the Nixon administration who were not convinced of the virtues of SALT I. Secretary of Defense Melvin Laird and Chairman of the Joint Chiefs of Staff Thomas Moorer conditioned their approval of the SALT I agreements to the continued development of new strategic weapons systems including the Trident submarine and missile system, the B-1 bomber, the Washington, D. C., ABM site, and the submarine-launched cruise missile.[36] The Laird-Moorer quid pro quo — their support of the agreements in exchange for the administration's support of new strategic weapons systems — was not unprecedented; the military had demanded similar assurances in 1963 in exchange for its support of the Limited Test Ban Treaty.

Following congressional approval of the ABM Treaty and the Interim Agreement, virtually all of the senior officials of the Arms Control and Disarmament Agency (ACDA) were replaced. This action may have been a concession to hardliners who opposed the agreements. In any event, Fred Iklé replaced Gerard Smith as ACDA director, and U. Alexis Johnson, a career diplomat with little previous arms-control experience, was appointed chief SALT negotiator.

SALT II

The second phase of the Strategic Arms Limitation Talks (SALT II) began on November 21, 1972, in Geneva, where all subsequent interdelegation negotiating sessions were held. By early 1973, the United States completed the process of appointing new delegation members and the two sides got to work. Whereas SALT I imposed quantitative limitations on weapons, the major task of SALT II was to develop qualitative limitations. Most experts agree that the latter task is far more difficult to achieve for many reasons. For example, verification of qualitative limitations is problematic. Satellites can readily verify the number of missile launchers that a country has; however, given present technology, they cannot determine whether the missiles are equipped with MIRVs.

In June 1973, President Nixon and Secretary Brezhnev signed the Agreement on the Prevention of Nuclear War during Brezhnev's visit to the United States. In addition, the two leaders signed a communiqué pledging to reach a SALT II agreement within the year. Throughout the last half of 1973 and 1974, criticism of the Nixon administration as a result of the Watergate affair became intense. Hoping to conclude a SALT II agreement and to divert the public's attention from Watergate, President Nixon visited Moscow in June 1974. He and Brezhnev signed a protocol to the ABM Treaty limiting each side to one ABM site. They also signed a communiqué stipulating that a SALT agreement covering the period from 1974 to 1985 and dealing with both quantitative and qualitative limitations should be completed prior to the 1977 expiration date of the Interim Agreement. These modest agreements were not enough to stem the tide of domestic criticism and on August 8, 1974, President Nixon resigned from office.

Anxious to reestablish the credibility of the presidency both domestically and internationally, President Gerald Ford ordered the U.S. SALT delegation to press forward with the achievement of a long-term strategic arms-control agreement. In November 1974, President Ford met Secretary Brezhnev at Vladivostok to sign an "agreement in principle," which constituted a list of objectives to be achieved in the SALT II negotiations. The two leaders agreed that each of their countries should be limited to 2,400 strategic delivery vehicles (long-range bombers, ICBMs, plus SLBMs) and of this total a maximum of 1,320 could be MIRVed warheads. The new agreement was supposed to cover the period from October 1977, the date the Interim Agreement expired, through December 1985.

When the terms of the Vladivostok *aide mémoire* were made public, neither the proponents nor the opponents of SALT were satisfied with the results. From the perspective of the supporters of arms control, the total aggregate number of strategic nuclear vehicles as well as the MIRV sublimit were set too high. And even though the agreement set equal limits for both the United States and Soviet Union, Senator Jackson was displeased with it since the Soviets would be able to threaten the survivability of the American ICBM force if they deployed all 1,320 warheads allowed by the agreement.

As the negotiators returned to Geneva, they were faced with the problem of how to deal with new weapons systems. The Soviet Union began to deploy a new bomber, the Backfire, which had a range that would enable it to reach the continental United States from bases within the Soviet Union and to land in neutral territory (presumably Cuba) for refueling. The U.S. delegation contended that these bombers should be counted against the Soviets' 2,400-vehicle ceiling, a position that the Soviet delegation repeatedly rejected. The Soviets were also developing a new mobile version of the the SS-16, the SS-20, which if deployed in certain areas would have the range to reach the United States.

The United States was also working on a number of new weapons systems. As a means of matching the Soviet development and deployment of large (or "heavy") ICBMs, the Department of Defense advocated the building of a new large ICBM called the "missile experimental" or MX. In addition, research and development work proceeded on a sophisticated new warhead, "the maneuverable reentry vehicle" (MARV), which was designed not only to be independently targetable like MIRV but also to maneuver during the last part of its reentry into the atmosphere. Tests were conducted on an air-launched ICBM. President Ford supported the deployment of two new strategic systems: the B-I bomber and the Trident submarine.

Perhaps the American weapon causing the greatest controversy during the SALT II negotiations was the cruise missile, a subsonic, long-range missile capable of extremely high accuracy. The Soviets contended that these missiles, if deployed, should be counted against the 2,400 ceiling set at Vladivostok, but the United States rejected this position. Once deployed, cruise missiles would complicate the problem of verification considerably. For instance, one model of the cruise missile was designed to fit into the torpedo tubes of submarines. Since there would be no way short of on-site inspection to verify whether or not such missiles were deployed on American submarines, Soviet defense planners would probably make "worst case" assumptions and assume that all U.S. submarines were strategic launchers and, since torpedo tubes are reloadable, further assume that submarines were armed with multiple warheads.

In addition to the technological problems standing in the way of a SALT II agreement, U.S. domestic politics constituted a further obstacle to reaching an agreement. Ronald Reagan attacked the detente and arms-control policies of the Ford administration and came very close to wresting the Republican nomination away from an incumbent president. Even though Ford received the nomination, he was forced to accept a party platform that in many respects was a repudiation of his administration's policies toward the Soviet Union. All of the Democratic candidates attacked the Ford-Kissinger policies toward the Soviet Union.

In his inaugural address, Jimmy Carter indicated a desire to move toward the ambitious goal of nuclear *disarmament* and not simply arms control. Within several weeks of assuming office, Carter said that he wanted to conclude a SALT II agreement quickly and to move on to further limitations. Along with his support for arms control and disarmament, the president expressed his support for human rights activists in the Soviet Union by writing a personal letter to Andrei Sakharov and receiving Vladimir Bukovsky at the White House. Soviet leaders were greatly disturbed by Carter's actions and indicated that a SALT II agreement would be impossible to conclude if such "interference in domestic affairs" continued.

During a visit to Moscow in March 1977, Secretary of State Cyrus Vance presented two arms-control proposals. The "comprehensive proposal" called for a 20 percent reduction in the total of strategic nuclear launch vehicles (from 2,400 to 1,800-2,000) allowed under the Vladivostok *aide mémoire*. Sublimits were proposed for MIRVed and "heavy" ICBMs. Land-mobile ICBMs were to be prohibited and there was a proposed limit on ICBM and SLBM test firings. The second American proposal was a fall-back proposal calling for an agreement along the line of the Vladivostok agreement with the provision that the deployment of neither the Soviet Backfire bomber nor U.S. cruise missiles would be affected.

The Soviets rejected both of the American proposals almost immediately. They considered the "comprehensive proposal" as heavily favoring the United States and they objected to the failure to include cruise missiles in the fall-back position. In addition, the Soviets were disturbed and confused by the new "open diplomacy" and human rights policies of the Carter administration.

Over two years passed before the United States and the Soviet Union were able to negotiate a SALT II Treaty; however, on June 18, 1979, President Carter and General Secretary Brezhnev meeting in Vienna signed the SALT II agreement, which consisted of three parts: a treaty, a protocol, and a statement of principles. Designed to remain in effect from the time it entered into force until 1985, the treaty contained the following provisions:

- A limit of 2,400 strategic nuclear launch vehicles (ICBMs, SLBMs, air-to-surface ballistic missiles, and heavy bombers); to be lowered to 2,250 by the end of 1981.
- No more than 1,320 ICBMs, SLBMs, and heavy bombers may be equipped with MIRVs or long-range cruise missiles and within this sublimit there may be no more than 1,200 ICBMs, SLBMs, and air-to-surface ballistic missiles (ASBM).
- No more than 820 MIRVed ICBMs are allowed.
- Ceilings are placed on the throw weight and launch weight of light and heavy ICBMs.

• Each side may test and deploy only one new type of ICBM.
• A freeze on the number of reentry vehicles (RVs) on current types of ICBMs, a limit of 10 RVs on the one new type ICBM permitted for each side, a limit of 14 RVs on SLBMs, and a limit of 10 RVs on ASBMs.
• A limit of 28 on the testing and deployment of air-launched cruise missiles (ALCM) with ranges over 600 kilometers (375 miles) carried by aircraft other than those counted as heavy bombers.
• A ban on the construction of additional fixed ICBM launchers and any increase in the number of fixed heavy ICBM launchers (this limited the Soviet Union to 308 large modern ballistic missiles).
• A ban on heavy mobile ICBMs, heavy SLBMs, and heavy ASBMs.
• A ban on certain types of strategic offensive systems not yet deployed by either side such as ballistic missiles with ranges over 600 kilometers on surface ships.
• An agreement to exchange data regularly on the numbers of weapons covered in the treaty.
• Advance notification of certain ICBM test launches.

The second part of the SALT II agreement was a protocol designed to remain in effect from the entry into force of the treaty through 1981. The protocol called for:

• The prohibition of flight testing and the deployment of ICBMs from mobile launch platforms (this provision was sought by the United States to keep the Soviet Union from deploying the SS-16).
• The prohibition of the deployment of land-based or sea-based long-range cruise missiles with a range of more than 600 kilometers.
• A ban on the testing and deployment of air-to-surface missiles.

The third part of the SALT agreement consisted of a joint statement of principles for the SALT III negotiations. The two sides agreed to pursue further negotiations, to resolve the issues covered in the protocol, and to bring up other relevant topics.

As noted previously, the Soviet Backfire bomber was one of the major points of contention in the SALT II negotiations. Although limitations on the Backfire were not part of the formal SALT II Treaty, the Soviet Union in a letter accompanying the treaty committed itself to the production of no more than 30 planes per year and to limit the upgrading capabilities of the Backfire. According to the State Department, these limitations "have the same legal force as the rest of the SALT II agreement," and "if the Soviet Union were to violate these commitments, the United States could withdraw from the treaty."

In support of the SALT II agreement, the Carter administration argued that the agreement would: (1) establish limits on building new types of weapons and the improvement of existing strategic arms; (2) set equal ceilings on all major intercontinental strategic nuclear delivery systems; (3) impose an upper limit on the number of warheads that could be placed on ICBMs and SLBMs; (4) limit the expansion of the arms race; (5) place significant limits on programs that the Soviet Union might develop in the absence of SALT; (6) require the reduction of approximately 250 Soviet missiles and/or bombers; (7) forbid any interference with efforts to verify compliance with the agreement; (8) continue the process of improving relations with the Soviet Union; and (9) enable the United States to save as much as $30 billion over the decade that followed.[37]

Opponents of the SALT II agreement argued that, if ratified, the agreement would: (1) grant the Soviet Union important military advantages in categories of weapons such as heavy ICBMs; (2) restrict the development of significant U.S. strategic arms designed to rectify the Soviet-American strategic imbalance; (3) not result in any substantial monetary savings for the United States; (4) reduce the stability of the strategic nuclear balance; (5) be unverifiable; (6) increase the Soviet drive for expansion of its influence; and (7) mark a significant decline in American power.[38]

The Senate held hearings on the SALT II agreement during the summer of 1979.[39] On November 9, 1979, the Senate Foreign Relations Committee voted 9 to 6 to recommend that the treaty be ratified. The Senate Select Committee on Intelligence found that the agreement "enhances the ability of the United States to monitor those components of Soviet strategic weapons forces which are subject to the limitations of the Treaty."[40] Only the Senate Armed Services Committee was critical of the treaty.

During the fall, it appeared that the treaty would be approved by the Senate. However, Senator Frank Church (D-Idaho) dramatically announced in August that U.S. intelligence agencies had identified a Soviet "combat brigade" in Cuba and that these troops would have to be withdrawn before the treaty could be approved. The Soviet Union repeatedly stressed that the unit had been in Cuba for a number of years and was a training, as opposed to combat, unit. Furthermore, the Soviets refused to consider the U.S. demand that the unit be removed from Cuba. The author of an excellent case study of the Cuban brigade crisis and SALT has concluded that if a Senate vote on SALT had been taken in August, the treaty would probably have passed; however, after the Cuban brigade became a public issue, passage of the agreement became doubtful.[41]

Events seemingly unrelated to arms control and disarmament can have a significant effect on arms limitation negotiations and the congressional consideration of such agreements. In November 1979, a group of anti-American Iranians took over the U.S. Embassy in Teheran and American personnel were taken hostage. The ensuing crisis, although unrelated to SALT, caused many to conclude that the United States could not compromise with the Soviet Union in any way, including the conclusion of the SALT II Treaty.

The final blow to SALT II came in December 1979 when the Soviet Union invaded Afghanistan. Because of this action, President Carter asked the Senate to delay indefinitely consideration of the SALT II Treaty. Despite the fact that the treaty was withdrawn from consideration, it was not forgotten. During the 1980 presidential campaign, Ronald Reagan claimed that the treaty was "fatally flawed" and that it "legitimized the arms race."[42] Following his election, however, President Reagan indicated that the United States would observe the SALT II limitations as long as the Soviet Union did so.

START and INF

During their initial months in office, President Reagan and his advisors were more concerned about building up U.S. military forces than in engaging the Soviet Union in arms-control negotiations. In a press conference on March 31, 1982, the president indicated his concern: "On balance the Soviet Union does have a definite margin of superiority — enough so that there is risk and there is what I have called . . . several times, a window of vulnerability."[43] This was the first time that any American president since the end of World War II had publicly made such a claim. The president's concern about the "window of vulnerability" referred to his fear that the U.S. land-based ICBMs were vulnerable to Soviet attack. To remedy these weaknesses, members of the Reagan administration argued that the United States needed to build up its forces and then negotiate. In addition, the administration contended that the Soviet Union had to behave internationally, or the United States would not engage the Soviet Union in arms-control negotiations.

During his first two years, President Reagan was successful in getting his defense requests through the Congress. However, in the fall of 1981, signs of dissent appeared, first in Europe and then in the United States. In October, millions of Europeans demonstrated in opposition to the deployment of American Pershing 2 and ground-launched cruise missiles that were scheduled to be deployed there starting in December 1983. Allied leaders pressured the United States to engage the Soviet Union in arms-control negotiations to defuse the pressure. On November 18, 1981, President Reagan announced his "zero-zero option": if the Soviet Union would agree to dismantle its 340 new SS-20 and 260 older SS-4 and SS-5 intermediate- and medium-range ballistic missiles, the United States would not deploy its 108 Pershing 2s and 464 ground-

launched cruise missiles in Europe.[44] The Soviet Union immediately rejected this proposal. Since that time, the United States and the Soviet
Union have each presented several proposals at the INF negotiations,
but no agreement has been reached.

Despite the opening of these negotiations, members of the public and
Congress continued to express concern about the administration's nuclear policies. This concern was no doubt fueled in part by the rhetoric of
the administration. During the 1980 presidential campaign, George Bush
stated that a limited nuclear war was possible. The Undersecretary of
Defense, T. K. Jones, told a reporter that all that was needed to survive a
nuclear attack was a hole, an old door, some dirt, and a shovel. [45]

During the spring of 1982, a number of events focused public attention
on the nuclear war issue. Jonathan Schell's influential book *The Fate of
the Earth* was published and was widely read.[46] In March, Senators
Edward Kennedy (D-Mass.) and Mark Hatfield (R-Oreg.) introduced a
resolution to freeze the production and deployment of nuclear weapons.
And in April, Ground Zero — a nonpartisan, nuclear war education
organization — sponsored educational activities in hundreds of cities,
colleges, and schools across the country. [47] On the first day of Ground
Zero Week (April 18), President Reagan remarked: "A nuclear war cannot
be won and must never be fought. So to those who protest against
nuclear war, I can only say, I'm with you." [48]

The president sought to back up these words with action on May 9,
1982, when he delivered the commencement address at his alma mater
(Eureka College in Peoria, Illinois) and announced a new approach to
limiting strategic nuclear arms control. Saying "we've given up on SALT,"
President Reagan announced that the United States and Soviet Union
would conduct Strategic Arms Reduction Talks (START). The United
States' initial START proposal was based on a two-phase approach.
During the first phase, the United States and the Soviet Union would
each be required to reduce the number of ballistic missile warheads by
one-third: from 7,500 to 5,000. The U.S. proposal also called for a
reduction of the number of deployed ballistic missiles (ICBMs and
SLBMs) on each side to 850 missiles. In the second phase of the negotiations, the United States would seek further reductions in these forces,
equal levels of destructive power for both sides, and a ceiling on throw
weight.

Following the death of Leonid Brezhnev in November 1982, Yuri Andropov was named the head of the Communist party of the Soviet Union,
the most important political position in the Soviet Union. Five weeks after
he assumed office, Andropov made a two-pronged proposal: (1) a reduction of Soviet intermediate-range nuclear missiles (SS-4, SS-5, and
SS-20) from 600 to 162 providing that the United States not deploy any

Pershing 2 or ground-launched cruise missiles to Europe; and (2) a 25 percent reduction of total strategic nuclear launch vehicles (ICBMs, SLBMs, and long-range bombers) from 2,500 to 1,800. The United States, Great Britain, and France immediately rejected the Soviet proposal.

American and Soviet negotiators have continued to meet in Geneva at the INF and START talks. In addition, U.S. and Soviet negotiators, along with representatives from the other 11 NATO states and six Warsaw Pact members, have met in Vienna since 1973 at the Mutual and Balanced Force Reduction (MBFR) negotiations. The prospects for reaching significant agreements in these negotiations is remote.

The Reagan administration has advocated a substantial military buildup as an attempt to influence the Soviet Union to negotiate seriously at START. A key element of this build-up is the MX missile. Facing significant congressional opposition to the MX, President Reagan named a prestigious commission consisting of former high government officials from both parties and chaired by retired Air Force general and President Ford's national security affairs advisor, Brent Scowcroft. In April 1982, the commission made the following recommendations: (1) to build 100 MX missiles each with 10 warheads and to place them in existing ICBM silos, and (2) to develop a smaller, single-warhead missile (dubbed the "Midgetman") for deployment in the 1990s.[49] In May, President Reagan accepted these recommendations and pledged to the Congress that he would earnestly seek to conclude arms-control agreements with the Soviet Union. Accepting the quid pro quo (the president's promise in exchange for the MX), the Congress voted to fund the MX.

By the fall of 1982, however, it was unclear whether agreements would be concluded at either the INF or START negotiations. The effects on the negotiations of the deployment of Pershing 2 missiles and ground-launched cruise missiles in West Germany (scheduled to begin in December 1983) and the development of the MX were seen by many as reducing the probability that the United States and the Soviet Union would reach any agreement. But members of the Reagan administration argued that these developments would pressure the Soviets into concluding an agreement at Geneva.

Conclusion

There are 21 formal agreements contained in this volume. Ten of these are bilateral U.S.-Soviet agreements, while the other 11 are multilateral agreements signed by a number of states. All but one of these 21 agreements are arms-control agreements; the lone disarmament agreement is the Biological Weapons Convention. The agreements in this volume concern a number of different issues from Antarctica and anthrax to nuclear weapon-free zones. I have described these agreements according to the norms and procedures that are established by them. A typology of the agreements is contained in the following table.

Given the inherently competitive nature of international politics, the number, variety, and the quality of the arms-control and disarmament agreements that have been concluded are remarkable. Statesmen have not concluded these agreements for purely idealistic or humanitarian reasons. Rather, these agreements represent a means to insure and even improve national security. But arms-control agreements, as the history of the Washington Naval Treaty attests, are fragile and can be made irrelevant by advances in technology. The task of statesmen is to keep up with the scientists.

The U.S. Arms Control and Disarmament Agency performs a valuable service in compiling this volume. ACDA also publishes an annual report that describes the current state of the various arms-control and disarmament negotiations in which the United States is engaged.[50] The introduction of this book as well as the narrative sections preceding each agreement have been written by staff members of ACDA. This is the fifth edition of this book. Hopefully, ACDA will continue to update and publish this book so that students, analysts, and scholars will have access to a valuable reference on what is the single most important issue of our time.

A Typology of Arms-Control and Disarmament Agreements

Types of Agreements and Norms Established	Agreements/Year Signed
1. Nuclear Weapon-Free Areas: Nuclear weapons should not be deployed in certain agreed-upon areas.	1-1. Antarctica Treaty (1959) 1-2. Outer Space Treaty (1967) 1-3. Latin American Nuclear Free Zone Treaty (1967) 1-4. Seabed Treaty (1971)
2. Nuclear Testing Limitations: Nuclear tests should be limited.	2-1. Limited Test Ban Treaty (1963) 2-2. Threshold Test Ban Treaty (1974) 2-3. Peaceful Nuclear Explosions Treaty (1976)
3. Crisis Management and Crisis Prevention: In crisis situations, the leaders of the U.S. and U.S.S.R. should communicate directly with one another to reduce the risk of escalation.	3-1. Hot Line Agreement (1963) 3-2. "Accidents Measures" Agreement (1971) 3-3. Hot Line Modernization Agreement (1971) 3-4. Basic Principles (1972) 3-5. Agreement on the Prevention of Nuclear War (1973)
4. Nonproliferation: The spread of nuclear weapons should be controlled.	4-1. Nonproliferation Treaty (1968) 4-2. U.S.-IAEA Safeguards Agreement (1977) 4-3. Convention on the Physical Protection of Nuclear Material
5. Disarmament: The production and use of certain weapons should be prohibited.	5-1. Geneva Protocol (1925) 5-2. Biological Weapons Convention (1972)
6. Environmental Protection: The detonation of nuclear weapons in certain areas should be prohibited in order to protect the environment.	6-1. Antarctica Treaty (1959) 6-2. Limited Test Ban Treaty (1963) 6-3. Environmental Modification Agreement (1977)
7. Strategic Nuclear Arms Limitations: Limitations should be placed on strategic nuclear weapons systems.	7-1. ABM Treaty (1972) 7-2. Interim Agreement (1972) 7-3. ABM Protocol (1974) 7-4. SALT II Treaty (1979)

Notes

1. I would like to thank Greg Conklin, Mark Garrison, and Peter Staugaard for their comments on an earlier version of this introduction. I would also like to thank the Center for Foreign Policy Development at Brown University for supporting the writing of this essay.
2. Gordon A. Craig, *Europe Since 1815,* third edition (New York: Holt, Rinehart and Winston, 1971), p. 465.
3. See Hedley Bull, *Strategic Arms Limitation: The Precedent of the Washington and London Naval Treaties,* Occasional Paper (Chicago: University of Chicago, 1971).
4. Frederick S. Dunn, "The Common Problem," in Bernard Brodie, *The Absolute Weapon: Atomic Power and World Order* (New York: Harcourt, Brace and Company, 1946), p. 4.
5. For a comparative history of the London Subcommittee and SALT I negotiations, see chapter 5 of Dan Caldwell, *American-Soviet Relations: From 1947 to the Nixon-Kissinger Grand Design* (Westport, Conn.: Greenwood Press, 1981), pp. 145-180.
6. Raymond L. Garthoff, "The Meaning of the Missiles," *The Washington Quarterly* 5, no. 4 (Autumn 1982), p. 79.
7. For an excellent summary of the Antarctica, Outer Space, and Seabed treaties, see John Barton and Lawrence Weiler (eds.), *International Arms Control: Issues and Agreements* (Stanford: Stanford University Press, 1976), pp. 96-101.
8. Despite its role in stimulating interest in the Latin American Nuclear Free Zone Treaty, Brazil has not signed the agreement. In addition, Argentina, Chile, and Cuba have not signed.
9. John F. Kennedy, "Commencement Address at American University, Washington, D.C., June 10, 1963," in *Public Papers of the Presidents of the United States: John F. Kennedy, 1963* (Washington, D.C.: U.S. Government Printing Office, 1964), pp. 459-464.
10. Elizabeth Young, *A Farewell to Arms Control?* (London: Penguin, 1972).
11. Herbert York and G. Allen Greb, *The Comprehensive Nuclear Test Ban* (Santa Monica, Calif.: California Seminar on Arms Control and Foreign Policy, June 1979).
12. Letter from Nikita Khrushchev to John F. Kennedy, October 28, 1962 (official translation), in *Department of State Bulletin* (November 19, 1973), p. 653.
13. Phil Williams, *Crisis Management: Confrontation and Diplomacy in the Nuclear Age* (New York: John Wiley, 1976), p. 118.
14. Henry Kissinger, *White House Years* (Boston: Little, Brown, 1979), p. 909.
15. Desmond Ball, *Can Nuclear War Be Controlled?* Adelphi Paper 169 (London: International Institute for Strategic Studies, 1981), p. 22.
16. Ibid., cited.
17. The text of the Basic Principles is reprinted in the *Department of State Bulletin* (June 26, 1972), pp. 898-899.
18. Ibid. For an excellent analysis of this agreement, see Alexander L. George, "The Basic Principles Agreement of 1972: Origins and Expectations," in Alexander L. George (ed.), *Managing U.S.-Soviet Rivalry: Problems of Crisis Prevention* (Boulder, Colo.: Westview Press, 1983), pp. 107-118.
19. The text of the Agreement on the Prevention of Nuclear War is contained in this volume, pp. 159-160.
20. Kissinger, *Years of Upheaval,* p. 285.
21. George, *Managing U.S.-Soviet Rivalry.*
22. "Press Conference of President John F. Kennedy, March 21, 1963," in *Public Papers of the Presidents: John F. Kennedy,* p. 273.

23. Lewis A. Dunn, *Controlling the Bomb: Nuclear Proliferation in the 1980s* (New Haven: Yale University Press, 1983), pp. 48-49.

24. William C. Potter, *Nuclear Power and Nonproliferation: An Interdisciplinary Perspective* (Cambridge, Mass.: Oelgeschlager, Gunn and Hain, 1982), p. 3.

25. Ibid., p. 44.

26. Ibid., p. 1.

27. Richard Halloran, "Spread of Nuclear Arms is Seen by 2000," *New York Times* (November 15, 1982), p. A3.

28. Leslie H. Gelb, "Keeping an Eye on Russia," *New York Times Magazine* (November 29, 1981).

29. See U.S. Department of State, *Chemical Warfare in Southeast Asia and Afghanistan: Report to the Congress from Secretary of State Alexander M. Haig, Jr.,* Special Report No. 98 (March 22, 1982); U.S. Department of State, *Chemical Warfare in Southeast Asia and Afghanistan: An Update: Report from Secretary of State George P. Schultz,* Special Report No. 104 (November 1982); and U.S. Department of State, *Yellow Rain: The Arms Control Implications,* Current Policy No. 458 (February 24, 1983).

30. Philip M. Boffey, "Source of 'Yellow Rain' Linked to Waste of Bees," *New York Times* (June 1, 1983), p. A16.

31. *The Military Balance, 1980-81* (London: The International Institute for Strategic Studies, 1980), pp. 90-91.

32. The view of the negotiations from the perspective of the U.S. delegation is given by the American chief negotiator in Gerard Smith, *Doubletalk: The Story of SALT I* (Garden City, N.Y.: Doubleday, 1980). The "back-channel" negotiations are described by Henry Kissinger in *White House Years* and by John Newhouse, *Cold Dawn: The Story of SALT* (New York: Holt, Rinehart and Winston, 1973).

33. Thomas W. Wolfe, *The SALT Experience* (Cambridge, Mass.: Ballinger Publishing Company, 1979).

34. Newhouse, *Cold Dawn,* p. 192.

35. President Nixon's briefing of congressional leaders, in U.S. Congress, Senate Committee on Foreign Relations, *Strategic Arms Limitation Agreements,* Hearings on S.J. Res. 242, 92nd Cong., 2nd sess., 1972, p. 392.

36. See Melvin Laird's testimony in U.S. Congress, Senate Armed Services Committee, *Military Implications of the Treaty on the Limitations of Anti-Ballistic Missile Systems and the Interim Agreement on the Limitation of Strategic Offensive Arms,* Hearings on S. J. Res. 241 and S. J. Res. 242, 92nd Cong., 2nd sess, 1972, p. 4.

37. This list is a summary of testimony to the Senate Foreign Relations Committee by senior members of the Carter administration; see *SALT II Senate Testimony,* Current Policy, no. 72A (Washington, D.C.: U.S. Department of State, 1979).

38. See the testimony of Paul Nitze, Edward Rowny, Thomas Moorer, Elmo Zumwalt, and Eugene Rostow in the Senate Foreign Relations and Armed Services Committees' hearings cited in notes 35 and 36 above.

39. See notes 35 and 36 above.

40. U.S. Congress, Senate Select Committee on Intelligence, *Capabilities of the United States to Monitor the SALT II Treaty* (Washington, D.C.: U.S. Government Printing Office, 1979).

41. Gloria Duffy, "Crisis Prevention in Cuba," in Alexander L. George (ed.), *Managing U.S.-Soviet Rivalry: Problems of Crisis Prevention* (Boulder, Colo.: Westview Press, 1983), pp. 285-318.

42. Robert C. Toth, "Carter, Reagan Display Wide Foreign Policy Gap," *Los Angeles Times* (October 19, 1980), part 1, p. 22.

43. *New York Times* (April 1, 1982).

44. *New York Times* (November 19, 1981).
45. Robert Scheer, *With Enough Shovels: Reagan, Bush and Nuclear War* (New York: Random House, 1982), pp. 24, 29.
46. Jonathan Schell, *The Fate of the Earth* (New York: Alfred A. Knopf, 1982).
47. Directed by former National Security Council staff member Roger Molander, the Ground Zero organization produced a "nuclear war primer"; see Ground Zero, *Nuclear War: What's in It for You?* (New York: Pocket Books, 1982).
483 *New York Times* (April 18, 1982), p. 16.
49. "Excerpts from Report of the Commission on Strategic Forces," *New York Times* (April 12, 1983), p. 18.
50. The reports prior to 1981 were published and distributed by the Arms Control Disarmament Agency. After 1981, the reports were published by the Senate Committee on Foreign Relations and the House Committee on Foreign Affairs.

Introduction

Efforts to prevent or limit war have a long history and have taken many forms. Men have tried to erect religious and ethical barriers against war, to outlaw it, to create codes and tribunals for peaceful arbitration and settlement of disputes. Nations have tried to avert war by withdrawing into isolation or neutrality, or by joining with others in leagues and alliances for the collective defense of peace and security.

In past eras efforts to control weapons of war were seldom successful or lasting. The coming of the nuclear era, however, brought such vast new dimensions of potential destructiveness that concepts of waging war and keeping the peace were transformed.

Until comparatively recent times, disarmament and arms control were chiefly measures imposed by the victors on the vanquished. Only rarely was arms limitation the result of freely negotiated agreement.

A notable example of freely negotiated and successful arms control in "modern" times was the Rush-Bagot agreement of 1817 between the United States and Great Britain, limiting naval forces on the Great Lakes and Lake Champlain to a few vessels on each side.

In the late 19th century the control of armaments took on new importance. The techniques of industrialization applied to the manufacture of weapons, mounting imperialist rivalries, nationalism, competing alliance systems—all contributed to an increasingly dangerous and costly arms race.

At the invitation of Tsar Nicholas II, International Peace Conferences met at The Hague in 1899 and 1907. The Hague Conferences brought advances in codifying the rules of war and in establishing institutions and procedures for settling international disputes—notably the Permanent Court of Arbitration at The Hague, antecedent of the Permanent Court of International Justice and of the present International Court of Justice.

Declarations signed at the 1899 conference prohibited the use of dum-dum bullets, asphyxiating gases, and the launching of projectiles and explosives from balloons or by other new methods of similar nature. The use of poison or poisoned weapons was forbidden by regulations annexed to both the 1899 and 1907 conventions; and a convention prohibiting or restricting the use of specific automatic contact mines and torpedoes was adopted in 1907.

The Hague Conferences were the first attempts at a worldwide approach to the problems of war and peace. They were the outgrowth of recognition that the control of modern weapons and the effects of modern warfare concerned the interests of all nations and required their collective action. Plans for a third conference, however, fell victim to the antagonisms and military competition that preceded World War I, as did many of the arms control declarations.

World War I was fought on a scale previously unknown and new weapons—tanks, submarines, aircraft, poison gas—increased its deadliness. The war gave fresh momentum to the creation of international peacekeeping institutions and to negotiations for disarmament. Following the cessation of hostilities, the Covenant of the League of Nations declared that "the maintenance of peace requires the reduction of national armaments to the lowest point consistent with national safety and the enforcement by common action of international obligations." The Treaty of Versailles imposed drastic limitations on Germany's armament and demilitarized the Rhineland. And in a series of postwar negotiations the Allied powers sought to impose agreed restrictions on certain weapons.

In 1921, on American initiative, a conference was convened at Washington to discuss arms limitations, one of its purposes being to curb an emerging naval race among the victorious allies. The resulting agreement established fixed ratios and tonnage limits for the capital ships of the leading naval powers, and a freeze on naval fortifications and bases in the western Pacific. In 1930 a subsequent treaty signed in London limited other classes of warships and provided for a third naval conference in 1935. That conference was unable to reach any effective agreement, and the naval treaties expired in 1936, following Japanese refusal to continue the arrangements.

The use of poison gas in the battles of World War I had evoked especially strong condemnation. In 1925, as the result of a U.S. initiative, a protocol was signed at Geneva prohibiting the use in war of poison gas and bacteriological weapons. By World War II most countries had ratified it, including all the great powers except the United States and Japan. The protocol was generally observed during that war, although Italy used poison gas in the Ethiopian war. Japan ratified the protocol in 1970; U.S. ratification took place in 1975. When the protocol was originally submitted to the U.S. Senate in 1926, there was strong lobbying against it, and Senate action was not completed. It was resubmitted by President Nixon in 1970, but disagreement about the protocol's application to riot-control agents and herbicides delayed Senate consent to ratification. (The administration took the position that the protocol did not apply to these.)

In 1928 the Kellogg-Briand Pact, initiated by the United States and France and signed by 63 nations, renounced war as an instrument of national policy. The pact included no provisions for insuring compliance with its obligations, and many signatories attached sweeping qualifications or unilateral interpretations, which made the agreement meaningless.

In 1932, after 7 years of preparation, a general disarmament conference was held under the auspices of the League of Nations. A wide variety of measures to limit armed forces, weapons, and expenditures was proposed, including a French proposal for an international police force under the League, a Soviet proposal for general and complete disarmament, and a U.S. plan to reduce forces and to abolish chemical warfare, tanks, bombers, and heavy artillery. No agreement was achieved. Germany demanded the right to rearm unless other nations disarmed to her level, and after Hitler came to power, Germany left the conference and the League. Sporadic sessions of the conference continued until 1937, when it dissolved in deadlock.

New levels of violence and devastation were reached in World War II. Even before its close, the nations fighting the Axis powers began a new effort to prevent war through a system of collective security. The U.N. Charter envisaged international forces under the Security Council to keep the peace. "Armed forces, assistance, and facilities" were to be contributed by all U.N. members. Unlike the Covenant of the League, the Charter gave disarmament no immediate priority; the five great powers would maintain their armaments, policing the disarmament of Germany and Japan and maintaining the peace until the United Nations had developed its own effective military forces. Under Article 11 the General Assembly was "to consider the general principles of cooperation in the maintenance of international peace and security, including the principles governing disarmament and the regulation of armaments," and make recommendations to the Security Council. Article 47 provided that the Military Staff Committee would advise the Security Council on "the regulation of armaments and possible disarmament." Only in these two articles does the word "disarmament" occur.

The Charter of the United Nations was signed at San Francisco on June 26, 1945; on August 6, a new weapon exploded over Hiroshima. Its stupendous power, shattering old concepts of war and weaponry, imposed new urgencies and demanded new perspectives on international efforts to control armaments.

The first American proposal for the control of nuclear weapons recognized that this new force involved the interests of the entire world community. In 1946 the U.S. Representative to the U.N. Atomic Energy Commission, Bernard Baruch, presented a U.S. plan that called for placing all the atomic resources of the world under the ownership or control of an independent international authority. It would have exclusive authority over all the stages of nuclear production, from mining to manufacture, and over the eventual destruction of all nuclear weapons. If the plan were adopted, the United States, the only nuclear power, would give up its atomic arsenal. All nations would submit to inspection by the international authority. If violations called for action by the Security Council, the veto could not be exercised. The plan was to be carried out in stages; the control system was to be in effective operation before the nuclear weapons were removed from the U.S. arsenal.

Although the plan was endorsed by a large majority of U.N. members, the Soviet Union objected to the ownership, staging, and enforcement provisions. Soviet counterproposals left nuclear activities under the control of national governments. The international authority would be empowered only to conduct periodic inspection of declared nuclear facilities. The United States and most other nations considered the Soviet plan's verification provisions altogether inadequate, and negotiations became deadlocked.

Meanwhile, the development of technology brought new dangers and complexities. In September 1949 President Truman announced that the Soviet Union had detonated a nuclear device. In 1952 the United States exploded the first hydrogen device. The first atomic bomb had had the power of 15,000 tons of TNT—15 kilotons. The destructive power of the new weapons was measured in megatons, the equivalent of millions of tons of TNT. In 1953 the Soviet Union announced that they too had exploded a hydrogen bomb. Rivalry in nuclear weapons was paralleled by rivalry in the development of delivery systems.

Among earlier efforts of the nuclear era to control armaments were broad, inclusive proposals, including (by 1959) proposals for "General and Complete Disarmament," with carefully interlocked stages for reducing or eliminating weapons and armed forces, and with precisely stipulated timing to assure that the process of disarming would not leave any nation's security weakened. This exacting requirement for establishing the pace and order of reductions and assuring their equitable impact put great difficulties in the way of agreements. Each nation defined its security needs differently; each possessed differing arrays of weapons and armed forces designed to defend its particular interests. Disparities and differences were accompanied by strong ideological conflicts that intensified wariness and suspicion. And the obstacle of verification stubbornly persisted.

The General Assembly's sessions devoted increasing attention to disarmament issues, and the nonnuclear powers demonstrated heightened concern as the spread of nuclear technology and the continued testing of weapons sharpened world awareness of the implications of nuclear warfare. Successive subsidiary bodies were created as forums for arms control negotiations. The U.N. Disarmament Commission, created in 1952, operated at first chiefly through a Subcommittee of Five—the United States, Great Britain, France, Canada, and the Soviet Union. As debates continued without agreement, membership in disarmament bodies was broadened and efforts were made to blunt the sharpness of East-West division by the participation of nonaligned, nonnuclear nations. The Eighteen Nation Disarmament Committee (ENDC), which began meeting in 1962, became the Conference of the Committee on Disarmament (CCD) in 1969, when its membership was enlarged. The ENDC and the CCD played important roles in achieving the multinational agreements that finally emerged. The Committee on Disarmament (CD), a still larger forum comprising 40 member states, was established in 1978 and began negotiations in 1979. France was a member of both the ENDC and the CCD but had never taken its seat in either. It is an active participant in CD meetings. China has also been an active participant since January 1980.

The creation of such active organizations for multilateral negotiations marked a step forward; so did the convening of special meetings with the participation of experts to deal with particular issues, such as the Geneva Conference on the Discontinuance of Nuclear Tests. The broad continuing effort was supported by active diplomatic exchanges and high-level meetings among the nuclear powers. The special responsibility of the major nuclear powers was subsequently manifested in the bilateral Strategic Arms Limitation Talks (SALT) between the United States and the Soviet Union that began in 1969.

By the middle of the 1950s, past production of nuclear materials could no longer be reliably accounted for, and control systems could not assure that none had been diverted to clandestine weapons manufacture or illegal stockpiles. A point of no return seemed to have been passed. As negotiations and debate continued, emphasis thus shifted gradually from programs of comprehensive disarmament to more limited measures. This brought a new flexibility and pragmatism into negotiations and, while general and complete disarmament remained a goal, willingness to consider partial solutions of limited scope helped to make solid step-by-step progress possible.

Moreover, advanced technology brought qualitative and quantitative changes in weaponry that radically altered concepts of national security and supplied a compelling incentive for pursuing arms control agreements. In the past it was the generally accepted assumption that more armed strength equaled more security. But this equation is no longer valid for the United States and the Soviet Union, which possess arsenals able to destroy the other many times over. More armaments do not guarantee more security. They may in fact have an opposite effect, creating new dangers by causing a potential adversary to overreact in his own weapons program—in response to what he perceives as a threat to his own security. The continuing arms race also increases the possibility of an accident.

Arms control is no longer an intermittent enterprise. It has become a central and continuing concern of governments and an integral aspect of foreign policy and national security. Thus the United States—the first government to do so—established a separate agency in 1961 to deal with disarmament issues. The U.S. Arms Control and Disarmament Agency (ACDA) is charged with formulating, coordinating, and carrying out arms control policies; for conducting and coordinating research; for preparation and management of U.S. participation in negotiations; and for public dissemination of information about arms control.

Some of the agreements printed here have been signed by almost all the world's nations. Others have been negotiated among the chief nuclear powers, who bear the greatest responsibility for averting conflict that would tragically affect nations and peoples everywhere. Some of the treaties are essentially "nonarmament" agreements, designed to keep free of conflict and nuclear weaponry the environments that science has made newly accessible and significant, and whose resources must be preserved for all—for example, outer space or the seabed—or geographic regions where nuclear weapons have not been introduced—Antarctica and Latin America. Some agreements reflect a growing concern with the need to prevent a war that might occur through accident, unauthorized or lawless action, human error, or mechanical failure. And some reflect a conscious decision by the major nuclear powers to limit their own strategic offensive and defensive weapons.

Protocol for the Prohibition of the Use in War of Asphyxiating, Poisonous or Other Gases, and of Bacteriological Methods of Warfare

At the end of World War I, the victorious Allies decided to reaffirm in the Versailles treaty (1919) the prewar prohibition of the use of poisonous gases (see Introduction) and to forbid Germany to manufacture or import them. Similar provisions were included in the peace treaties with Austria, Bulgaria, and Hungary.

Drawing upon the language of these peace treaties, the United States—at the Washington Disarmament Conference of 1922—took the initiative of introducing a similar provision into a treaty on submarines and noxious gases. The U.S. Senate gave its advice and consent to ratification of this treaty without a dissenting vote. It never entered into force, however, since French ratification was necessary, and France objected to the submarine provisions.

At the 1925 Geneva Conference for the Supervision of the International Traffic in Arms, the United States similarly took the initiative of seeking to prohibit the export of gases for use in war. At French suggestion, it was decided to draw up a protocol on non-use of poisonous gas; and at the suggestion of Poland, the prohibition was extended to bacteriological weapons. Signed on June 17, 1925, the Geneva Protocol thus restated the prohibition previously laid down by the Versailles and Washington treaties and added a ban on bacteriological warfare.

Before World War II the protocol was ratified by many countries, including all the great powers except the United States and Japan. When they ratified or acceded to the protocol, some nations—including the United Kingdom, France, and the U.S.S.R.—declared that it would cease to be binding on them if their enemies, or the allies of their enemies, failed to respect the prohibitions of the protocol. Although Italy was a party to the protocol, it used poison gas in the Ethiopian war. On the other hand, the protocol was generally observed in World War II. Referring to reports that the Axis powers were considering the use of gas, President Roosevelt said on June 8, 1943:

Use of such weapons has been outlawed by the general opinion of civilized mankind. This country has not used them, and I hope that we never will be compelled to use them. I state categorically that we shall under no circumstances resort to the use of such weapons unless they are first used by our enemies.

Although the Senate Foreign Relations Committee had favorably reported the protocol in 1926, there was strong lobbying against it, and the Senate had never voted on it. After the war, President Truman withdrew it from the Senate, together with other inactive older treaties. Little attention was paid to the protocol for several years thereafter. During the Korean war, however, the Communist side falsely accused the United States of using bacteriological weapons in Korea; however, they rejected American proposals for international investigation of their charges. In the Security Council, the Soviet Union introduced a draft resolution calling on all U.N. members to ratify the protocol. At that time, the United States was not willing to agree to prohibit the use of any weapons of mass destruction unless they could be eliminated through a disarmament agreement with effective safeguards. On June 26, 1952, the Soviet resolution was rejected by a vote of 1 to 0, with 10 abstentions (including the United States, the United Kingdom, and France).

In 1966 the Communist countries strongly criticized the United States for using tear gas and chemical herbicides in Vietnam. In the General Assembly, Hungary charged that the use in war of these agents was prohibited by the protocol and other provisions of international law. The United States denied that the protocol applied to nontoxic gases or chemical herbicides. Joined by Canada, Italy, and the United Kingdom, the United States introduced amendments to a Hungarian resolution that would have made the use of any chemical and bacteriological weapons an international crime. In its final form, the resolution called for "strict observance by all states of the principles and objectives" of the protocol, condemned "all actions contrary to those objectives," and invited all states to accede to the protocol. During the debate, the U.S. Representative stated that it would be up to each country to decide whether or how to adhere to the protocol, "in the light of constitutional and other considerations."

Interpretation of the protocol remained a thorny problem. In his foreword to a U.N. report on chemical and biological weapons (July 1, 1969), Secretary General Thant recommended a renewed appeal for accession to the protocol and a "clear affirmation" that it covered the use in war of all chemical and biological weapons, including tear gas and other harassing agents. Discussion in the Conference of the Committee on Disarmament (CCD) showed that most members agreed with the Thant recommendations. Swedish Ambassador Myrdal, a strong advocate of the broad interpretation, stressed the danger of escalation if nonlethal chemical agents were permitted. She also pointed out that the military use of tear gases should be distinguished from their use for riot control and that there was a similar difference between using herbicides in war and employing them for peaceful purposes. On the other hand, U.K. Disarmament

Minister Mulley held that only the parties to the protocol were entitled to say what it meant.

In the General Assembly, the 12 nonaligned members of the CCD, joined by 9 other nations, introduced a resolution condemning as contrary to international law the use in international armed conflict of all chemical and biological agents. Opposing the resolution, the U.S. Representative reaffirmed the American interpretation of the protocol and took the position that it was inappropriate for the General Assembly to interpret treaties by means of a resolution. The 21-nation resolution was adopted on December 16, 1969, by a vote of 80 to 3 (Australia, Portugal, the United States), and 36 abstentions (including France and the United Kingdom). France and many other abstainers accepted the broad interpretation of the protocol but considered the resolution undesirable on other grounds.

While the General Assembly debate was still underway, President Nixon announced on November 25, 1969, that he would resubmit the protocol to the Senate. He reaffirmed U.S. renunciation of the first use of lethal chemical weapons and extended this renunciation to incapacitating chemicals. It was on this occasion that he also announced the unilateral U.S. renunciation of bacteriological (biological) methods of warfare.

Some support for the American interpretation of the protocol now came from the United Kingdom and Japan. During the 1930 discussion at Geneva in the Preparatory Commission for the Disarmament Conference, the United Kingdom had taken the position that the protocol covered tear gas. In February 1970 the British Foreign Secretary told Parliament that this was still the British position, but that the riot-control agent CS, unlike older tear gases, was not harmful to man and was therefore not covered by the protocol. During the Diet debate on Japanese ratification of the protocol, Foreign Minister Aichi took the position that it did not prohibit riot-control agents and herbicides. Japan ratified the protocol in May 1970.

In a report of August 11, 1970, to the President, Secretary of State Rogers recommended that the protocol be ratified with a reservation of the right to retaliate with gas if an enemy state or its allies violated the protocol. He also reaffirmed the position that the protocol did not apply to the use in war of riot-control agents and herbicides. President Nixon resubmitted the protocol to the Senate on August 19.

The Foreign Relations Committee did not accept the Administration's interpretation regarding riot-control agents and herbicides. In a letter of April 15, 1971, to the President, Senator Fulbright (Dem., Ark.), the Chairman, said many members thought that it would be in the interest of the United States either to ratify the protocol without "restrictive understandings" or to postpone action until this became possible. The Committee thus deferred action. It also held in abeyance the Biological Weapons Convention, which was submitted to it on August 10, 1972, pending resolution of this issue.

In the latter part of 1974, the Ford Administration launched a new initiative to obtain Senate consent to ratification of the protocol (and, simultaneously, of the Biological Weapons Convention). The new approach was set forth to the Committee by ACDA Director Fred Ikle on December 10, when he announced that the President, while reaffirming the Administration's view as to the scope of the protocol, was prepared "to renounce as a matter of national policy: (1) first use of herbicides in war except use, under regulations applicable to their domestic use, for control of vegetation within U.S. bases and installations or around their immediate defensive perimeters; (2) first use of riot-control agents in war except in defensive military modes to save lives such as:

(a) Use of riot-control agents in riot-control circumstances to include controlling rioting prisoners of war. This exception would permit use of riot-control agents in riot situations in areas under direct and distinct U.S. military control;
(b) Use of riot-control agents in situations where civilian casualties can be reduced or avoided. This use would be restricted to situations in which civilians are used to mask or screen attacks;
(c) Use of riot-control agents in rescue missions. The use of riot-control agents would be permissible in the recovery of remotely isolated personnel such as downed aircrews (and passengers);
(d) Use of riot-control agents in rear echelon areas outside the combat zone to protect convoys from civil disturbances, terrorists and paramilitary organizations."

In addition, Dr. Ikle testified that "the President, under an earlier directive still in force, must approve in advance any use of riot-control agents and chemical herbicides in war."

Two days later, on December 12, the Committee voted unanimously to send the protocol and the convention to the Senate floor, and on December 16 the Senate voted its approval, also unanimously. The Committee, in recommending advice and consent to ratification of the protocol indicated that it attached particular importance to Dr. Ikle's response to the following question posed in connection with his December 10 testimony:

Question: "Assuming the Senate were to give its advice and consent to ratification on the grounds proposed by the Administration, what legal impediment would there be to subsequent Presidential decisions broadening the permissible uses of herbicides and riot-control agents?

Answer: "There would be no formal legal impediment to such a decision. However, the policy which was presented to the Committee will be inextricably linked with the history of Senate consent to ratification of the Protocol with its consent dependent upon its observance. If a future administration should change this policy without Senate consent whether in practice or by a formal policy change, it would be inconsistent with the history of the ratification, and could have extremely grave political repercussions and as a result is extremely unlikely to happen."

The protocol and the convention were ratified by President Ford on January 22, 1975. The U.S. instrument of ratification of the convention was deposited on March 26, 1975, and of the protocol on April 10, 1975.

Protocol for the Prohibition of the Use in War of Asphyxiating, Poisonous or Other Gases, and of Bacteriological Methods of Warfare

Signed at Geneva June 17, 1925
Entered into force February 8, 1928
Ratification advised by the U.S. Senate December 16, 1974
Ratified by U.S. President January 22, 1975
U.S. ratification deposited with the Government of France April 10, 1975
Proclaimed by U.S. President April 29, 1975

The Undersigned Plenipotentiaries, in the name of their respective Governments:

Whereas the use in war of asphyxiating, poisonous or other gases, and of all analogous liquids, materials or devices, has been justly condemned by the general opinion of the civilized world; and

Whereas the prohibition of such use has been declared in Treaties to which the majority of Powers of the World are Parties; and

To the end that this prohibition shall be universally accepted as a part of International Law, binding alike the conscience and the practice of nations;

Declare:

That the High Contracting Parties, so far as they are not already Parties to Treaties prohibiting such use, accept this prohibition, agree to extend this prohibition to the use of bacteriological methods of warfare and agree to be bound as between themselves according to the terms of this declaration.

The High Contracting Parties will exert every effort to induce other States to accede to the present Protocol. Such accession will be notified to the Government of the French Republic, and by the latter to all signatory and acceding Powers, and will take effect on the date of the notification by the Government of the French Republic.

The present Protocol, of which the French and English texts are both authentic, shall be ratified as soon as possible. It shall bear today's date.

The ratifications of the present Protocol shall be addressed to the Government of the French Republic, which will at once notify the deposit of such ratification to each of the signatory and acceding Powers.

The instruments of ratification of and accession to the present Protocol will remain deposited in the archives of the Government of the French Republic.

The present Protocol will come into force for each signatory Power as from the date of deposit of its ratification, and, from that moment, each Power will be bound as regards other powers which have already deposited their ratifications.

IN WITNESS WHEREOF the Plenipotentiaries have signed the present Protocol.

DONE at Geneva in a single copy, this seventeenth day of June, One Thousand Nine Hundred and Twenty-Five.

States Parties to the Protocol for the Prohibition of the Use in War of Asphyxiating, Poisonous or Other Gases, and of Bacteriological Methods of Warfare, Done at Geneva June 17, 1925

States which have deposited instruments of ratification or accession, or continue to be bound as the result of succession agreements concluded by them or by reason of notification given by them to the Secretary-General of the United Nations:

	Argentina—May 12, 1969
1 a b	Australia—Jan. 22, 1930
	Austria—May 9, 1928
1 a b 2	Bahamas, The
2	Barbados—June 22, 1976
1 a b	Belgium—Dec. 4, 1928
6	Bhutan—June 12, 1978[6]
1 a b 2	Botswana
	Brazil—Aug. 28, 1970
1 a b	Bulgaria—Mar. 7, 1934
1 a b 2	Burma
1 a b	Canada—May 6, 1930
	Central African Republic—July 31, 1970
1 a b	Chile—July 2, 1935
1 a b	China, People's Republic of—Aug. 9, 1952
	China (Taiwan)—Aug. 7, 1929
7	Comoros
	Cuba—June 24, 1966
	Cyprus—Dec. 12, 1966
1 b	Czechoslovakia—Aug. 16, 1938
	Denmark—May 5, 1930
7	Djibouti
	Dominican Republic—Dec. 8, 1970
	Ecuador—Sept. 16, 1970
	Egypt—Dec. 6, 1928
1 a b	Estonia—Aug. 28, 1931
	Ethiopia—Sept. 18, 1935
1 a b	Fiji—Mar. 21, 1973
	Finland—June 26, 1929
1 a b 3	France—May 9, 1926
	Gambia, The—Nov. 16, 1966
	German Democratic Republic
	Germany, Federal Republic of—Apr. 25, 1929
	Ghana—May 3, 1967
	Greece—May 30, 1931

See footnotes page 18.

1 a b   Grenada
1 a b 2   Guyana

               Holy See—Oct. 18, 1966
               Hungary—Oct. 11, 1952

               Iceland—Nov. 2, 1967
1 a b   India—Apr. 9, 1930
               Indonesia—Jan. 26, 1971
               Iran—July 4, 1929
1 a b   Iraq—Sept. 8, 1931
               Ireland—Aug. 18, 1930
1 a b   Israel—Feb. 20, 1969
               Italy—Apr. 3, 1928
               Ivory Coast—July 27, 1970

               Jamaica—July 31, 1970
               Japan—May 21, 1970
1 a b d   Jordan—Jan. 20, 1977

               Kenya—July 6, 1970
1 a b d   Kuwait—Dec. 15, 1971

               Latvia—June 3, 1931
               Lebanon—Apr. 17, 1969
               Lesotho—Mar. 15, 1972
               Liberia—Apr. 2, 1927
1 b d   Libya—Dec. 29, 1971
               Lithuania—June 15, 1933
               Luxembourg—Sept. 1, 1936

               Madagascar—Aug. 12, 1967
               Malawi—Sept. 14, 1970
               Malaysia—Dec. 10, 1970
               Maldive Islands—Jan. 6, 1967
               Mali—Nov. 19, 1966
               Malta—Oct. 15, 1970
               Mauritius—Jan. 8, 1971
               Mexico—Mar. 15, 1932
               Monaco—Jan. 6, 1967
1   b   Mongolia—Dec. 6, 1968
               Morocco—Oct. 13, 1970

               Nepal—May 9, 1969
1 c 4   Netherlands—Oct. 31, 1930
1 a b   New Zealand—Jan. 22, 1930
               Niger—Apr. 19, 1967
1 a b   Nigeria—Oct. 15, 1968
               Norway—July 27, 1932

               Pakistan—June 9, 1960

See footnotes page 18.

	Panama—Dec. 4, 1970
1 a b	Papua New Guinea—Sept. 16, 1975
	Paraguay—Jan. 14, 1969
	Philippines—May 29, 1973
	Poland—Feb. 4, 1929
1 a b	Portugal—July 1, 1930
	Qatar—Sept. 16, 1976
1 a b	Romania—Aug. 23, 1929
	Rwanda—June 25, 1964
	Saudi Arabia—Jan. 27, 1971
1 a b 2	Seychelles
	Sierra Leone—Mar. 20, 1967
1 a b 2	Singapore
1 a b	South Africa—Jan. 22, 1930
1 a b	Spain—Aug. 22, 1929
	Sri Lanka—Jan. 20, 1954
	Sudan—Dec. 17, 1980
1 c 4	Suriname
1 a b 2	Swaziland
	Sweden—Apr. 25, 1930
	Switzerland—July 12, 1932
1 d	Syrian Arab Republic—Dec. 17, 1968
	Tanzania—Apr. 22, 1963
	Thailand—June 6, 1931
	Togo—Apr. 5, 1971
	Tonga—July 28, 1971
	Trinidad and Tobago—Nov. 30, 1970
	Tunisia—July 12, 1967
	Turkey—Oct. 5, 1929
	Uganda—May 24, 1965
1 a b	Union of Soviet Socialist Republics—Apr. 5, 1928
1 a b 5	United Kingdom—Apr. 9, 1930
1 c	United States—Apr. 10, 1975
	Upper Volta—Mar. 3, 1971
	Uruguay—Apr. 12, 1977
	Venezuela—Feb. 8, 1928
1 a b	Vietnam—Sept. 23, 1980
1 b	Yemen Arab Republic (Sana)—Mar. 17, 1971
	Yugoslavia—Apr. 12, 1929
1 a b 2	Zambia

1 a, b, c, d With reservations to Protocol as follows:

  a—binding only as regards relations with other parties.
  b—to cease to be binding in regard to any enemy States whose armed forces or allies do not observe provisions.
  c—to cease to be binding as regards use of chemical agents with respect to any enemy State whose armed forces or allies do not observe provisions.
  d—does not constitute recognition of or involve treaty relations with Israel.

[2]By virtue of agreement with former parent State or notification to the Secretary General of the United Nations of succession to treaty rights and obligations upon independence.

[3]Applicable to all French territories.

[4]Applicable to Suriname and Curacao.

[5]It does not bind India or any British Dominion which is a separate member of the League of Nations and does not separately sign or adhere to the Protocol. It is applicable to all colonies.

[6]Deposited accession on June 12, 1978, but the French Government asked that accession take effect on date of notification by them—Feb. 19, 1979.

[7]Included in declaration by France. Continued application has apparently not been determined.

The Antarctic Treaty

The Antarctic Treaty, the earliest of the post-World War II arms limitation agreements, has significance both in itself and as a precedent. It internationalized and demilitarized the Antarctic Continent and provided for its cooperative exploration and future use. It has been cited as an example of nations exercising foresight and working in concert to prevent conflict before it develops. Based on the premise that to exclude armaments is easier than to eliminate or control them once they have been introduced, the treaty served as a model, in its approach and even provisions, for later "nonarmament" treaties—the treaties that excluded nuclear weapons from outer space, from Latin America, and from the seabed.

By the 1950s seven nations—Argentina, Australia, Chile, France, New Zealand, Norway, and the United Kingdom—claimed sovereignty over areas of Antarctica, on the basis of discovery, exploration, or geographic propinquity. Claims of Argentina, Chile, and the United Kingdom overlapped. Eight other nations—the United States, the Soviet Union, Belgium, Germany, Poland, Sweden, Japan, and South Africa—had engaged in exploration but had put forward no specific claims. The United States did not recognize the claims of other governments and reserved the right to assert claims based on exploration by its citizens. The Soviet Union took a similar position.

Activities in the Antarctic had generally been conducted peacefully and cooperatively. Yet the possibility that exploitable economic resources might be found meant the possibility of future rivalry for their control. Moreover, isolated and uninhabited, the continent might at some time become a potential site for emplacing nuclear weapons.

Fortunately, scientific interests rather than political, economic, or military concerns dominated the expeditions sent to Antarctica after World War II. Fortunately, too, international scientific associations were able to work out arrangements for effective cooperation. In 1956 and 1957, for example, American meteorologists "wintered over" at the Soviet post, Mirnyy, while Soviet meteorologists "wintered over" at Little America. These cooperative activities culminated in the International Geophysical Year of 1957-1958 (IGY), a joint scientific effort by 12 nations—Argentina, Australia, Belgium, Chile, France, Japan, New Zealand, Norway, South Africa, the Soviet Union, the United Kingdom, and the United States—to conduct studies of the Earth and its cosmic environment.

In these years the desire to keep the continent demilitarized was general and some diplomatic discussion of the possibility had taken place. On May 3, 1958, the United States proposed to the other 11 nations participating in the IGY that a conference be held, based on the points of agreement that had been reached in informal discussions:

(1) that the legal *status quo* of the Antarctic Continent remain unchanged;
(2) that scientific cooperation continue;
(3) that the continent be used for peaceful purposes only.

All accepted the U.S. invitation. The Washington Conference on Antarctica met from October 15 to December 1, 1959. No insurmountable conflicts or issues divided the conference, and negotiations culminated in a treaty signed by all 12 nations on December 1, 1959. Approved by the U.S. Senate, U.S. ratification was deposited August 18, 1960, and the treaty entered into force on June 23, 1961, when the formal ratifications of all the participating nations had been received.

The treaty provides that Antarctica shall be used for peaceful purposes only. It specifically prohibits "any measures of a military nature, such as the establishment of military bases and fortifications, the carrying out of military maneuvers, as well as the testing of any type of weapons." Military personnel or equipment, however, may be used for scientific research or for any other peaceful purpose. Nuclear explosions and the disposal of radioactive waste material in Antarctica are prohibited, subject to certain future international agreements of these subjects. All Contracting Parties entitled to participate in the meetings referred to in Article IX of the treaty have the right to designate observers to carry out inspections in all areas of Antarctica, including all stations, installations and equipment, and ships and aircraft at discharge or embarkation points. Each observer has complete freedom of access at any time to any or all areas of Antarctica. Contracting Parties may also carry out aerial inspections. There are provisions for amending the treaty; for referring disputes that cannot be handled by direct talks, mediation, arbitration, or other peaceful means to the International Court of Justice; and for calling a conference in 30 years to review the operation of the treaty if any parties request it.

Argentina, Australia, New Zealand, the United Kingdom, and the United States have all exercised the right of inspection. The United States in 1964 inspected stations operated by six nations—Argentina, Chile, France, New Zealand, the United Kingdom, and the Soviet Union; in 1967, eight stations operated by seven nations were visited during a 5-week, 8,500-mile voyage; inspections have taken place in 1971, 1975, 1977, and 1980. All American inspections included Soviet facilities. They reported essentially the same findings. No military activities, armaments, or prohibited nuclear activities were observed, and all scientific programs were in accord with previously published plans. The observed activities at each station were in compliance with the provisions and spirit of the Antarctic Treaty.

Eleven consultative meetings have been held in accordance with Article IX of the treaty. Numerous recommendations on measures in furtherance of the principles and objectives of the treaty have been adopted, many of which have now entered into force. The Contracting Parties entitled to participate in these meetings are the 12 original signatory states, as well as Poland and the Federal Republic of Germany, whose entitlements to consultative status, pursuant to paragraph 2 of Article IX, were recognized at a special consultative meeting in London in July 1977, and at the preparatory meeting for the eleventh consultative meeting held from February 20 to March 3, 1981, respectively.

The Antarctic Treaty

Signed at Washington December 1, 1959
Ratification advised by U.S. Senate August 10, 1960
Ratified by U.S. President August 18, 1960
U.S. ratification deposited at Washington August 18, 1960
Proclaimed by U.S. President June 23, 1961
Entered into force June 23, 1961

The Governments of Argentina, Australia, Belgium, Chile, the French Republic, Japan, New Zealand, Norway, the Union of South Africa, the Union of Soviet Socialist Republics, the United Kingdom of Great Britain and Northern Ireland, and the United States of America,

Recognizing that it is in the interest of all mankind that Antarctica shall continue forever to be used exclusively for peaceful purposes and shall not become the scene or object of international discord;

Acknowledging the substantial contributions to scientific knowledge resulting from international cooperation in scientific investigation in Antarctica;

Convinced that the establishment of a firm foundation for the continuation and development of such cooperation on the basis of freedom of scientific investigation in Antarctica as applied during the International Geophysical Year accords with the interests of science and the progress of all mankind;

Convinced also that a treaty ensuring the use of Antarctica for peaceful purposes only and the continuance of international harmony in Antarctica will further the purposes and principles embodied in the Charter of the United Nations;

Have agreed as follows:

Article I

1. Antarctica shall be used for peaceful purposes only. There shall be prohibited, *inter alia,* any measures of a military nature, such as the establishment of military bases and fortifications, the carrying out of military maneuvers, as well as the testing of any type of weapons.

2. The present Treaty shall not prevent the use of military personnel or equipment for scientific research or for any other peaceful purposes.

Article II

Freedom of scientific investigation in Antarctica and cooperation toward that end, as applied during the International Geophysical Year, shall continue, subject to the provisions of the present Treaty.

Article III

1. In order to promote international cooperation in scientific investigation in Antarctica, as provided for in Article II of the present Treaty, the Contracting Parties agree that, to the greatest extent feasible and practicable:

(a) information regarding plans for scientific programs in Antarctica shall be exchanged to permit maximum economy and efficiency of operations;

(b) scientific personnel shall be exchanged in Antarctica between expeditions and stations;

(c) scientific observations and results from Antarctica shall be exchanged and made freely available.

2. In implementing this Article, every encouragement shall be given to the establishment of cooperative working relations with those Specialized Agencies of the United Nations and other international organizations having a scientific or technical interest in Antarctica.

Article IV

1. Nothing contained in the present Treaty shall be interpreted as:

(a) a renunciation by any Contracting Party of previously asserted rights of or claims to territorial sovereignty in Antarctica;

(b) a renunciation or diminution by any Contracting Party of any basis of claim to territorial sovereignty in Antarctica which it may have whether as a result of its activities or those of its nationals in Antarctica, or otherwise;

(c) prejudicing the position of any Contracting Party as regards its recognition or non-recognition of any other State's right of or claim or basis of claim to territorial sovereignty in Antarctica.

2. No acts or activities taking place while the present Treaty is in force shall constitute a basis for asserting, supporting or denying a claim to territorial sovereignty in Antarctica or create any rights of sovereignty in Antarctica. No new claim, or enlargement of an existing claim, to territorial sovereignty in Antarctica shall be asserted while the present Treaty is in force.

Article V

1. Any nuclear explosions in Antarctica and the disposal there of radioactive waste material shall be prohibited.

2. In the event of the conclusion of international agreements concerning the use of nuclear energy, including nuclear explosions and the disposal of radioactive waste material, to which all of the Contracting Parties whose representatives are entitled to participate in the meetings provided for under Article IX are parties, the rules established under such agreements shall apply in Antarctica.

Article VI

The provisions of the present Treaty shall apply to the area south of 60° South Latitude, including all ice shelves, but nothing in the present Treaty shall prejudice or in any way affect the rights, or the exercise of the rights, of any State under international law with regard to the high seas within that area.

Article VII

1. In order to promote the objectives and ensure the observance of the provisions of the present Treaty, each Contracting Party whose representatives are entitled to participate in the meetings referred to in Article IX of the Treaty shall have the right to designate observers to carry out any inspection provided for by the present Article. Observers shall be nationals of the Contracting Parties which designate them. The names of observers shall be communicated to every other Contracting Party having the right to designate observers, and like notice shall be given of the termination of their appointment.

2. Each observer designated in accordance with the provisions of paragraph 1 of this Article shall have complete freedom of access at any time to any or all areas of Antarctica.

3. All areas of Antarctica, including all stations, installations and equipment within those areas, and all ships and aircraft at points of discharging or embarking cargoes or personnel in Antarctica, shall be open at all times to inspection by any observers designated in accordance with paragraph 1 of this Article.

4. Aerial observation may be carried out at any time over any or all areas of Antarctica by any of the Contracting Parties having the right to designate observers.

5. Each Contracting Party shall, at the time when the present Treaty enters into force for it, inform the other Contracting Parties, and thereafter shall give them notice in advance, of

(a) all expeditions to and within Antarctica, on the part of its ships or nationals, and all expeditions to Antarctica organized in or proceeding from its territory;

(b) all stations in Antarctica occupied by its nationals; and

(c) any military personnel or equipment intended to be introduced by it into Antarctica subject to the conditions prescribed in paragraph 2 of Article I of the present Treaty.

Article VIII

1. In order to facilitate the exercise of their functions under the present Treaty, and without prejudice to the respective positions of the Contracting Parties relating to jurisdiction over all other persons in Antarctica, observers designated under paragraph 1 of Article VII and scientific personnel exchanged under subparagraph 1(b) of Article III of the Treaty, and members of the staffs accompanying any such persons, shall be subject only to the jurisdiction of the Contracting Party of which they are nationals in respect of all acts or omissions occurring while they are in Antarctica for the purpose of exercising their functions.

2. Without prejudice to the provisions of paragraph 1 of this Article, and pending the adoption of measures in pursuance of subparagraph 1(e) of Article IX, the Contracting Parties concerned in any case of dispute with regard to the exercise of jurisdiction in Antarctica shall immediately consult together with a view to reaching a mutually acceptable solution.

Article IX

1. Representatives of the Contracting Parties named in the preamble to the present Treaty shall meet at the City of Canberra within two months after the date of entry into force of the Treaty, and thereafter at suitable intervals and places, for the purpose of exchanging information, consulting together on matters of common interest pertaining to Antarctica, and formulating and considering, and recommending to their Governments, measures in furtherance of the principles and objectives of the Treaty, including measures regarding:

(a) use of Antarctica for peaceful purposes only;

(b) facilitation of scientific research in Antarctica;

(c) facilitation of international scientific cooperation in Antarctica;

(d) facilitation of the exercise of the rights of inspection provided for in Article VII of the Treaty;

(e) questions relating to the exercise of jurisdiction in Antarctica;

(f) preservation and conservation of living resources in Antarctica.

2. Each Contracting Party which has become a party to the present Treaty by accession under Article XIII shall be entitled to appoint representatives to participate in the meetings referred to in paragraph 1 of the present Article, during such time as that Contracting Party demonstrates its interest in Antarctica by conducting substantial scientific research activity there, such as the establishment of a scientific station or the despatch of a scientific expedition.

3. Reports from the observers referred to in Article VII of the present Treaty shall be transmitted to the representatives of the Contracting Parties participating in the meetings referred to in paragraph 1 of the present Article.

4. The measures referred to in paragraph 1 of this Article shall become effective when approved by all the Contracting Parties whose representatives were entitled to participate in the meetings held to consider those measures.

5. Any or all of the rights established in the present Treaty may be exercised as from the date of entry into force of the Treaty whether or not any measures facilitating the exercise of such rights have been proposed, considered or approved as provided in this Article.

Article X

Each of the Contracting Parties undertakes to exert appropriate efforts, consistent with the Charter of the United Nations, to the end that no one engages in any activity in Antarctica contrary to the principles or purposes of the present Treaty.

Article XI

1. If any dispute arises between two or more of the Contracting Parties concerning the interpretation or application of the present Treaty, those Contracting Parties shall consult among themselves with a view to having the dispute resolved by negotiation, inquiry, mediation, conciliation, arbitration, judicial settlement or other peaceful means of their own choice.

2. Any dispute of this character not so resolved shall, with the consent, in each case, of all parties to the dispute, be referred to the International Court of Justice for settlement; but failure to reach agreement on reference to the International Court shall not absolve parties to the dispute from the responsibility of continuing to seek to resolve it by any of the various peaceful means referred to in paragraph 1 of this Article.

Article XII

1. (a) The present Treaty may be modified or amended at any time by unanimous agreement of the Contracting Parties whose representatives are entitled to participate in the meetings provided for under Article IX. Any such modification or amendment shall enter into force when the depositary Government has received notice from all such Contracting Parties that they have ratified it.

(b) Such modification or amendment shall thereafter enter into force as to any other Contracting Party when notice of ratification by it has been received by the depositary Government. Any such Contracting Party from which no notice of ratification is received within a period of two years from the date of entry into force of the modification or amendment in accordance with the provisions of subparagraph 1(a) of this Article shall be deemed to have withdrawn from the present Treaty on the date of the expiration of such period.

2. (a) If after the expiration of thirty years from the date of entry into force of the present Treaty, any of the Contracting Parties whose representatives are entitled to participate in the meetings provided for under Article IX so requests by a communication addressed to the depositary Government, a Conference of all the

Contracting Parties shall be held as soon as practicable to review the operation of the Treaty.

(b) Any modification or amendment to the present Treaty which is approved at such a Conference by a majority of the Contracting Parties there represented, including a majority of those whose representatives are entitled to participate in the meetings provided for under Article IX, shall be communicated by the depositary Government to all the Contracting Parties immediately after the termination of the Conference and shall enter into force in accordance with the provisions of paragraph 1 of the present Article.

(c) If any such modification or amendment has not entered into force in accordance with the provisions of subparagraph 1(a) of this Article within a period of two years after the date of its communication to all the Contracting Parties, any Contracting Party may at any time after the expiration of that period give notice to the depositary Government of its withdrawal from the present Treaty; and such withdrawal shall take effect two years after the receipt of the notice of the depositary Government.

Article XIII

1. The present Treaty shall be subject to ratification by the signatory States. It shall be open for accession by any State which is a Member of the United Nations, or by any other State which may be invited to accede to the Treaty with the consent of all the Contracting Parties whose representatives are entitled to participate in the meetings provided for under Article IX of the Treaty.

2. Ratification of or accession to the present Treaty shall be effected by each State in accordance with its constitutional processes.

3. Instruments of ratification and instruments of accession shall be deposited with the Government of the United States of America, hereby designated as the depositary Government.

4. The depositary Government shall inform all signatory and acceding States of the date of each deposit of an instrument of ratification or accession, and the date of entry into force of the Treaty and of any modification or amendment thereto.

5. Upon the deposit of instruments of ratification by all the signatory States, the present Treaty shall enter into force for those States and for States which have deposited instruments of accession. Thereafter the Treaty shall enter into force for any acceding State upon the deposit of its instrument of accession.

6. The present Treaty shall be registered by the depositary Government pursuant to Article 102 of the Charter of the United Nations.

Article XIV

The present Treaty, done in the English, French, Russian and Spanish languages, each version being equally authentic, shall be deposited in the archives of the Government of the United States of America, which shall transmit duly certified copies thereof to the Governments of the signatory and acceding States.

IN WITNESS WHEREOF the undersigned Plenipotentiaries, duly authorized, have signed the present Treaty.

DONE at Washington this first day of December, one thousand nine hundred and fifty-nine.

Antarctic Treaty

Country	Date of Signature	Date of Deposit of Ratification	Date of Deposit of Accession
Argentina	12/1/59	6/23/61	
Australia	12/1/59	6/23/61	
Belgium	12/1/59	7/26/60	
Brazil			5/16/75
Bulgaria			9/11/78
Chile	12/1/59	6/23/61	
Czechoslovakia			6/14/62
Denmark			5/20/65
France	12/1/59	9/16/60	
German Democratic Republic			11/19/74
Germany, Federal Republic of			2/5/79
Japan	12/1/59	8/4/60	
Netherlands			3/30/67
New Zealand	12/1/59	11/1/60	
Norway	12/1/59	8/24/60	
Peru			4/10/81
Poland			6/8/61
Romania			9/15/71
South Africa	12/1/59	6/21/60	
Union of Soviet Socialist Republics	12/1/59	11/2/60	
United Kingdom	12/1/59	5/31/60	
United States	12/1/59	8/18/60	
Uruguay			1/11/80
Total	12	12	11

Memorandum of Understanding Between the United States of America and the Union of Soviet Socialist Republics Regarding the Establishment of a Direct Communications Link (With Annex)

The need for assuring quick and reliable communication directly between the heads of government of nuclear-weapons states first emerged in the context of efforts to reduce the danger that accident, miscalculation, or surprise attack might trigger a nuclear war. These risks, arising out of conditions which are novel in history and peculiar to the nuclear-armed missile age, can of course threaten all countries, directly or indirectly.

The Soviet Union had been the first nation to propose, in 1954, specific safeguards against surprise attack; it also expressed concern about the danger of accidental war. At Western initiative, a Conference of Experts on Surprise Attack was held in Geneva in 1958, but recessed without achieving conclusive results, although it stimulated technical research on the issues involved.

In its "Program for General and Complete Disarmament in a Peaceful World," presented to the General Assembly by President Kennedy on September 25, 1961, the United States proposed a group of measures to reduce the risks of war. These included advance notification of military movements and maneuvers, observation posts at major transportation centers and air bases, and additional inspection arrangements. An international commission would be established to study possible further measures to reduce risks, including "failure of communication."

The United States draft treaty outline submitted to the ENDC[1] on April 18, 1962, added a proposal for the exchange of military missions to improve communications and understanding. It also proposed "establishment of rapid and reliable communications" among the heads of governments and with the Secretary General of the United Nations.

The Soviet draft treaty on general and complete disarmament (March 15, 1962) offered no provisions covering the risk of war by

---

[1] Eighteen-Nation Disarmament Committee, which met at Geneva from 1962 on. In 1969, with the addition of new members, the name was changed to Conference of the Committee on Disarmament (CCD). A yet larger group, the Committee on Disarmament, was established in 1978–79.

surprise attack, miscalculation, or accident; on July 16, however, it introduced amendments to its draft that called for (1) a ban on joint maneuvers involving the forces of two or more states and advance notification of substantial military movements, (2) exchange of military missions, and (3) improved communications between heads of governments and with the U.N. Secretary General. These measures were not separable, however, from the rest of the Soviet program.

The Cuban missile crisis of October 1962 compellingly underscored the importance of prompt, direct communication between heads of states. On December 12 of that year, a United States working paper submitted to the ENDC urged consideration of a number of measures to reduce the risk of war; these measures, the United States argued, offered opportunities for early agreement and could be undertaken either as a group or separately. Included was establishment of communication links between major capitals to insure rapid and reliable communication in times of crisis. The working paper suggested that it did not appear either necessary or desirable to specify in advance all the situations in which a special communications link might be used:

> . . . In the view of the United States, such a link should, as a general matter, be reserved for emergency use; that is to say, for example, that it might be reserved for communications concerning a military crisis which might appear directly to threaten the security of either of the states involved and where such developments were taking place at a rate which appeared to preclude the use of normal consultative procedures. Effectiveness of the link would not be degraded through use for other matters.

On June 20, 1963, at Geneva the American and Soviet representatives to the ENDC completed negotiations and signed the "Memorandum of Understanding Between the United States of America and the Union of Soviet Socialist Republics Regarding the Establishment of a Direct Communications Link." The memorandum provided that each government should be responsible for arrangements for the link on its own territory, including continuous functioning of the link and prompt delivery of communications to its head of government. An annex set forth the routing and components of the link and provided for allocation of costs, exchange of equipment, and other technical matters. The direct communications link would comprise:

(1) two terminal points with teletype equipment,
(2) a full-time duplex wire telegraph circuit (Washington-London-Copenhagen-Stockholm-Helsinki-Moscow),
(3) a full-time duplex radiotelegraph circuit (Washington-Tangier-Moscow).

If the wire circuit should be interrupted, messages would be transmitted by the radio circuit. If experience showed the need for an additional wire circuit, it might be established by mutual agreement.

The "Hot Line" agreement, the first bilateral agreement between the United States and the Soviet Union that gave concrete recognition to the perils implicit in modern nuclear-weapons systems, was a limited but practical step to bring those perils under rational control.

The communications link has proved its worth since its installation. During the Arab-Israeli war in 1967, for example, the United States used it to prevent possible misunderstanding of U.S. fleet movements in the Mediterranean. It was used again during the 1973 Arab-Israeli war. The significance of the hot line is further attested by the 1971 agreement to modernize it.

Memorandum of Understanding Between the United States of America and the Union of Soviet Socialist Republics Regarding the Establishment of a Direct Communications Link

Signed at Geneva June 20, 1963
Entered into force June 20, 1963

For use in time of emergency the Government of the United States of America and the Government of the Union of Soviet Socialist Republics have agreed to establish as soon as technically feasible a direct communications link between the two Governments.

Each Government shall be responsible for the arrangements for the link on its own territory. Each Government shall take the necessary steps to ensure continuous functioning of the link and prompt delivery to its head of government of any communications received by means of the link from the head of government of the other party.

Arrangements for establishing and operating the link are set forth in the Annex which is attached hereto and forms an integral part hereof.

DONE in duplicate in the English and Russian languages at Geneva, Switzerland, this 20th day of June, 1963.

FOR THE GOVERNMENT OF THE UNITED STATES OF AMERICA:

CHARLES C. STELLE

Acting Representative of the United States of America to the Eighteen-Nation Committee on Disarmament

FOR THE GOVERNMENT OF THE UNION OF SOVIET SOCIALIST REPUBLICS:

SEMYON K. TSARAPKIN

Acting Representative of the Union of Soviet Socialist Republics to the Eighteen-Nation Committee on Disarmament

(SEAL)

Annex

To the Memorandum of Understanding Between the United States of America and the Union of Soviet Socialist Republics Regarding the Establishment of a Direct Communications Link

The direct communications link between Washington and Moscow established in accordance with the Memorandum, and the operation of such link, shall be governed by the following provisions:

1. The direct communications link shall consist of:

a. Two terminal points with telegraph-teleprinter equipment between which communications shall be directly exchanged;

b. One full-time duplex wire telegraph circuit, routed Washington-London-Copenhagen-Stockholm-Helsinki-Moscow, which shall be used for the transmission of messages;

c. One full-time duplex radiotelegraph circuit, routed Washington-Tangier-Moscow, which shall be used for service communications and for coordination of operations between the two terminal points.

If experience in operating the direct communications link should demonstrate that the establishment of an additional wire telegraph circuit is advisable, such circuit may be established by mutual agreement between authorized representatives of both Governments.

2. In case of interruption of the wire circuit, transmission of messages shall be effected via the radio circuit, and for this purpose provision shall be made at the terminal points for the capability of prompt switching of all necessary equipment from one circuit to another.

3. The terminal points of the link shall be so equipped as to provide for the transmission and reception of messages from Moscow to Washington in the Russian language and from Washington to Moscow in the English language. In this connection, the USSR shall furnish the United States four sets of telegraph terminal equipment, including page printers, transmitters, and reperforators, with one year's supply of spare parts and all necessary special tools, test equipment, operating instructions, and other technical literature, to provide for transmission and reception of messages in the Russian language.

The United States shall furnish the Soviet Union four sets of telegraph terminal equipment, including page printers, transmitters, and reperforators, with one year's supply of spare parts and all necessary special tools, test equipment, operating instructions and other technical literature, to provide for transmission and reception of messages in the English language.

The equipment described in this paragraph shall be exchanged directly between the parties without any payment being required therefor.

4. The terminal points of the direct communications link shall be provided with encoding equipment. For the terminal point in the USSR, four sets of such equipment (each capable of simplex operation), with one year's supply of spare parts, with all

necessary special tools, test equipment, operating instructions and other technical literature, and with all necessary blank tape, shall be furnished by the United States to the USSR against payment of the cost thereof by the USSR.

The USSR shall provide for preparation and delivery of keying tapes to the terminal point of the link in the United States for reception of messages from the USSR. The United States shall provide for the preparation and delivery of keying tapes to the terminal point of the link in the USSR for reception of messages from the United States. Delivery of prepared keying tapes to the terminal points of the link shall be effected through the Embassy of the USSR in Washington (for the terminal of the link in the USSR) and through the Embassy of the United States in Moscow (for the terminal of the link in the United States).

5. The United States and the USSR shall designate the agencies responsible for the arrangements regarding the direct communications link, for its technical maintenance, continuity and reliability, and for the timely transmission of messages.

Such agencies may, by mutual agreement, decide matters and develop instructions relating to the technical maintenance and operation of the direct communications link and effect arrangements to improve the operation of the link.

6. The technical parameters of the telegraph circuits of the link and of the terminal equipment, as well as the maintenance of such circuits and equipment, shall be in accordance with CCITT and CCIR recommendations.

Transmission and reception of messages over the direct communications link shall be effected in accordance with applicable recommendations of international telegraph and radio communications regulations, as well as with mutually agreed instructions.

7. The costs of the direct communications link shall be borne as follows:

a. The USSR shall pay the full cost of leasing the portion of the telegraph circuit from Moscow to Helsinki and 50% of the cost of leasing the portion of the telegraph circuit from Helsinki to London. The United States shall pay the full cost of leasing the portion of the telegraph circuit from Washington to London and 50% of the cost of leasing the portion of the telegraph circuit from London to Helsinki.

b. Payment of the cost of leasing the radio telegraph circuit between Washington and Moscow shall be effected without any transfer of payments between the parties. The USSR shall bear the expenses relating to the transmission of messages from Moscow to Washington. The United States shall bear the expenses relating to the transmission of messages from Washington to Moscow.

Treaty Banning Nuclear Weapon Tests in the Atmosphere, in Outer Space and Under Water

The test ban treaty of 1963 prohibits nuclear weapons tests "or any other nuclear explosion" in the atmosphere, in outer space, and under water. While not banning tests underground, the treaty does prohibit nuclear explosions in this environment if they cause "radioactive debris to be present outside the territorial limits of the State under whose jurisdiction or control" the explosions were conducted. In accepting limitations on testing, the nuclear powers accepted as a common goal "an end to the contamination of man's environment by radioactive substances."

Efforts to achieve a test ban agreement had extended over 8 years. They involved complex technical problems of verification and the difficulties of reconciling deep-seated differences in approach to arms control and security. The uneven progress of the negotiations reflected, moreover, contemporaneous fluctuations in East-West political relationships.

Prior to SALT, no arms control measure since World War II had enlisted so intensely the sustained interest of the international community. The United States in November 1952, and the Soviet Union in August of the following year, exploded their first hydrogen devices, and rising concern about radioactive fallout and the prospect of even more powerful explosions spurred efforts to halt testing. Succeeding events gave the dangers of fallout concrete and human meaning. In March 1954 the United States exploded an experimental thermonuclear device at Bikini atoll, expected to have the power of 8 million tons of TNT. The actual yield was almost double that predicted—about 15 megatons, and the area of dangerous fallout greatly exceeded original estimates. A Japanese fishing vessel, the *Lucky Dragon,* was accidentally contaminated, and its crew suffered from radiation sickness, as did the inhabitants of an atoll in the area. In another such accident, radioactive rain containing debris from a Soviet hydrogen bomb test fell on Japan.

As knowledge of the nature and effects of fallout increased, and as it became apparent that no region was untouched by radioactive debris, the issue of continued nuclear tests drew widened and intensified public attention. Apprehension was expressed about the possibility of a cumulative contamination of the environment and of resultant genetic damage.

Efforts to negotiate an international agreement to end nuclear tests began in the Subcommittee of Five (the United States, the United Kingdom, Canada, France, and the U.S.S.R.) of the U.N. Disarmament Commission in May 1955, when the Soviet Union included discontinuance of weapons tests in its proposals.

Public interest in the course of the negotiations was active and sustained. In individual statements and proposals, and in international meetings, governments pressed for discontinuance of nuclear tests. A dozen resolutions of the General Assembly addressed the issue, repeatedly urging conclusion of an agreement to ban tests under a system of international controls.

Test Ban and General Disarmament

The relation of a test ban to other aspects of disarmament was for a time a troubling issue. The initial Soviet proposal of a test ban on May 10, 1955, was part of a comprehensive plan to reduce conventional forces and armaments and to eliminate nuclear weapons. Later that year in the General Assembly, the U.S.S.R. advocated a separate test ban. The three Western powers, over the next 3 years, made discontinuance of tests contingent on progress in other measures of arms control, particularly a cut-off in the production of fissionable materials for weapons and safeguards against surprise attack, and insisted that a test ban could not be enforced "in the absence of more general control agreements."

In January 1959 the United States and the United Kingdom dropped the linkage between a test ban and other arms control agreements; France, however, did not. The French continued to maintain that until there was agreement on nuclear disarmament— including an end to weapons production, reconversion of stocks, and a ban on possession and use—French plans to conduct tests would go forward. The Soviet Union abruptly reversed its position in June 1961, when Premier Khrushchev declared during his meeting with President Kennedy in Vienna that the test-ban question must be linked with general and complete disarmament. The Soviet Union refused to modify this position until November, when it proposed a separate test ban with no controls whatever, pending agreement on general and complete disarmament.

Verification

The central and most persistent barrier to a treaty on cessation of tests, however, was the issue of verifying compliance, of agreeing to establish a system of controls and inspection—particularly with regard to underground explosions—that could guarantee against testing in secret. The Western powers were determined to assure that no agreement would be liable to clandestine violation. In test-ban negotiations, as well as in other arms control efforts, they considered that it would be dangerous to their security to accept simple pledges without the means of knowing that they would be observed.

It was further believed that such pledges would mislead concerned world opinion with illusions of secure progress toward disarmament.

Writing to President Eisenhower on October 17, 1956, Premier Bulganin had stated the fundamental Soviet position. "Since any explosion of an atomic or hydrogen bomb cannot, in the present state of scientific knowledge, be produced without being recorded in other countries," he said, there could be an immediate agreement to prohibit tests without any provision for international control:

> Would not the best guarantee against the violation of such an agreement be the mere fact that secret testing of nuclear weapons is impossible and that consequently a government undertaking the solemn obligation to stop making tests could not violate it without exposing itself to the entire world as the violator of an international agreement?

The western countries were not convinced that existing technology for detecting nuclear explosions was adequate to monitor compliance, or that the mere force of world opinion would provide assurance against violations. In his response, President Eisenhower stated that "to be effective, and not simply a mirage," disarmament plans required systems of inspection and control. And in a public statement a few days later, he said

> A simple agreement to stop H-bomb tests cannot be regarded as automatically self-enforcing on the unverified assumption that such tests can instantly and surely be detected. It is true that tests of very large weapons would probably be detected when they occur . . . It is, however, impossible—in my view of the vast Soviet land-mass that can screen future tests—to have positive assurance of such detection, except in the case of the largest weapons.

On June 14, 1957, the Soviet Union for the first time offered test ban proposals that included international control. The proposals were very general: establishment of an international supervisory commission and control posts, on the basis of reciprocity, on the territories of the three nuclear powers and in the Pacific Ocean area. The Western powers suggested that a group of experts work out the details of a control system, while the delegates considered a temporary test ban in relation to other disarmament measures.

The Soviet Union continued to press for an immediate suspension of tests, and the United States for agreement on a control system as a necessary accompanying measure. In March 1958 the Soviet Union announced that it was discontinuing all tests and appealed to the parliaments of other nuclear powers to take similar action. It added, however, that the Soviet Union would "naturally be free" to resume testing if other nuclear powers did not stop their tests. Succeeding Bulganin as Premier, Nikita Khrushchev called on President Eisenhower to end tests. President Eisenhower rejected the proposal, stating that some tests could be conducted "under conditions of secrecy," and renewed the proposal for an experts' group to study control problems. After further summit correspondence and diplomatic exchange, Khrushchev agreed to a conference of experts. Meanwhile U.S. and British tests continued.

The Geneva Conference of Experts met in July and August 1958, attended by representatives from the United States, the United Kingdom, Canada, France, the U.S.S.R., Poland, Czechoslovakia, and Romania. They agreed on the technical characteristics of a control system to monitor a ban on tests in the atmosphere, under water, and underground. Their report proposed an elaborate network of 170–180 land control posts and 10 shipborne posts, as well as regular and special aircraft flights. It recognized that on-site inspections would be needed to determine whether some seismic events were caused by earthquakes or explosions.

The United States and Britain welcomed the experts' report and declared their willingness to negotiate an agreement for suspension of tests and the establishment of an international control system on the basis of the report. They were prepared to suspend tests for a year from the beginning of negotiations unless the U.S.S.R. resumed testing. The suspension could continue on a year-to-year basis, provided that the inspection system was installed and functioning, and "satisfactory progress" was being made on major arms-control measures. Premier Khrushchev's response was to attack the Americans and British for continuing their tests, and for linking the test ban to other matters; he announced that the Soviet Union was released from its self-imposed pledge. The U.S.S.R. resumed tests, and the series continued until November 3.

The negotiating powers refrained from testing for the next 3 years. The "moratorium" was marked by several public statements of intent, by the United States, the United Kingdom, and the Soviet Union, in varying degrees of specificity and with various caveats. At the end of December 1959, President Eisenhower announced that the United States would no longer consider itself bound by the "voluntary moratorium" but would give advance notice if it decided to resume testing. The Soviet Union, with dramatic effect, resumed testing in September of 1961. The United States resumed testing 2 weeks later.

Throughout the various conferences and exchanges on a test ban, the complexity of the central problem brought successive deadlocks, break-offs, and renewals of discussion, shifts in position, searches for compromise and new approaches, and for new techniques of verifications, and successive suspensions and resumptions of tests. The United States continued to be unwilling to accept the Soviet basic proposition that a test ban could be agreed to and controls instituted subsequently, or to accept indefinite test suspensions that were tantamount to endorsing an uncontrolled prohibition. New data from American underground tests, moreover, had shown that techniques recommended earlier for distinguishing between explosions and earthquakes were less effective than had been believed and that a reliable control system to monitor seismic events that registered under 4.75 on the Richter scale required further research and confirmed the need for on-site inspections.

Among the salient points of disagreement on a control system were:

The Veto. The U.S.S.R. initially sought to have all substantive operations of the system subject to veto; the United States insisted that the fact-finding process of inspection, to be effective, must be as automatic as possible.

On-Site Inspections. The Soviet Union placed a limit on permitted inspections in its territory, refusing to allow more than three per year. The United States and the United Kingdom held that the number must be determined by scientific fact and detection capability. As new information became available, the United States eventually indicated that it could accept a minimum of seven, but the U.S.S.R. rejected this quota. There was disagreement, as well, over the size of the area to be inspected, the nationality and composition of inspection teams, and the criteria for identifying events that required inspection.

Control Posts. Although the United States and the United Kingdom had originally proposed that the control posts should be internationally owned and operated, they later agreed to national ownership and operation of the posts, as the U.S.S.R. insisted, with international monitoring and supervision.

There were unresolved differences about the number and location of posts and about the number and location of the automatic seismic observation stations ("black boxes") with which it was proposed to supplement them. The U.S.S.R. also claimed that national control posts and automatic observation devices made any international inspection unnecessary, a position that the United States and the United Kingdom were not willing to accept.

The Organization of the Control Commission. In March 1961 the Soviet Union recommended replacing the single administrator of the proposed Control Commission with a "troika," a tripartite administrative council, consisting of one neutral, one Western, and one Communist member (a proposal paralleling the Soviet effort the previous year to replace the U.N. Secretary General with a tripartite commission). This three-headed administration would be able to function even in routine matters only by unanimous agreement, an arrangement that the Western powers argued was unworkable and would make the Control Commission helpless. The Soviet Union eventually abandoned this demand.

The effort to achieve a test ban, and to resolve the stubborn issues involved, had been pursued in a wide variety of channels. Successive General Assembly sessions had debated the issue. It had been a major item on the agenda of the U.N. Disarmament Commission and its Subcommittee of Five (later ten). The United States, the United Kingdom, and the Soviet Union had engaged in a long tripartite effort—The Conference on the Discontinuance of Nuclear Weapons Tests—in almost continuous session in Geneva from October 31, 1958, to January 29, 1962. Under its auspices three technical working groups of experts had investigated and reported on various aspects of control: one on high altitude tests, another on underground tests, the third on seismic research programs to improve detection capabilities.

After the three-power conference adjourned in January 1962, unable to complete the drafting of a treaty because of the Soviet Union's claim that national means of detection were adequate for all environments, the principal forum for negotiations became the newly formed Eighteen-Nation Disarmament Committee (ENDC), which began its meetings at Geneva under the aegis of the General Assembly in March 1962. On the U.S. side, overall direction of the negotiations was assumed by William C. Foster, first Director of the newly created U.S. Arms Control and Disarmament Agency. Soviet insistence that the West accept Premier Khrushchev's quota of three annual inspections, however, brought these talks to an impasse. The United States and the United Kingdom, in high-level correspondence with the Soviet Union, then sought to arrange three-power talks. Finally, on June 10, 1963, President Kennedy announced that agreement had been reached to hold three-power meetings on the test ban in Moscow. He also pledged that the United States would not be the first to resume tests in the atmosphere.

At this time a shift of Soviet interest to a ban that did not deal with underground tests emerged, although the Soviet Union had rejected an Anglo-American proposal for an agreement of this kind the year before. Premier Khrushchev disclosed this in a speech on July 2, 1963, when he called for an agreement outlawing tests in the atmosphere, in outer space, and under water—environments where both sides agreed their existing verification systems could adequately police a ban.

The three-power meetings began on July 15. The long years of discussion had clarified views and greatly reduced areas of disagreement, and a treaty was negotiated within 10 days. It was initialed on July 25 and formally signed at Moscow on August 5, 1963, by U.S. Secretary of State Dean Rusk; the Foreign Minister of the U.S.S.R., Andrei Gromyko; and the Foreign Minister of the U.K., Lord Home. On September 24, after extensive hearings and almost 3 weeks of floor debate, the Senate consented to ratification of the treaty by a vote of 80 to 19. It was ratified by President Kennedy on October 7, 1963, and entered into force on October 10 when the three original signatories deposited their instruments of ratification.

The parties to the treaty undertake "not to carry out any nuclear weapon test explosion, or any other nuclear explosion," in the atmosphere, under water, or in outer space, or in any other environment if the explosion would cause radioactive debris to be present outside the borders of the state conducting the explosion. As explained by Acting Secretary of State Ball in a subsequent report to President Kennedy, "The phrase 'any other nuclear explosion' includes explosions for peaceful purposes. Such explosions are prohibited by the treaty because of the difficulty of differentiating between weapon test explosions and peaceful explosions without additional controls."

The treaty is of unlimited duration, with provisions for amendment or withdrawal. Article III opens the treaty to all states, and most of the countries of the world have now signed it (108 nations are parties, 15 nations have signed but not ratified it). The treaty has not been signed by France or by the People's Republic of China.

Treaty Banning Nuclear Weapon Tests in the Atmosphere, in Outer Space and Under Water

Signed at Moscow August 5, 1963
Ratification advised by U.S. Senate September 24, 1963
Ratified by U.S. President October 7, 1963
U.S. ratification deposited at Washington, London, and Moscow October 10, 1963
Proclaimed by U.S. President October 10, 1963
Entered into force October 10, 1963

The Governments of the United States of America, the United Kingdom of Great Britain and Northern Ireland, and the Union of Soviet Socialist Republics, hereinafter referred to as the "Original Parties,"

Proclaiming as their principal aim the speediest possible achievement of an agreement on general and complete disarmament under strict international control in accordance with the objectives of the United Nations which would put an end to the armaments race and eliminate the incentive to the production and testing of all kinds of weapons, including nuclear weapons.

Seeking to achieve the discontinuance of all test explosions of nuclear weapons for all time, determined to continue negotiations to this end, and desiring to put an end to the contamination of man's environment by radioactive substances,

Have agreed as follows:

Article I

1. Each of the Parties to this Treaty undertakes to prohibit, to prevent, and not to carry out any nuclear weapon test explosion, or any other nuclear explosion, at any place under its jurisdiction or control:

(a) in the atmosphere; beyond its limits, including outer space; or under water, including territorial waters or high seas; or

(b) in any other environment if such explosion causes radioactive debris to be present outside the territorial limits of the State under whose jurisdiction or control such explosion is conducted. It is understood in this connection that the provisions of this subparagraph are without prejudice to the conclusion of a treaty resulting in the permanent banning of all nuclear test explosions, including all such explosions underground, the conclusion of which, as the Parties have stated in the Preamble to this Treaty, they seek to achieve.

2. Each of the Parties to this Treaty undertakes furthermore to refrain from causing, encouraging, or in any way participating in, the carrying out of any nuclear weapon test explosion, or any other nuclear explosion, anywhere which would take place in any of the environments described, or have the effect referred to, in paragraph 1 of this Article.

Article II

1. Any Party may propose amendments to this Treaty. The text of any proposed amendment shall be submitted to the Depositary Governments which shall circulate it to all Parties to this Treaty. Thereafter, if requested to do so by one-third or more of the

Parties, the Depositary Governments shall convene a conference, to which they shall invite all the Parties, to consider such amendment.

2. Any amendment to this Treaty must be approved by a majority of the votes of all the Parties to this Treaty, including the votes of all of the Original Parties. The amendment shall enter into force for all Parties upon the deposit of instruments of ratification by a majority of all the Parties, including the instruments of ratification of all of the Original Parties.

Article III

1. This Treaty shall be open to all States for signature. Any State which does not sign this Treaty before its entry into force in accordance with paragraph 3 of this Article may accede to it at any time.

2. This Treaty shall be subject to ratification by signatory States. Instruments of ratification and instruments of accession shall be deposited with the Governments of the Original Parties—the United States of America, the United Kingdom of Great Britain and Northern Ireland, and the Union of Soviet Socialist Republics—which are hereby designated the Depositary Governments.

3. This Treaty shall enter into force after its ratification by all the Original Parties and the deposit of their instruments of ratification.

4. For States whose instruments of ratification or accession are deposited subsequent to the entry into force of this Treaty, it shall enter into force on the date of the deposit of their instruments of ratification or accession.

5. The Depositary Governments shall promptly inform all signatory and acceding States of the date of each signature, the date of deposit of each instrument of ratification of and accession to this Treaty, the date of its entry into force, and the date of receipt of any requests for conferences or other notices.

6. This Treaty shall be registered by the Depositary Governments pursuant to Article 102 of the Charter of the United Nations.

Article IV

This Treaty shall be of unlimited duration.

Each Party shall in exercising its national sovereignty have the right to withdraw from the Treaty if it decides that extraordinary events, related to the subject matter of this Treaty, have jeopardized the supreme interests of its country. It shall give notice of such withdrawal to all other Parties to the Treaty three months in advance.

Article V

This Treaty, of which the English and Russian texts are equally authentic, shall be deposited in the archives of the Depositary Governments. Duly certified copies of this Treaty shall be transmitted by the Depositary Governments to the Governments of the signatory and acceding States.

IN WITNESS WHEREOF the undersigned, duly authorized, have signed this Treaty.

DONE in triplicate at the city of Moscow the fifth day of August, one thousand nine hundred and sixty-three.

For the Government of the United States of America	For the Government of the United Kingdom of Great Britain and Northern Ireland	For the Government of the Union of Soviet Socialist Republics
DEAN RUSK	**HOME**	**A. GROMYKO**

Limited Test Ban Treaty

Country	Date of[1] Signature	Date of Deposit[1] of Ratification	Date of Deposit[1] of Accession
Afghanistan	8/8/63	3/12/64	
Algeria	8/14/63		
Argentina	8/8/63		
Australia	8/8/63	11/12/63	
Austria	9/11/63	7/17/64	
Bahamas, The			8/13/76
Belgium	8/8/63	3/1/66	
Benin	8/27/63	12/15/64	
Bhutan			6/8/78
Bolivia	8/8/63	8/4/65	
Botswana			1/5/68
Brazil	8/8/63	12/15/64	
Bulgaria	8/8/63	11/13/63	
Burma	8/14/63	11/15/63	
Burundi	10/4/63		
Byelorussian S.S.R.[2]	10/8/63	12/16/63	
Cameroon	8/27/63		
Canada	8/8/63	1/28/64	
Cape Verde			10/24/79
Central African Republic			12/22/64
Chad	8/26/63	3/1/65	
Chile	8/8/63	10/6/65	
China (Taiwan)	8/23/63	5/18/64	
Colombia	8/16/63		
Costa Rica	8/9/63	7/10/67	
Cyprus	8/8/63	4/15/65	
Czechoslovakia	8/8/63	10/14/63	
Denmark	8/9/63	1/15/64	
Dominican Republic	9/16/63	6/3/64	
Ecuador	9/27/63	5/6/64	
Egypt	8/8/63	1/10/64	
El Salvador	8/21/63	12/3/64	
Ethiopia	8/9/63		
Fiji			7/18/72
Finland	8/8/63	1/9/64	
Gabon	9/10/63	2/20/64	
Gambia, The			4/27/65
German Democratic Republic	8/8/63	12/30/63	

See footnotes on page 290.

Country	Date of[1] Signature	Date of Deposit[1] of Ratification	Date of Deposit[1] of Accession
Germany, Federal Republic of	8/19/63	12.1/64	
Ghana	8/8/63	11/27/63	
Greece	8/8/63	12/18/63	
Guatemala	9/23/63	1/6/64	
Haiti	10/9/63		
Honduras	8/8/63	10/2/64	
Hungary	8/8/63	10/21/63	
Iceland	8/12/63	4/29/64	
India	8/8/63	10/10/63	
Indonesia	8/23/63	1/20/64	
Iran	8/8/63	5/5/64	
Iraq	8/13/63	11/30/64	
Ireland	8/8/63	12/18/63	
Israel	8/8/63	1/15/64	
Italy	8/8/63	12/10/64	
Ivory Coast	9/5/63	2/5/65	
Jamaica	8/13/63		
Japan	8/14/63	6/15/64	
Jordan	8/12/63	5/29/64	
Kenya			6/10/65
Korea, Republic of	8/30/63	7/24/64	
Kuwait	8/20/63	5/20/65	
Laos	8/12/63	2/10/65	
Lebanon	8/12/63	5/14/65	
Liberia	8/8/63	5/19/64	
Libya	8/9/63	7/15/68	
Luxembourg	8/13/63	2/10/65	
Madagascar	9/23/63	3/15/65	
Malawi			11/26/64
Malaysia	8/8/63	7/15/64	
Mali	8/23/63		
Malta			11/25/64
Mauritania	9/13/63	4/6/64	
Mauritius			4/30/69
Mexico	8/8/63	12/27/63	
Mongolia	8/8/63	11/1/63	
Morocco	8/27/63	2/1/66	
Nepal	8/26/63	10/7/64	
Netherlands	8/9/63	9/14/64	
New Zealand	8/8/63	10/10/63	

See footnotes on page 290.

Country	Date of[1] Signature	Date of Deposit[1] of Ratification	Date of Deposit[1] of Accession
Nicaragua	8/13/63	1/26/65	
Niger	9/24/63	7/3/64	
Nigeria	8/30/63	2/17/67	
Norway	8/9/63	11/21/63	
Pakistan	8/14/63		
Panama	9/20/63	2/24/66	
Papua New Guinea			11/13/80
Paraguay	8/15/63		
Peru	8/23/63	7/20/64	
Philippines	8/8/63	11/10/65	
Poland	8/8/63	10/14/63	
Portugal	10/9/63		
Romania	8/8/63	12/12/63	
Rwanda	9/19/63	12/27/63	
San Marino	9/17/63	7/3/64	
Senegal	9/20/63	5/6/64	
Sierra Leone	9/4/63	2/21/64	
Singapore			7/12/68
Somalia	8/19/63		
South Africa			10/10/63
Spain	8/13/63	12/17/64	
Sri Lanka	8/22/63	2/5/64	
Sudan	8/9/63	3/4/66	
Swaziland			5/29/69
Sweden	8/12/63	12/9/63	
Switzerland	8/26/63	1/16/64	
Syrian Arab Republic	8/13/63	6/1/64	
Tanzania	9/16/63	2/6/64	
Thailand	8/8/63	11/15/63	
Togo	9/18/63	12/7/64	
Tonga			7/7/71
Trinidad & Tobago	8/12/63	7/14/64	
Tunisia	8/8/63	5/26/65	
Turkey	8/9/63	7/8/65	
Uganda	8/29/63	3/24/64	
Ukrainian S.S.R.[2]	10/8/63	12/30/63	
Union of Soviet Socialist Republics	8/5/63	10/10/63	
United Kingdom	8/5/63	10/10/63	
United States	8/5/63	10/10/63	
Upper Volta	8/30/63		
Uruguay	8/12/63	2/25/63	

See footnotes on page 290.

Country	Date of[1] Signature	Date of Deposit[1] of Ratification	Date of Deposit[1] of Accession
Venezuela	8/16/63	2/22/65	
Western Samoa	9/5/63	1/15/65	
Yemen Arab Republic (Sana)	8/13/63		
Yemen, People's Democratic Republic of (Aden)			6/1/79
Yugoslavia	8/8/63	1/15/64	
Zaire	8/8/63	10/28/63	
Zambia			1/11/65
Total	106	91	18

See footnotes on page 290.

Treaty on Principles Governing the Activities of States in the Exploration and Use of Outer Space, Including the Moon and Other Celestial Bodies

The treaty on outer space and celestial bodies was the second of the so-called "nonarmament" treaties; its concepts and some of its provisions were modeled on its predecessor, the Antarctic Treaty. Like that treaty it sought to prevent "a new form of colonial competition" and the possible damage that self-seeking exploitation might cause.

In early 1957, even before the launching of Sputnik in October, developments in rocketry had led the United States to propose international verification of the testing of space objects. And the development of an inspection system for outer space was part of a Western proposal for partial disarmament put forward in August 1957. The U.S.S.R., however, in the midst of testing its first ICBM and about to orbit its first Earth satellite, did not accept these proposals.

Between 1959 and 1962 the Western powers made a series of proposals that would bar the use of outer space for military purposes. Their successive plans for general and complete disarmament included provisions to ban the orbiting and stationing in outer space of weapons of mass destruction. Addressing the General Assembly on September 22, 1960, President Eisenhower proposed that the principles of the Antarctic Treaty be applied to outer space and celestial bodies.

Soviet plans for general and complete disarmament between 1960 and 1962 included provisions for insuring the peaceful use of outer space. The Soviet Union, however, would not separate outer space from other disarmament issues. It declined to agree to restrict outer space to peaceful uses unless American foreign bases, where short-range and medium-range missiles were stationed, were eliminated also.

The Western powers declined to accept the Soviet approach; the linkage, they held, would upset the military balance and weaken the security of the West.

After the signing of the limited test ban treaty, the Soviet Union's position changed. It ceased to link an agreement on outer space with the question of foreign bases. On September 19, 1963, Foreign

Minister Gromyko told the General Assembly that the Soviet Union wished to conclude an agreement banning the orbiting of objects carrying nuclear weapons. Ambassador Stevenson stated that the United States had no intention of orbiting weapons of mass destruction, installing them on celestial bodies or stationing them in outer space. The General Assembly unanimously adopted a resolution on October 17, 1963, welcoming the Soviet and American statements and calling upon all states to refrain from introducing weapons of mass destruction into outer space.

The United States supported the resolution, despite the absence of any provisions for verification; the capabilities of its space-tracking systems, it was estimated, were adequate for detecting launchings and devices in orbit.

Seeking to sustain the momentum for arms control agreements, the United States in 1965 and 1966 pressed for a treaty that would give further substance to the U.N. resolution.

On June 16, 1966, both the United States and the Soviet Union submitted draft treaties. The American draft dealt only with celestial bodies; the Soviet draft covered the whole outer space environment. The United States accepted the Soviet position on the scope of the treaty, and by September agreement had been reached in discussions at Geneva on most treaty provisions. Differences on the few remaining issues—chiefly involving access to facilities on celestial bodies, reporting on space activities, and the use of military equipment and personnel in space exploration—were satisfactorily resolved in private consultations during the General Assembly session by December.

On the 19th of that month the General Assembly approved by acclamation a resolution commending the treaty. It was opened for signature at Washington, London, and Moscow on January 27, 1967. On April 25 the Senate gave unanimous consent to its ratification, and the treaty entered into force on October 10, 1967.

The substance of the arms control provisions is in Article IV. This article restricts military activities in two ways:

First, it contains an undertaking not to place in orbit around the Earth, install on the moon or any other celestial body, or otherwise station in outer space nuclear or any other weapons of mass destruction.

Second, it limits the use of the moon and other celestial bodies exclusively to peaceful purposes and expressly prohibits their use for establishing military bases, installations, or fortifications; testing weapons of any kind; or conducting military maneuvers.

In the years since the treaty came into force, space exploration has been conducted in an increasingly cooperative spirit, as manifested in United States and Soviet collaboration in jointly planned and manned space enterprises.

Treaty on Principles Governing the Activities of States in the Exploration and Use of Outer Space, Including the Moon and Other Celestial Bodies

Signed at Washington, London, Moscow, January 27, 1967
Ratification advised by U.S. Senate April 25, 1967
Ratified by U.S. President May 24, 1967
U.S. ratification deposited at Washington, London, and Moscow October 10, 1967
Proclaimed by U.S. President October 10, 1967
Entered into force October 10, 1967

The States Parties to this Treaty,

Inspired by the great prospects opening up before mankind as a result of man's entry into outer space,

Recognizing the common interest of all mankind in the progress of the exploration and use of outer space for peaceful purposes.

Believing that the exploration and use of outer space should be carried on for the benefit of all peoples irrespective of the degree of their economic or scientific development,

Desiring to contribute to broad international co-operation in the scientific as well as the legal aspects of the exploration and use of outer space for peaceful purposes,

Believing that such co-operation will contribute to the development of mutual understanding and to the strengthening of friendly relations between States and peoples,

Recalling resolution 1962 (XVIII), entitled "Declaration of Legal Principles Governing the Activities of States in the Exploration and Use of Outer Space," which was adopted unanimously by the United Nations General Assembly on 13 December 1963,

Recalling resolution 1884 (XVIII), calling upon States to refrain from placing in orbit around the Earth any objects carrying nuclear weapons or any other kinds of weapons of mass destruction or from installing such weapons on celestial bodies, which was adopted unanimously by the United Nations General Assembly on 17 October 1963,

Taking account of United Nations General Assembly resolution 110 (II) of 3 November 1947, which condemned propaganda designed or likely to provoke or encourage any threat to the peace, breach of the peace or act of aggression, and considering that the aforementioned resolution is applicable to outer space,

Convinced that a Treaty on Principles Governing the Activities of States in the Exploration and Use of Outer Space, including the Moon and Other Celestial Bodies, will further the Purposes and Principles of the Charter of the United Nations,

Have agreed on the following:

Article I

The exploration and use of outer space, including the moon and other celestial bodies, shall be carried out for the benefit and in the interests of all countries, irrespective of their degree of economic or scientific development, and shall be the province of all mankind.

Outer space, including the moon and other celestial bodies, shall be free for exploration and use by all States without discrimination of any kind, on a basis of equality and in accordance with international law, and there shall be free access to all areas of celestial bodies.

There shall be freedom of scientific investigation in outer space, including the moon and other celestial bodies, and States shall facilitate and encourage international co-operation in such investigation.

Article II

Outer space, including the moon and other celestial bodies, is not subject to national appropriation by claim of sovereignty, by means of use or occupation, or by any other means.

Article III

States Parties to the Treaty shall carry on activities in the exploration and use of outer space, including the moon and other celestial bodies, in accordance with international law, including the Charter of the United Nations, in the interest of maintaining international peace and security and promoting international co-operation and understanding.

Article IV

States Parties to the Treaty undertake not to place in orbit around the Earth any objects carrying nuclear weapons or any other kinds of weapons of mass destruction, install such weapons on celestial bodies, or station such weapons in outer space in any other manner.

The moon and other celestial bodies shall be used by all States Parties to the Treaty exclusively for peaceful purposes. The establishment of military bases, installations and fortifications, the testing of any type of weapons and the conduct of military maneuvers on celestial bodies shall be forbidden. The use of military personnel for scientific research or for any other peaceful purposes shall not be prohibited. The use of any equipment or facility necessary for peaceful exploration of the moon and other celestial bodies shall also not be prohibited.

Article V

States Parties to the Treaty shall regard astronauts as envoys of mankind in outer space and shall render to them all possible assistance in the event of accident, distress, or emergency landing on the territory of another State Party or on the high seas. When astronauts make such a landing, they shall be safely and promptly returned to the State of registry of their space vehicle.

In carrying on activities in outer space and on celestial bodies, the astronauts of one State Party shall render all possible assistance to the astronauts of other States Parties.

States Parties to the Treaty shall immediately inform the other States Parties to the Treaty or the Secretary-General of the United Nations of any phenomena they discover in outer space, including the moon and other celestial bodies, which could constitute a danger to the life or health of astronauts.

Article VI

States Parties to the Treaty shall bear international responsibility for national activities in outer space, including the moon and other celestial bodies, whether such activities are carried on by governmental agencies or by non-governmental entities, and for assuring that national activities are carried out in conformity with the provisions set forth in the present Treaty. The activities of non-governmental entities in outer space, including the moon and other celestial bodies, shall require authorization and continuing supervision by the appropriate State Party to the Treaty. When activities are carried on in outer space, including the moon and other celestial bodies, by an international organization, responsibility for compliance with this Treaty shall be borne both by the international organization and by the States Parties to the Treaty participating in such organization.

Article VII

Each State Party to the Treaty that launches or procures the launching of an object into outer space, including the moon and other celestial bodies, and each State Party from whose territory or facility an object is launched, is internationally liable for damage to another State Party to the Treaty or to its natural or juridical persons by such object or its component parts on the Earth, in air space or in outer space, including the moon and other celestial bodies.

Article VIII

A State Party to the Treaty on whose registry an object launched into outer space is carried shall retain jurisdiction and control over such object, and over any personnel thereof, while in outer space or on a celestial body. Ownership of objects launched into outer space, including objects landed or constructed on a celestial body, and of their component parts, is not affected by their presence in outer space or on a celestial body or by their return to the Earth. Such objects or component parts found beyond the limits of the State Party to the Treaty on whose registry they are carried shall be returned to that State Party, which shall, upon request, furnish identifying data prior to their return.

Article IX

In the exploration and use of outer space, including the moon and other celestial bodies, States Parties to the Treaty shall be guided by the principle of co-operation and mutual assistance and shall conduct all their activities in outer space, including the moon and other celestial bodies, with due regard to the corresponding interests of all other States Parties to the Treaty. States Parties to the Treaty shall pursue studies of outer space, including the moon and other celestial bodies, and conduct exploration of them so as to avoid their harmful contamination and also adverse changes in the environment of the Earth resulting from the introduction of extraterrestrial matter and, where necessary, shall adopt appropriate measures for this purpose. If a State Party to the Treaty has reason to believe that an activity or experiment planned by it or its nationals in outer space, including the moon and other celestial bodies, would cause potentially harmful interference with activities of other States Parties in the peaceful exploration and use of outer space, including the moon and other celestial bodies, it shall undertake appropriate international consultations before proceeding with any such activity or experiment. A State Party to the Treaty which has reason to believe that an activity or experiment planned by another State Party in outer space, including the moon and other celestial bodies, would cause potentially harmful interference with activities in the peaceful exploration and use of outer space, including the moon and other celestial bodies, may request consultation concerning the activity or experiment.

Article X

In order to promote international co-operation in the exploration and use of outer space, including the moon and other celestial bodies, in conformity with the purposes of this Treaty, the States Parties to the Treaty shall consider on a basis of equality any requests by other States Parties to the Treaty to be afforded an opportunity to observe the flight of space objects launched by those States.

The nature of such an opportunity for observation and the conditions under which it could be afforded shall be determined by agreement between the States concerned.

Article XI

In order to promote international co-operation in the peaceful exploration and use of outer space, States Parties to the Treaty conducting activities in outer space, including the moon and other celestial bodies, agree to inform the Secretary-General of the United Nations as well as the public and the international scientific community, to the greatest extent feasible and practicable, of the nature, conduct, locations and results of such activities. On receiving the said information, the Secretary-General of the United Nations should be prepared to disseminate it immediately and effectively.

Article XII

All stations, installations, equipment and space vehicles on the moon and other celestial bodies shall be open to representatives of other States Parties to the Treaty on a basis of reciprocity. Such representatives shall give reasonable advance notice of a projected visit, in order that appropriate consultations may be held and that maximum precautions may be taken to assure safety and to avoid interference with normal operations in the facility to be visited.

Article XIII

The provisions of this Treaty shall apply to the activities of States Parties to the Treaty in the exploration and use of outer space, including the moon and other celestial bodies, whether such activities are carried on by a single State Party to the Treaty or jointly with other States, including cases where they are carried on within the framework of international inter-governmental organizations.

Any practical questions arising in connection with activities carried on by international inter-governmental organizations in the exploration and use of outer space, including the moon and other celestial bodies, shall be resolved by the States Parties to the Treaty either with the appropriate international organization or with one or more States members of that international organization, which are Parties to this Treaty.

Article XIV

1. This Treaty shall be open to all States for signature. Any State which does not sign this Treaty before its entry into force in accordance with paragraph 3 of this article may accede to it at any time.

2. This Treaty shall be subject to ratification by signatory States. Instruments of ratification and instruments of accession shall be deposited with the Governments of the United States of America, the United Kingdom of Great Britain and Northern Ireland and the Union of Soviet Socialist Republics, which are hereby designated the Depositary Governments.

3. This Treaty shall enter into force upon the deposit of instruments of ratification by five Governments including the Governments designated as Depositary Governments under this Treaty.

4. For States whose instruments of ratification or accession are deposited subsequent to the entry into force of this Treaty, it shall enter into force on the date of the deposit of their instruments of ratification or accession.

5. The Depositary Governments shall promptly inform all signatory and acceding States of the date of each signature, the date of deposit of each instrument of ratification of and accession to this Treaty, the date of its entry into force and other notices.

6. This Treaty shall be registered by the Depositary Governments pursuant to Article 102 of the Charter of the United Nations.

Article XV

Any State Party to the Treaty may propose amendments to this Treaty. Amendments shall enter into force for each State Party to the Treaty accepting the amendments upon their acceptance by a majority of the States Parties to the Treaty and thereafter for each remaining State Party to the Treaty on the date of acceptance by it.

Article XVI

Any State Party to the Treaty may give notice of its withdrawal from the Treaty one year after its entry into force by written notification to the Depositary Governments. Such withdrawal shall take effect one year from the date of receipt of this notification.

Article XVII

This Treaty, of which the English, Russian, French, Spanish and Chinese texts are equally authentic, shall be deposited in the archives of the Depositary Governments. Duly certified copies of this Treaty shall be transmitted by the Depositary Governments to the Governments of the signatory and acceding States.

IN WITNESS WHEREOF the undersigned, duly authorized, have signed this Treaty.

DONE in triplicate, at the cities of Washington, London and Moscow, this twenty-seventh day of January one thousand nine hundred sixty-seven.

Outer Space Treaty

Country	Date of[1] Signature	Date of Deposit[1] of Ratification	Date of Deposit[1] of Accession
Afghanistan	1/27/67		
Argentina	1/27/67	3/26/69	
Australia	1/27/67	10/10/67	
Austria	2/20/67	2/26/68	
Bahamas, The			8/11/76
Barbados			9/12/68
Belgium	1/27/67	3/30/73	
Bolivia	1/27/67		
Botswana	1/27/67		
Brazil	1/30/67	3/5/69	
Bulgaria	1/27/67	3/28/67	
Burma	5/22/67	3/18/70	
Burundi	1/27/67		
Byelorussian S.S.R.[2]	2/10/67	10/31/67	
Cameroon	1/27/67		
Canada	1/27/67	10/10/67	
Central African Republic	1/27/67		
Chile	1/27/67	10/8/81	
China (Taiwan)	1/27/67	7/24/70	
Colombia	1/27/67		
Cyprus	1/27/67	7/5/72	
Czechoslovakia	1/27/67	5/11/67	
Denmark	1/27/67	10/10/67	
Dominican Republic	1/27/67	11/21/68	
Ecuador	1/27/67	3/7/69	
Egypt	1/27/67	10/10/67	
El Salvador	1/27/67	1/15/69	
Ethiopia	1/27/67		
Fiji			7/14/72
Finland	1/27/67	7/12/67	
France	9/25/67	8/5/70	
Gambia, The	6/2/67		
German Democratic Republic	1/27/67	2/2/67	
Germany, Federal Republic of	1/27/67	2/10/71	
Ghana	1/27/67		
Greece	1/27/67	1/19/71	
Guyana	2/3/67		

See footnotes on page 290.

Country	Date of[1] Signature	Date of Deposit[1] of Ratification	Date of Deposit[1] of Accession
Haiti	1/27/67		
Holy See	4/5/67		
Honduras	1/27/67		
Hungary	1/27/67	6/26/67	
Iceland	1/27/67	2/5/68	
India	3/3/67	1/18/82	
Indonesia	1/27/67		
Iran	1/27/67		
Iraq	2/27/67	12/4/68	
Ireland	1/27/67	7/17/68	
Israel	1/27/67	2/18/77	
Italy	1/27/67	5/4/72	
Jamaica	6/29/67	8/6/70	
Japan	1/27/67	10/10/67	
Jordan	2/2/67		
Korea, Republic of	1/27/67	10/13/67	
Kuwait			6/7/72
Laos	1/27/67	11/27/72	
Lebanon	2/23/67	3/31/69	
Lesotho	1/27/67		
Libya			7/3/68
Luxembourg	1/27/67		
Madagascar			8/22/68
Malaysia	2/20/67		
Mali			6/11/68
Mauritius			4/7/69
Mexico	1/27/67	1/31/68	
Mongolia	1/27/67	10/10/67	
Morocco			12/21/67
Nepal	2/3/67	10/10/67	
Netherlands	2/10/67	10/10/69	
New Zealand	1/27/67	5/31/68	
Nicaragua	1/27/67		
Niger	2/1/67	4/17/67	
Nigeria			11/14/67
Norway	2/3/67	7/1/69	
Pakistan	9/12/67	4/8/68	
Panama	1/27/67		
Papua New Guinea			10/27/80
Peru	6/30/67	2/28/79	

See footnotes on page 290.

Country	Date of[1] Signature	Date of Deposit[1] of Ratification	Date of Deposit[1] of Accession
Philippines	1/27/67		
Poland	1/27/67	1/30/68	
Romania	1/27/67	4/9/68	
Rwanda	1/27/67		
San Marino	4/21/67	10/29/68	
Saudi Arabia			12/17/76
Seychelles			1/5/78
Sierra Leone	1/27/67	7/13/67	
Singapore			9/10/76
Somalia	2/2/67		
South Africa	3/1/67	9/30/68	
Spain			11/27/68
Sri Lanka	3/10/69		
Sweden	1/27/67	10/11/67	
Switzerland	1/27/67	12/18/69	
Syrian Arab Republic			11/19/68
Thailand	1/27/67	9/5/68	
Togo	1/27/67		
Tonga			6/22/71
Trinidad & Tobago	7/24/67		
Tunisia	1/27/67	3/28/68	
Turkey	1/27/67	3/27/68	
Uganda			4/24/68
Ukrainian S.S.R.[2]	2/10/67	10/31/67	
Union of Soviet Socialist Republics	1/27/67	10/10/67	
United Kingdom	1/27/67	10/10/67	
United States	1/27/67	10/10/67	
Upper Volta	3/3/67	6/18/68	
Uruguay	1/27/67	8/31/70	
Venezuela	1/27/67	3/3/70	
Vietnam			6/20/80
Yemen, People's Democratic Republic of (Aden)			6/1/79
Yugoslavia	1/27/67		
Zaire	1/27/67		
Zambia			8/20/73
Total[3]	89	59	21

See footnotes on page 290.

Treaty for the Prohibition of Nuclear Weapons in Latin America

The Treaty for the Prohibition of Nuclear Weapons in Latin America, like the Antarctic Treaty and the Outer Space Treaty, seeks to limit the spread of nuclear weapons by preventing their introduction into areas hitherto free of them. Unlike the other treaties, the Latin American Treaty concerns itself with a populated area— over 7½ million square miles, inhabited by nearly 200 million people. Besides the agreement among the Latin American countries themselves, there are two Additional Protocols dealing with matters that concern non-Latin American countries. Protocol I involves an undertaking by non-Latin American countries that have possessions in the nuclear-free zone. Protocol II involves an undertaking by those powers which possess nuclear weapons. The United States is a party to both Protocols.

The United States has favored the establishment of nuclear-free zones where they would not disturb existing security arrangements and where provisions for investigating alleged violations would give reasonable assurance of compliance. It has also considered it important that the initiative for such zones originate in the geographical area concerned and that all states important to the denuclearization of the area participate. Considering that Soviet proposals for the denuclearization of Central Europe and other areas did not meet these criteria, the United States opposed them. From the start, however, the United States gave support and encouragement to Latin American countries in this undertaking.

Even before the Cuban missile crisis, the Brazilian representative to the U.N. General Assembly had suggested making Latin America a nuclear-weapon-free zone. During the crisis, he submitted a draft resolution calling for such a zone. While asserting support for the principle, Cuba stipulated certain conditions, including the requirement that Puerto Rico and the Panama Canal Zone be included in the zone, and that foreign military bases, especially Guantanamo Naval Base, be eliminated. The draft resolution was not put to a vote at the General Assembly that year.

The Cuban missile crisis of October 1962 brought home to Latin American countries the dangers of nuclear war, and in April 1963 the Presidents of five Latin American countries—Bolivia, Brazil, Chile, Ecuador, and Mexico—announced that they were prepared to sign a multilateral agreement that would make Latin America a nuclear-weapon-free zone. On November 27, 1963, this declaration received the support of the U.N. General Assembly, with the United States voting in the affirmative.

The Latin American nations followed this initiative by extensive and detailed negotiations among themselves. At the Mexico City Conference (November 23–27, 1965) a Preparatory Commission for the Denuclearization of Latin America was created, with instructions to prepare a draft treaty. Important differences among the Latin American countries emerged over questions of defining the boundaries of the nuclear-weapon-free zone, transit, guarantees, and safeguards on peaceful nuclear activities. Most of these differences were eventually resolved.

On February 14, 1967, the treaty was signed at the regional meeting of Latin American countries at Tlatelolco, a section of Mexico City. On December 5, 1967, the U.N. General Assembly endorsed the Treaty of Tlatelolco by a vote of 82–0 with 28 abstentions, the United States voting in support of the treaty. Thus far Cuba has refused to sign. (A question has been raised as to whether Guyana is eligible to sign.) Argentina has signed the treaty and publicly announced its intention to ratify. Although Brazil and Chile have ratified, the treaty is not yet in force for them because they did not waive the entry-into-force provision which, *inter alia*, requires ratification by all eligible countries.

The basic obligations of the treaty are contained in Article I:

1. The Contracting Parties hereby undertake to use exclusively for peaceful purposes the nuclear material and facilities which are under their jurisdiction, and to prohibit and prevent in their respective territories:

   (a) The testing, use, manufacture, production or acquisition by any means whatsoever of any nuclear weapons, by the Parties themselves, directly or indirectly, on behalf of anyone else or in any other way, and

   (b) The receipt, storage, installation, deployment and any form of possession of any nuclear weapons, directly or indirectly, by the Parties themselves, by anyone on their behalf or in any other way.

2. The Contracting Parties also undertake to refrain from engaging in, encouraging or authorizing directly or indirectly, or in any way participating in the testing, use, manufacture, production, possession or control of any nuclear weapon.

Important provisions of the treaty deal with verification. Treaty parties undertake to negotiate agreements with the International Atomic Energy Agency for application of its safeguards to their peaceful nuclear activities. In addition, the treaty establishes an organization to ensure compliance with treaty provisions—the Agency for the Prohibition of Nuclear Weapons in Latin America. The Council, one of the principal organs of the Agency, is empowered to perform "special inspections."

Of the accompanying protocols, Protocol I calls on nations outside the treaty zone to apply the denuclearization provisions of the treaty to their territories in the zone. All four powers having such territories have signed—the United Kingdom, the Netherlands, France, and the United States. All except France have ratified.

Within the Latin American nuclear-weapon-free zone lie the Canal Zone, the Guantanamo Naval Base in Cuba, the Virgin Islands, and Puerto Rico—four areas with differing relationships to the United States. For some time, the United States had indicated that it would be prepared to have the Canal Zone included in the treaty, subject to a clear understanding that the well-established rights of transit through the zone would not be affected, and to have Guantanamo included if Cuba joined the treaty. It had not been prepared to include Puerto Rico and the Virgin Islands. President Carter decided that it was in the net interest of the United States to allow these areas to be included, and he signed Protocol I in 1977. President Reagan also supported U.S. adherence to Protocol I. In November 1981, the Senate gave its advice and consent to ratification, President Reagan ratified it, and Secretary of State Haig deposited the U.S. instrument of ratification in Mexico City.

Senate advice and consent to ratification of Protocol I was made subject to three understandings:

— That the provisions of the Treaty made applicable by the Protocol do not affect the rights of the Contracting Parties to grant or deny transport and transit privileges to their own or other vessels or aircraft regardless of cargo or armaments;
— That the provisions of the Treaty made applicable by the Protocol do not affect the rights of the Contracting Parties regarding the exercise of freedom of the seas or passage through or over waters subject to the sovereignty of a State;
— That the understandings and declarations the United States attached to ratification of Protocol II apply also to its ratification of Protocol I.

In Protocol II, nuclear-weapons states undertake (1) to respect the denuclearized status of the zone, (2) not to contribute to acts involving violation of obligations of the parties, and (3) not to use or threaten to use nuclear weapons against the Contracting Parties. France, the United Kingdom, the United States, the People's Republic of China, and the Soviet Union have adhered to Protocol II.

When President Nixon transmitted Protocol II to the Senate on August 13, 1970, he recommended that the Senate give its advice and consent to ratification subject to a statement containing the following understandings and declarations:

— The Treaty and its Protocols have no effect upon the international status of territorial claims.
— The Treaty does not affect the rights of the Contracting Parties to grant or deny transport and transit privileges to non-Contracting Parties.
— With respect to the undertaking in Article 3 of Protocol II not to use or threaten to use nuclear weapons against the Treaty parties, the United States would "have to consider that an armed attack by a Contracting Party, in which it was assisted by a nuclear-weapon state, would be incompatible with the Contracting Party's corresponding obligations under Article I of the Treaty."
— Considering the technology for producing explosive devices for peaceful purposes to be indistinguishable from that for making nuclear weapons, the United States regards the Treaty's prohibitions as applying to all nuclear explosive devices. However, the Treaty would not prevent the United States, as a nuclear-weapon state, from making nuclear explosion services for peaceful purposes available "in a manner consistent with our policy of not contributing to the proliferation of nuclear weapons capabilities."
— Although not required to do so, the United States will act, with respect to the territories of Protocol I adherents that are within the treaty zone, in the same way as Protocol II requires it to act toward the territories of the Latin American treaty parties.

The statement was slightly revised by the Senate Foreign Relations Committee during its hearings on the Protocol in September 1970 and February 1971. The Senate made its consent to ratification subject to the statement, which was included in the U.S. instrument of ratification. The President ratified the Protocol and the United States deposited the instrument of ratification in May 1971.

This was the first time the United States had ever entered into an obligation that restricted the use of nuclear weapons. The Treaty, however, significantly enhances U.S. national security. It includes an undertaking by the Latin American countries party to the treaty to prevent the type of deployment of nuclear weapons in their territory that occurred in the Cuban missile crisis. It provides for verification of compliance with this undertaking not only by the parties themselves, but by the regional organization they have established and given the right to make special inspections. It requires IAEA safeguards on all nuclear materials and facilities under the jurisdiction of the parties. And this regional initiative to curb the spread of nuclear weapons gave important support to efforts to obtain a universal non-proliferation treaty.

Treaty for the Prohibition of Nuclear Weapons in Latin America

Signed at Mexico City February 14, 1967
Entered into force April 22, 1968

Preamble

In the name of their peoples and faithfully interpreting their desires and aspirations, the Governments of the States which sign the Treaty for the Prohibition of Nuclear Weapons in Latin America,

Desiring to contribute, so far as lies in their power, towards ending the armaments race, especially in the field of nuclear weapons, and towards strengthening a world at peace, based on the sovereign equality of States, mutual respect and good neighbourliness,

Recalling that the United Nations General Assembly, in its Resolution 808 (IX), adopted unanimously as one of the three points of a coordinated programme of disarmament "the total prohibition of the use and manufacture of nuclear weapons and weapons of mass destruction of every type,"

Recalling that militarily denuclearized zones are not an end in themselves but rather a means for achieving general and complete disarmament at a later stage,

Recalling United Nations General Assembly Resolution 1911 (XVIII), which established that the measures that should be agreed upon for the denuclearization of Latin America should be taken "in the light of the principles of the Charter of the United Nations and of regional agreements,"

Recalling United Nations General Assembly Resolution 2028 (XX), which established the principle of an acceptable balance of mutual responsibilities and duties for the nuclear and non-nuclear powers, and

Recalling that the Charter of the Organization of American States proclaims that it is an essential purpose of the Organization to strengthen the peace and security of the hemisphere,

Convinced:

That the incalculable destructive power of nuclear weapons has made it imperative that the legal prohibition of war should be strictly observed in practice if the survival of civilization and of mankind itself is to be assured,

That nuclear weapons, whose terrible effects are suffered, indiscriminately and inexorably, by military forces and civilian population alike, constitute, through the persistence of the radioactivity they release, an attack on the integrity of the human species and ultimately may even render the whole earth uninhabitable,

That general and complete disarmament under effective international control is a vital matter which all the peoples of the world equally demand,

That the proliferation of nuclear weapons, which seems inevitable unless States, in the exercise of their sovereign rights, impose restrictions on themselves in order to prevent it, would make any agreement on disarmament enormously difficult and would increase the danger of the outbreak of a nuclear conflagration,

That the establishment of militarily denuclearized zones is closely linked with the maintenance of peace and security in the respective regions,

That the military denuclearization of vast geographical zones, adopted by the sovereign decision of the States comprised therein, will exercise a beneficial influence on other regions where similar conditions exist.

That the privileged situation of the signatory States, whose territories are wholly free from nuclear weapons, imposes upon them the inescapable duty of preserving that situation both in their own interests and for the good of mankind,

That the existence of nuclear weapons in any country of Latin America would make it a target for possible nuclear attacks and would inevitably set off, throughout the region, a ruinous race in nuclear weapons which would involve the unjustifiable diversion, for warlike purposes, of the limited resources required for economic and social development,

That the foregoing reasons, together with the traditional peace-loving outlook of Latin America, give rise to an inescapable necessity that nuclear energy should be used in that region exclusively for peaceful purposes, and that the Latin American countries should use their right to the greatest and most equitable possible access to this new source of energy in order to expedite the economic and social development of their peoples,

Convinced finally:

That the military denuclearization of Latin America—being understood to mean the undertaking entered into internationally in this Treaty to keep their territories forever free from nuclear weapons—will constitute a measure which will spare their peoples from the squandering of their limited resources on nuclear armaments and will protect them against possible nuclear attacks on their territories, and will also constitute a significant contribution towards preventing the proliferation of nuclear weapons and a powerful factor for general and complete disarmament, and

That Latin America, faithful to its tradition of universality, must not only endeavour to banish from its homelands the scourge of a nuclear war, but must also strive to promote the well-being and advancement of its peoples, at the same time co-operating in the fulfilment of the ideals of mankind, that is to say, in the consolidation of a permanent peace based on equal rights, economic fairness and social justice for all, in accordance with the principles and purposes set forth in the Charter of the United Nations and in the Charter of the Organization of American States,

Have agreed as follows:

Obligations

Article I

1. The Contracting Parties hereby undertake to use exclusively for peaceful purposes the nuclear material and facilities which are under their jurisdiction, and to prohibit and prevent in their respective territories:

   (a) The testing, use, manufacture, production or acquisition by any means whatsoever of any nuclear weapons, by the Parties themselves, directly or indirectly, on behalf of anyone else or in any other way, and

   (b) The receipt, storage, installation, deployment and any form of possession of any nuclear weapons, directly or indirectly, by the Parties themselves, by anyone on their behalf or in any other way.

2. The Contracting Parties also undertake to refrain from engaging in, encouraging or authorizing, directly or indirectly, or in any way participating in the testing, use, manufacture, production, possession or control of any nuclear weapon.

Definition of the Contracting Parties

Article 2

For the purposes of this Treaty, the Contracting Parties are those for whom the Treaty is in force.

Definition of territory

Article 3

For the purposes of this Treaty, the term "territory" shall include the territorial sea, air space and any other space over which the State exercises sovereignty in accordance with its own legislation.

Zone of application

Article 4

1. The zone of application of this Treaty is the whole of the territories for which the Treaty is in force.

2. Upon fulfilment of the requirements of article 28, paragraph 1, the zone of application of this Treaty shall also be that which is situated in the western hemisphere within the following limits (except the continental part of the territory of the United States of America and its territorial waters): starting at a point located at 35° north latitude, 75° west longitude; from this point directly southward to a point at 30° north latitude, 75° west longitude; from there, directly eastward to a point at 30° north latitude, 50° west longitude; from there, along a loxodromic line to a point at 5° north latitude, 20° west longitude; from there, directly southward to a point at 60° south latitude, 20° west longitude; from there, directly westward to a point at 60° south latitude, 115° west longitude; from there, directly northward to a point at 0 latitude, 115° west longitude; from there, along a loxodromic line to a point at 35° north latitude, 150° west longitude; from there, directly eastward to a point at 35° north latitude, 75° west longitude.

Definition of nuclear weapons

Article 5

For the purposes of this Treaty, a nuclear weapon is any device which is capable of releasing nuclear energy in an uncontrolled manner and which has a group of characteristics that are appropriate for use for warlike purposes. An instrument that may be used for the transport or propulsion of the device is not included in this definition if it is separable from the device and not an indivisible part thereof.

Meeting of signatories

Article 6

At the request of any of the signatory States or if the Agency established by article 7 should so decide, a meeting of all the signatories may be convoked to consider in common questions which may affect the very essence of this instrument, including possible amendments to it. In either case, the meeting will be convoked by the General Secretary.

Organization

Article 7

1. In order to ensure compliance with the obligations of this Treaty, the Contracting Parties hereby establish an international organization to be known as the "Agency for the Prohibition of Nuclear Weapons in Latin America," hereinafter referred to as "the Agency." Only the Contracting Parties shall be affected by its decisions.

2. The Agency shall be responsible for the holding of periodic or extraordinary consultations among Member States on matters relating to the purposes, measures and procedures set forth in this Treaty and to the supervision of compliance with the obligations arising therefrom.

3. The Contracting Parties agree to extend to the Agency full and prompt co-operation in accordance with the provisions of this Treaty, of any agreements they may conclude with the Agency and of any agreements the Agency may conclude with any other international organization or body.

4. The headquarters of the Agency shall be in Mexico City.

Organs

Article 8

1. There are hereby established as principal organs of the Agency a General Conference, a Council and a Secretariat.

2. Such subsidiary organs as are considered necessary by the General Conference may be established within the purview of this Treaty.

The General Conference

Article 9

1. The General Conference,the supreme organ of the Agency, shall be composed of all the Contracting Parties; it shall hold regular sessions every two years, and may also hold special sessions whenever this Treaty so provides or, in the opinion of the Council, the circumstances so require.

2. The General Conference:

(a) May consider and decide on any matters or questions covered by this Treaty, within the limits thereof, including those referring to powers and functions of any organ provided for in this Treaty.

(b) Shall establish procedures for the control system to ensure observance of this Treaty in accordance with its provisions.

(c) Shall elect the Members of the Council and the General Secretary.

(d) May remove the General Secretary from office if the proper functioning of the Agency so requires.

(e) Shall receive and consider the biennial and special reports submitted by the Council and the General Secretary.

(f) Shall initiate and consider studies designed to facilitate the optimum fulfilment of the aims of this Treaty, without prejudice to the power of the General Secretary independently to carry out similar studies for submission to and consideration by the Conference.

(g) Shall be the organ competent to authorize the conclusion of agreements with Governments and other international organizations and bodies.

3. The General Conference shall adopt the Agency's budget and fix the scale of financial contributions to be paid by Member States, taking into account the systems and criteria used for the same purpose by the United Nations.

4. The General Conference shall elect its officers for each session and may establish such subsidiary organs as it deems necessary for the performance of its functions.

5. Each Member of the Agency shall have one vote. The decisions of the General Conference shall be taken by a two-thirds majority of the Members present and voting in the case of matters relating to the control system and measures referred to in article 20, the admission of new Members, the election or removal of the General Secretary, adoption of the budget and matters related thereto. Decisions on other matters, as well as procedural questions and also determination of which questions must be decided by a two-thirds majority, shall be taken by a simple majority of the Members present and voting.

6. The General Conference shall adopt its own rules of procedure.

The Council

Article 10

1. The Council shall be composed of five Members of the Agency elected by the General Conference from among the Contracting Parties, due account being taken of equitable geographic distribution.

2. The Members of the Council shall be elected for a term of four years. However, in the first election three will be elected for two years. Outgoing Members may not be re-elected for the following period unless the limited number of States for which the Treaty is in force so requires.

3. Each Member of the Council shall have one representative.

4. The Council shall be so organized as to be able to function continuously.

5. In addition to the functions conferred upon it by this Treaty and to those which may be assigned to it by the General Conference, the Council shall, through the General Secretary, ensure the proper operation of the control system in accordance with the provisions of this Treaty and with the decisions adopted by the General Conference.

6. The Council shall submit an annual report on its work to the General Conference as well as such special reports as it deems necessary or which the General Conference requests of it.

7. The Council shall elect its officers for each session.

8. The decisions of the Council shall be taken by a simple majority of its Members present and voting.

9. The Council shall adopt its own rules of procedure.

The Secretariat

Article 11

1. The Secretariat shall consist of a General Secretary, who shall be the chief administrative officer of the Agency, and of such staff as the Agency may require. The term of office of the General Secretary shall be four years and he may be re-elected for a single additional term. The General Secretary may not be a national of the country in which the Agency has its headquarters. In case the office of General Secretary becomes vacant, a new election shall be held to fill the office for the remainder of the term.

2. The staff of the Secretariat shall be appointed by the General Secretary, in accordance with rules laid down by the General Conference.

3. In addition to the functions conferred upon him by this Treaty and to those which may be assigned to him by the General Conference, the General Secretary shall ensure, as provided by article 10, paragraph 5, the proper operation of the control system established by this Treaty, in accordance with the provisions of the Treaty and the decisions taken by the General Conference.

4. The General Secretary shall act in that capacity in all meetings of the General Conference and of the Council and shall make an annual report to both bodies on the work of the Agency and any special reports requested by the General Conference or the Council or which the General Secretary may deem desirable.

5. The General Secretary shall establish the procedures for distributing to all Contracting Parties information received by the Agency from governmental sources and such information from non-governmental sources as may be of interest to the Agency.

6. In the performance of their duties the General Secretary and the staff shall not seek or receive instructions from any Government or from any other authority external to the Agency and shall refrain from any action which might reflect on their position as international officials responsible only to the Agency; subject to their responsibility to the Agency, they shall not disclose any industrial secrets or other confidential information coming to their knowledge by reason of their official duties in the Agency.

7. Each of the Contracting Parties undertakes to respect the exclusively international character of the responsibilities of the General Secretary and the staff and not to seek to influence them in the discharge of their responsibilities.

Control system

Article 12

1. For the purpose of verifying compliance with the obligations entered into by the Contracting Parties in accordance with article 1, a control system shall be established which shall be put into effect in accordance with the provisions of articles 13–18 of this Treaty.

2. The control system shall be used in particular for the purpose of verifying:

(a) That devices, services and facilities intended for peaceful uses of nuclear energy are not used in the testing or manufacture of nuclear weapons,

(b) That none of the activities prohibited in article 1 of this Treaty are carried out in the territory of the Contracting Parties with nuclear materials or weapons introduced from abroad, and

(c) That explosions for peaceful purposes are compatible with article 18 of this Treaty.

IAEA safeguards

Article 13

Each Contracting Party shall negotiate multilateral or bilateral agreements with the International Atomic Energy Agency for the application of its safeguards to its nuclear activities. Each Contracting Party shall initiate negotiations within a period of 180 days after the date of the deposit of its instrument of ratification of this Treaty. These agreements shall enter into force, for each Party, not later than eighteen months after the date of the initiation of such negotiations except in case of unforeseen circumstances or *force majeure*.

Reports of the Parties

Article 14

1. The Contracting Parties shall submit to the Agency and to the International Atomic Energy Agency, for their information, semi-annual reports stating that no activity prohibited under this Treaty has occurred in their respective territories.

2. The Contracting Parties shall simultaneously transmit to the Agency a copy of any report they may submit to the International Atomic Energy Agency which relates to matters that are the subject of this Treaty and to the application of safeguards.

3. The Contracting Parties shall also transmit to the Organization of American States, for its information, any reports that may be of interest to it, in accordance with the obligations established by the Inter-American System.

Special reports requested by the General Secretary

Article 15

1. With the authorization of the Council, the General Secretary may request any of the Contracting Parties to provide the Agency with complementary or supplementary information regarding any event or circumstance connected with compliance with this Treaty, explaining his reasons. The Contracting Parties undertake to co-operate promptly and fully with the General Secretary.

2. The General Secretary shall inform the Council and the Contracting Parties forthwith of such requests and of the respective replies.

Special inspections

Article 16

1. The International Atomic Energy Agency and the Council established by this Treaty have the power of carrying out special inspections in the following cases:

(a) In the case of the International Atomic Energy Agency, in accordance with the agreements referred to in article 13 of this Treaty;

(b) In the case of the Council:

(i) When so requested, the reasons for the request being stated, by any Party which suspects that some activity prohibited by this Treaty has been carried out or is about to be carried out, either in the territory of any other Party or in any other place on such latter Party's behalf, the Council shall immediately arrange for such an inspection in accordance with article 10, paragraph 5.

(ii) When requested by any Party which has been suspected of or charged with having violated this Treaty, the Council shall immediately arrange for the special inspection requested in accordance with article 10, paragraph 5.

The above requests will be made to the Council through the General Secretary.

2. The costs and expenses of any special inspection carried out under paragraph 1, sub-paragraph (b), sections (i) and (ii) of this article shall be borne by the requesting Party or Parties, except where the Council concludes on the basis of the report on the special inspection that, in view of the circumstances existing in the case, such costs and expenses should be borne by the agency.

3. The General Conference shall formulate the procedures for the organization and execution of the special inspections carried out in accordance with paragraph 1, sub-paragraph (b), sections (i) and (ii) of this article.

4. The Contracting Parties undertake to grant the inspectors carrying out such special inspections full and free access to all places and all information which may be necessary for the performance of their duties and which are directly and intimately connected with the suspicion of violation of this Treaty. If so requested by the authorities of the Contracting Party in whose territory the inspection is carried out, the inspectors designated by the General Conference shall be accompanied by representatives of said authorities, provided that this does not in any way delay or hinder the work of the inspectors.

5. The Council shall immediately transmit to all the Parties, through the General Secretary, a copy of any report resulting from special inspections.

6. Similarly, the Council shall send through the General Secretary to the Secretary-General of the United Nations, for transmission to the United Nations Security Council and General Assembly, and to the Council of the Organization of American States, for its information, a copy of any report resulting from any special inspection carried out in accordance with paragraph 1, sub-paragraph (b), sections (i) and (ii) of this article.

7. The Council may decide, or any Contracting Party may request, the convening of a special session of the General Conference for the purpose of considering the reports resulting from any special inspection. In such a case, the General Secretary shall take immediate steps to convene the special session requested.

8. The General Conference, convened in special session under this article, may make recommendations to the Contracting Parties and submit reports to the Secretary-General of the United Nations to be transmitted to the United Nations Security Council and the General Assembly.

Use of nuclear energy for peaceful purposes

Article 17

Nothing in the provisions of this Treaty shall prejudice the rights of the Contracting Parties, in conformity with this Treaty, to use nuclear energy for peaceful purposes, in particular for their economic development and social progress.

Explosions for peaceful purposes

Article 18

1. The Contracting Parties may carry out explosions of nuclear devices for peaceful purposes—including explosions which involve devices similar to those used in nuclear weapons—or collaborate with third parties for the same purpose, provided that they do so in accordance with the provisions of this article and the other articles of the Treaty, particularly articles 1 and 5.

2. Contracting Parties intending to carry out, or to cooperate in carrying out, such an explosion shall notify the Agency and the International Atomic Energy Agency, as far in advance as the circumstances require, of the date of the explosion and shall at the same time provide the following information:

(a) The nature of the nuclear device and the source from which it was obtained,

(b) The place and purpose of the planned explosion,

(c) The procedures which will be followed in order to comply with paragraph 3 of this article.

(d) The expected force of the device, and

(e) The fullest possible information on any possible radioactive fall-out that may result from the explosion or explosions, and measures which will be taken to avoid danger to the population, flora, fauna and territories of any other Party or Parties.

3. The General Secretary and the technical personnel designated by the Council and the International Atomic Energy Agency may observe all the preparations, including the explosion of the device, and shall have unrestricted access to any area in the vicinity of the site of the explosion in order to ascertain whether the device and the procedures followed during the explosion are in conformity with the information supplied under paragraph 2 of this article and the other provisions of this Treaty.

4. The Contracting Parties may accept the collaboration of third parties for the purpose set forth in paragraph 1 of the present article, in accordance with paragraphs 2 and 3 thereof.

Relations with other international organizations

Article 19

1. The Agency may conclude such agreements with the International Atomic Energy Agency as are authorized by the General Conference and as it considers likely to facilitate the efficient operation of the control system established by this Treaty.

2. The Agency may also enter into relations with any international organization or body, especially any which may be established in the future to supervise disarmament or measures for the control of armaments in any part of the world.

3. The Contracting Parties may, if they see fit, request the advice of the Inter-American Nuclear Energy Commission on all technical matters connected with the application of this Treaty with which the Commission is competent to deal under its Statute.

Measures in the event of violation of the Treaty

Article 20

1. The General Conference shall take note of all cases in which, in its opinion, any Contracting Party is not complying fully with its obligations under this Treaty and shall draw the matter to the attention of the Party concerned, making such recommendations as it deems appropriate.

2. If, in its opinion, such non-compliance constitutes a violation of this Treaty which might endanger peace and security, the General Conference shall report thereon simultaneously to the United Nations Security Council and the General Assembly through the Secretary-General of the United Nations, and to the Council of the Organization of American States. The General Conference shall likewise report to the International Atomic Energy Agency for such purposes as are relevant in accordance with its Statute.

United Nations and Organization of American States

Article 21

None of the provisions of this Treaty shall be construed as impairing the rights and obligations of the Parties under the Charter of the United Nations or, in the case of States Members of the Organization of American States, under existing regional treaties.

Privileges and immunities

Article 22

1. The Agency shall enjoy in the territory of each of the Contracting Parties such

legal capacity and such privileges and immunities as may be necessary for the exercise of its functions and the fulfilment of its purposes.

2. Representatives of the Contracting Parties accredited to the Agency and officials of the Agency shall similarly enjoy such privileges and immunities as are necessary for the performance of their functions.

3. The Agency may conclude agreements with the Contracting Parties with a view to determining the details of the application of paragraphs 1 and 2 of this article.

Notification of other agreements

Article 23

Once this Treaty has entered into force, the Secretariat shall be notified immediately of any international agreement concluded by any of the Contracting Parties on matters with which this Treaty is concerned; the Secretariat shall register it and notify the other Contracting Parties.

Settlement of disputes

Article 24

Unless the Parties concerned agree on another mode of peaceful settlement, any question or dispute concerning the interpretation or application of this Treaty which is not settled shall be referred to the International Court of Justice with the prior consent of the Parties to the controversy.

Signature

Article 25

1. This Treaty shall be open indefinitely for signature by:

(a) All the Latin American Republics, and
(b) All other sovereign States situated in their entirety south of latitude 35° north in the western hemisphere; and, except as provided in paragraph 2 of this article, all such States which become sovereign, when they have been admitted by the General Conference.

2. The General Conference shall not take any decision regarding the admission of a political entity part or all of whose territory is the subject, prior to the date when this Treaty is opened for signature, of a dispute or claim between an extra-continental country and one or more Latin American States, so long as the dispute has not been settled by peaceful means.

Ratification and deposit

Article 26

1. This Treaty shall be subject to ratification by signatory States in accordance with their respective constitutional procedures.

2. This Treaty and the instruments of ratification shall be deposited with the Government of the Mexican United States, which is hereby designated the Depositary Government.

3. The Depositary Government shall send certified copies of this Treaty to the Governments of signatory States and shall notify them of the deposit of each instrument of ratification.

Reservations

Article 27

This Treaty shall not be subject to reservations.

Entry into force

Article 28

1. Subject to the provisions of paragraph 2 of this article, this Treaty shall enter into force among the States that have ratified it as soon as the following requirements have been met:

(a) Deposit of the instruments of ratification of this Treaty with the Depositary Government by the Governments of the States mentioned in article 25 which are in existence on the date when this Treaty is opened for signature and which are not affected by the provisions of article 25, paragraph 2;

(b) Signature and ratification of Additional Protocol I annexed to this Treaty by all extra-continental or continental States having *de jure* or *de facto* international responsibility for territories situated in the zone of application of the Treaty;

(c) Signature and ratification of the Additional Protocol II annexed to this Treaty by all powers possessing nuclear weapons;

(d) Conclusion of bilateral or multilateral agreements on the application of the Safeguards System of the International Atomic Energy Agency in accordance with article 13 of this Treaty.

2. All signatory States shall have the imprescriptible right to waive, wholly or in part, the requirements laid down in the preceding paragraph. They may do so by means of a declaration which shall be annexed to their respective instrument of ratification and which may be formulated at the time of deposit of the instrument or subsequently. For those States which exercise this right, this Treaty shall enter into force upon deposit of the declaration, or as soon as those requirements have been met which have not been expressly waived.

3. As soon as this Treaty has entered into force in accordance with the provisions of paragraph 2 for eleven States, the Depositary Government shall convene a preliminary meeting of those States in order that the Agency may be set up and commence its work.

4. After the entry into force of this Treaty for all the countries of the zone, the rise of a new power possessing nuclear weapons shall have the effect of suspending the execution of this Treaty for those countries which have ratified it without waiving requirements of paragraph 1, sub-paragraph (c) of this article, and which request such suspension; the Treaty shall remain suspended until the new power, on its own initiative or upon request by the General Conference, ratifies the annexed Additional Protocol II.

Amendments

Article 29

1. Any Contracting Party may propose amendments to this Treaty and shall submit its proposals to the Council through the General Secretary, who shall transmit them to

all the other Contracting Parties and, in addition, to all other signatories in accordance with article 6. The Council, through the General Secretary, shall immediately following the meeting of signatories convene a special session of the General Conference to examine the proposals made, for the adoption of which a two-thirds majority of the Contracting Parties present and voting shall be required.

2. Amendments adopted shall enter into force as soon as the requirements set forth in article 28 of this Treaty have been complied with.

Duration and denunciation

Article 30

1. This Treaty shall be of a permanent nature and shall remain in force indefinitely, but any Party may denounce it by notifying the General Secretary of the Agency if, in the opinion of the denouncing State, there have arisen or may arise circumstances connected with the content of this Treaty or of the annexed Additional Protocols I and II which affect its supreme interests or the peace and security of one or more Contracting Parties.

2. The denunciation shall take effect three months after the delivery to the General Secretary of the Agency of the notification by the Government of the signatory State concerned. The General Secretary shall immediately communicate such notification to the other Contracting Parties and to the Secretary-General of the United Nations for the information of the United Nations Security Council and the General Assembly. He shall also communicate it to the Secretary-General of the Organization of American States.

Authentic texts and registration

Article 31

This Treaty, of which the Spanish, Chinese, English, French, Portuguese and Russian texts are equally authentic, shall be registered by the Depositary Government in accordance with article 102 of the United Nations Charter. The Depositary Government shall notify the Secretary-General of the United Nations of the signatures, ratifications and amendments relating to this Treaty and shall communicate them to the Secretary-General of the Organization of American States for its information.

Transitional Article

Denunciation of the declaration referred to in article 28, paragraph 2, shall be subject to the same procedures as the denunciation of this Treaty, except that it will take effect on the date of delivery of the respective notification.

IN WITNESS WHEREOF the undersigned Plenipotentiaries, having deposited their full powers, found in good and due form, sign this Treaty on behalf of their respective Governments.

DONE at Mexico, Distrito Federal, on the Fourteenth day of February, one thousand nine hundred and sixty-seven.

Additional Protocol I to the Treaty for the Prohibition of Nuclear Weapons in Latin America

Signed by the United States at Washington May 26, 1977
Ratification advised by U.S. Senate November 13, 1981
Ratified by U.S. President November 19, 1981
U.S. ratification deposited at Mexico City November 23, 1981
Proclaimed by U.S. President December 4, 1981

The undersigned Plenipotentiaries, furnished with full powers by their respective Governments,

Convinced that the Treaty for the Prohibition of Nuclear Weapons in Latin America, negotiated and signed in accordance with the recommendations of the General Assembly of the United Nations in Resolution 1911 (XVIII) of 27 November 1963, represents an important step towards ensuring the non-proliferation of nuclear weapons,

Aware that the non-proliferation of nuclear weapons is not an end in itself but, rather, a means of achieving general and complete disarmament at a later stage, and

Desiring to contribute, so far as lies in their power, towards ending the armaments race, especially in the field of nuclear weapons, and towards strengthening a world at peace, based on mutual respect and sovereign equality of States,

Have agreed as follows:

Article 1. To undertake to apply the statute of denuclearization in respect of warlike purposes as defined in articles 1, 3, 5 and 13 of the Treaty for the Prohibition of Nuclear Weapons in Latin America in territories for which, *de jure* or *de facto*, they are internationally responsible and which lie within the limits of the geographical zone established in that Treaty.

Article 2. The duration of this Protocol shall be the same as that of the Treaty for the Prohibition of Nuclear Weapons in Latin America of which this Protocol is an annex, and the provisions regarding ratification and denunciation contained in the Treaty shall be applicable to it.

Article 3. This Protocol shall enter into force, for the States which have ratified it, on the date of the deposit of their respective instruments of ratification.

IN WITNESS WHEREOF the undersigned Plenipotentiaries, having deposited their full powers, found in good and due form, sign this Protocol on behalf of their respective Governments.

Additional Protocol II to the Treaty for the Prohibition of Nuclear Weapons in Latin America

Signed by the United States at Mexico City April 1, 1968
Ratification advised by U.S. Senate April 19, 1971
Ratified by U.S. President May 8, 1971
U.S. ratification deposited at Mexico City May 12, 1971
Proclaimed by U.S. President June 11, 1971

The Undersigned Plenipotentiaries, furnished with full powers by their respective Governments,

Convinced that the Treaty for the Prohibition of Nuclear Weapons in Latin America, negotiated and signed in accordance with the recommendations of the General Assembly of the United Nations in Resolution 1911 (XVIII) of 27 November 1963, represents an important step towards ensuring the non-proliferation of nuclear weapons,

Aware that the non-proliferation of nuclear weapons is not an end in itself but, rather, a means of achieving general and complete disarmament at a later stage, and

Desiring to contribute, so far as lies in their power, towards ending the armaments race, especially in the field of nuclear weapons, and towards promoting and strengthening a world at peace, based on mutual respect and sovereign equality of States,

Have agreed as follows:

Article 1. The statute of denuclearization of Latin America in respect of warlike purposes, as defined, delimited and set forth in the Treaty for the Prohibition of Nuclear Weapons in Latin America of which this instrument is an annex, shall be fully respected by the Parties to this Protocol in all its express aims and provisions.

Article 2. The Governments represented by the undersigned Plenipotentiaries undertake, therefore, not to contribute in any way to the performance of acts involving a violation of the obligations of article 1 of the Treaty in the territories to which the Treaty applies in accordance with article 4 thereof.

Article 3. The Governments represented by the undersigned Plenipotentiaries also undertake not to use or threaten to use nuclear weapons against the Contracting Parties of the Treaty for the Prohibition of Nuclear Weapons in Latin America.

Article 4. The duration of this Protocol shall be the same as that of the Treaty for the Prohibition of Nuclear Weapons in Latin America of which this Protocol is an annex, and the definitions of territory and nuclear weapons set forth in articles 3 and 5 of the Treaty shall be applicable to this Protocol, as well as the provisions regarding ratification, reservations, denunciation, authentic texts and registration contained in articles 26, 27, 30 and 31 of the Treaty.

Article 5. This Protocol shall enter into force, for the States which have ratified it, on the date of the deposit of their respective instruments of ratification.

IN WITNESS WHEREOF the undersigned Plenipotentiaries, having deposited their full powers, found in good and due form, sign this Additional Protocol on behalf of their respective Governments.

Proclamation by President Nixon on Ratification of Additional Protocol II to the Treaty for the Prohibition of Nuclear Weapons in Latin America

BY THE PRESIDENT OF THE UNITED STATES OF AMERICA

A PROCLAMATION

Considering that:

Additional Protocol II to the Treaty for the Prohibition of Nuclear Weapons in Latin America, done at the City of Mexico on February 14, 1967, was signed on behalf of the United States of America on April 1, 1968, the text of which Protocol is word for word as follows:

[The text of the Protocol appears here.]

The Senate of the United States of America by its resolution of April 19, 1971, two-thirds of the Senators present concurring, gave its advice and consent to the ratification of Additional Protocol II, with the following understandings and declarations:

I

That the United States Government understands the reference in Article 3 of the treaty to "its own legislation" to relate only to such legislation as is compatible with the rules of international law and as involves an exercise of sovereignty consistent with those rules, and accordingly that ratification of Additional Protocol II by the United States Government could not be regarded as implying recognition, for the purposes of this treaty and its protocols or for any other purpose, of any legislation which did not, in the view of the United States, comply with the relevant rules of international law.

That the United States Government takes note of the Preparatory Commission's interpretation of the treaty, as set forth in the Final Act, that, governed by the principles and rules of international law, each of the Contracting Parties retains exclusive power and legal competence, unaffected by the terms of the treaty, to grant or deny non-Contracting Parties transit and transport privileges.

That as regards the undertaking in Article 3 of Protocol II not to use or threaten to use nuclear weapons against the Contracting Parties, the United States Government would have to consider that an armed attack by a Contracting Party, in which it was assisted by a nuclear-weapon state, would be incompatible with the Contracting Party's corresponding obligations under Article I of the Treaty.

II

That the United States Government considers that the technology of making nuclear explosive devices for peaceful purposes is indistinguishable from the technology of making nuclear weapons, and that nuclear weapons and nuclear explosive devices for peaceful purposes are both capable of releasing nuclear energy in an uncontrolled manner and have the common group of characteristics of large amounts of energy generated instantaneously from a compact source. Therefore, the United States

Government understands the definition contained in Article 5 of the treaty as necessarily encompassing all nuclear explosive devices. It is also understood that Articles 1 and 5 restrict accordingly the activities of the Contracting Parties under paragraph 1 of Article 18.

That the United States Government understands that paragraph 4 of Article 18 of the Treaty permits, and that United States adherence to Protocol II will not prevent, collaboration by the United States with Contracting Parties for the purpose of carrying out explosions of nuclear devices for peaceful purposes in a manner consistent with a policy of not contributing to the proliferation of nuclear weapons capabilities. In this connection, the United States Government notes Article V of the Treaty on the Non-Proliferation of Nuclerar Weapons, under which it joined in an undertaking to take appropriate measures to ensure that potential benefits of peaceful applications of nuclear explosions would be made available to non-nuclear-weapon states party to that treaty, and reaffirms its willingness to extend such undertaking, on the same basis, to states precluded by the present treaty from manufacturing or acquiring any nuclear explosive device.

III

That the United States Government also declares that, although not required by Protocol II, it will act with respect to such territories of Protocol I adherents as are within the geographical area defined in paragraph 2 of Article 4 of the treaty in the same manner as Protocol II requires it to act with respect to the territories of Contracting Parties.

The President ratified Additional Protocol II on May 8, 1971, with the above-recited understandings and declarations, in pursuance of the advice and consent of the Senate.

It is provided in Article 5 of Additional Protocol II that the Protocol shall enter into force, for the States which have ratified it, on the date of the deposit of their respective instruments of ratification.

The instrument of ratification of the United Kingdom of Great Britain and Northern Ireland was deposited on December 11, 1969 with understandings and a declaration, and the instrument of ratification of the United States of America was deposited on May 12, 1971 with the above-recited understandings and declarations.

In accordance with Article 5 of Additional Protocol II, the Protocol entered into force for the United States of America on May 12, 1971, subject to the above recited under-standings and declarations.

NOW, THEREFORE, I, Richard Nixon, President of the United States of America, proclaim and make public Additional Protocol II to the Treaty for the Prohibition of Nuclear Weapons in Latin America to the end that it shall be observed and fulfilled with good faith, subject to the above-recited understandings and declarations, on and after May 12, 1971 by the United States of America and by the citizens of the United States of America and all other persons subject to the jurisdiction thereof.

IN TESTIMONY WHEREOF, I have signed this proclamation and caused the Seal of the United States of America to be affixed.

DONE at the city of Washington this eleventh day of June in the year of our Lord one thousand nine hundred seventy-one and of the Independence of the United States of America the one hundred ninety-fifth.

(SEAL)

Treaty for the Prohibition of Nuclear Weapons in Latin America

Country	Date of Signature	Date of Deposit of Ratification
Argentina	9/27/67	
Bahamas, The		7/16/76[a]
Barbados	10/18/68	4/25/69
Bolivia	2/14/67	2/18/69
Brazil	5/ 9/67	1/29/68[b]
Chile	2/14/67	10/ 9/74[b]
Colombia	2/14/67	8/ 4/72
Costa Rica	2/14/67	8/25/69
Dominican Republic	7/29/67	6/14/68
Ecuador	2/14/67	2/11/69
El Salvador	2/14/67	4/22/68
Grenada	4/29/75	6/20/75
Guatemala	2/14/67	2/ 6/70
Haiti	2/14/67	5/23/69
Honduras	2/14/67	9/23/68
Jamaica	10/26/67	6/26/69
Mexico	2/14/67	9/20/67
Nicaragua	2/15/67	10/24/68
Panama	2/14/67	6/11/71
Paraguay	4/26/67	3/19/69
Peru	2/14/67	3/ 4/69
Suriname	2/13/76	6/10/77
Trinidad & Tobago	6/27/67	12/ 3/70[c]
Uruguay	2/14/67	8/20/68
Venezuela	2/14/67	3/23/70
Total	24	24

[a]This is date of notification of succession. The declaration of waiver was deposited 4/26/77, which is date of entry into force for The Bahamas.

[b]Not in force. No declaration of waiver under Art. 28, para. 2.

[c]The declaration of waiver was deposited 6/27/75, which is date of entry into force for Trinidad and Tobago.

Additional Protocol I to the Treaty for the Prohibition of Nuclear Weapons in Latin America

Country	Date of Signature	Date of Deposit of Ratification
France	3/2/79	
Netherlands	4/ 1/68	7/26/71
United Kingdom	12/20/67	12/11/69
United States	5/26/77	11/23/81

Additional Protocol II to the Treaty for the Prohibition of Nuclear Weapons in Latin America

Country	Date of Signature	Date of Deposit of Ratification
China, People's Republic of	8/21/73	6/12/74
France	7/18/73	3/22/74
Union of Soviet Socialist Republics	5/18/78	1/ 8/79
United Kingdom	12/20/67	12/11/69
United States	4/ 1/68	5/12/71

Treaty on the Non-Proliferation of Nuclear Weapons

The need to prevent the spread of nuclear weapons was evident from the first days of the nuclear era. On November 15, 1945, the United States, the United Kingdom, and Canada proposed the establishment of a U.N. Atomic Energy Commission for the purpose of "entirely eliminating the use of atomic energy for destructive purposes." The Baruch plan of 1946, offered by the United States, sought to forestall nuclear arms proliferation by placing all nuclear resources under international ownership and control.

But the early postwar efforts to achieve agreement on nuclear disarmament failed. The Soviet Union in 1949, the United Kingdom in 1952, France in 1960, and the People's Republic of China in 1964, became nuclear-weapons states. And increasingly it was becoming apparent that earlier assumptions about the scarcity of nuclear materials and the difficulty of mastering nuclear technology were inaccurate.

Other developments and prospects further underscored the threat of nuclear proliferation. In the early 1960s the search for peaceful applications of nuclear energy had brought advances in the technology of nuclear reactors for the generation of electric power. By 1966 such nuclear reactors were operating or under construction in five countries. It was estimated that by 1985 more than 300 nuclear power reactors would be operating, under construction, or on order. Nuclear reactors produce not only power, but plutonium—a fissionable material which can be chemically separated and used in the manufacture of nuclear weapons. By 1985 the quantity of plutonium being produced would make possible the construction of 15 to 20 nuclear bombs daily, depending upon the level of the technology employed.

If the diversion of nuclear materials from peaceful purposes were not prevented by an international system of safeguards, and if a growing number of nations came to possess nuclear arsenals, the risks of nuclear war as a result of accident, unauthorized use, or escalation of regional conflicts would greatly increase. The possession of nuclear weapons by many countries would add a grave new dimension of threat to world security.

A succession of initiatives by both nuclear and nonnuclear powers sought to check proliferation. Indeed the effort to achieve a test ban—culminating in the treaty of 1963—had as one of its main purposes inhibiting the spread of nuclear weapons. But much before that, in

August 1957, the Western powers (Canada, France, the United Kingdom, and the United States) submitted a "package" of measures, in the Subcommittee of the United Nations Disarmament Commission, which included a commitment "not to transfer out of its control any nuclear weapons, or to accept transfer to it of such weapons," except for self-defense.

Although the Soviet Union opposed proliferation, it claimed that this Western formula would allow an aggressor to judge his own actions, and to use nuclear weapons "under cover of the alleged right of self-defense." It sought to couple a ban on transfer of nuclear weapons to other states with a prohibition on stationing nuclear weapons in foreign countries.

In 1961 the General Assembly unanimously approved an Irish resolution calling on all states, particularly the nuclear powers, to conclude an international agreement to refrain from transfer or acquisition of nuclear weapons. Moreover, the general disarmament plans which had been submitted by the United States and the Soviet Union during the period 1960–62 included provisions banning the transfer and acquisition of nuclear weapons.

The United States, on January 21, 1964, outlined a program to halt the nuclear arms race in a message from President Johnson to the Eighteen-Nation Disarmament Committee (ENDC). This program, unlike the 1957 proposal, was not a "package." It included a nondissemination and nonacquisition proposal—based on the Irish resolution—and safeguards on international transfers of nuclear materials for peaceful purposes, combined with acceptance by the major nuclear powers that their peaceful nuclear activities undergo increasingly "the same inspection they recommend for other states."

An issue that was to be the principal stumbling block for the next 3 years was the proposed multilateral nuclear force (MLF) then under discussion by the United States and its NATO allies. The Soviet Union strongly objected to this plan and maintained that no agreement could be reached on non-proliferation so long as the United States held open the possibility of such nuclear-sharing arrangements in NATO. These would constitute proliferation, the Soviet Union contended, and were devices for giving the Federal Republic of Germany access to or control of nuclear weapons.

On August 17, 1965, the United States submitted a draft non-proliferation treaty to the ENDC. This draft would oblige the nuclear-weapons powers not to transfer nuclear weapons to the national control of any country not having them. Nonnuclear nations would undertake to facilitate the application of International Atomic Energy Agency or equivalent safeguards to their peaceful nuclear activities.

A Soviet draft treaty was submitted to the General Assembly on

September 24. In an accompanying memorandum, the Soviet Union declared that the greatest danger of proliferation was posed by the MLF and the alternative British proposal for an Atlantic nuclear force (ANF). The Soviet draft prohibited the transfer of nuclear weapons "directly or indirectly, through third States or groups of States not possessing nuclear weapons." It would also bar nuclear powers from transferring "nuclear weapons, or control over them or their emplacement or use" to military units of nonnuclear allies, even if these were placed under joint command. The draft included no safeguards provisions.

In March 1966 the United States tabled amendments to its draft treaty in the ENDC, seeking to clarify and emphasize the Western view that collective defense arrangements would not violate the principle of non-proliferation. The U.S. representative stressed that the United States would not relinquish its veto over the use of U.S. weapons. The Soviet Union objected that the amendments did not prevent the transfer of nuclear weapons through such alliance arrangements as the MLF, the ANF, or units placed under joint command. The U.S. retention of a veto, the Soviet representative argued, did not provide security against dissemination.

Despite strong disagreement on the issue of collective defense arrangements, it was apparent that both sides recognized the desirability of an agreement on non-proliferation. Moreover, the interest of nonnuclear powers was increasingly manifest. It was shown in 1964 at the African summit conference and at the Cairo conference of nonaligned states and expressed in a series of resolutions in the General Assembly urging that non-proliferation receive priority attention. In May 1966 the U.S. Senate unanimously passed a resolution, sponsored by Senator Pastore of Rhode Island and 55 other Senators, commending efforts to reach a non-proliferation agreement and supporting continued efforts.

In the fall of 1966 the U.S. and Soviet co-chairmen of the ENDC began private talks, and by the end of the year they had reached tentative agreement on the basic nontransfer and nonacquisition provisions of a treaty, as well as on a number of other aspects.

There followed a long and arduous series of consultations between the United States and its allies. The allies raised a number of questions regarding the effect of the treaty on NATO nuclear defense arrangements, and the United States gave its interpretations. The United States considered that the treaty covered nuclear weapons or explosive devices but not delivery systems. It would not prohibit NATO consultation and planning on nuclear defense, nor ban deployment of U.S.-owned and -controlled nuclear weapons on the territory of nonnuclear NATO members. It would not "bar succession by a new federated European state to the nuclear status of one of its members." The allies' questions and the United States answers were provided to the Soviet Union, which did not challenge the U.S. interpretations.

On August 24, 1967, the United States and the Soviet Union were able to submit separate but identical texts of a draft treaty to the ENDC. Other ENDC members proposed numerous amendments, largely reflecting the concerns of the nonnuclear states. In response to these, the drafts underwent several revisions, and the co-chairmen tabled a joint draft on March 11, 1968. With additional revisions, the joint draft was submitted to the General Assembly, where it was extensively debated. Further suggestions for strengthening the treaty were made, and in the light of these the United States and the Soviet Union submitted a new revised version—the seventh—to the First Committee of the General Assembly on May 31. The General Assembly on June 12 approved a resolution commending the text and requesting the depositary governments to open it for signature. France abstained in the General Assembly vote, stating that while France would not sign the treaty, it "would behave in the future in this field exactly as the States adhering to the treaty."

In the course of these extended negotiations, the concerns of the nonnuclear powers centered particularly on three main issues:

Safeguards. There was general agreement that the treaty should include provisions designed to detect and deter the diversion of nuclear materials from peaceful to weapons use. Two problems were involved. One was to reconcile the Soviet insistence that all nonnuclear parties accept IAEA[1] safeguards with the desire of the nonnuclear members of EURATOM[2] (Belgium, the Federal Republic of Germany, Italy, Luxembourg, and the Netherlands) to preserve their regional system. To meet this concern, the final draft provided that nonnuclear parties could negotiate safeguards agreements with IAEA either individually or together with other states.[3]

The other problem was to satisfy the widespread concern among nonnuclear states that IAEA safeguards might place them at a commercial and industrial disadvantage in developing nuclear energy for peaceful use, since the nuclear powers would not be required to accept safeguards. To help allay these misgivings, the United States offered, on December 2, 1967, to permit the IAEA

---

[1]International Atomic Energy Agency, a U.N.-sponsored agency headquartered at Vienna.

[2]European Atomic Energy Community, an organization established by the original European Common Market partners for cooperation in nuclear energy matters.

[3]EURATOM and the IAEA began negotiations in 1971. An IAEA-EURATOM safeguards agreement was signed in April 1973 and entered into force on February 21, 1977.

to apply its safeguards, when such safeguards were applied under the NPT, in all nuclear facilities in the United States, excluding only those with "direct national security significance." The United Kingdom announced that it would take similar action. Its safeguards agreement with the IAEA was concluded in 1976 and is now in force. The U.S.-IAEA agreement, signed on November 18, 1977, was submitted by the President to the Senate for its advice and consent to ratification on February 9, 1978, and entered into force on December 9, 1980. In 1977, France opened negotiations with the IAEA, and a safeguards agreement entered into force on September 12, 1981. In June 1982, the Soviet Union announced its readiness to put some of its nuclear installations under IAEA been willing to accept safeguards on its nuclear facilities.

Balanced Obligations. Throughout the negotiations most nonnuclear states held that their renunciation of nuclear weapons should be accompanied by a commitment on the part of the nuclear powers to reduce their nuclear arsenals and to make progress on measures of comprehensive disarmament. General provisions were attached to the treaty affirming the intentions of the parties to negotiate in good faith to achieve a cessation of the nuclear arms race, nuclear disarmament, and general and complete disarmament.

Further, to meet objections about possible discriminatory effects, the treaty stipulated that parties were to participate in and have fullest access to materials and information for peaceful uses of nuclear energy. The treaty also provided that any potential benefits of nuclear explosions for peaceful purposes would be made available to nonnuclear weapons parties on a nondiscriminatory basis.

Security Assurances. Nonnuclear-weapons states sought guarantees that renunciation of nuclear arms would not place them at a permanent military disadvantage and make them vulnerable to nuclear intimidation. But, it was argued, the security interests of the various states, and groups of states, were not identical; an effort to frame provisions within the treaty that would meet this diversity of requirements—for unforeseeable future contingencies—would create inordinate complexities. To resolve the issue, the United States, the Soviet Union, and the United Kingdom submitted in the ENDC, on March 7, 1968, a tripartite proposal that security assurances take the form of a U.N. Security Council resolution, supported by declarations of the three powers. The resolution, noting the security concerns of states wishing to subscribe to the Non-Proliferation Treaty, would recognize that nuclear aggression, or the threat of nuclear aggression, created a situation requiring immediate action by the Security Council, especially its permanent members.

Following submission of the treaty itself to the General Assembly, the tripartite resolution was submitted to the Security Council. In a formal declaration the United States asserted its intention to seek immediate Security Council actions to provide assistance to any nonnuclear-weapons state party to the treaty that was the object of nuclear aggression or threats. The Soviet Union and the United Kingdom made similar declarations. France abstained from voting on the Security Council resolution; the French representative said that France did not intend its abstention to be an obstacle to adoption of the tripartite proposal, but that France did not believe the nations would receive adequate security guarantees without nuclear disarmament.

In addition to this "positive" security assurance, the United States in 1978 issued a policy statement on "negative" security assurances in connection with the U.N. Special Session on Disarmament. Secretary of State Vance made the following statement on June 12, 1978:

> After reviewing the current status of the discussions in the United Nations Special Session on Disarmament, after consultations with our principal allies, and on the basis of studies made in preparation for the Special Session, the President has decided to elaborate the U.S. position on the question of security assurances. His objective is to encourage support for halting the spread of nuclear weapons, to increase international security and stability, and to create a more positive environment for success of the Special Session. To this end, the President declares:
>
> > "The United States will not use nuclear weapons against any non-nuclear weapons state party to the NPT or any comparable internationally binding commitment not to acquire nuclear explosive devices, except in the case of an attack on the United States, its territorities or armed forces, or its allies, by such a state allied to a nuclear weapons state, or associated with a nuclear weapons state in carrying out or sustaining the attack."

It is the President's view that this formulation preserves our security commitments and advances our collective security as well as enhances the prospect for more effective arms control and disarmament.

The treaty was opened for signature on July 1, 1968, and signed on that date by the United States, the United Kingdom, the Soviet Union, and 59 other countries. On July 9, President Johnson transmitted it to the Senate, but prospects for early U.S. ratification dimmed after the Soviet invasion of Czechoslovakia in August. The Senate adjourned without voting on the Treaty. In February 1969 President Nixon requested Senate approval of the treaty, and in March the Senate gave its advice and consent to ratification. The treaty entered into force with the deposit of U.S. ratification on March 5, 1970.

In broadest outline, the basic provisions of the treaty are designed to

— prevent the spread of nuclear weapons (Articles I and II);
— provide assurance, through international safeguards, that the peaceful nuclear activities of states which have not already developed nuclear weapons will not be diverted to making such weapons (Article III);
— promote, to the maximum extent consistent with the other purposes of the treaty, the peaceful uses of nuclear energy through full cooperation—with the potential benefits of any peaceful application of nuclear explosion technology being made available to nonnuclear parties under appropriate international observation (Articles IV and V);
— express the determination of the parties that the treaty should lead to further progress in comprehensive arms control and nuclear disarmament measures (Article VI).

Article VIII provides for a conference "to review the operation of this Treaty with a view to assuring that the Purposes of the Preamble and the provisions of the Treaty are being realized." The NPT Review Conference, held in Geneva in May 1975, produced a number of significant recommendations. It expressed strong support for IAEA safeguards and called for greater efforts to make them universal and effective. There was general agreement that safeguards do not hamper peaceful nuclear activities. The final declaration of the conference, accepted by consensus, urged all states with peaceful nuclear activities to maintain effective accounting and control systems, noting the readiness of the International Atomic Energy Agency to assist them and the importance of such systems to effective IAEA monitoring. It recommended that safeguards be of adequate duration (which had not always been the case in the past); and that they preclude the diversion of safeguarded material to any nuclear explosive device, regardless of its stated purpose. It recommended that support be given to improving safeguards techniques, instrumentation, data handling, and implementation.

The conference urged common export requirements designed to extend safeguards, in all available ways, to all peaceful nuclear activities in importing states not party to the treaty, and urged all suppliers and recipients to accept these requirements.

The conference recommended better physical protection of nuclear materials, giving weight to NPT adherence in decisions on nuclear assistance and credit arrangements, and also recommended the study of the potential advantages of multinational fuel cycle centers.

The conference emphasized the need for further study of

"peaceful" nuclear explosions (PNEs) by the IAEA (which subsequently established an international advisory group on this subject) and for considering arms control implications of PNEs by the Conference of the Committee on Disarmament (which subsequently held a meeting of experts on this aspect of the subject).

At the second review conference which was held in Geneva August 11–September 7, 1980, a thorough exchange of views on progress toward fulfillment of the treaty's objectives was heard. While the participants failed to agree on a final document, the consensus of the parties shows positive signs for the viability of the NPT. The participants did agree to hold another review conference in 1985. (It should also be noted that Article X of the NPT calls for a conference to be held 25 years after entry into force [1995] to determine whether the treaty shall be extended indefinitely, or for an additional fixed period of time.)

The following can be said about implementation of the Treaty Articles:

Articles I and II: No nuclear-weapon state party to the Treaty has transferred nuclear explosive devices or has assisted any nonnuclear-weapon state in acquiring or manufacturing a nuclear explosive device. No nonnuclear-weapon state party to the Treaty has acquired or manufactured a nuclear explosive device.

Article III: The IAEA has developed an extensive system of safeguards which ensures that nuclear materials located in nonnuclear-weapon states party to the Treaty are used solely for nonexplosive purposes. Safeguards agreements required by the NPT have entered into force for 68 countries. For 44 nonnuclear-weapon states party to the Treaty, the relevant safeguards agreements have not yet entered into force; however, none of these states has significant nuclear activities. In 1974 a number of NPT parties indicated which nuclear exports would require IAEA safeguards under Article III.2 of the NPT. Since then a total of 18 nuclear suppliers which are party to the NPT have expanded the list of items which trigger safeguards under this article.

Article IV: The United States has been in the forefront of nations which have provided technical assistance in the nuclear field. At the United Nations Special Session on Disarmament in 1978, the United States announced that it would be expanding technical assistance through the IAEA for NPT parties. In 1977 President Carter proposed the International Nuclear Fuel Cycle Evaluation to study how nuclear energy can be used in peaceful applications while minimizing the danger of proliferation. Over 40 nations participated in this 2-year study.

Article V: No nuclear explosions for peaceful purposes have been conducted under this Article. It is the view of the United States that there are no potential benefits to be derived from such explosions.

Article VI: Article VI is one of the most contentious articles of the NPT. The United States and the Soviet Union have pointed to the U.S.-Soviet talks on limiting and reducing strategic and intermediate-range nuclear weapons as evidence that they are implementing this Article. While the nonnuclear-weapon states have welcomed the SALT talks and agreements reached to date, they have noted that the number of nuclear weapons has increased on both sides since the NPT came into force. A Comprehensive Test Ban Treaty prohibiting the testing of nuclear explosives is viewed by many non-nuclear-weapon states as a *sine qua non* for preventing the emergence of additional nuclear-weapon states and for preserving the NPT regime.

Treaty on the Non-Proliferation of Nuclear Weapons

Signed at Washington, London, and Moscow July 1, 1968
Ratification advised by U.S. Senate March 13, 1969
Ratified by U.S. President November 24, 1969
U.S. ratification deposited at Washington, London, and Moscow March 5, 1970
Proclaimed by U.S. President March 5, 1970
Entered into force March 5, 1970

The States concluding this Treaty, hereinafter referred to as the "Parties to the Treaty",

Considering the devastation that would be visited upon all mankind by a nuclear war and the consequent need to make every effort to avert the danger of such a war and to take measures to safeguard the security of peoples,

Believing that the proliferation of nuclear weapons would seriously enhance the danger of nuclear war,

In conformity with resolutions of the United Nations General Assembly calling for the conclusion of an agreement on the prevention of wider dissemination of nuclear weapons,

Undertaking to cooperate in facilitating the application of International Atomic Energy Agency safeguards on peaceful nuclear activities,

Expressing their support for research, development and other efforts to further the application, within the framework of the International Atomic Energy Agency safeguards system, of the principle of safeguarding effectively the flow of source and special fissionable materials by use of instruments and other techniques at certain strategic points,

Affirming the principle that the benefits of peaceful applications of nuclear technology, including any technological by-products which may be derived by nuclear-weapon States from the development of nuclear explosive devices, should be available for peaceful purposes to all Parties of the Treaty, whether nuclear-weapon or non-nuclear weapon States,

Convinced that, in furtherance of this principle, all Parties to the Treaty are entitled to participate in the fullest possible exchange of scientific information for, and to contribute alone or in cooperation with other States to, the further development of the applications of atomic energy for peaceful purposes,

Declaring their intention to achieve at the earliest possible date the cessation of the nuclear arms race and to undertake effective measures in the direction of nuclear disarmament,

Urging the cooperation of all States in the attainment of this objective,

Recalling the determination expressed by the Parties to the 1963 Treaty banning nuclear weapon tests in the atmosphere, in outer space and under water in its Preamble to seek to achieve the discontinuance of all test explosions of nuclear weapons for all time and to continue negotiations to this end,

Desiring to further the easing of international tension and the strengthening of trust between States in order to facilitate the cessation of the manufacture of nuclear weapons, the liquidation of all their existing stockpiles, and the elimination from national arsenals of nuclear weapons and the means of their delivery pursuant to a treaty on general and complete disarmament under strict and effective international control,

Recalling that, in accordance with the Charter of the United Nations, States must refrain in their international relations from the threat or use of force against the territorial integrity or political independence of any State, or in any other manner inconsistent with the Purposes of the United Nations, and that the establishment and maintenance of international peace and security are to be promoted with the least diversion for armaments of the world's human and economic resources,

Have agreed as follows:

Article I

Each nuclear-weapon State Party to the Treaty undertakes not to transfer to any recipient whatsoever nuclear weapons or other nuclear explosive devices or control over such weapons or explosive devices directly, or indirectly; and not in any way to assist, encourage, or induce any non-nuclear-weapon State to manufacture or otherwise acquire nuclear weapons or other nuclear explosive devices, or control over such weapons or explosive devices.

Article II

Each non-nuclear-weapon State Party to the Treaty undertakes not to receive the transfer from any transferor whatsoever of nuclear weapons or other nuclear explosive devices or of control over such weapons or explosive devices directly, or indirectly; not to manufacture or otherwise acquire nuclear weapons or other nuclear explosive devices; and not to seek or receive any assistance in the manufacture of nuclear weapons or other nuclear explosive devices.

Article III

1. Each non-nuclear-weapon State Party to the Treaty undertakes to accept safeguards, as set forth in an agreement to be negotiated and concluded with the International Atomic Energy Agency in accordance with the Statute of the International Atomic Energy Agency and the Agency's safeguards system, for the exclusive purpose of verification of the fulfillment of its obligations assumed under this Treaty with a view to preventing diversion of nuclear energy from peaceful uses to nuclear weapons or other nuclear explosive devices. Procedures for the safeguards required by this article shall be followed with respect to source or special fissionable material whether it is being produced, processed or used in any principal nuclear facility or is outside any such facility. The safeguards required by this article shall be applied to all source or special fissionable material in all peaceful nuclear activities within the territory of such State, under its jurisdiction, or carried out under its control anywhere.

2. Each State Party to the Treaty undertakes not to provide: (a) source or special fissionable material, or (b) equipment or material especially designed or prepared for the processing, use or production of special fissionable material, to any non-nuclear-weapon State for peaceful purposes, unless the source or special fissionable material shall be subject to the safeguards required by this article.

3. The safeguards required by this article shall be implemented in a manner designed to comply with article IV of this Treaty, and to avoid hampering the economic or technological development of the Parties or international cooperation in the field of peaceful nuclear activities, including the international exchange of nuclear material and equipment for the processing, use or production of nuclear material for peaceful purposes in accordance with the provisions of this article and the principle of safeguarding set forth in the Preamble of the Treaty.

4. Non-nuclear-weapon States Party to the Treaty shall conclude agreements with the International Atomic Energy Agency to meet the requirements of this article either

individually or together with other States in accordance with the Statute of the International Atomic Energy Agency. Negotiation of such agreements shall commence within 180 days from the original entry into force of this Treaty. For States depositing their instruments of ratification or accession after the 180-day period, negotiation of such agreements shall commence not later than the date of such deposit. Such agreements shall enter into force not later than eighteen months after the date of initiation of negotiations.

Article IV

1. Nothing in this Treaty shall be interpreted as affecting the inalienable right of all the Parties to the Treaty to develop research, production and use of nuclear energy for peaceful purposes without discrimination and in conformity with articles I and II of this Treaty.

2. All the Parties to the Treaty undertake to facilitate, and have the right to participate in, the fullest possible exchange of equipment, materials and scientific and technological information for the peaceful uses of nuclear energy. Parties to the Treaty in a position to do so shall also cooperate in contributing alone or together with other States or international organizations to the further development of the applications of nuclear energy for peaceful purposes, especially in the territories of non-nuclear-weapon States Party to the Treaty, with due consideration for the needs of the developing areas of the world.

Article V

Each party to the Treaty undertakes to take appropriate measures to ensure that, in accordance with this Treaty, under appropriate international observation and through appropriate international procedures, potential benefits from any peaceful applications of nuclear explosions will be made available to non-nuclear-weapon States Party to the Treaty on a nondiscriminatory basis and that the charge to such Parties for the explosive devices used will be as low as possible and exclude any charge for research and development. Non-nuclear-weapon States Party to the Treaty shall be able to obtain such benefits, pursuant to a special international agreement or agreements, through an appropriate international body with adequate representation of non-nuclear-weapon States. Negotiations on this subject shall commence as soon as possible after the Treaty enters into force. Non-nuclear-weapon States Party to the Treaty so desiring may also obtain such benefits pursuant to bilateral agreements.

Article VI

Each of the Parties to the Treaty undertakes to pursue negotiations in good faith on effective measures relating to cessation of the nuclear arms race at an early date and to nuclear disarmament, and on a treaty on general and complete disarmament under strict and effective international control.

Article VII

Nothing in this Treaty affects the right of any group of States to conclude regional treaties in order to assure the total absence of nuclear weapons in their respective territories.

Article VIII

1. Any Party to the Treaty may propose amendments to this Treaty. The text of any proposed amendment shall be submitted to the Depositary Governments which shall

circulate it to all Parties to the Treaty. Thereupon, if requested to do so by one-third or more of the Parties to the Treaty, the Depositary Governments shall convene a conference, to which they shall invite all the Parties to the Treaty, to consider such an amendment.

2. Any amendment to this Treaty must be approved by a majority of the votes of all the Parties to the Treaty, including the votes of all nuclear-weapon States Party to the Treaty and all other Parties which, on the date the amendment is circulated, are members of the Board of Governors of the International Atomic Energy Agency. The amendment shall enter into force for each Party that deposits its instrument of ratification of the amendment upon the deposit of such instruments of ratification by a majority of all the Parties, including the instruments of ratification of all nuclear-weapon States Party to the Treaty and all other Parties which, on the date the amendment is circulated, are members of the Board of Governors of the International Atomic Energy Agency. Thereafter, it shall enter into force for any other Party upon the deposit of its instrument of ratification of the amendment.

3. Five years after the entry into force of this Treaty, a conference of Parties to the Treaty shall be held in Geneva, Switzerland, in order to review the operation of this Treaty with a view to assuring that the purposes of the Preamble and the provisions of the Treaty are being realized. At intervals of five years thereafter, a majority of the Parties to the Treaty may obtain, by submitting a proposal to this effect to the Depositary Governments, the convening of further conferences with the same objective of reviewing the operation of the Treaty.

Article IX

1. This Treaty shall be open to all States for signature. Any State which does not sign the Treaty before its entry into force in accordance with paragraph 3 of this article may accede to it at any time.

2. This Treaty shall be subject to ratification by signatory States. Instruments of ratification and instruments of accession shall be deposited with the Governments of the United States of America, the United Kingdom of Great Britain and Northern Ireland and the Union of Soviet Socialist Republics, which are hereby designated the Depositary Governments.

3. This Treaty shall enter into force after its ratification by the States, the Governments of which are designated Depositaries of the Treaty, and forty other States signatory to this Treaty and the deposit of their instruments of ratification. For the purposes of this Treaty, a nuclear-weapon State is one which has manufactured and exploded a nuclear weapon or other nuclear explosive device prior to January 1, 1967.

4. For States whose instruments of ratification or accession are deposited subsequent to the entry into force of this Treaty, it shall enter into force on the date of the deposit of their instruments of ratification or accession.

5. The Depositary Governments shall promptly inform all signatory and acceding States of the date of each signature, the date of deposit of each instrument of ratification or of accession, the date of the entry into force of this Treaty, and the date of receipt of any requests for convening a conference or other notices.

6. This Treaty shall be registered by the Depositary Governments pursuant to article 102 of the Charter of the United Nations.

Article X

1. Each Party shall in exercising its national sovereignty have the right to withdraw from the Treaty if it decides that extraordinary events, related to the subject matter of this Treaty, have jeopardized the supreme interests of its country. It shall give notice of

such withdrawal to all other Parties to the Treaty and to the United Nations Security Council three months in advance. Such notice shall include a statement of the extraordinary events it regards as having jeopardized its supreme interests.

2. Twenty-five years after the entry into force of the Treaty, a conference shall be convened to decide whether the Treaty shall continue in force indefinitely, or shall be extended for an additional fixed period or periods. This decision shall be taken by a majority of the Parties to the Treaty.

Article XI

This Treaty, the English, Russian, French, Spanish and Chinese texts of which are equally authentic, shall be deposited in the archives of the Depositary Governments. Duly certified copies of this Treaty shall be transmitted by the Depositary Governments to the Governments of the signatory and acceding States.

IN WITNESS WHEREOF the undersigned, duly authorized, have signed this Treaty.

DONE in triplicate, at the cities of Washington, London and Moscow, this first day of July one thousand nine hundred sixty-eight.

Non-Proliferation Treaty

Country	Date of[1] Signature	Date of Deposit[1] of Ratification	Date of Deposit[1] of Accession
Afghanistan	7/1/68	2/4/70	
Australia	2/27/70	1/23/73	
Austria	7/1/68	6/27/69	
Bahamas, The			8/11/76
Bangladesh			8/31/79
Barbados	7/1/68	2/21/80	
Belgium	8/20/68	5/2/75	
Benin	7/1/68	10/31/72	
Bolivia	7/1/68	5/26/70	
Botswana	7/1/68	4/28/69	
Bulgaria	7/1/68	9/5/69	
Burundi			3/19/71
Cameroon	7/17/68	1/8/69	
Canada	7/23/68	1/8/69	
Cape Verde			10/24/79
Central African Republic			10/25/70
Chad	7/1/68	3/10/71	
China (Taiwan)	7/1/68	1/27/70	
Colombia	7/1/68		
Congo, People's Republic of (Brazzaville)			10/23/78
Costa Rica	7/1/68	3/3/70	
Cyprus	7/1/68	2/10/70	
Czechoslovakia	7/1/68	7/22/69	
Denmark	7/1/68	1/3/69	
Dominican Republic	7/1/68	7/24/71	
Ecuador	7/9/68	3/7/69	
Egypt	7/1/68	2/26/81	
El Salvador	7/1/68	7/11/72	
Ethiopia	9/5/68	2/5/70	
Fiji			7/14/72
Finland	7/1/68	2/5/69	
Gabon			2/19/74
Gambia, The	9/4/68	5/12/75	
German Democratic Republic	7/1/68	10/31/69	
Germany, Federal Republic of	11/28/69	5/2/75	
Ghana	7/1/68	5/4/70	
Greece	7/1/68	3/11/70	
Grenada			9/2/75
Guatemala	7/26/68	9/22/70	
Guinea-Bissau			8/20/76

See footnotes on page 290.

Country	Date of[1] Signature	Date of Deposit[1] of Ratification	Date of Deposit[1] of Accession
Haiti	7/1/68	6/2/70	
Holy See			2/25/71
Honduras	7/1/68	5/16/73	
Hungary	7/1/68	5/27/69	
Iceland	7/1/68	7/18/69	
Indonesia	3/2/70	7/12/79	
Iran	7/1/68	2/2/70	
Iraq	7/1/68	10/29/69	
Ireland	7/1/68	7/1/68	
Italy	1/28/69	5/2/75	
Ivory Coast	7/1/68	3/6/73	
Jamaica	4/14/69	3/5/70	
Japan	2/3/70	6/8/76	
Jordan	7/10/68	2/11/70	
Kampuchea			6/2/72
Kenya	7/1/68	6/11/70	
Korea, Republic of	7/1/68	4/23/75	
Kuwait	8/15/68		
Laos	7/1/68	2/20/70	
Lebanon	7/1/68	7/15/70	
Lesotho	7/9/68	5/20/70	
Liberia	7/1/68	3/5/70	
Libya	7/18/68	5/26/75	
Liechtenstein			4/20/78
Luxembourg	8/14/68	5/2/75	
Madagascar	8/22/68	10/8/70	
Malaysia	7/1/68	3/5/70	
Maldive Islands	9/11/68	4/7/70	
Mali	7/14/69	2/10/70	
Malta	4/17/69	2/6/70	
Mauritius	7/1/68	4/8/69	
Mexico	7/26/68	1/21/69	
Mongolia	7/1/68	5/14/69	
Morocco	7/1/68	11/27/70	
Nepal	7/1/68	1/5/70	
Netherlands	8/20/68	5/2/75	
New Zealand	7/1/68	9/10/69	
Nicaragua	7/1/68	3/6/73	
Nigeria	7/1/68	9/27/68	
Norway	7/1/68	2/5/69	
Panama	7/1/68	1/13/77	
Papua New Guinea			1/25/82

See footnotes on page 290.

Country	Date of[1] Signature	Date of Deposit[1] of Ratification	Date of Deposit[1] of Accession
Paraguay	7/1/68	2/4/70	
Peru	7/1/68	3/3/70	
Philippines	7/1/68	10/5/72	
Poland	7/1/68	6/12/69	
Portugal			12/15/77
Romania	7/1/68	2/4/70	
Rwanda			5/20/75
San Marino	7/1/68	8/10/70	
St. Lucia			12/28/79
Senegal	7/1/68	12/17/70	
Sierra Leone			2/26/75
Singapore	2/5/70	3/10/76	
Somalia	7/1/68	3/5/70	
Sri Lanka	7/1/68	3/5/79	
Sudan	12/24/68	10/31/73	
Suriname			6/30/76[a]
Swaziland	6/24/69	12/11/69	
Sweden	8/19/68	1/9/70	
Switzerland	11/27/69	3/9/77	
Syrian Arab Republic	7/1/68	9/24/69	
Thailand			12/2/72
Togo	7/1/68	2/26/70	
Tonga			7/7/71[1]
Trinidad and Tobago	8/20/68		
Tunisia	7/1/68	2/26/70	
Turkey	1/28/69	4/17/80	
Tuvalu			1/19/79[1]
Union of Soviet Socialist Republics	7/1/68	3/5/70	
United Kingdom	7/1/68	11/27/68	
United States	7/1/68	3/5/70	
Upper Volta	11/25/68	3/3/70	
Uruguay	7/1/68	8/31/70	
Venezuela	7/1/68	9/25/75	
Western Samoa			3/17/75
Yemen Arab Republic (Sana)	9/23/68		
Yemen, People's Democratic Republic of (Aden)	11/14/68	6/1/79	
Yugoslavia	7/10/68	3/4/70	
Zaire	7/22/68	8/4/70	
Total[3]	97	93	23

See footnotes on page 290.

[a]Effective 11/25/75.

Treaty on the Prohibition of the Emplacement of Nuclear Weapons and Other Weapons of Mass Destruction on the Seabed and the Ocean Floor and in the Subsoil Thereof

Like the Antarctic Treaty, the Outer Space Treaty, and the Latin American Nuclear-Free Zone, the Seabed Treaty sought to prevent the introduction of international conflict and nuclear weapons into an area hitherto free of them. Reaching agreement on the seabed, however, involved problems not met in framing the other two agreements.

In the 1960s advances in the technology of oceanography and greatly increased interest in the vast and virtually untapped resources of the ocean floor led to concern that the absence of clearly established rules of law might lead to strife. And there were concurrent fears that nations might use the seabed as a new environment for military installations, including those capable of launching nuclear weapons.

In keeping with a proposal submitted to the U.N. Secretary General by Ambassador Pardo of Malta in August 1967, the U.N. General Assembly, on December 18, 1967, established an *ad hoc* committee to study ways of reserving the seabed for peaceful purposes, with the objective of assuring "that the exploration and use of the seabed and the ocean floor should be conducted in accordance with the principles and purposes of the Charter of the United Nations, in the interests of maintaining international peace and security and for the benefit of all mankind." The Committee was given permanent status the following year. At the same time, seabed-related military and arms control issues were referred to the ENDC and its successor, the CCD.[1] In a message of March 18, 1969, President Nixon said the American delegation to the ENDC should seek discussion of the factors necessary for an international agreement prohibiting the emplacement of weapons of mass destruction on the seabed and ocean floor and pointed out that an agreement of this kind would, like the Antarctic and outer space treaties, "prevent an arms race before it has a chance to start."

On March 18, 1969, the Soviet Union presented a draft treaty that provided for the complete demilitarization of the seabed beyond a 12-

---

[1]As noted elsewhere, the Geneva-based ENDC (Eighteen-Nation Disarmament Committee) became known as the CCD (Conference of the Committee on Disarmament) after its enlargement in 1969.

mile limit and making all seabed installations open to treaty parties on the basis of reciprocity. The U.S. draft treaty, submitted on May 22, prohibited the emplacement of nuclear weapons and other weapons of mass destruction on the seabed and ocean floor beyond a 3-mile band. This, the United States held, was the urgent problem, and complete demilitarization would not be verifiable.

As can be seen, the two drafts differed importantly on what was to be prohibited. The Soviet draft would have banned *all* military uses of the seabed. It would have precluded, for example, submarine surveillance systems that were fixed to the ocean floor. The United States regarded these as essential to its defense.

The two drafts also differed on the issue of verification. Using as a model the provisions for verification in the Outer Space Treaty, the Soviets proposed that all installations and structures be open to inspection, provided that reciprocal rights to inspect were granted. The United States contended that on the moon no claims of national jurisdiction existed and that provisions suitable for the moon would not be adequate for the seabed, where many claims of national jurisdiction already existed and many kinds of activities were in progress or possible. Moreover, the United States felt that to attempt to inspect for the emplacement of *all* kinds of weapons would make the problems connected with verification virtually insuperable.

On the other hand, the United States stated the case that any structure capable of handling nuclear devices would necessarily be large and elaborate; their installation would require extensive activity, difficult to conceal; and there would probably be a number of devices involved, as it would not be worth violating the treaty simply to install one or two weapons. Violations, therefore, would be readily observed and evoke the appropriate steps—first an effort to deal directly with the problem through consultations with the country violating the treaty; if that failed, recourse to cooperative action; and, as a last resort, appeal to the Security Council.

Comments on the two drafts in the ENDC, U.S. consultations with its NATO allies, and private U.S.-Soviet talks at the ENDC eventually led to the framing of a joint draft by the United States and the Soviet Union, submitted on October 7, 1969, to the CCD. This joint draft underwent intensive discussion and was three times revised in response to suggestions made in the CCD and at the United Nations.

Discussion centered on a few difficult issues. In international law there is much confusion about how territorial waters are to be defined. Some countries claim up to 200 miles, and even international conventions on the subject contain ambiguities. In its final form the treaty adopted a 12-mile limit to define the seabed area.

The verification provisions also were a subject of intensive discussion. Coastal states were concerned about whether their rights would be protected. Smaller states had doubts as to their ability to check on violations. Some felt that the United Nations should play a larger role. Some wondered whether the verification procedures would really be effective. Reassurances were given to the coastal states. Smaller states could apply for assistance to another state to help it in case of a suspected violation.

The verification procedures are set forth in Article III. Parties may undertake verification using their own means, with the assistance of other parties, or through appropriate international procedures within the framework of the United Nations and in accordance with its Charter. These provisions permit parties to assure themselves the treaty obligations are being fulfilled without interfering with legitimate seabed activities.

After more than 2 years of negotiation, the final draft was approved by the U.N. General Assembly on December 7, 1970, by a vote of 104 to 2 (El Salvador, Peru), with 2 abstentions (Ecuador and France).

Article I sets forth the principal obligation of the treaty. It prohibits parties from emplacing nuclear weapons or weapons of mass destruction on the seabed and the ocean floor beyond a 12-mile coastal zone. Article II provides that the "seabed zone" is to be measured in accordance with the provisions of the 1958 Convention on the Territorial Sea and the Contiguous Zone. To make clear that none of the treaty's provisions should be interpreted as supporting or prejudicing the positions of any party regarding law-of-the-sea issues, a broad disclaimer provision to this effect was included as Article IV.

In recognition of the feeling that efforts to achieve a more comprehensive agreement should continue, Article V of the treaty bound parties to work for further measures to prevent an arms race on the seabed.

The Seabed Arms Control Treaty was opened for signature in Washington, London, and Moscow on February 11, 1971. It entered into force May 18, 1972, when the United States, the United Kingdom, the U.S.S.R., and more than 22 nations had deposited instruments of ratification.

Article VII included a provision for a review conference to be held in 5 years. The Seabed Arms Control Treaty Review Conference was held in Geneva June 20–July 1, 1977. The Conference concluded that the first 5 years in the life of the treaty had demonstrated its effectiveness. It decided that a further review conference should be held in Geneva in 1982, unless a majority of the treaty parties wanted it postponed for up to 2 years. In view of the full calendar of disarmament activities requiring the attention of the parties in 1982, a proposal has been made by the depositaries to postpone the next review conference until 1983 or 1984. The parties plan to consult further on this matter in New York at the time of the U.N. General Assembly in the fall of 1982.

Treaty on the Prohibition of the Emplacement of Nuclear Weapons and Other Weapons of Mass Destruction on the Seabed and the Ocean Floor and in the Subsoil Thereof

Signed at Washington, London, and Moscow February 11, 1971
Ratification advised by U.S. Senate February 15, 1972
Ratified by U.S. President April 26, 1972
U.S. ratification deposited at Washington, London, and Moscow May 18, 1972
Proclaimed by U.S. President May 18, 1972
Entered into force May 18, 1972

The States Parties to this Treaty,

Recognizing the common interest of mankind in the progress of the exploration and use of the seabed and the ocean floor for peaceful purposes,

Considering that the prevention of a nuclear arms race on the seabed and the ocean floor serves the interests of maintaining world peace, reduces international tensions and strengthens friendly relations among States,

Convinced that this Treaty constitutes a step towards the exclusion of the seabed, the ocean floor and the subsoil thereof frcm the arms race,

Convinced that this Treaty constitutes a step towards a treaty on general and complete disarmament under strict and effective international control, and determined to continue negotiations to this end,

Convinced that this Treaty will further the purposes and principles of the Charter of the United Nations, in a manner consistent with the principles of international law and without infringing the freedoms of the high seas,

Have agreed as follows:

Article I

1. The States Parties to this Treaty undertake not to emplant or emplace on the sea-bed and the ocean floor and in the subsoil thereof beyond the outer limit of a seabed zone, as defined in article II, any nuclear weapons or any other types of weapons of mass destruction as well as structures, launching installations or any other facilities specifically designed for storing, testing or using such weapons.

2. The undertakings of paragraph 1 of this article shall also apply to the seabed zone referred to in the same paragraph, except that within such seabed zone, they shall not apply either to the coastal State or to the seabed beneath its territorial waters.

3. The States Parties to this Treaty undertake not to assist, encourage or induce any State to carry out activities referred to in paragraph 1 of this article and not to participate in any other way in such actions.

Article II

For the purpose of this Treaty, the outer limit of the seabed zone referred to in article I shall be coterminous with the twelve-mile outer limit of the zone referred to in part II of the Convention on the Territorial Sea and the Contiguous Zone, signed at Geneva on

April 29, 1958, and shall be measured in accordance with the provisions of part I, section II, of that Convention and in accordance with international law.

Article III

1. In order to promote the objectives of and insure compliance with the provisions of this Treaty, each State Party to the Treaty shall have the right to verify through observations the activities of other States Parties to the Treaty on the seabed and the ocean floor and in the subsoil thereof beyond the zone referred to in article I, provided that observation does not interfere with such activities.

2. If after such observation reasonable doubts remain concerning the fulfillment of the obligations assumed under the Treaty, the State Party having such doubts and the State Party that is responsible for the activities giving rise to the doubts shall consult with a view to removing the doubts. If the doubts persist, the State Party having such doubts shall notify the other States Parties, and the Parties concerned shall cooperate on such further procedures for verification as may be agreed, including appropriate inspection of objects, structures, installations or other facilities that reasonably may be expected to be of a kind described in article I. The Parties in the region of the activities, including any coastal State, and any other Party so requesting, shall be entitled to participate in such consultation and cooperation. After completion of the further procedures for verification, an appropriate report shall be circulated to other Parties by the Party that initiated such procedures.

3. If the State responsible for the activities giving rise to the reasonable doubts is not identifiable by observation of the object, structure, installation or other facility, the State Party having such doubts shall notify and make appropriate inquiries of States Parties in the region of the activities and of any other State Party. If it is ascertained through these inquiries that a particular State Party is responsible for the activities, that State Party shall consult and cooperate with other Parties as provided in paragraph 2 of this article. If the identity of the State responsible for the activities cannot be ascertained through these inquiries, then further verification procedures, including inspection, may be undertaken by the inquiring State Party, which shall invite the participation of the Parties in the region of the activities, including any coastal State, and of any other Party desiring to cooperate.

4. If consultation and cooperation pursuant to paragraphs 2 and 3 of this article have not removed the doubts concerning the activities and there remains a serious question concerning fulfillment of the obligations assumed under this Treaty, a State Party may, in accordance with the provisions of the Charter of the United Nations, refer the matter to the Security Council, which may take action in accordance with the Charter.

5. Verification pursuant to this article may be undertaken by any State Party using its own means, or with the full or partial assistance of any other State Party, or through appropriate international procedures within the framework of the United Nations and in accordance with its Charter.

6. Verification activities pursuant to this Treaty shall not interfere with activities of other States Parties and shall be conducted with due regard for rights recognized under international law, including the freedoms of the high seas and the rights of coastal States with respect to the exploration and exploitation of their continental shelves.

Article IV

Nothing in this Treaty shall be interpreted as supporting or prejudicing the position of any State Party with respect to existing international conventions, including the 1958

Convention on the Territorial Sea and the Contiguous Zone, or with respect to rights or claims which such State Party may assert, or with respect to recognition or non-recognition of rights or claims asserted by any other State, related to waters off its coasts, including, *inter alia,* territorial seas and contiguous zones, or to the seabed and the ocean floor, including continental shelves.

Article V

The Parties to this Treaty undertake to continue negotiations in good faith concerning further measures in the field of disarmament for the prevention of an arms race on the seabed, the ocean floor and the subsoil thereof.

Article VI

Any State Party may propose amendments to this Treaty. Amendments shall enter into force for each State Party accepting the amendments upon their acceptance by a majority of the States Parties to the Treaty and, thereafter, for each remaining State Party on the date of acceptance by it.

Article VII

Five years after the entry into force of this Treaty, a conference of Parties to the Treaty shall be held at Geneva, Switzerland, in order to review the operation of this Treaty with a view to assuring that the purposes of the preamble and the provisions of the Treaty are being realized. Such review shall take into account any relevant technological developments. The review conference shall determine, in accordance with the views of a majority of those Parties attending, whether and when an additional review conference shall be convened.

Article VIII

Each State Party to this Treaty shall in exercising its national sovereignty have the right to withdraw from this Treaty if it decides that extraordinary events related to the subject matter of this Treaty have jeopardized the supreme interests of its country. It shall give notice of such withdrawal to all other States Parties to the Treaty and to the United Nations Security Council three months in advance. Such notice shall include a statement of the extraordinary events it considers to have jeopardized its supreme interests.

Article IX

The provisions of this Treaty shall in no way affect the obligations assumed by States Parties to the Treaty under international instruments establishing zones free from nuclear weapons.

Article X

1. This Treaty shall be open for signature to all States. Any State which does not sign the Treaty before its entry into force in accordance with paragraph 3 of this article may accede to it at any time.

2. This Treaty shall be subject to ratification by signatory States. Instruments of ratification and of accession shall be deposited with the Governments of the United States of America, the United Kingdom of Great Britain and Northern Ireland, and the Union of Soviet Socialist Republics, which are hereby designated the Depositary Governments.

3. This Treaty shall enter into force after the deposit of instruments of ratification by twenty-two Governments, including the Governments designated as Depositary Governments of this Treaty.

4. For states whose instruments of ratification or accession are deposited after the entry into force of this Treaty, it shall enter into force on the date of the deposit of their instruments of ratification or accession.

5. The Depositary Governments shall promptly inform the Governments of all signatory and acceding States of the date of each signature, of the date of deposit of each instrument of ratification or of accession, of the date of the entry into force of this Treaty, and of the receipt of other notices.

6. This Treaty shall be registered by the Depositary Governments pursuant to Article 102 of the Charter of the United Nations.

Article XI

This Treaty, the English, Russian, French, Spanish and Chinese texts of which are equally authentic, shall be deposited in the archives of the Depositary Governments. Duly certified copies of this Treaty shall be transmitted by the Depositary Governments to the Governments of the States signatory and acceding thereto.

IN WITNESS WHEREOF the undersigned, being duly authorized thereto, have signed this Treaty.

DONE in triplicate, at the cities of Washington, London and Moscow, this eleventh day of February, one thousand nine hundred seventy-one.

Seabed Arms Control Treaty

Country	Date of[1] Signature	Date of Deposit[1] of Ratification	Date of Deposit[1] of Accession
Afghanistan	2/11/71	4/22/71	
Argentina	9/3/71		
Australia	2/11/71	1/23/73	
Austria	2/11/71	8/10/72	
Belgium	2/11/71	11/20/72	
Benin	3/18/71		
Bolivia	2/11/71		
Botswana	2/11/71	11/10/72	
Brazil	9/3/71		
Bulgaria	2/11/71	4/16/71	
Burma	2/11/71		
Burundi	2/11/71		
Byelorussian S.S.R.[2]	3/3/71	9/14/71	
Cameroon	11/11/71		
Canada	2/11/71	5/17/72	
Cape Verde			10/24/79
Central African Republic	2/11/71	7/9/81	
China (Taiwan)	2/11/71	2/22/72	
Colombia	2/11/71		
Congo, People's Republic of (Brazzaville)			10/23/78
Costa Rica	2/11/71		
Cyprus	2/11/71	11/17/71	
Czechoslovakia	2/11/71	1/11/72	
Denmark	2/11/71	6/15/71	
Dominican Republic	2/11/71	2/11/72	
Equatorial Guinea	6/4/71		
Ethiopia	2/11/71	7/14/77	
Finland	2/11/71	6/8/71	
Gambia, The	5/18/71		
German Democratic Republic	2/11/71	7/27/71	
Germany, Federal Republic of	6/8/71	11/18/75	
Ghana	2/11/71	8/9/72	
Greece	2/11/71		
Guatemala	2/11/71		
Guinea	2/11/71		
Guinea-Bissau			8/20/76

See footnotes on page 290.

Country	Date of[1] Signature	Date of Deposit[1] of Ratification	Date of Deposit[1] of Accession
Honduras	2/11/71		
Hungary	2/11/71	8/13/71	
Iceland	2/11/71	5/30/72	
India			7/20/73
Iran	2/11/71	8/26/71	
Iraq	2/22/71	9/13/72	
Ireland	2/11/71	8/19/71	
Italy	2/11/71	9/3/74	
Ivory Coast			1/14/72
Jamaica	10/11/71		
Japan	2/11/71	6/21/71	
Jordan	2/11/71	8/17/71	
Kampuchea	2/11/71		
Korea, Republic of	2/11/71		
Laos	2/11/71	10/19/71	
Lebanon	2/11/71		
Lesotho	9/8/71	4/3/73	
Liberia	2/11/71		
Luxembourg	2/11/71		
Madagascar	9/14/71		
Malaysia	5/20/71	6/21/72	
Mali	2/11/71		
Malta	2/11/71	5/4/71	
Mauritius	2/11/71	4/23/71	
Mongolia	2/11/71	10/8/71	
Morocco	2/11/71	7/26/71	
Nepal	2/11/71	7/6/71	
Netherlands	2/11/71	1/14/76	
New Zealand	2/11/71	2/24/72	
Nicaragua	2/11/71	2/7/73	
Niger	2/11/71	8/9/71	
Norway	2/11/71	6/28/71	
Panama	2/11/71	3/20/74	
Paraguay	2/23/71		
Poland	2/11/71	11/15/71	
Portugal			6/24/75
Qatar			11/12/74

See footnotes on page 290.

Country	Date of[1] Signature	Date of Deposit[1] of Ratification	Date of Deposit[1] of Accession
Romania	2/11/71	7/10/72	
Rwanda	2/11/71	5/20/75	
São Tome and Principé			8/24/79
Saudi Arabia	1/7/72	6/23/72	
Senegal	3/17/71		
Seychelles			6/29/76[1]
Sierra Leone	2/11/71		
Singapore	5/5/71	9/10/76	
South Africa	2/11/71	11/14/73	
Sudan	2/11/71		
Swaziland	2/11/71	8/9/71	
Sweden	2/11/71	4/28/72	
Switzerland	2/11/71	5/4/76	
Tanzania	2/11/71		
Togo	4/2/71	6/28/71	
Tunisia	2/11/71	10/22/71	
Turkey	2/25/71	10/19/72	
Ukrainian S.S.R.[2]	3/3/71	9/3/71	
Union of Soviet Socialist Republics	2/11/71	5/18/72	
United Kingdom	2/11/71	5/18/72	
United States	2/11/71	5/18/72	
Uruguay	2/11/71		
Vietnam			6/20/80
Yemen Arab Republic (Sana)	2/23/71		
Yemen, People's Democratic Republic of (Aden)	2/23/71	6/1/79	
Yugoslavia	3/2/71	10/25/73	
Zambia			10/9/72
Total[3]	87	57	11

See footnotes on page 290.

Agreement on Measures To Reduce the Risk of Outbreak of Nuclear War Between the United States of America and the Union of Soviet Socialist Republics

The very existence of nuclear-weapons systems, even under the most sophisticated command-and-control procedures, obviously is a source of constant concern. Despite the most elaborate precautions, it is conceivable that technical malfunction or human failure, a misinterpreted incident or unauthorized action, could trigger a nuclear disaster or nuclear war. In the course of the Strategic Arms Limitation Talks (SALT), the United States and the Soviet Union reached two agreements that manifest increasing recognition of the need to reduce such risks, and that complement the central goal of the negotiations.

In early sessions, discussions parallel to the main SALT negotiations showed a degree of mutual concern regarding the problem of accidental war that indicated encouraging prospects of accord. These preliminary explorations resulted in the establishme. ᵗ of two special working groups under the direction of the two SALT delegations. One group focused on arrangements for exchanging information to reduce uncertainties and prevent misunderstandings in the event of a nuclear incident. The other addressed a related topic—ways to improve the direct communications link between Washington and Moscow. By the summer of 1971, major substantive issues had been resolved, and draft international agreements were referred by the SALT delegations to their governments. Both agreements were signed in Washington on September 30, 1971, and came into force on that date.

The "Agreement on Measures To Reduce the Risk of Outbreak of Nuclear War between the United States of America and the Union of Soviet Socialist Republics" covers three main areas:

— A pledge by both sides to take measures each considers necessary to maintain and improve its organizational and technical safeguards against accidental or unauthorized use of nuclear weapons.

— Arrangements for immediate notification should a risk of nuclear war arise from such incidents, from detection of unidentified objects on early warning systems, or from any accidental, unauthorized, or other unexplained incident involving a possible detonation of a nuclear weapon.

— Advance notification of any planned missile launches beyond the territory of the launching party and in the direction of the other party.

The agreement provides that for urgent communication "in situations requiring prompt clarification" the "Hot Line" will be used. The duration of the agreement is not limited, and the parties undertake to consult on questions that may arise and to discuss possible amendments aimed at further reduction of risks.

Agreement on Measures To Reduce the Risk of Outbreak of Nuclear War Between the United States of America and the Union of Soviet Socialist Republics

Signed at Washington September 30, 1971
Entered into force September 30, 1971

The United States of America and the Union of Soviet Socialist Republics, hereinafter referred to as the Parties:

Taking into account the devastating consequences that nuclear war would have for all mankind, and recognizing the need to exert every effort to avert the risk of outbreak of such a war, including measures to guard against accidental or unauthorized use of nuclear weapons,

Believing that agreement on measures for reducing the risk of outbreak of nuclear war serves the interests of strengthening international peace and security, and is in no way contrary to the interests of any other country,

Bearing in mind that continued efforts are also needed in the future to seek ways of reducing the risk of outbreak of nuclear war,

Have agreed as follows:

Article 1

Each Party undertakes to maintain and to improve, as it deems necessary, its existing organizational and technical arrangements to guard against the accidental or unauthorized use of nuclear weapons under its control.

Article 2

The Parties undertake to notify each other immediately in the event of an accidental, unauthorized or any other unexplained incident involving a possible detonation of a nuclear weapon which could create a risk of outbreak of nuclear war. In the event of such an incident, the Party whose nuclear weapon is involved will immediately make every effort to take necessary measures to render harmless or destroy such weapon without its causing damage.

Article 3

The Parties undertake to notify each other immediately in the event of detection by missile warning systems of unidentified objects, or in the event of signs of interference with these systems or with related communications facilities, if such occurrences could create a risk of outbreak of nuclear war between the two countries.

Article 4

Each Party undertakes to notify the other Party in advance of any planned missile launches if such launches will extend beyond its national territory in the direction of the other Party.

Article 5

Each Party, in other situations involving unexplained nuclear incidents, undertakes to act in such a manner as to reduce the possibility of its actions being misinterpreted by the other Party. In any such situation, each Party may inform the other Party or request information when, in its view, this is warranted by the interests of averting the risk of outbreak of nuclear war.

Article 6

For transmission of urgent information, notifications and requests for information in situations requiring prompt clarification, the Parties shall make primary use of the Direct Communications Link between the Governments of the United States of America and the Union of Soviet Socialist Republics.

For transmission of other information, notifications and requests for information, the Parties, at their own discretion, may use any communications facilities, including diplomatic channels, depending on the degree of urgency.

Article 7

The Parties undertake to hold consultations, as mutually agreed, to consider questions relating to implementation of the provisions of this Agreement, as well as to discuss possible amendments thereto aimed at further implementation of the purposes of this Agreement.

Article 8

This Agreement shall be of unlimited duration.

Article 9

This Agreement shall enter into force upon signature.

DONE at Washington on September 30, 1971, in two copies, each in the English and Russian languages, both texts being equally authentic.

FOR THE UNITED STATES OF AMERICA:

FOR THE UNION OF SOVIET SOCIALIST REPUBLICS:

WILLIAM P. ROGERS

A. GROMYKO

Agreement Between the United States of America and the Union of Soviet Socialist Republics on Measures To Improve the USA-USSR Direct Communications Link (With Annex, Supplementing and Modifying the Memorandum of Understanding With Annex, of June 20,1963)

The United States and the Soviet Union had agreed in 1963 to establish, for use in time of emergency, a direct communications link between the two governments. The original "Hot Line" (see "Hot Line" section) agreement provided for a wire telegraph circuit, routed Washington-London-Copenhagen-Stockholm-Helsinki-Moscow, and as a backup system a radio telegraph circuit routed Washington-Tangier-Moscow. These circuits had one terminal in the United States and one in the U.S.S.R.

Concern about the risk that nuclear accidents, ambiguous incidents, or unauthorized actions might lead to the outbreak of nuclear war contributed to concern about the reliability and survivability of the "Hot Line," which had shown its value in emergency situations. The advances in satellite communications technology that had occurred since 1963, moveover, offered the possibility of greater reliability than the arrangements originally agreed upon. Hence, when the SALT delegations established a special working group under their direction to work on "accidents measures," a similar group was established to consider ways to improve the Washington-Moscow direct communications link.

The understandings reached by this group were reported to the SALT delegations in the summer of 1971 and became a formal agreement to improve the "Hot Line" at the same time that the related agreement on steps to reduce the risks of accidental war was concluded.

The terms of the agreement, with its annex detailing the specifics of operation, equipment, and allocation of costs, provided for establishment of two satellite communications circuits between the United States and the U.S.S.R., with a system of multiple terminals in each country. The United States was to provide one circuit via the Intelsat system, and the Soviet Union a circuit via its Molniya II system. The agreement of 1963 was to remain in force "except to the extent that its provisions are modified by this Agreement and Annex thereto." The original circuits were to be maintained until it was agreed that the operation of the satellite circuits made them no longer necessary.

On September 30, 1971, the agreement was signed in Washington. The two satellite communications circuits became operational in January 1978. The radio circuit provided for in the 1963 agreement was then terminated, but the wire telegraph circuit has been retained as a backup.

Agreement Between the United States of America and the Union of Soviet Socialist Republics on Measures To Improve the USA-USSR Direct Communications Link

Signed at Washington September 30, 1971
Entered into force September 30, 1971

The United States of America and the Union of Soviet Socialist Republics, hereinafter referred to as the Parties,

Noting the positive experience gained in the process of operating the existing Direct Communications Link between the United States of America and the Union of Soviet Socialist Republics, which was established for use in time of emergency pursuant to the Memorandum of Understanding Regarding the Establishment of a Direct Communications Link, signed on June 20, 1963,

Having examined, in a spirit of mutual understanding, matters relating to the improvement and modernization of the Direct Communications Link,

Having agreed as follows:

Article 1

1. For the purpose of increasing the reliability of the Direct Communications Link, there shall be established and put into operation the following:

(a) two additional circuits between the United States of America and the Union of Soviet Socialist Republics each using a satellite communications system, with each Party selecting a satellite communications system of its own choice,

(b) a system of terminals (more than one) in the territory of each Party for the Direct Communications Link, with the locations and number of terminals in the United States of America to be determined by the United States side, and the locations and number of terminals in the Union of Soviet Socialist Republics to be determined by the Soviet side.

2. Matters relating to the implementation of the aforementioned improvements of the Direct Communications Link are set forth in the Annex which is attached hereto and forms an integral part hereof.

Article 2

Each Party confirms its intention to take all possible measures to assure the continuous and reliable operation of the communications circuits and the system of terminals of the Direct Communications Link for which it is responsible in accordance with this Agreement and the Annex hereto, as well as to communicate to the head of its Government any messages received via the Direct Communications Link from the head of Government of the other Party.

Article 3

The Memorandum of Understanding Between the United States of America and the Union of Soviet Socialist Republics Regarding the Establishment of a Direct Communications Link, signed on June 20, 1963, with the Annex thereto, shall remain in force, except to the extent that its provisions are modified by this Agreement and Annex hereto.

Article 4

The undertakings of the Parties hereunder shall be carried out in accordance with their respective Constitutional processes.

Article 5

This Agreement, including the Annex hereto, shall enter into force upon signature.

DONE at Washington on September 30, 1971, in two copies, each in the English and Russian languages, both texts being equally authentic.

FOR THE UNITED STATES   **FOR THE UNION OF SOVIET**
OF AMERICA: **SOCIALIST REPUBLICS:**

WILLIAM P. ROGERS   **A. GROMYKO**

Annex to the Agreement Between the United States of America and the Union of Soviet Socialist Republics on Measures To Improve the USA-USSR Direct Communications Link

Improvements to the USA-USSR Direct Communications Link shall be implemented in accordance with the provisions set forth in this Annex.

I. CIRCUITS

(a) Each of the original circuits established pursuant to paragraph 1 of the Annex to the Memorandum of Understanding, dated June 20, 1963, shall continue to be maintained and operated as part of the Direct Communications Link until such time, after the satellite communications circuits provided for herein become operational, as the agencies designated pursuant to paragraph III (hereinafter referred to as the "designated agencies") mutually agree that such original circuit is no longer necessary. The provisions of paragraph 7 of the Annex to the Memorandum of Understanding, dated June 20, 1963, shall continue to govern the allocation of the costs of maintaining and operating such original circuits.

(b) Two additional circuits shall be established using two satellite communications systems. Taking into account paragraph I (e) below, the United States side shall provide one circuit via the Intelsat system and the Soviet side shall provide one circuit via the Molniya II system. The two circuits shall be duplex telephone band-width circuits conforming to CCITT standards, equipped for secondary telegraphic multiplexing. Transmission and reception of messages over the Direct Communications Link shall be effected in accordance with applicable recommendations of international communications regulations, as well as with mutually agreed instructions.

(c) When the reliability of both additional circuits has been established to the mutual satisfaction of the designated agencies, they shall be used as the primary circuits of the Direct Communications Link for transmission and reception of teleprinter messages between the United States and the Soviet Union.

(d) Each satellite communications circuit shall utilize an earth station in the territory of the United States, a communications satellite transponder, and an earth station in the territory of the Soviet Union. Each Party shall be responsible for linking the earth stations in its territory to its own terminals of the Direct Communications Link.

(e) For the circuits specified in paragraph I (b):

—The Soviet side will provide and operate at least one earth station in its territory for the satellite communications circuit in the Intelsat system, and will also arrange for the use of suitable earth station facilities in its territory for the satellite communications circuit in the Molniya II system. The United States side, through a governmental agency or other United States legal entity, will make appropriate arrangements with Intelsat with regard to access for the Soviet Intelsat earth station to the Intelsat space segment, as well as for the use of the applicable portion of the Intelsat space segment.

—The United States side will provide and operate at least one earth station in its territory for the satellite communications circuit in the Molniya II system, and will also arrange for the use of suitable earth station facilities in its territory for the satellite communications circuit in the Intelsat system.

(f) Each earth station shall conform to the performance specifications and operating procedures at the corresponding satellite communications system and the ratio of antenna gain to the equivalent noise temperature should be no less than 31 decibels. Any deviation from these specifications and procedures which may be required in any unusual situation shall be worked out and mutually agreed upon by the designated agencies of both Parties after consultation.

(g) The operational commissioning dates for the satellite communications circuits based on the Intelsat and Molniya II systems shall be as agreed upon by the designated agencies of the Parties through consultations.

(h) The United States side shall bear the costs of: (1) providing and operating the Molniya II earth station in its territory; (2) the use of the Intelsat earth station in its territory; and (3) the transmission of messages via the Intelsat system. The Soviet side shall bear the costs of: (1) providing and operating the Intelsat earth station in its territory; (2) the use of the Molniya II earth station in its territory; and (3) the transmission of messages via the Molniya II system. Payment of the costs of the satellite communications circuits shall be effected without any transfer of payments between the Parties.

(i) Each Party shall be responsible for providing to the other Party notification of any proposed modification or replacement of the communications satellite system containing the circuit provided by it that might require accommodation by earth stations using that system or otherwise affect the maintenance or operation of the Direct Communications Link. Such notification should be given sufficiently in advance to enable the designated agencies to consult and to make, before the modification or replacement is effected, such preparation as may be agreed upon for accommodation by the affected earth stations.

II. TERMINALS

(a) Each Party shall establish a system of terminals in its territory for the exchange of messages with the other Party, and shall determine the locations and number of terminals in such a system. Terminals of the Direct Communications Link shall be designated "USA" and "USSR."

(b) Each Party shall take necessary measures to provide for rapidly switching circuits among terminal points in such a manner that only one terminal location is connected to the circuits at any one time.

(c) Each Party shall use teleprinter equipment from its own sources to equip the additional terminals for the transmission and reception of messages from the United States to the Soviet Union in the English language and from the Soviet Union to the United States in the Russian language.

(d) The terminals of the Direct Communications Link shall be provided with encoding equipment. One-time tape encoding equipment shall be used for transmissions via the Direct Communications Link. A mutually agreed quantity of encoding equipment of a modern and reliable type selected by the United States side, with spares, test equipment, technical literature and operating supplies, shall be furnished by the United States side to the Soviet side against payment of the cost thereof by the Soviet side; additional spares for the encoding equipment supplied will be furnished as necessary.

(e) Keying tapes shall be supplied in accordance with the provisions set forth in paragraph 4 of the Annex to the Memorandum of Understanding, dated June 20, 1963. Each Party shall be responsible for reproducing and distributing additional keying tapes for its system of terminals and for implementing procedures which ensure that the required synchronization of encoding equipment can be effected from any one terminal at any time.

III. OTHER MATTERS

Each Party shall designate the agencies responsible for arrangements regarding the establishment of the additional circuits and the systems of terminals provided for in this Agreement and Annex, for their operation and for their continuity and reliability. These agencies shall, on the basis of direct contacts:

(a) arrange for the exchange of required performance specifications and operating procedures for the earth stations of the communications systems using Intelsat and Molniya II satellites;

(b) arrange for testing, acceptance and commissioning of the satellite circuits and for operation of these circuits after commissioning; and,

(c) decide matters and develop instructions relating to the operation of the secondary teleprinter multiplex system used on the satellite circuits.

Convention on the Prohibition of the Development, Production and Stockpiling of Bacteriological (Biological) and Toxin Weapons and on Their Destruction

Biological and chemical weapons have generally been associated in the public mind, and the extensive use of poison gas in World War I (resulting in over a million casualties and over 100,000 deaths) led to the Geneval Protocol of 1925 prohibiting the use of both poison gas *and* bacteriological methods in warfare. At the 1932–1937 Disarmament Conference, unsuccessful attempts were made to work out an agreement that would prohibit the production and stockpiling of biological and chemical weapons. During World War II, new and more toxic nerve gases were developed, and research and development was begun on biological weapons. Neither side used such weapons. President Roosevelt, in a statement warning the Axis powers against the use of chemical weapons, declared:

> Use of such weapons has been outlawed by the general opinion of civilized mankind. This country has not used them, and I hope we never will be compelled to use them. I state categorically that we shall under no circumstances resort to the use of such weapons unless they are first used by our enemies.

In the postwar negotiations on general disarmament, biological and chemical weapons were usually considered together with nuclear and conventional weapons. Both the United States and Soviet Union, in the 1962 sessions of the Eighteen-Nation Disarmament Committee (ENDC), offered plans for general and complete disarmament that included provisions for eliminating chemical and biological weapons.

An issue that long hindered progress was whether chemical and biological weapons should continue to be linked. A British draft convention submitted to the ENDC on July 10, 1969, concentrated on the elimination of biological weapons only. A draft convention proposed in the General Assembly by the Soviet Union and its allies on September 19 dealt with both chemical and biological weapons. The Soviet representative argued that they had been treated together in the Geneva Protocol and in the General Assembly resolutions and report, and should continue to be dealt with in the same instrument. A separate biological weapons convention, he warned, might serve to intensify the chemical arms race.

The United States supported the British position and stressed the difference between the two kinds of weapons. Unlike biological weapons, chemical weapons had actually been used in modern warfare. Many states maintained chemical weapons in their arsenals to deter the use of this type of weapons against them, and to provide a retaliatory capability if deterrence failed. Many of these nations, the United States pointed out, would be reluctant to give up this capability without reliable assurance that other nations were not developing, producing, and stockpiling chemical weapons.

While the United States did not consider prohibition of one of these classes of weapons less urgent or important than the other, it held that biological weapons presented less intractable problems, and an agreement on banning them should not be delayed until agreement on reliable prohibition of chemical weapons could be reached.

Shortly after President Nixon took office, he ordered a review of U.S. policy and programs regarding biological and chemical warfare. On November 25, 1969, the President declared that the United States unilaterally renounced first use of lethal or incapacitating chemical agents and weapons and unconditionally renounced all methods of biological warfare. Henceforth the U.S. biological program would be confined to research on strictly defined measures of defense, such as immunization. The Department of Defense was ordered to draw up a plan for the disposal of existing stocks of biological agents and weapons. On February 14, 1970, the White House announced extension of the ban to cover toxins (substances falling between biologicals and chemicals in that they act like chemicals but are ordinarily produced by biological or microbic processes).

The American action was widely welcomed internationally, and the example was followed by others. Canada, Sweden, and the United Kingdom stated that they had no biological weapons and did not intend to produce any. It was generally recognized, however, that unilateral actions could not take the place of a binding international commitment. A number of nations, including the Soviet Union and its allies, continued to favor a comprehensive agreement covering both chemical and biological weapons.

Discussion throughout 1970 in the General Assembly and the Conference of the Committee on Disarmament (CCD)—as the ENDC was named after its enlargement to 26 members in August 1969—produced no agreement. A breakthrough came on March 30, 1971, however, when the Soviet Union and its allies changed their position and introduced a revised draft convention limited to biological weapons and toxins. It then became possible for the co-chairmen of the CCD—the U.S. and Soviet representatives—to work out an agreed draft, as they had done with the non-proliferation and the seabed treaties. On

August 5, the United States and the Soviet Union submitted separate but identical texts.

On December 16, the General Assembly approved a resolution, adopted by a vote of 110 to 0, commending the convention and expressing hope for the widest possible adherence.

The French representative abstained, explaining that the convention, though a step forward, might weaken the Geneval Protocol ban on the use of chemical weapons, and he did not consider that adequate international controls were provided. He announced, however, that France would enact domestic legislation prohibiting biological weapons, and this was done in June of the next year.

The People's Republic of China did not participate in the negotiations on the convention and did not sign it. At the 1972 General Assembly its representative attacked the convention as a "sham," and criticized it for not prohibiting chemical weapons.

The convention was opened for signature at Washington, London, and Moscow on April 10, 1972. President Nixon submitted it to the Senate on August 10, calling it "the first international agreement since World War II to provide for the actual elimination of an entire class of weapons from the arsenals of nations." The Senate Foreign Relations Committee delayed action on the convention, however, holding it for consideration after resolution of the herbicide and riot-control issues involved in the Geneva Protocol (see section on the Geneva Protocol).

In the latter part of 1974 the Ford Administration undertook a new initiative to obtain Senate consent to ratification of both the Geneva Protocol and the Biological Weapons Convention, and ACDA Director Fred Ikle testified with respect to both instruments before the Senate Foreign Relations Committee on December 10. Soon thereafter the Committee voted unanimously to send the two measures to the Senate floor, and on December 16 the Senate voted its approval, also unanimously.

President Ford signed instruments of ratification for the two measures on January 22, 1975.

Under the terms of the convention, the parties undertake not to develop, produce, stockpile, or acquire biological agents or toxins "of types and in quantities that have no justification for prophylactic, protective, and other peaceful purposes," as well as weapons and means of delivery. All such materiel is to be destroyed within 9 months of the convention's entry into force. In January 1976, all heads of Federal departments and agencies certified to the President that as of December 26, 1975, their respective departments and agencies were in full compliance with the convention.

The parties are to consult and cooperate in solving any problems that arise. Complaints of a breach of obligations may be lodged with the Security Council, and parties undertake to cooperate with any investigation the Council initiates. If the Security Council finds that a state has been endangered by a violation, the parties are to provide any assistance requested.

Nothing in the convention is to be interpreted as lessening the obligations imposed by the Geneva Protocol, and the parties undertake to pursue negotiations for a ban on chemical weapons.

In addition, articles provide for exchange of information on peaceful uses, amendment and review, and accession and withdrawal. The convention is of unlimited duration.

Convention on the Prohibition of the Development, Production and Stockpiling of Bacteriological (Biological) and Toxin Weapons and on Their Destruction

Signed at Washington, London, and Moscow April 10, 1972
Ratification advised by U.S. Senate December 16, 1974
Ratified by U.S. President January 22, 1975
U.S. ratification deposited at Washington, London, and Moscow March 26, 1975
Proclaimed by U.S. President March 26, 1975
Entered into force March 26, 1975

The States Parties to this Convention,

Determined to act with a view to achieving effective progress towards general and complete disarmament, including the prohibition and elimination of all types of weapons of mass destruction, and convinced that the prohibition of the development, production and stockpiling of chemical and bacteriological (biological) weapons and their elimination, through effective measures, will facilitate the achievement of general and complete disarmament under strict and effective international control,

Recognizing the important significance of the Protocol for the Prohibition of the Use in War of Asphyxiating, Poisonous or Other Gases, and of Bacteriological Methods of Warfare, signed at Geneva on June 17, 1925, and conscious also of the contribution which the said Protocol has already made, and continues to make, to mitigating the horrors of war,

Reaffirming their adherence to the principles and objectives of that Protocol and calling upon all States to comply strictly with them,

Recalling that the General Assembly of the United Nations has repeatedly condemned all actions contrary to the principles and objectives of the Geneva Protocol of June 17, 1925,

Desiring to contribute to the strengthening of confidence between peoples and the general improvement of the international atmosphere,

Desiring also to contribute to the realization of the purposes and principles of the Charter of the United Nations,

Convinced of the importance and urgency of eliminating from the arsenals of States, through effective measures, such dangerous weapons of mass destruction as those using chemical or bacteriological (biological) agents,

Recognizing that an agreement on the prohibition of bacteriological (biological) and toxin weapons represents a first possible step towards the achievement of agreement on effective measures also for the prohibition of the development, production and stockpiling of chemical weapons, and determined to continue negotiations to that end,

Determined, for the sake of all mankind, to exclude completely the possibility of bacteriological (biological) agents and toxins being used as weapons,

Convinced that such use would be repugnant to the conscience of mankind and that no effort should be spared to minimize this risk,

Have agreed as follows:

Article I

Each State Party to this Convention undertakes never in any circumstances to develop, produce, stockpile or otherwise acquire or retain:

(1) Microbial or other biological agents, or toxins whatever their origin or method of production, of types and in quantities that have no justification for prophylactic, protective or other peaceful purposes;

(2) Weapons, equipment or means of delivery designed to use such agents or toxins for hostile purposes or in armed conflict.

Article II

Each State Party to this Convention undertakes to destroy, or to divert to peaceful purposes, as soon as possible but not later than nine months after the entry into force of the Convention, all agents, toxins, weapons, equipment and means of delivery specified in article I of the Convention, which are in its possession or under its jurisdiction or control. In implementing the provisions of this article all necessary safety precautions shall be observed to protect populations and the environment.

Article III

Each State Party to this Convention undertakes not to transfer to any recipient whatsoever, directly or indirectly, and not in any way to assist, encourage, or induce any State, group of States or international organizations to manufacture or otherwise acquire any of the agents, toxins, weapons, equipment or means of delivery specified in article I of the Convention.

Article IV

Each State Party to this Convention shall, in accordance with its constitutional processes, take any necessary measures to prohibit and prevent the development, production, stockpiling, acquisition, or retention of the agents, toxins, weapons, equipment and means of delivery specified in article I of the Convention, within the territory of such State, under its jurisdiction or under its control anywhere.

Article V

The States Parties to this Convention undertake to consult one another and to cooperate in solving any problems which may arise in relation to the objective of, or in the application of the provisions of, the Convention. Consultation and cooperation pursuant to this article may also be undertaken through appropriate international procedures within the framework of the United Nations and in accordance with its Charter.

Article VI

(1) Any State Party to this Convention which finds that any other State Party is acting in breach of obligations deriving from the provisions of the Convention may lodge a complaint with the Security Council of the United Nations. Such a complaint should include all possible evidence confirming its validity, as well as a request for its consideration by the Security Council.

(2) Each State Party to this Convention undertakes to cooperate in carrying out any investigation which the Security Council may initiate, in accordance with the provisions of the Charter of the United Nations, on the basis of the complaint received

by the Council. The Security Council shall inform the States Parties to the Convention of the results of the investigation.

Article VII

Each State Party to this Convention undertakes to provide or support assistance, in accordance with the United Nations Charter, to any Party to the Convention which so requests, if the Security Council decides that such Party has been exposed to danger as a result of violation of the Convention.

Article VIII

Nothing in this Convention shall be interpreted as in any way limiting or detracting from the obligations assumed by any State under the Protocol for the Prohibition of the Use in War of Asphyxiating, Poisonous or Other Gases, and of Bacteriological Methods of Warfare, signed at Geneva on June 17, 1925.

Article IX

Each State Party to this Convention affirms the recognized objective of effective prohibition of chemical weapons and, to this end, undertakes to continue negotiations in good faith with a view to reaching early agreement on effective measures for the prohibition of their development, production and stockpiling and for their destruction, and on appropriate measures concerning equipment and means of delivery specifically designed for the production or use of chemical agents for weapons purposes.

Article X

(1) The States Parties to this Convention undertake to facilitate, and have the right to participate in, the fullest possible exchange of equipment, materials and scientific and technological information for the use of bacteriological (biological) agents and toxins for peaceful purposes. Parties to the Convention in a position to do so shall also cooperate in contributing individually or together with other States or international organizations to the further development and application of scientific discoveries in the field of bacteriology (biology) for prevention of disease, or for other peaceful purposes.

(2) This Convention shall be implemented in a manner designed to avoid hampering the economic or technological development of States Parties to the Convention or international cooperation in the field of peaceful bacteriological (biological) activities, including the international exchange of bacteriological (biological) agents and toxins and equipment for the processing, use or production of bacteriological (biological) agents and toxins for peaceful purposes in accordance with the provisions of the Convention.

Article XI

Any State Party may propose amendments to this Convention. Amendments shall enter into force for each State Party accepting the amendments upon their acceptance by a majority of the States Parties to the Convention and thereafter for each remaining State Party on the date of acceptance by it.

Article XII

Five years after the entry into force of this Convention, or earlier if it is requested by a majority of Parties to the Convention by submitting a proposal to this effect to the

Depositary Governments, a conference of States Parties to the Convention shall be held at Geneva, Switzerland, to review the operation of the Convention, with a view to assuring that the purposes of the preamble and the provisions of the Convention, including the provisions concerning negotiations on chemical weapons, are being realized. Such review shall take into account any new scientific and technological developments relevant to the Convention.

Article XIII

(1) This Convention shall be of unlimited duration.

(2) Each State Party to this Convention shall in exercising its national sovereignty have the right to withdraw from the Convention if it decides that extraordinary events, related to the subject matter of the Convention, have jeopardized the supreme interests of its country. It shall give notice of such withdrawal to all other States Parties to the Convention and to the United Nations Security Council three months in advance. Such notice shall include a statement of the extraordinary events it regards as having jeopardized its supreme interests.

Article XIV

(1) This Convention shall be open to all States for signature. Any State which does not sign the Convention before its entry into force in accordance with paragraph (3) of this Article may accede to it at any time.

(2) This Convention shall be subject to ratification by signatory States. Instruments of ratification and instruments of accession shall be deposited with the Governments of the United States of America, the United Kingdom of Great Britain and Northern Ireland and the Union of Soviet Socialist Republics, which are hereby designated the Depositary Governments.

(3) This Convention shall enter into force after the deposit of instruments of ratification by twenty-two Governments, including the Governments designated as Depositaries of the Convention.

(4) For States whose instruments of ratification or accession are deposited subsequent to the entry into force of this Convention, it shall enter into force on the date of the deposit of their instruments of ratification or accession.

(5) The Depositary Governments shall promptly inform all signatory and acceding States of the date of each signature, the date of deposit of each instrument of ratification or of accession and the date of the entry into force of this Convention, and of the receipt of other notices.

(6) This Convention shall be registered by the Depositary Governments pursuant to Article 102 of the Charter of the United Nations.

Article XV

This Convention, the English, Russian, French, Spanish and Chinese texts of which are equally authentic, shall be deposited in the archives of the Depositary Governments. Duly certified copies of the Convention shall be transmitted by the Depositary Governments to the Governments of the signatory and acceding states.

IN WITNESS WHEREOF the undersigned, duly authorized, have signed this Convention.

DONE in triplicate, at the cities of Washington, London and Moscow, this tenth day of April, one thousand nine hundred and seventy-two.

Biological Weapons Convention

Country	Date of[1] Signature	Date of Deposit[1] of Ratification	Date of Deposit[1] of Accession
Afghanistan	4/10/72	3/26/75	
Argentina	8/1/72	11/27/79	
Australia	4/10/72	10/5/77	
Austria	4/10/72	8/10/73	
Barbados	2/16/73	2/16/73	
Belgium	4/10/72	3/15/79	
Benin	4/10/72	4/25/75	
Bhutan			6/8/78
Bolivia	4/10/72	10/30/75	
Botswana	4/10/72		
Brazil	4/10/72	2/27/73	
Bulgaria	4/10/72	8/2/72	
Burma	4/10/72		
Burundi	4/10/72		
Byelorussian S.S.R.[2]	4/10/72	3/26/75	
Canada	4/10/72	9/18/72	
Cape Verde			10/20/77
Central African Republic	4/10/72		
Chile	4/10/72		
China (Taiwan)	4/10/72	2/9/73	
Colombia	4/10/72		
Congo, People's Republic of (Brazzaville)			10/23/78
Costa Rica	4/10/72	12/17/73	
Cuba	4/12/72	4/21/76	
Cyprus	4/10/72	11/6/73	
Czechoslovakia	4/10/72	4/30/73	
Denmark	4/10/72	3/1/73	
Dominican Republic	4/10/72	2/23/73	
Ecuador	6/14/72	3/12/75	
Egypt	4/10/72		
El Salvador	4/10/72		
Ethiopia	4/10/72	6/26/75	
Fiji	2/22/73	9/4/73	
Finland	4/10/72	2/4/74	
Gabon	4/10/72		
Gambia, The	6/2/72		
German Democratic Republic	4/10/72	11/28/72	

See footnotes on page 290.

Country	Date of[1] Signature	Date of Deposit[1] of Ratification	Date of Deposit[1] of Accession
Germany, Federal Republic of	4/10/72		
Ghana	4/10/72	6/6/75	
Greece	4/10/72	12/10/75	
Guatemala	5/9/72	9/19/73	
Guinea-Bissau			8/20/76
Guyana	1/3/73		
Haiti	4/10/72		
Honduras	4/10/72	3/14/79	
Hungary	4/10/72	12/27/72	
Iceland	4/10/72	2/15/73	
India	1/15/73	7/15/74	
Indonesia	6/20/72		
Iran	4/10/72	8/22/73	
Iraq	5/11/72		
Ireland	4/10/72	10/27/72	
Italy	4/10/72	5/30/75	
Ivory Coast	5/23/72		
Jamaica			8/13/75
Japan	4/10/72		
Jordan	4/10/72	6/2/75	
Kampuchea	4/10/72		
Kenya			9/30/81
Korea, Republic of	4/10/72		
Kuwait	4/14/72	7/18/72	
Laos	4/10/72	3/20/73	
Lebanon	4/10/72	6/13/75	
Lesotho	4/10/72		
Liberia	4/10/72		
Libya			1/19/82
Luxembourg	4/10/72	3/23/76	
Madagascar	10/13/72		
Malawi	4/10/72		
Malaysia	4/10/72		
Mali	4/10/72		
Malta	9/11/72	4/7/75	
Mauritius	4/10/72	8/7/72	
Mexico	4/10/72	4/8/74	
Mongolia	4/10/72	9/5/72	
Morocco	5/2/72		
Nepal	4/10/72		
Netherlands	4/10/72	6/22/81	

See footnotes on page 290.

Country	Date of[1] Signature	Date of Deposit[1] of Ratification	Date of Deposit[1] of Accession
New Zealand	4/10/72	12/13/72	
Nicaragua	4/10/72	8/7/75	
Niger	4/21/72	6/23/72	
Nigeria	7/3/72	7/3/73	
Norway	4/10/72	8/1/73	
Pakistan	4/10/72	9/25/74	
Panama	5/2/72	3/20/74	
Papua New Guinea			10/27/80
Paraguay			6/9/76
Peru	4/10/72		
Philippines	4/10/72	5/21/73	
Poland	4/10/72	1/25/73	
Portugal	6/29/72	5/15/75	
Qatar	11/14/72	4/17/75	
Romania	4/10/72	7/25/79	
Rwanda	4/10/72	5/20/75	
San Marino	9/12/72	3/11/75	
São Tome and Principe			8/24/79
Saudi Arabia	4/12/72	5/24/72	
Senegal	4/10/72	3/26/75	
Sierra Leone	11/7/72	6/29/76	
Seychelles			10/24/79
Singapore	6/19/72	12/2/75	
Somalia	7/3/72		
South Africa	4/10/72	11/3/75	
Spain	4/10/72	6/20/79	
Sri Lanka	4/10/72		
Sweden	2/27/75	2/5/76	
Switzerland	4/10/72	5/4/76	
Syrian Arab Republic	4/14/72		
Tanzania	8/16/72		
Thailand	1/17/73	5/28/75	
Togo	4/10/72	11/10/76	
Tonga			9/30/81
Tunisia	4/10/72	5/18/73	
Turkey	4/10/72	11/5/74	
Ukrainian S.S.R.[2]	4/10/72	3/26/75	
Union of Soviet Socialist Republics	4/10/72	3/26/75	
United Arab Emirates	9/28/72		
United Kingdom	4/10/72	3/26/75	
United States	4/10/72	3/26/75	
Uruguay			4/16/81

See footnotes on page 290.

Country	Date of[1] Signature	Date of Deposit[1] of Ratification	Date of Deposit[1] of Accession
Venezuela	4/10/72	10/18/78	
Vietnam			6/20/80
Yemen Arab Republic (Sana)	4/10/72		
Yemen, People's Democratic Republic of (Aden)	4/26/72	6/1/79	
Yugoslavia	4/10/72	10/25/73	
Zaire	4/10/72	9/16/75	
Total[3]	111	76	14

See footnotes on page 290.

Strategic Arms Limitation Talks (SALT I)

SALT I, the first series of Strategic Arms Limitation Talks, extended from November 1969 to May 1972. During that period the United States and the Soviet Union negotiated the first agreements to place limits and restraints on some of their central and most important armaments. In a "Treaty...on the Limitation of Anti-Ballistic Missile Systems," they moved to end an emerging competition in defensive systems that threatened to spur offensive competition to still greater heights. In an "Interim Agreement...on Certain Measures With Respect to the Limitation of Strategic Offensive Arms," the two nations took the first steps to check the rivalry in their most powerful land- and submarine-based offensive nuclear weapons.

The earliest efforts to halt the growth in strategic arms had met with no success. Strategic weapons had been included in the U.S. and Soviet proposals for general and complete disarmament. But the failure of these comprehensive schemes left strategic arms unrestrained. The United States was the first to suggest dissociating them from comprehensive disarmament plans—proposing, at the Geneva-based Eighteen-Nation Disarmament Committee in January 1964, that the two sides should "explore a verified freeze of the number and characteristics of their strategic nuclear offensive and defensive vehicles."

The competition in offensive and defensive armaments continued. By 1966 the Soviet Union had begun to deploy an antiballistic missile defense around Moscow; and that year the People's Republic of China successfully tested a nuclear missile. In the United States, research and development were leading to U.S. deployment of its own ABM system.

In March 1967, after an exchange of communications with Soviet leaders, President Johnson announced that Premier Kosygin had indicated a willingness to begin discussions. Attempts to get talks underway, however, were not successful.

On September 18, 1967, the United States announced that it would begin deployment of a "thin" antiballistic missile (ABM) system. The Administration emphasized that the deployment was intended to meet a possible limited Chinese ICBM threat, to underscore U.S. security assurances to its allies by reinforcing the U.S. deterrent, and to add protection against "the improbable but possible accidental launch of an intercontinental missile by one of the nuclear powers." This program for limited ABM defense brought sharply divided views in public and congressional debate regarding the efficacy and desirability of an ABM system and its possible effects on the arms race.

In announcing the U.S. decision, Secretary of Defense McNamara said,

> Let me emphasize—and I cannot do so too strongly—that our decision to go ahead with a limited ABM deployment in no way indicates that we feel an agreement with the Soviet Union on the limitation of strategic nuclear offensive and defensive forces is in any way less urgent or desirable.

Through diplomatic channels in Washington and Moscow, discussions with Soviet representatives in the ENDC, and exchanges at the highest levels of the two governments, the United States continued to press for a Soviet commitment to discuss strategic arms limitation. But it was not until the following year that evidence of a Soviet reassessment of its position emerged. On July 1, 1968, President Johnson announced, at the signing of the Non-Proliferation Treaty, that agreement had been reached with the Soviet Union to begin discussions on limiting and reducing both strategic nuclear weapons delivery systems and defenses against ballistic missiles. The date and place for the talks had not yet been announced, when, on August 20, the Soviet Union began its invasion of Czechoslovakia, and the talks were indefinitely postponed.

On January 20, 1969, the day that President Nixon assumed office, a statement by the Soviet Foreign Ministry expressed willingness to discuss strategic arms limitations. The new President promptly voiced his support for talks, and initiated, under the aegis of the National Security Council, an extensive and detailed review of the strategic, political, and verification aspects of the problem.

In October, the White House and the Kremlin announced that the Strategic Arms Limitation Talks would begin in Helsinki on November 17, 1969, "for preliminary discussion of the questions involved." The Director of ACDA, Gerard Smith, was named to head the U.S. delegation and led it throughout the 2½-year series of SALT I negotiations.

In the first session of the talks, from November 17 to December 22, each side gained a better understanding of the other's views and of the range of questions to be considered. It was agreed that the talks would be private, to encourage a free and frank exchange, and the stage was set for the main negotiations, which opened in Vienna in April 1970. Sessions thereafter alternated between Helsinki and Vienna until the first accords were reached in May 1972. (When SALT II began, in November 1972, to reduce the administrative burdens involved in shifting sites it was agreed to hold them henceforth in one place—Geneva.)

Soviet and American weapons systems were far from symmetrical. The Soviet Union had continued its development and deployment of heavy ballistic missiles and had overtaken the U.S. lead in land-based ICBMs. During the SALT I years alone its ICBMs rose from around 1,000 to around 1,500, and they were being deployed at the rate of some 200 annually. Soviet submarine-based launchers had quadrupled. The huge payload capacity of some Soviet missiles ("throw-weight") was seen as a possible threat to U.S. land-based strategic missiles even in heavily protected ("hardened") launch-sites.

The United States had not increased its deployment of strategic missiles since 1967, when its ICBMs numbered 1,054 and its SLBMs, 656, but it was conducting a vigorous program of substituting missiles with "Multiple Independently-targeted Re-entry Vehicles" (MIRV). These MIRVs permit an individual missile to carry a number of warheads directed at separate targets. MIRVs gave the United States a lead in numbers of warheads, and the United States retained a lead in long-range bombers. The Soviet Union had a limited ABM system around Moscow; the United States had shifted from its earlier plan for a "thin" ABM defense of certain American cities and had begun to deploy ABMs at two land-based (ICBM) missile sites to protect its retaliatory forces. (The full program envisaged 12 ABM complexes.)

Besides these asymmetries in their strategic forces, the defense needs and commitments of the two parties differed materially. The United States had obligations for the defense of allies overseas, such as Western Europe and Japan, while the Soviet Union's allies were its near neighbors. All these circumstances made for difficulties in equating specific weapons, or categories of weapons, and in defining overall strategic equivalence.

Two initial disagreements presented obstacles. The Soviet representatives sought to define as "strategic"—i.e., negotiable in SALT—any U.S. or Soviet weapons system capable of reaching the territory of the other side. This would have included U.S. "forward-based systems," chiefly short-range or medium-range bombers on aircraft carriers or based in Europe, but it would have excluded, for example, Soviet intermediate-range missiles aimed at Western Europe. The United States held that weapons to be negotiated in SALT comprised intercontinental systems. Its forward-based forces served to counter Soviet medium-range missiles and aircraft aimed at U.S. allies. To accept the Soviet approach would have prejudiced alliance commitments.

After initial attempts to reach a comprehensive agreement failed, the Soviets sought to restrict negotiations to antiballistic missile systems, maintaining that limitation on offensive systems should be deferred. The U.S. position was that to limit ABM systems but allow the unrestricted growth of offensive weapons would be incompatible with the basic objectives of SALT and that it was essential to make at least a beginning at limiting offensive systems as well. A long deadlock on the question was finally broken by exchanges at the highest levels of both governments. On May 20, 1971, Washington and Moscow announced that an understanding had been reached to concentrate on a permanent treaty to limit ABM systems, but at the same time to work out certain limitations on offensive systems, and to continue negotiations for a more comprehensive and long-term agreement on the latter.

In a summit meeting in Moscow, after 2½ years of negotiation, the first round of SALT was brought to a conclusion on May 26, 1972, when President Nixon and General Secretary Brezhnev signed the ABM Treaty and the Interim Agreement on strategic offensive arms.

Intensive research had gone into finding ways of verifying possible agreements without requiring access to the territory of the other side. Both the ABM Treaty and the Interim Agreement stipulate that compliance is to be assured by "national technical means of verification." Moreover, the agreements include provisions that are important steps to strengthen assurance against violations: both sides undertake not to interfere with national technical means of verification. In addition, both countries agree not to use deliberate concealment measures to impede verification.

The basic provisions of each SALT I agreement are briefly reviewed in sections that follow. The two accords differ in their duration and inclusiveness. The ABM Treaty "shall be of unlimited duration," but each party has the right to withdraw on 6 months' notice if it decides that its supreme interests are jeopardized by "extraordinary events related to the subject matter of this Treaty." The Interim Agreement was for a 5-year span, and covered only certain major aspects of strategic weaponry. The agreements are linked not only in their strategic effects, but in their relationship to future negotiations for limitations on strategic offensive arms. A formal statement by the United States stressed the critical importance it attaches to achieving more complete limitations on strategic offensive arms.

The two agreements were accompanied by a number of "Agreed Statements" that were agreed upon and initialed by the Heads of the Delegations. When the two agreements were submitted to the U.S. Congress, they were also accompanied by common understandings reached and unilateral statements made during the negotiations.

These were intended to clarify specific provisions of the agreements or parts of the negotiating record. The three groups of items are reproduced here with the texts of the agreements.

Treaty Between the United States of America and the Union of Soviet Socialist Republics on the Limitation of Anti-Ballistic Missile Systems

In the Treaty on the Limitation of Anti-Ballistic Missile Systems the United States and the Soviet Union agree that each may have only two ABM deployment areas,[1] so restricted and so located that they cannot provide a nationwide ABM defense or become the basis for developing one. Each country thus leaves unchallenged the penetration capability of the other's retaliatory missile forces.

The treaty permits each side to have one limited ABM system to protect its capital and another to protect an ICBM launch area. The two sites defended must be at least 1,300 kilometers apart, to prevent the creation of any effective regional defense zone or the beginnings of a nationwide system.

Precise quantitative and qualitative limits are imposed on the ABM systems that may be deployed. At each site there may be no more than 100 interceptor missiles and 100 launchers. Agreement on the number and characteristics of radars to be permitted had required extensive and complex technical negotiations, and the provisions governing these important components of ABM systems are spelled out in very specific detail in the treaty and further clarified in the "Agreed Statements" accompanying it.

Both parties agreed to limit qualitative improvement of their ABM technology, e.g., not to develop, test, or deploy ABM launchers capable of launching more than one interceptor missile at a time or modify existing launchers to give them this capability, and systems for rapid reload of launchers are similarly barred. These provisions, the Agreed Statements clarify, also ban interceptor missiles with more than one independently guided warhead.

There had been some concern over the possibility that surface-to-air missiles (SAMs) intended for defense against aircraft might be improved, along with their supporting radars, to the point where they could effectively be used against ICBMs and SLBMs, and the treaty prohibits this. While further deployment of radars intended to give early warning of strategic ballistic missile attack is not prohibited, they must be located along the territorial boundaries of each country

---

[1]Subsequently reduced to one area (see section on ABM Protocol).

and oriented outward, so that they do not contribute to an effective ABM defense of points in the interior.

Further, to decrease the pressures of technological change and its unsettling impact on the strategic balance, both sides agree to prohibit development, testing, or deployment of sea-based, air-based, or space-based ABM systems and their components, along with mobile land-based ABM systems. Should future technology bring forth new ABM systems "based on other physical principles" than those employed in current systems, it was agreed that limiting such systems would be discussed, in accordance with the treaty's provisions for consultation and amendment.

The treaty also provides for a U.S.-Soviet Standing Consultative Commission to promote its objectives and implementation. The commission was established during the first negotiating session of SALT II, by a Memorandum of Understanding dated December 21, 1972. Since then both the United States and the Soviet Union have raised a number of questions in the Commission relating to each side's compliance with the SALT I agreements. In each case raised by the United States, the Soviet activity in question has either ceased or additional information has allayed U.S. concern.

Article XIV of the treaty calls for review of the treaty 5 years after its entry into force, and at 5-year intervals thereafter. The first such review was conducted by the Standing Consultative Commission at its special session in the fall of 1977. At this session, the United States and the Soviet Union agreed that the treaty had operated effectively during its first 5 years, that it had continued to serve national security interests, and that it did not need to be amended at that time.

Treaty Between the United States of America and the Union of Soviet Socialist Republics on the Limitation of Anti-Ballistic Missile Systems

Signed at Moscow May 26, 1972
Ratification advised by U.S. Senate August 3, 1972
Ratified by U.S. President September 30, 1972
Proclaimed by U.S. President October 3, 1972
Instruments of ratification exchanged October 3, 1972
Entered into force October 3, 1972

The United States of America and the Union of Soviet Socialist Republics, hereinafter referred to as the Parties,

Proceeding from the premise that nuclear war would have devastating consequences for all mankind,

Considering that effective measures to limit anti-ballistic missile systems would be a substantial factor in curbing the race in strategic offensive arms and would lead to a decrease in the risk of outbreak of war involving nuclear weapons,

Proceeding from the premise that the limitation of anti-ballistic missile systems, as well as certain agreed measures with respect to the limitation of strategic offensive arms, would contribute to the creation of more favorable conditions for further negotiations on limiting strategic arms,

Mindful of their obligations under Article VI of the Treaty on the Non-Proliferation of Nuclear Weapons,

Declaring their intention to achieve at the earliest possible date the cessation of the nuclear arms race and to take effective measures toward reductions in strategic arms, nuclear disarmament, and general and complete disarmament,

Desiring to contribute to the relaxation of international tension and the strengthening of trust between States,

Have agreed as follows:

Article I

1. Each party undertakes to limit anti-ballistic missile (ABM) systems and to adopt other measures in accordance with the provisions of this Treaty.

2. Each Party undertakes not to deploy ABM systems for a defense of the territory of its country and not to provide a base for such a defense, and not to deploy ABM systems for defense of an individual region except as provided for in Article III of this Treaty.

Article II

1. For the purpose of this Treaty an ABM system is a system to counter strategic ballistic missiles or their elements in flight trajectory, currently consisting of:

(a) ABM interceptor missiles, which are interceptor missiles constructed and deployed for an ABM role, or of a type tested in an ABM mode;

139

(b) ABM launchers, which are launchers constructed and deployed for launching ABM interceptor missiles; and

(c) ABM radars, which are radars constructed and deployed for an ABM role, or of a type tested in an ABM mode.

2. The ABM system components listed in paragraph 1 of this Article include those which are:

(a) operational;
(b) under construction;
(c) undergoing testing;
(d) undergoing overhaul, repair or conversion; or
(e) mothballed.

Article III

Each Party undertakes not to deploy ABM systems or their components except that:

(a) within one ABM system deployment area having a radius of one hundred and fifty kilometers and centered on the Party's national capital, a Party may deploy: (1) no more than one hundred ABM launchers and no more than one hundred ABM interceptor missiles at launch sites, and (2) ABM radars within no more than six ABM radar complexes, the area of each complex being circular and having a diameter of no more than three kilometers; and

(b) within one ABM system deployment area having a radius of one hundred and fifty kilometers and containing ICBM silo launchers, a Party may deploy: (1) no more than one hundred ABM launchers and no more than one hundred ABM interceptor missiles at launch sites, (2) two large phased-array ABM radars comparable in potential to corresponding ABM radars operational or under construction on the date of signature of the Treaty in an ABM system deployment area containing ICBM silo launchers, and (3) no more than eighteen ABM radars each having a potential less than the potential of the smaller of the above-mentioned two large phased-array ABM radars.

Article IV

The limitations provided for in Article III shall not apply to ABM systems or their components used for development or testing, and located within current or additionally agreed test ranges. Each Party may have no more than a total of fifteen ABM launchers at test ranges.

Article V

1. Each Party undertakes not to develop, test, or deploy ABM systems or components which are sea-based, air-based, space-based, or mobile land-based.

2. Each Party undertakes not to develop, test, or deploy ABM launchers for launching more than one ABM interceptor missile at a time from each launcher, not to modify deployed launchers to provide them with such a capability, not to develop, test, or deploy automatic or semi-automatic or other similar systems for rapid reload of ABM launchers.

Article VI

To enhance assurance of the effectiveness of the limitations on ABM systems and their components provided by the Treaty, each Party undertakes:

(a) not to give missiles, launchers, or radars, other than ABM interceptor missiles, ABM launchers, or ABM radars, capabilities to counter strategic ballistic missiles or their elements in flight trajectory, and not to test them in an ABM mode; and

(b) not to deploy in the future radars for early warning of strategic ballistic missile attack except at locations along the periphery of its national territory and oriented outward.

Article VII

Subject to the provisions of this Treaty, modernization and replacement of ABM systems or their components may be carried out.

Article VIII

ABM systems or their components in excess of the numbers or outside the areas specified in this Treaty, as well as ABM systems or their components prohibited by this Treaty, shall be destroyed or dismantled under agreed procedures within the shortest possible agreed period of time.

Article IX

To assure the viability and effectiveness of this Treaty, each Party undertakes not to transfer to other States, and not to deploy outside its national territory, ABM systems or their components limited by this Treaty.

Article X

Each Party undertakes not to assume any international obligations which would conflict with this Treaty.

Article XI

The Parties undertake to continue active negotiations for limitations on strategic offensive arms.

Article XII

1. For the purpose of providing assurance of compliance with the provisions of this Treaty, each Party shall use national technical means of verification at its disposal in a manner consistent with generally recognized principles of international law.

2. Each Party undertakes not to interfere with the national technical means of verification of the other Party operating in accordance with paragraph 1 of this Article.

3. Each Party undertakes not to use deliberate concealment measures which impede verification by national technical means of compliance with the provisions of this Treaty. This obligation shall not require changes in current construction, assembly, conversion, or overhaul practices.

Article XIII

1. To promote the objectives and implementation of the provisions of this Treaty, the Parties shall establish promptly a Standing Consultative Commission, within the framework of which they will:

(a) consider questions concerning compliance with the obligations assumed and related situations which may be considered ambiguous;

(b) provide on a voluntary basis such information as either Party considers necessary to assure confidence in compliance with the obligations assumed;

(c) consider questions involving unintended interference with national technical means of verification;

(d) consider possible changes in the strategic situation which have a bearing on the provisions of this Treaty;

(e) agree upon procedures and dates for destruction or dismantling of ABM systems or their components in cases provided for by the provisions of this Treaty;

(f) consider, as appropriate, possible proposals for further increasing the viability of this Treaty; including proposals for amendments in accordance with the provisions of this Treaty;

(g) consider, as appropriate, proposals for further measures aimed at limiting strategic arms.

2. The Parties through consultation shall establish, and may amend as appropriate, Regulations for the Standing Consultative Commission governing procedures, composition and other relevant matters.

Article XIV

1. Each Party may propose amendments to this Treaty. Agreed amendments shall enter into force in accordance with the procedures governing the entry into force of this Treaty.

2. Five years after entry into force of this Treaty, and at five-year intervals thereafter, the Parties shall together conduct a review of this Treaty.

Article XV

1. This Treaty shall be of unlimited duration.

2. Each Party shall, in exercising its national sovereignty, have the right to withdraw from this Treaty if it decides that extraordinary events related to the subject matter of this Treaty have jeopardized its supreme interests. It shall give notice of its decision to the other Party six months prior to withdrawal from the Treaty. Such notice shall include a statement of the extraordinary events the notifying Party regards as having jeopardized its supreme interests.

Article XVI

1. This Treaty shall be subject to ratification in accordance with the constitutional procedures of each Party. The Treaty shall enter into force on the day of the exchange of instruments of ratification.

2. This Treaty shall be registered pursuant to Article 102 of the Charter of the United Nations.

DONE at Moscow on May 26, 1972, in two copies, each in the English and Russian languages, both texts being equally authentic.

FOR THE UNITED STATES OF AMERICA

FOR THE UNION OF SOVIET SOCIALIST REPUBLICS

RICHARD NIXON

L. I. BREZHNEV

President of the United States of America

General Secretary of the Central Committee of the CPSU

Agreed Statements, Common Understandings, and Unilateral Statements Regarding the Treaty Between the United States of America and the Union of Soviet Socialist Republics on the Limitation of Anti-Ballistic Missiles

1. Agreed Statements

The document set forth below was agreed upon and initialed by the Heads of the Delegations on May 26, 1972 (letter designations added);

AGREED STATEMENTS REGARDING THE TREATY BETWEEN THE UNITED STATES OF AMERICA AND THE UNION OF SOVIET SOCIALIST REPUBLICS ON THE LIMITATION OF ANTI-BALLISTIC MISSILE SYTEMS

[A]

The Parties understand that, in addition to the ABM radars which may be deployed in accordance with subparagraph (a) of Article III of the Treaty, those non-phased- array ABM radars operational on the date of signature of the Treaty within the ABM system deployment area for defense of the national capital may be retained.

[B]

The Parties understand that the potential (the product of mean emitted power in watts and antenna area in square meters) of the smaller of the two large phased-array ABM radars referred to in subparagraph (b) of Article III of the Treaty is considered for purposes of the Treaty to be three million.

[C]

The Parties understand that the center of the ABM system deployment area centered on the national capital and the center of the ABM system deployment area containing ICBM silo launchers for each Party shall be separated by no less than thirteen hundred kilometers.

[D]

In order to insure fulfillment of the obligation not to deploy ABM systems and their components except as provided in Article III of the Treaty, the Parties agree that in the event ABM systems based on other physical principles and including components capable of substituting for ABM interceptor missiles, ABM launchers, or ABM radars are created in the future, specific limitations on such systems and their components would be subject to discussion in accordance with Article XIII and agreement in accordance with Article XIV of the Treaty.

[E]

The Parties understand that Article V of the Treaty includes obligations not to develop, test or deploy ABM interceptor missiles for the delivery by each ABM interceptor missile of more than one independently guided warhead.

[F]

The Parties agree not to deploy phased-array radars having a potential (the product of mean emitted power in watts and antenna area in square meters) exceeding three million, except as provided for in Articles III, IV and VI of the Treaty, or except for the purposes of tracking objects in outer space or for use as national technical means of verification.

[G]

The Parties understand that Article IX of the Treaty includes the obligation of the US and the USSR not to provide to other States technical descriptions or blue prints specially worked out for the construction of ABM systems and their components limited by the Treaty.

2. Common Understandings

Common understanding of the Parties on the following matters was reached during the negotiations:

A.   Location of ICBM Defenses

The U.S. Delegation made the following statement on May 26, 1972:

Article III of the ABM Treaty provides for each side one ABM system deployment area centered on its national capital and one ABM system deployment area containing ICBM silo launchers. The two sides have registered agreement on the following statement: "The Parties understand that the center of the ABM system deployment area centered on the national capital and the center of the ABM system deployment area containing ICBM silo launchers for each Party shall be separated by no less than thirteen hundred kilometers." In this connection, the U.S. side notes that its ABM system deployment area for defense of ICBM silo launchers, located west of the Mississippi River, will be centered in the Grand Forks ICBM silo launcher deployment area. (See Agreed Statement [C].)

B.   ABM Test Ranges

The U.S. Delegation made the following statement on April 26, 1972:

Article IV of the ABM Treaty provides that "the limitations provided for in Article III shall not apply to ABM systems or their components used for development or testing, and located within current or additionally agreed test ranges." We believe it would be useful to assure that there is no misunderstanding as to current ABM test ranges. It is our understanding that ABM test ranges encompass the area within which ABM components are located for test purposes. The current U.S. ABM test ranges are at White Sands, New Mexico, and at Kwajalein Atoll, and the current Soviet ABM test range is near Sary Shagan in Kazakhstan. We consider that non-phased array radars of types used for range safety or instrumentation purposes may be located outside of ABM test ranges. We interpret the reference in Article IV to "additionally agreed test ranges" to mean that ABM components will not be located at any other test ranges without prior agreement between our Governments that there will be such additional ABM test ranges.

On May 5, 1972, the Soviet Delegation stated that there was a common understanding on what ABM test ranges were, that the use of the types of non-ABM radars for range safety or instrumentation was not limited under the Treaty, that the reference in Article IV to "additionally agreed" test ranges was sufficiently clear, and that national means permitted identifying current test ranges.

C. Mobile ABM Systems

On January 29, 1972, the U.S. Delegation made the following statement:

Article V(1) of the Joint Draft Text of the ABM Treaty includes an undertaking not to develop, test, or deploy mobile land-based ABM systems and their components. On May 5, 1971, the U.S. side indicated that, in its view, a prohibition on deployment of mobile ABM systems and components would rule out the deployment of ABM launchers and radars which were not permanent fixed types. At that time, we asked for the Soviet view of this interpretation. Does the Soviet side agree with the U.S. side's interpretation put forward on May 5, 1971?

On April 13, 1972, the Soviet Delegation said there is a general common understanding on this matter.

D. Standing Consultative Commission

Ambassador Smith made the following statement on May 22, 1972:

The United States proposes that the sides agree that, with regard to initial implementation of the ABM Treaty's Article XIII on the Standing Consultative Commission (SCC) and of the consultation Articles to the Interim Agreement on offensive arms and the Accidents Agreement,[1] agreement establishing the SCC will be worked out early in the follow-on SALT negotiations; until that is completed, the following arrangements will prevail: when SALT is in session, any consultation desired by either side under these Articles can be carried out by the two SALT Delegations; when SALT is not in session, ad hoc arrangements for any desired consultations under these Articles may be made through diplomatic channels.

Minister Semenov replied that, on an ad referendum basis, he could agree that the U.S. statement corresponded to the Soviet understanding.

E. Standstill

On May 6, 1972, Minister Semenov made the following statement:

In an effort to accommodate the wishes of the U.S. side, the Soviet Delegation is prepared to proceed on the basis that the two sides will in fact observe the obligations of both the Interim Agreement and the ABM Treaty beginning from the date of signature of these two documents.

In reply, the U.S. Delegation made the following statement on May 20, 1972:

---

[1]See Article 7 of Agreement to Reduce the Risk of Outbreak of Nuclear War Between the United States of America and the Union of Soviet Socialist Republics, signed Sept. 30, 1971.

The U.S. agrees in principle with the Soviet statement made on May 6 concerning observance of obligations beginning from date of signature but we would like to make clear our understanding that this means that, pending ratification and acceptance, neither side would take any action prohibited by the agreements after they had entered into force. This understanding would continue to apply in the absence of notification by either signatory of its intention not to proceed with ratification or approval.

The Soviet Delegation indicated agreement with the U.S. statement.

3. Unilateral Statements

The following noteworthy unilateral statements were made during the negotiations by the United States Delegation:

A. Withdrawal from the ABM Treaty

On May 9, 1972, Ambassador Smith made the following statement:

The U.S. Delegation has stressed the importance the U.S. Government attaches to achieving agreement on more complete limitations on strategic offensive arms, following agreement on an ABM Treaty and on an Interim Agreement on certain measures with respect to the limitation of strategic offensive arms. The U.S. Delegation believes that an objective of the follow-on negotiations should be to constrain and reduce on a long-term basis threats to the survivability of our respective strategic retaliatory forces. The USSR Delegation has also indicated that the objectives of SALT would remain unfulfilled without the achievement of an agreement providing for more complete limitations on strategic offensive arms. Both sides recognize that the initial agreements would be steps toward the achievement of more complete limitations on strategic arms. If an agreement providing for more complete strategic offensive arms limitations were not achieved within five years, U.S. supreme interests could be jeopardized. Should that occur, it would constitute a basis for withdrawal from the ABM Treaty. The U.S. does not wish to see such a situation occur, nor do we believe that the USSR does. It is because we wish to prevent such a situation that we emphasize the importance the U.S. Government attaches to achievement of more complete limitations on strategic offensive arms. The U.S. Executive will inform the Congress, in connection with Congressional consideration of the ABM Treaty and the Interim Agreement, of this statement of the U.S. position.

B. Tested in ABM Mode

On April 7, 1972, the U.S. Delegation made the following statement:

Article II of the Joint Text Draft uses the term "tested in an ABM mode," in defining ABM components, and Article VI includes certain obligations concerning such testing. We believe that the sides should have a common understanding of this phrase. First, we would note that the testing provisions of the ABM Treaty are intended to apply to testing which occurs after the date of signature of the Treaty, and not to any testing which may have occurred in the past. Next, we would amplify the remarks we have made on this subject during the previous Helsinki phase by setting forth the objectives which govern the U.S. view on the subject, namely, while prohibiting testing of non-ABM components for ABM purposes: not to prevent testing of ABM components, and not to prevent testing of non-ABM components for non-ABM purposes. To clarify our interpretation of "tested in an ABM mode," we note that we would consider a launcher, missile or radar to be "tested in an ABM mode" if, for example, any of the following events occur: (1) a launcher is used to launch an ABM interceptor missile, (2) an interceptor missile is flight tested against a target vehicle which has a flight trajectory with characteristics of a strategic ballistic missile flight trajectory, or is flight tested in conjunction with the test of an ABM interceptor missile or an ABM radar at the same test range, or is flight tested to an altitude inconsistent with interception of targets against which air defenses are deployed, (3) a radar makes measurements on a cooperative target vehicle of the kind referred to in item (2) above during the reentry portion of its trajectory or makes measurements in conjunction with the test of an ABM interceptor missile or an ABM radar at the same test range. Radars used for purposes such as range safety or instrumentation would be exempt from application of these criteria.

C. No-Transfer Article of ABM Treaty

On April 18, 1972, the U.S. Delegation made the following statement:

In regard to this Article [IX], I have a brief and I believe self-explanatory statement to make. The U.S. side wishes to make clear that the provisions of this Article do not set a precedent for whatever provision may be considered for a Treaty on Limiting Strategic Offensive Arms. The question of transfer of strategic offensive arms is a far more complex issue, which may require a different solution.

D. No Increase in Defense of Early Warning Radars

On July 28, 1970, the U.S. Delegation made the following statement:

Since Hen House radars [Soviet ballistic missile early warning radars] can detect and track ballistic missile warheads at great distances, they have a significant ABM potential. Accordingly, the U.S. would regard any increase in the defenses of such radars by surface-to-air missiles as inconsistent with an agreement.

Interim Agreement Between the United States of America and the Union of Soviet Socialist Republics on Certain Measures With Respect to the Limitation of Strategic Offensive Arms

As its title suggests, the "Interim Agreement Between the United States and the Union of Soviet Socialist Republics on Certain Measures With Respect to the Limitation of Offensive Arms" was limited in duration and scope. It was intended to remain in force for 5 years. (See preceding section on SALT.) Both countries undertook to continue negotiations for a more comprehensive agreement as soon as possible, and the scope and terms of any new agreement were not to be prejudiced by the provisions of the 1972 accord.

Thus the Interim Agreement was set essentially as a holding action, designed to complement the ABM Treaty by limiting competition in offensive strategic arms and to provide time for further negotiations. The agreement essentially freezes at existing levels the number of strategic ballistic missile launchers, operational or under construction, on each side, and permits an increase in SLBM launchers up to an agreed level for each party only with the dismantling or destruction of a corresponding number of older ICBM or SLBM launchers.

In view of the many asymmetries in the two countries' forces, imposing equivalent limitations required rather complex and precise provisions. At the date of signing, the United States had 1,054 operational land-based ICBMs, and none under construction; the Soviet Union had an estimated 1,618, operational and under construction. Launchers under construction could be completed. Neither side would start construction of additional fixed land-based ICBM launchers during the period of the agreement—this, in effect, also bars relocation of existing launchers. Launchers for light or older ICBMs cannot be converted into launchers for modern heavy ICBMs. This prevents the U.S.S.R. from replacing older missiles with missiles such as the SS-9, which in 1972 was the largest and most powerful missile in the Soviet inventory and a source of particular concern to the United States.

Within these limitations, modernization and replacement are permitted, but in the process of modernizing, the dimensions of silo launchers cannot be significantly increased.

Mobile ICBMs are not covered. The Soviet Union held that since neither side had such systems, a freeze should not apply to them; it also opposed banning them in a future comprehensive agreement. The United States held they should be banned because of the verification difficulties they presented. In a formal statement, the U.S. delegation declared that the United States would consider deployment of land-mobile ICBMs during the period of the agreement as inconsistent with its objectives.

Article III and the protocol limit launchers for submarine-launched ballistic missiles (SLBMs) and modern ballistic missile submarines. The United States is permitted to reach a ceiling of 710 SLBM launchers on 44 submarines, from its base level of 656 SLBM launchers on 41 ballistic missile submarines, by replacing 54 older ICBM launchers. The Soviet Union, beyond the level of 740 SLBM launchers on modern nuclear-powered submarines, may increase to 950. But these additional launchers are permitted only as replacements for older ICBM or SLBM launchers, which must be dismantled or destroyed under agreed procedures.

In a unilateral statement, the Soviet Union asserted that if U.S. NATO allies increased the number of their modern submarines, the Soviet Union would have a right to increase the number of its submarines correspondingly. The United States declared that it did not accept this claim.

Interim Agreement Between the United States of America and the Union of Soviet Socialist Republics on Certain Measures With Respect to the Limitation of Strategic Offensive Arms

Signed at Moscow May 26, 1972
Approval authorized by U.S. Congress September 30, 1972
Approved by U.S. President September 30, 1972
Notices of acceptance exchanged October 3, 1972
Entered into force October 3, 1972

The United States of America and the Union of Soviet Socialist Republics, hereinafter referred to as the Parties,

Convinced that the Treaty on the Limitation of Anti-Ballistic Missile Systems and this Interim Agreement on Certain Measures with Respect to the Limitation of Strategic Offensive Arms will contribute to the creation of more favorable conditions for active negotiations on limiting strategic arms as well as to the relaxation of international tension and the strengthening of trust between States,

Taking into account the relationship between strategic offensive and defensive arms,

Mindful of their obligations under Article VI of the Treaty on the Non-Proliferation of Nuclear Weapons,

Have agreed as follows:

Article I

The Parties undertake not to start construction of additional fixed land-based intercontinental ballistic missile (ICBM) launchers after July 1, 1972.

Article II

The Parties undertake not to convert land-based launchers for light ICBMs, or for ICBMs of older types deployed prior to 1964, into land-based launchers for heavy ICBMs of types deployed after that time.

Article III

The Parties undertake to limit submarine-launched ballistic missile (SLBM) launchers and modern ballistic missile submarines to the numbers operational and under construction on the date of signature of this Interim Agreement, and in addition to launchers and submarines constructed under procedures established by the Parties as replacements for an equal number of ICBM launchers of older types deployed prior to 1964 or for launchers on older submarines.

Article IV

Subject to the provisions of this Interim Agreement, modernization and replacement of strategic offensive ballistic missiles and launchers covered by this Interim Agreement may be undertaken.

Article V

1. For the purpose of providing assurance of compliance with the provisions of this Interim Agreement, each Party shall use national technical means of verification at its disposal in a manner consistent with generally recognized principles of international law.

2. Each party undertakes not to interfere with the national technical means of verification of the other Party operating in accordance with paragraph 1 of this Article.

3. Each Party undertakes not to use deliberate concealment measures which impede verification by national technical means of compliance with the provisions of this Interim Agreement. This obligation shall not require changes in current construction, assembly, conversion, or overhaul practices.

Article VI

To promote the objectives and implementation of the provisions of this Interim Agreement, the Parties shall use the Standing Consultative Commission established under Article XIII of the Treaty on the Limitation of Anti-Ballistic Missile Systems in accordance with the provisions of that Article.

Article VII

The Parties undertake to continue active negotiations for limitations on strategic offensive arms. The obligations provided for in this Interim Agreement shall not prejudice the scope or terms of the limitations on strategic offensive arms which may be worked out in the course of further negotiations.

Article VIII

1. This Interim Agreement shall enter into force upon exchange of written notices of acceptance by each Party, which exchange shall take place simultaneously with the exchange of instruments of ratification of the Treaty on the Limitation of Anti-Ballistic Missile Systems.

2. This Interim Agreement shall remain in force for a period of five years unless replaced earlier by an agreement on more complete measures limiting strategic offensive arms. It is the objective of the Parties to conduct active follow-on negotiations with the aim of concluding such an agreement as soon as possible.

3. Each Party shall, in exercising its national sovereignty, have the right to withdraw from this Interim Agreement if it decides that extraordinary events related to the subject matter of this Interim Agreement have jeopardized its supreme interests. It shall give notice of its decision to the other Party six months prior to withdrawal from this Interim Agreement. Such notice shall include a statement of the extraordinary events the notifying Party regards as having jeopardized its supreme interests.

DONE at Moscow on May 26, 1972, in two copies, each in the English and Russian languages, both texts being equally authentic.

FOR THE UNITED STATES OF AMERICA

FOR THE UNION OF SOVIET SOCIALIST REPUBLICS

RICHARD NIXON

L. I. BREZHNEV

President of the United States of America

General Secretary of the Central Committee of the CPSU

Protocol to the Interim Agreement Between the United States of America and the Union of Soviet Socialist Republics on Certain Measures With Respect to the Limitation of Strategic Offensive Arms

The United States of America and the Union of Soviet Socialist Republics, hereinafter referred to as the Parties,

Having agreed on certain limitations relating to submarine-launched ballistic missile launchers and modern ballistic missile submarines, and to replacement procedures, in the Interim Agreement,

Have agreed as follows:

The Parties understand that, under Article III of the Interim Agreement, for the period during which that Agreement remains in force:

The U.S. may have no more than 710 ballistic missile launchers on submarines (SLBMs) and no more than 44 modern ballistic missile submarines. The Soviet Union may have no more than 950 ballistic missile launchers on submarines and no more than 62 modern ballistic missile submarines.

Additional ballistic missile launchers on submarines up to the above-mentioned levels, in the U.S.—over 656 ballistic missile launchers on nuclear-powered submarines, and in the U.S.S.R.—over 740 ballistic missile launchers on nuclear-powered submarines, operational and under construction, may become operational as replacements for equal numbers of ballistic missile launchers of older types deployed prior to 1964 or of ballistic missile launchers on older submarines.

The deployment of modern SLBMs on any submarine, regardless of type, will be counted against the total level of SLBMs permitted for the U.S. and the U.S.S.R.

This Protocol shall be considered an integral part of the Interim Agreement.

DONE at Moscow this 26th day of May, 1972

FOR THE UNITED STATES OF AMERICA	**FOR THE UNION OF SOVIET SOCIALIST REPUBLICS**
RICHARD NIXON	**L. I. BREZHNEV**
President of the *United States of America*	*General Secretary of the* *Central Committee of the CPSU*

Agreed Statements, Common Understandings, and Unilateral Statements Regarding the Interim Agreement Between the United States of America and the Union of Soviet Socialist Republics on Certain Measures With Respect to the Limitation of Strategic Offensive Arms

1. Agreed Statements

The document set forth below was agreed upon and initialed by the Heads of the Delegations on May 26, 1972 (letter designations added):

AGREED STATEMENTS REGARDING THE INTERIM AGREEMENT BETWEEN THE UNITED STATES OF AMERICA AND THE UNION OF SOVIET SOCIALIST REPUBLICS ON CERTAIN MEASURES WITH RESPECT TO THE LIMITATION OF STRATEGIC OFFENSIVE ARMS

[A]

The Parties understand that land-based ICBM launchers referred to in the Interim Agreement are understood to be launchers for strategic ballistic missiles capable of ranges in excess of the shortest distance between the northeastern border of the continental U.S. and the northwestern border of the continental USSR.

[B]

The Parties understand that fixed land-based ICBM launchers under active construction as of the date of signature of the Interim Agreement may be completed.

[C]

The Parties understand that in the process of modernization and replacement the dimensions of land-based ICBM silo launchers will not be significantly increased.

[D]

The Parties understand that during the period of the Interim Agreement there shall be no significant increase in the number of ICBM or SLBM test and training launchers, or in the number of such launchers for modern land-based heavy ICBMs. The Parties further understand that construction or conversion of ICBM launchers at test ranges shall be undertaken only for purposes of testing and training.

[E]

The Parties understand that dismantling or destruction of ICBM launchers of older types deployed prior to 1964 and ballistic missile launchers on older submarines being replaced by new SLBM launchers on modern submarines will be initiated at the time of the beginning of sea trials of a replacement submarine, and will be completed in the shortest possible agreed period of time. Such dismantling or destruction, and timely notification thereof, will be accomplished under procedures to be agreed in the Standing Consultative Commission.

2. Common Understandings

Common understanding of the Parties on the following matters was reached during the negotiations:

A. Increase in ICBM Silo Dimensions

Ambassador Smith made the following statement on May 26, 1972:

The Parties agree that the term "significantly increased" means that an increase will not be greater than 10-15 percent of the present dimensions of land-based ICBM silo launchers.

Minister Semenov replied that this statement corresponded to the Soviet understanding.

B. Standing Consultative Commission

Ambassador Smith made the following statement on May 22, 1972:

The United States proposes that the sides agree that, with regard to initial implementation of the ABM Treaty's Article XIII on the Standing Consultative Commission (SCC) and of the consultation Articles to the Interim Agreement on offensive arms and the Accidents Agreement,[1] agreement establishing the SCC will be worked out early in the follow-on SALT negotiations; until that is completed, the following arrangements will prevail: when SALT is in session, any consultation desired by either side under these Articles can be carried out by the two SALT Delegations; when SALT is not in session, ad hoc arrangements for any desired consultations under these Articles may be made through diplomatic channels.

Minister Semenov replied that, on an ad referendum basis, he could agree that the U.S. statement corresponded to the Soviet understanding.

C. Standstill

On May 6, 1972, Minister Semenov made the following statement:

In an effort to accommodate the wishes of the U.S. side, the Soviet Delegation is prepared to proceed on the basis that the two sides will in fact observe the obligations of both the Interim Agreement and the ABM Treaty beginning from the date of signature of these two documents.

In reply, the U.S. Delegation made the following statement on May 20, 1972:

The U.S. agrees in principle with the Soviet statement made on May 6 concerning observance of obligations beginning from date of signature but we would like to make clear our understanding that this means that, pending ratification and acceptance, neither side would take any action prohibited by the agreements after

---

[1]See Article 7 of Agreement to Reduce the Risk of Outbreak of Nuclear War Between the United States of America and the Union of Soviet Socialist Republics, signed Sept. 30, 1971.

they had entered into force. This understanding would continue to apply in the absence of notification by either signatory of its intention not to proceed with ratification or approval.

The Soviet Delegation indicated agreement with the U.S. statement.

3. Unilateral Statements

(a) The following noteworthy unilateral statements were made during the negotiations by the United States Delegation:

A. Withdrawal from the ABM Treaty

On May 9, 1972, Ambassador Smith made the following statement:

The U.S. Delegation has stressed the importance the U.S. Government attaches to achieving agreement on more complete limitations on strategic offensive arms, following agreement on an ABM Treaty and on an Interim Agreement on certain measures with respect to the limitation of strategic offensive arms. The U.S. Delegation believes that an objective of the follow-on negotiations should be to constrain and reduce on a long-term basis threats to the survivability of our respective strategic retaliatory forces. The USSR Delegation has also indicated that the objectives of SALT would remain unfulfilled without the achievement of an agreement providing for more complete limitations on strategic offensive arms. Both sides recognize that the initial agreements would be steps toward the achievement of more complete limitations on strategic arms. If an agreement providing for more complete strategic offensive arms limitations were not achieved within five years, U.S. supreme interests could be jeopardized. Should that occur, it would constitute a basis for withdrawal from the ABM Treaty. The U.S. does not wish to see such a situation occur, nor do we believe that the USSR does. It is because we wish to prevent such a situation that we emphasize the importance the U.S. Government attaches to achievement of more complete limitations on strategic offensive arms. The U.S. Executive will inform the Congress, in connection with Congressional consideration of the ABM Treaty and the Interim Agreement, of this statement of the U.S. position.

B. Land-Mobile ICBM Launchers

The U.S. Delegation made the following statement on May 20, 1972:

In connection with the important subject of land-mobile ICBM launchers, in the interest of concluding the Interim Agreement the U.S. Delegation now withdraws its proposal that Article I or an agreed statement explicitly prohibit the deployment of mobile land-based ICBM launchers. I have been instructed to inform you that, while agreeing to defer the question of limitation of operational land-mobile ICBM launchers to the subsequent negotiations on more complete limitations on strategic offensive arms, the U.S. would consider the deployment of operational land-mobile ICBM launchers during the period of the Interim Agreement as inconsistent with the objectives of that Agreement.

C. Covered Facilities

The U.S. Delegation made the following statement on May 20, 1972:

I wish to emphasize the importance that the United States attaches to the provisions of Article V, including in particular their application to fitting out or berthing submarines.

D. "Heavy" ICBM's

The U.S. Delegation made the following statement on May 26, 1972:

The U.S. Delegation regrets that the Soviet Delegation has not been willing to agree on a common definition of a heavy missile. Under these circumstances, the U.S. Delegation believes it necessary to state the following: The United States would consider any ICBM having a volume significantly greater than that of the largest light ICBM now operational on either side to be a heavy ICBM. The U.S. proceeds on the premise that the Soviet side will give due account to this consideration.

(b) The following noteworthy unilateral statement was made by the Delegation of the U.S.S.R. and is shown here with the U.S. reply:

On May 17, 1972, Minister Semenov made the following unilateral "Statement of the Soviet Side":

Taking into account that modern ballistic missile submarines are presently in the possession of not only the U.S., but also of its NATO allies, the Soviet Union agrees that for the period of effectiveness of the Interim 'Freeze' Agreement the U.S. and its NATO allies have up to 50 such submarines with a total of up to 800 ballistic missile launchers thereon (including 41 U.S. submarines with 656 ballistic missile launchers). However, if during the period of effectiveness of the Agreement U.S. allies in NATO should increase the number of their modern submarines to exceed the numbers of submarines they would have operational or under construction on the date of signature of the Agreement, the Soviet Union will have the right to a corresponding increase in the number of its submarines. In the opinion of the Soviet side, the solution of the question of modern ballistic missile submarines provided for in the Interim Agreement only partially compensates for the strategic imbalance in the deployment of the nuclear-powered missile submarines of the USSR and the U.S. Therefore, the Soviet side believes that this whole question, and above all the question of liquidating the American missile submarine bases outside the U.S., will be appropriately resolved in the course of follow-on negotiations.

On May 24, Ambassador Smith made the following reply to Minister Semenov:

The United States side has studied the "statement made by the Soviet side" of May 17 concerning compensation for submarine basing and SLBM submarines belonging to third countries. The United States does not accept the validity of the considerations in that statement.

On May 26 Minister Semenov repeated the unilateral statement made on May 17. Ambassador Smith also repeated the U.S. rejection on May 26.

Agreement Between the United States of America and the Union of Soviet Socialist Republics on the Prevention of Nuclear War

From the onset of the SALT negotiations between the United States and the Soviet Union, the two countries began the process of reshaping their relations on the basis of peaceful cooperation. One of the primary goals in this relationship was the prevention of war, especially nuclear war. During the last session of the Moscow summit meeting in May 1972, the countries exchanged some general ideas on how to accomplish this objective. These discussions were continued throughout the next year and were concluded in a formal agreement during General Secretary Brezhnev's visit to the United States on June 18-25, 1973.

In the Agreement on the Prevention of Nuclear War, signed in Washington on June 22, 1973, the United States and the Soviet Union agreed to make the removal of the danger of nuclear war and the use of nuclear weapons an "objective of their policies," to practice restraint in their relations toward each other and toward all countries, and to pursue a policy dedicated toward stability and peace. It was viewed as a preliminary step toward preventing the outbreak of nuclear war or military conflict by adopting an attitude of international cooperation.

The agreement basically covers two main areas:

1. It outlines the general conduct of both countries toward each other and toward third countries regarding the avoidance of nuclear war. In this respect it is a bilateral agreement with multilateral implications.

2. The parties agreed that in a situation in which the two great nuclear countries find themselves in a nuclear confrontation or in which, either as a result of their policies toward each other or as the result of developments elsewhere in the world, there is a danger of a nuclear confrontation between them or any other country, they are committed to consult with each other in order to avoid this risk.

The agreement further provides that these consultations may be communicated to the United Nations and to other countries, a clause the United States, of course, applies to its allies. Article VI stipulates that nothing in the agreement shall affect formal alliance obligations or the inherent right of countries to defend themselves.

Agreement Between the United States of America and the Union of Soviet Socialist Republics on the Prevention of Nuclear War

Signed at Washington June 22, 1973
Entered into force June 22, 1973

The United States of America and the Union of Soviet Socialist Republics, hereinafter referred to as the Parties,

Guided by the objectives of strengthening world peace and international security,

Conscious that nuclear war would have devastating consequences for mankind,

Proceeding from the desire to bring about conditions in which the danger of an outbreak of nuclear war anywhere in the world would be reduced and ultimately eliminated,

Proceeding from their obligations under the Charter of the United Nations regarding the maintenance of peace, refraining from the threat or use of force, and the avoidance of war, and in conformity with the agreements to which either Party has subscribed,

Proceeding from the Basic Principles of Relations between the United States of America and the Union of Soviet Socialist Republics signed in Moscow on May 29, 1972,

Reaffirming that the development of relations between the United States of America and the Union of Soviet Socialist Republics is not directed against other countries and their interests,

Have agreed as follows:

Article I

The United States and the Soviet Union agree that an objective of their policies is to remove the danger of nuclear war and of the use of nuclear weapons.

Accordingly, the Parties agree that they will act in such a manner as to prevent the development of situations capable of causing a dangerous exacerbation of their relations, as to avoid military confrontations, and as to exclude the outbreak of nuclear war between them and between either of the Parties and other countries.

Article II

The Parties agree, in accordance with Article I and to realize the objective stated in that Article, to proceed from the premise that each Party will refrain from the threat or use of force against the other Party, against the allies of the other Party and against other countries, in circumstances which may endanger international peace and security. The Parties agree that they will be guided by these considerations in the formulation of their foreign policies and in their actions in the field of international relations.

Article III

The Parties undertake to develop their relations with each other and with other countries in a way consistent with the purposes of this Agreement.

Article IV

If at any time relations between the Parties or between either Party and other countries appear to involve the risk of a nuclear conflict, or if relations between countries not parties to this Agreement appear to involve the risk of nuclear war between the United States of America and the Union of Soviet Socialist Republics or between either Party and other countries, the United States and the Soviet Union, acting in accordance with the provisions of this Agreement, shall immediately enter into urgent consultations with each other and make every effort to avert this risk.

Article V

Each Party shall be free to inform the Security Council of the United Nations, the Secretary General of the United Nations and the Governments of allied or other countries of the progress and outcome of consultations initiated in accordance with Article IV of this Agreement.

Article VI

Nothing in this Agreement shall affect or impair:

(a) the inherent right of individual or collective self-defense as envisaged by Article 51 of the Charter of the United Nations,*
(b) the provisions of the Charter of the United Nations, including those relating to the maintenance or restoration of international peace and security, and
(c) the obligations undertaken by either Party towards its allies or other countries in treaties, agreements, and other appropriate documents.

Article VII

This Agreement shall be of unlimited duration.

Article VIII

This Agreement shall enter into force upon signature.

DONE at Washington on June 22, 1973, in two copies, each in the English and Russian languages, both texts being equally authentic.

FOR THE UNITED STATES OF AMERICA:

RICHARD NIXON

President of the United States of America

FOR THE UNION OF SOVIET SOCIALIST REPUBLICS:

L. I. BREZHNEV

General Secretary of the Central Committee, CPSU

---

*TS 993; 59 Stat. 1044.

Protocol to the Treaty Between the United States of America and the Union of Soviet Socialist Republics on the Limitation of Anti-Ballistic Missile Systems

At the 1974 Summit meeting, the United States and the Soviet Union signed a protocol that further restrained deployment of strategic defensive armaments. The 1972 ABM Treaty had permitted each side two ABM deployment areas, one to defend its national capital and another to defend an ICBM field. The 1974 ABM Protocol limits each side to one site only.

The Soviet Union had chosen to maintain its ABM defense of Moscow, and the United States chose to maintain defense of its ICBM emplacements near Grand Forks, North Dakota. To allow some flexibility, the protocol allows each side to reverse its original choice of an ABM site. That is, the United States may dismantle or destroy its ABM system at Grand Forks and deploy an ABM defense of Washington. The Soviet Union, similarly, can decide to shift to an ABM defense of a missile field rather than of Moscow. Each side can make such a change only once. Advance notice must be given, and this may be done only during a year in which a review of the ABM Treaty is scheduled. The treaty prescribes reviews every 5 years; the first year for such a review began October 3, 1977.

Upon entry into force, the protocol became an integral part of the 1972 ABM Treaty, of which the verification and other provisions continue to apply. Thus the deployments permitted are governed by the treaty limitations on numbers and characteristics of interceptor missiles, launchers, and supporting radars. The system the United States chose to deploy (Grand Forks) has actually been on an inactive status since 1976.

Protocol to the Treaty Between the United States of America and the Union of Soviet Socialist Republics on the Limitation of Anti-Ballistic Missile Systems

Signed at Moscow July 3, 1974
Ratification advised by U.S. Senate November 10, 1975
Ratified by U.S. President March 19, 1976
Instruments of ratification exchanged May 24, 1976
Proclaimed by U.S. President July 6, 1976
Entered into force May 24, 1976

The United States of America and the Union of Soviet Socialist Republics, hereinafter referred to as the Parties,

Proceeding from the Basic Principles of Relations between the United States of America and the Union of Soviet Socialist Republics signed on May 29, 1972,

Desiring to further the objectives of the Treaty between the United States of America and the Union of Soviet Socialist Republics on the Limitation of Anti-Ballistic Missile Systems signed on May 26, 1972, hereinafter referred to as the Treaty,

Reaffirming their conviction that the adoption of further measures for the limitation of strategic arms would contribute to strengthening international peace and security,

Proceeding from the premise that further limitation of anti-ballistic missile systems will create more favorable conditions for the completion of work on a permanent agreement on more complete measures for the limitation of strategic offensive arms,

Have agreed as follows:

Article I

1. Each Party shall be limited at any one time to a single area out of the two provided in Article III of the Treaty for deployment of anti-ballistic missile (ABM) systems or their components and accordingly shall not exercise its right to deploy an ABM system or its components in the second of the two ABM system deployment areas permitted by Article III of the Treaty, except as an exchange of one permitted area for the other in accordance with Article II of this Protocol.

2. Accordingly, except as permitted by Article II of this Protocol: the United States of America shall not deploy an ABM system or its components in the area centered on its capital, as permitted by Article III(a) of the Treaty, and the Soviet Union shall not deploy an ABM system or its components in the deployment area of intercontinental ballistic missile (ICBM) silo launchers as permitted by Article III(b) of the Treaty.

Article II

1. Each Party shall have the right to dismantle or destroy its ABM system and the components thereof in the area where they are presently deployed and to deploy an ABM system or its components in the alternative area permitted by Article III of the Treaty, provided that prior to initiation of construction, notification is given in accord

162

with the procedure agreed to in the Standing Consultative Commission, during the year beginning October 3, 1977 and ending October 2, 1978, or during any year which commences at five year intervals thereafter, those being the years for periodic review of the Treaty, as provided in Article XIV of the Treaty. This right may be exercised only once.

2. Accordingly, in the event of such notice, the United States would have the right to dismantle or destroy the ABM system and its components in the deployment area of ICBM silo launchers and to deploy an ABM system or its components in an area centered on its capital, as permitted by Article III(a) of the Treaty, and the Soviet Union would have the right to dismantle or destroy the ABM system and its components in the area centered on its capital and to deploy an ABM system or its components in an area containing ICBM silo launchers, as permitted by Article III(b) of the Treaty.

3. Dismantling or destruction and deployment of ABM systems or their components and the notification thereof shall be carried out in accordance with Article VIII of the ABM Treaty and procedures agreed to in the Standing Consultative Commission.

Article III

The rights and obligations established by the Treaty remain in force and shall be complied with by the Parties except to the extent modified by this Protocol. In particular, the deployment of an ABM system or its components within the area selected shall remain limited by the levels and other requirements established by the Treaty.

Article IV

This Protocol shall be subject to ratification in accordance with the constitutional procedures of each Party. It shall enter into force on the day of the exchange of instruments of ratification and shall thereafter be considered an integral part of the Treaty.

DONE at Moscow on July 3, 1974, in duplicate, in the English and Russian languages, both texts being equally authentic.

For the United States of America:

RICHARD NIXON

President of the United States of America

For the Union of Soviet Socialist Republics:

L. I. BREZHNEV

General Secretary of the Central Committee of the CPSU

Treaty Between the United States of America and the Union of Soviet Socialist Republics on the Limitation of Underground Nuclear Weapon Tests (and Protocol Thereto)

The Treaty on the Limitation of Underground Nuclear Weapon Tests, also known as the Threshold Test Ban Treaty (TTBT), was signed in July 1974. It establishes a nuclear "threshold," by prohibiting tests having a yield exceeding 150 kilotons (equivalent to 150,000 tons of TNT).

The threshold is militarily important since it removes the possibility of testing new or existing nuclear weapons going beyond the fractional-megaton range. In the past decade, many tests above 150 kilotons have been conducted by both countries. The mutual restraint undertaken will significantly reduce the explosive force of new nuclear warheads and bombs which could otherwise be tested for weapon systems. Of particular significance is the relationship between explosive power of reliable, tested warheads and first-strike capability.

The task of negotiating a comprehensive test ban remains on the agenda of the U.S. Government, and, in Article I, the parties to the Threshold Test Ban Treaty undertook an obligation to continue negotiations toward that goal.

The first proposal for stopping nuclear weapon tests was made in 1955, and the first major negotiations with the Soviet Union for an effectively controlled test ban began in Geneva in 1958, with the United Kingdom also participating. The Conference on the Discontinuance of Nuclear Weapon Tests produced no agreement. The problem of working out verification procedures to insure compliance with a complete ban on nuclear weapon tests in all environments proved to be intractable at that time. The procedures deemed necessary by the United States and the United Kingdom were not acceptable to the Soviet Union.

In 1963 the Limited Test Ban Treaty (LTBT) was signed by the Soviet Union, the United States, and the United Kingdom. This treaty prohibits nuclear weapon testing in the atmosphere, in outer space and under water. The parties also agreed not to carry out any nuclear weapon test, or any other nuclear explosion, in any other environment—i.e., underground—that would cause radioactive debris to be present beyond the borders of the country in which the explosion took place.

Underground nuclear explosions were not prohibited by the 1963 treaty, although both in the treaty preamble and Article I, the LTBT parties pledged to seek "the discontinuance of all test explosions of nuclear weapons for all time...."

The United States and the Soviet Union agreed in the spring of 1974 to pursue the possibilities of further restrictions on nuclear testing. Accordingly, a team of U.S. experts was sent to Moscow for technical talks.

Agreement on the Threshold Test Ban Treaty was reached during the summit meeting in Moscow in July 1974. The test ban treaty includes a protocol which details technical data to be exchanged and which limits weapon testing to specific designated test sites to assist verification. The data to be exchanged include information on the geographical boundaries and geology of the testing areas. Geological data—including such factors as density of rock formation, water saturation, and depth of the water table—are useful in verifying test yields because the seismic signal produced by a given underground nuclear explosion varies with these factors at the test location. After an actual test has taken place, the geographic coordinates of the test location are to be furnished to the other party, to help in placing the test in the proper geological setting and thus in assessing the yield. Other information available to the United States will be used to cross-check the data provided.

The treaty also stipulates that data will be exchanged on a certain number of tests for calibration purposes. By establishing the correlation between stated yields of explosions at the specified sites and the seismic signals produced, this exchange will help improve assessments by both parties of the yields of explosions based primarily on the measurements derived from their seismic instruments. The tests used for calibration purposes may be tests which have been conducted in the past or may be new tests.

Agreement to exchange the detailed data described above represents a significant degree of direct cooperation by the two major nuclear powers in the effort to control nuclear weapons. For the first time, each party will make available to the other data relating to its nuclear weapons test program.

The technical problems associated with a yield threshold were recognized by the sides in the spring of 1974 during the negotiation of the TTB Treaty. In this context the U.S.S.R. mentioned the idea of some kind of a "mistakes" understanding concerning occasional, minor, unintended breaches. Discussions on the subject of such an understanding took place in the autumn of 1974 and in the spring of 1976. The U.S.S.R. was informed by the United States that the understanding reached would be included as part of the public record associated with submitting the TTB Treaty to the Senate for advice and consent to ratification. The entire understanding is as follows:

Both Parties will make every effort to comply fully with all the provisions of the TTB Treaty. However, there are technical uncertainties associated with predicting the precise yields of nuclear weapon tests. These uncertainties may result in slight, unintended breaches of the 150 kiloton threshold. Therefore, the two sides have discussed this problem and agreed that: (1) One or two slight, unintended breaches per year would not be considered a violation of the Treaty; (2) such breaches would be a cause for concern, however, and, at the request of either Party, would be the subject for consultations.

The U.S.S.R. was also informed that while the United States would not consider such a slight, unintentional breach a violation, the United States would carefully review each such breach to insure that it is not part of a general attempt to exceed the confines of the Treaty.

The understanding in its entirety was included in the transmittal documents which accompanied the TTB Treaty and the PNE Treaty when they were submitted to the Senate for advice and consent to ratification on July 29, 1976.

Although the TTBT was signed in 1974, it was not sent to the U.S. Senate for ratification until July 1976. Submission for ratification was held in abeyance until the companion treaty on underground nuclear explosions for peaceful purposes had been successfully negotiated in accordance with Article III of the TTBT. Both treaties are currently awaiting Senate action.

Treaty Between the United States of America and the Union of Soviet Socialist Republics on the Limitation of Underground Nuclear Weapon Tests

Signed at Moscow July 3, 1974

The United States of America and the Union of Soviet Socialist Republics, hereinafter referred to as the Parties,

Declaring their intention to achieve at the earliest possible date the cessation of the nuclear arms race and to take effective measures toward reductions in strategic arms, nuclear disarmament, and general and complete disarmament under strict and effective international control,

Recalling the determination expressed by the Parties to the 1963 Treaty Banning Nuclear Weapon Tests in the Atmosphere, in Outer Space and Under Water in its Preamble to seek to achieve the discontinuance of all test explosions of nuclear weapons for all time, and to continue negotiations to this end,

Noting that the adoption of measures for the further limitation of underground nuclear weapon tests would contribute to the achievement of these objectives and would meet the interests of strengthening peace and the further relaxation of international tension,

Reaffirming their adherence to the objectives and principles of the Treaty Banning Nuclear Weapon Tests in the Atmosphere, in Outer Space and Under Water and of the Treaty on the Non-Proliferation of Nuclear Weapons,

Have agreed as follows:

Article I

1. Each Party undertakes to prohibit, to prevent, and not to carry out any underground nuclear weapon test having a yield exceeding 150 kilotons at any place under its jurisdiction or control, beginning March 31, 1976.

2. Each Party shall limit the number of its underground nuclear weapon tests to a minimum.

3. The Parties shall continue their negotiations with a view toward achieving a solution to the problem of the cessation of all underground nuclear weapon tests.

Article II

1. For the purpose of providing assurance of compliance with the provisions of this Treaty, each Party shall use national technical means of verification at its disposal in a manner consistent with the generally recognized principles of international law.

2. Each Party undertakes not to interfere with the national technical means of verification of the other Party operating in accordance with paragraph 1 of this Article.

3. To promote the objectives and implementation of the provisions of this Treaty the Parties shall, as necessary, consult with each other, make inquiries and furnish information in response to such inquiries.

Article III

The provisions of this Treaty do not extend to underground nuclear explosions carried out by the Parties for peaceful purposes. Underground nuclear explosions for peaceful purposes shall be governed by an agreement which is to be negotiated and concluded by the Parties at the earliest possible time.

Article IV

This Treaty shall be subject to ratification in accordance with the constitutional procedures of each Party. This Treaty shall enter into force on the day of the exchange of instruments of ratification.

Article V

1. This Treaty shall remain in force for a period of five years. Unless replaced earlier by an agreement in implementation of the objectives specified in paragraph 3 of Article I of this Treaty, it shall be extended for successive five-year periods unless either Party notifies the other of its termination no later than six months prior to the expiration of the Treaty. Before the expiration of this period the Parties may, as necessary, hold consultations to consider the situation relevant to the substance of this Treaty and to introduce possible amendments to the text of the Treaty.

2. Each Party shall, in exercising its national sovereignty, have the right to withdraw from this Treaty if it decides that extraordinary events related to the subject matter of this Treaty have jeopardized its supreme interests. It shall give notice of its decision to the other Party six months prior to withdrawal from this Treaty. Such notice shall include a statement of the extraordinary events the notifying Party regards as having jeopardized its supreme interests.

3. This Treaty shall be registered pursuant to Article 102 of the Charter of the United Nations.

DONE at Moscow on July 3, 1974, in duplicate, in the English and Russian languages, both texts being equally authentic.

For the United States of America:

RICHARD NIXON,

The President of the United States of America

For the Union of Soviet Socialist Republics:

L. BREZHNEV,

General Secretary of the Central Committee of the CPSU.

Protocol to the Treaty Between the United States of America and the Union of Soviet Socialist Republics on the Limitation of Underground Nuclear Weapon Tests

The United States of America and the Union of Soviet Socialist Republics, hereinafter referred to as the Parties,
Having agreed to limit underground nuclear weapon tests,

Have agreed as follows:

1. For the Purpose of ensuring verification of compliance with the obligations of the Parties under the Treaty by national technical means, the Parties shall, on the basis of reciprocity, exchange the following data:

    a. The geographic coordinates of the boundaries of each test site and of the boundaries of the geophysically distinct testing areas therein.

    b. Information on the geology of the testing areas of the sites (the rock characteristics of geological formations and the basic physical properties of the rock, i.e., density, seismic velocity, water saturation, porosity and the depth of water table).

    c. The geographic coordinates of underground nuclear weapon tests, after they have been conducted.

    d. Yield, date, time, depth and coordinates for two nuclear weapon tests for calibration purposes from each geophysically distinct testing area where underground nuclear weapon tests have been and are to be conducted. In this connection the yield of such explosions for calibration purposes should be as near as possible to the limit defined in Article I of the Treaty and not less than one-tenth of that limit. In the case of testing areas where data are not available on two tests for calibration purposes, the data pertaining to one such test shall be exchanged, if available, and the data pertaining to the second test shall be exchanged as soon as possible after the second test having a yield in the above-mentioned range. The provisions of this Protocol shall not require the Parties to conduct tests solely for calibration purposes.

2. The Parties agree that the exchange of data pursuant to subparagraphs a, b, and d of paragraph 1 shall be carried out simultaneously with the exchange of instruments of ratification of the Treaty, as provided in Article IV of the Treaty, having in mind that the Parties shall, on the basis of reciprocity, afford each other the opportunity to familiarize themselves with these data before the exchange of instruments of ratification.

3. Should a Party specify a new test site or testing area after the entry into force of the Treaty, the data called for by subparagraphs a and b of paragraph 1 shall be transmitted to the other Party in advance of use of that site or area. The data called for by subparagraph d of paragraph 1 shall also be transmitted in advance of use of that site or area if they are available; if they are not available, they shall be transmitted as soon as possible after they have been obtained by the transmitting Party.

4. The Parties agree that the test sites of each Party shall be located at places under its jurisdiction or control and that all nuclear weapon tests shall be conducted solely within the testing areas specified in accordance with paragraph 1.

5. For the purposes of the Treaty, all underground nuclear explosions at the specified test sites shall be considered nuclear weapon tests and shall be subject to all the provisions of the Treaty relating to nuclear weapon tests. The provisions of Article III of the Treaty apply to all underground nuclear explosions conducted outside of the specified test sites, and only to such explosions.

This Protocol shall be considered an integral part of the Treaty.

DONE at Moscow on July 3, 1974.

For the United States of America:

RICHARD M. NIXON,

The President of the United States of America

For the Union of Soviet Socialist Republics:

L. BREZHNEV,

General Secretary of the Central Committee of the CPSU.

Treaty Between the United States of America and the Union of Soviet Socialist Republics on Underground Nuclear Explosions for Peaceful Purposes (and Protocol Thereto)

In preparing the Threshold Test Ban Treaty (TTBT) in July 1974, the United States and the Soviet Union recognized the need to establish an appropriate agreement to govern underground nuclear explosions for peaceful purposes (PNEs). There is no essential distinction between the technology of a nuclear explosive device which would be used as a weapon and the technology of a nuclear explosive device used for a peaceful purpose.

Negotiations on the PNE agreement contemplated in Article III of the TTBT began in Moscow on October 7, 1974, and after six negotiating sessions over a period of 18 months, resulted in the Treaty on Underground Nuclear Explosions for Peaceful Purposes in April 1976. The agreement consists of a treaty, a detailed protocol to the treaty, and an agreed statement delineating certain important activities which do not constitute a peaceful application as that term is used in the treaty.

The PNE Treaty will govern all nuclear explosions carried out at locations outside the weapons test sites specified under the Threshold Test Ban Treaty.

The two nations agreed: not to carry out any individual nuclear explosions having a yield exceeding 150 kilotons; not to carry out any group explosion (consisting of a number of individual explosions) having an aggregate yield exceeding 1,500 kilotons; and not to carry out any group explosion having an aggregate yield exceeding 150 kilotons unless the individual explosions in the group could be identified and measured by agreed verification procedures. The parties also reaffirmed their obligations to comply fully with the Limited Test Ban Treaty of 1963.

The parties reserve the right to carry out nuclear explosions for peaceful purposes in the territory of another country if requested to do so, but only in full compliance with the yield limitations and other provisions of the PNE Treaty and in accord with the Non-Proliferation Treaty.

Articles IV and V of the PNE Treaty set forth the agreed verification arrangements. In addition to the use of national technical means, the treaty states that information and access to sites of explosions will be provided by each side, and includes a commitment not to interfere with verification means and procedures.

The protocol to the PNE Treaty sets forth the specific agreed arrangements for assuring that no weapon-related benefits precluded by the Threshold Test Ban Treaty are derived by carrying out a nuclear explosion for peaceful purposes, including provisions for both detailed information and the rights and functions of observers.

The central problem to be solved through observation procedures is that of ensuring that no single nuclear device will be exploded with a yield exceeding 150 kilotons. Special procedures are required when the aggregate yield of a group explosion is larger than 150 kilotons. It is necessary for observers, using appropriate equipment, at the site of a group explosion to determine the yield of each of the individual explosive devices making up the group explosion.

The protocol spells out the procedures to be followed during the observation process, including such specifics as the number of observers, the geographical extent of their access, and the provision of certain information, such as maps of the area of the explosion, to assist in the planning of their activities.

In addition, the protocol provides for certain necessary privileges and immunities to be granted to observer personnel and their equipment, and for housing and working facilities to assure their freedom to carry out their rights and functions effectively.

The agreed statement that accompanies the treaty specifies that a "peaceful application" of an underground nuclear explosion would not include the developmental testing of any nuclear explosive. Such testing must be carried out at the nuclear weapon test sites specified by the terms of the TTBT, and therefore, is treated as the testing of a nuclear weapon.

The provisions of the PNE Treaty, together with those of the TTBT, establish a comprehensive system of regulations which will govern all underground nuclear explosions of the United States and the Soviet Union. The interrelationship of the TTBT and the PNE Treaty is further recognized by their identical 5-year durations, and by the provision that neither party may withdraw from the PNE Treaty while the TTBT remains in force. Conversely, either party may withdraw from the PNE Treaty upon termination of the TTBT.

A Joint Consultative Commission will be established to discuss any questions of compliance, to develop further details of the on-site inspection process as needed, and to facilitate cooperation in various areas related to PNEs which might be mutually beneficial.

Both treaties were submitted to the Senate on July 29, 1976, for advice and consent to ratification.

Treaty Between the United States of America and the Union of Soviet Socialist Republics on Underground Nuclear Explosions for Peaceful Purposes

Signed at Washington and Moscow May 28, 1976

The United States of America and the Union of Soviet Socialist Republics, hereinafter referred to as the Parties,

Proceeding from a desire to implement Article III of the Treaty between the United States of America and the Union of Soviet Socialist Republics on the Limitation of Underground Nuclear Weapon Tests, which calls for the earliest possible conclusion of an agreement on underground nuclear explosions for peaceful purposes,

Reaffirming their adherence to the objectives and principles of the Treaty Banning Nuclear Weapon Tests in the Atmosphere, in Outer Space and Under Water, the Treaty on Non-Proliferation of Nuclear Weapons, and the Treaty on the Limitation of Underground Nuclear Weapon Tests, and their determination to observe strictly the provisions of these international agreements,

Desiring to assure that underground nuclear explosions for peaceful purposes shall not be used for purposes related to nuclear weapons,

Desiring that utilization of nuclear energy be directed only toward peaceful purposes,

Desiring to develop appropriately cooperation in the field of underground nuclear explosions for peaceful purposes,

Have agreed as follows:

Article I

1. The Parties enter into this Treaty to satisfy the obligations in Article III of the Treaty on the Limitation of Underground Nuclear Weapon Tests, and assume additional obligations in accordance with the provisions of this Treaty.

2. This Treaty shall govern all underground nuclear explosions for peaceful purposes conducted by the Parties after March 31, 1976.

Article II

For the purposes of this Treaty:

(a) "explosion" means any individual or group underground nuclear explosion for peaceful purposes;

(b) "explosive" means any device, mechanism or system for producing an individual explosion;

(c) "group explosion" means two or more individual explosions for which the time interval between successive individual explosions does not exceed five seconds and for which the emplacement points of all explosives can be interconnected by straight line segments, each of which joins two emplacement points and each of which does not exceed 40 kilometers.

Article III

1. Each Party, subject to the obligations assumed under this Treaty and other international agreements, reserves the right to:

(a) carry out explosions at any place under its jurisdiction or control outside the geographical boundaries of test sites specified under the provisions of the Treaty on the Limitation of Underground Nuclear Weapon Tests; and

(b) carry out, participate or assist in carrying out explosions in the territory of another State at the request of such other State.

2. Each Party undertakes to prohibit, to prevent and not to carry out at any place under its jurisdiction or control, and further undertakes not to carry out, participate or assist in carrying out anywhere:

(a) any individual explosion having a yield exceeding 150 kilotons;

(b) any group explosion:

(1) having an aggregate yield exceeding 150 kilotons except in ways that will permit identification of each individual explosion and determination of the yield of each individual explosion in the group in accordance with the provisions of Article IV of and the Protocol to this Treaty;

(2) having an aggregate yield exceeding one and one-half megatons;

(c) any explosion which does not carry out a peaceful application;

(d) any explosion except in compliance with the provisions of the Treaty Banning Nuclear Weapon Tests in the Atmosphere, in Outer Space and Under Water, the Treaty on the Non-Proliferation of Nuclear Weapons, and other international agreements entered into by that Party.

3. The question of carrying out any individual explosion having a yield exceeding the yield specified in paragraph 2(a) of this article will be considered by the Parties at an appropriate time to be agreed.

Article IV

1. For the purpose of providing assurance of compliance with the provisions of this Treaty, each Party shall:

(a) use national technical means of verification at its disposal in a manner consistent with generally recognized principles of international law; and

(b) provide to the other Party information and access to sites of explosions and furnish assistance in accordance with the provisions set forth in the Protocol to this Treaty.

2. Each Party undertakes not to interfere with the national technical means of verification of the other Party operating in accordance with paragraph 1(a) of this article, or with the implementation of the provisions of paragraph 1(b) of this article.

Article V

1. To promote the objectives and implementation of the provisions of this Treaty, the Parties shall establish promptly a Joint Consultative Commission within the framework of which they will:

(a) consult with each other, make inquiries and furnish information in response to such inquiries, to assure confidence in compliance with the obligations assumed;

(b) consider questions concerning compliance with the obligations assumed and related situations which may be considered ambiguous;

(c) consider questions involving unintended interference with the means for assuring compliance with the provisions of this Treaty;

(d) consider changes in technology or other new circumstances which have a bearing on the provisions of this Treaty; and

(e) consider possible amendments to provisions governing underground nuclear explosions for peaceful purposes.

2. The Parties through consultation shall establish, and may amend as appropriate, Regulations for the Joint Consultative Commission governing procedures, composition and other relevant matters.

Article VI

1. The Parties will develop cooperation on the basis of mutual benefit, equality, and reciprocity in various areas related to carrying out underground nuclear explosions for peaceful purposes.

2. The Joint Consultative Commission will facilitate this cooperation by considering specific areas and forms of cooperation which shall be determined by agreement between the Parties in accordance with their constitutional procedures.

3. The Parties will appropriately inform the International Atomic Energy Agency of results of their cooperation in the field of underground nuclear explosions for peaceful purposes.

Article VII

1. Each Party shall continue to promote the development of the international agreement or agreements and procedures provided for in Article V of the Treaty on the Non-Proliferation of Nuclear Weapons, and shall provide appropriate assistance to the International Atomic Energy Agency in this regard.

2. Each Party undertakes not to carry out, participate or assist in the carrying out of any explosion in the territory of another State unless that State agrees to the implementation in its territory of the international observation and procedures contemplated by Article V of the Treaty on the Non-Proliferation of Nuclear Weapons and the provisions of Article IV of and the Protocol to this Treaty, including the provision by that State of the assistance necessary for such implementation and of the privileges and immunities specified in the Protocol.

Article VIII

1. This Treaty shall remain in force for a period of five years, and it shall be extended for successive five-year periods unless either Party notifies the other of its termination no later than six months prior to its expiration. Before the expiration of this period the Parties may, as necessary, hold consultations to consider the situation relevant to the substance of this Treaty. However, under no circumstances shall either Party be entitled to terminate this Treaty while the Treaty on the Limitation of Underground Nuclear Weapon Tests remains in force.

2. Termination of the Treaty on the Limitation of Underground Nuclear Weapon Tests shall entitle either Party to withdraw from this Treaty at any time.

3. Each Party may propose amendments to this Treaty. Amendments shall enter into force on the day of the exchange of instruments of ratification of such amendments.

Article IX

1. This Treaty including the Protocol which forms an integral part hereof, shall be subject to ratification in accordance with the constitutional procedures of each Party. This Treaty shall enter into force on the day of the exchange of instruments of ratification which exchange shall take place simultaneously with the exchange of instruments of ratification of the Treaty on the Limitation of Underground Nuclear Weapon Tests.

2. This Treaty shall be registered pursuant to Article 102 of the Charter of the United Nations.

DONE at Washington and Moscow, on May 28, 1976, in duplicate, in the English and Russian languages, both texts being equally authentic.

For the United States of America:

GERALD R. FORD,

The President of the United States of America.

For the Union of Soviet Socialist Republics:

L. BREZHNEV,

General Secretary of the Central Committee of the CPSU.

Protocol to the Treaty Between the United States of America and the Union of Soviet Socialist Republics on Underground Nuclear Explosions for Peaceful Purposes

The United States of America and the Union of Soviet Socialist Republics, hereinafter referred to as the Parties,

Having agreed to the provisions in the Treaty on Underground Nuclear Explosions for Peaceful Purposes, hereinafter referred to as the Treaty,

Have agreed as follows:

Article I

1. No individual explosion shall take place at a distance, in meters, from the ground surface which is less than 30 times the 3.4 root of its planned yield in kilotons.

2. Any group explosion with a planned aggregate yield exceeding 500 kilotons shall not include more than five individual explosions, each of which has a planned yield not exceeding 50 kilotons.

Article II

1. For each explosion, the Party carrying out the explosion shall provide the other Party:

(a) not later than 90 days before the beginning of emplacement of the explosives when the planned aggregate yield of the explosion does not exceed 100 kilotons, or not later than 180 days before the beginning of emplacement of the explosives when the planned aggregate yield of the explosion exceeds 100 kilotons, with the following information to the extent and degree of precision available when it is conveyed:

(1) the purpose of the planned explosion;

(2) the location of the explosion expressed in geographical coordinates with a precision of four or less kilometers, planned date and aggregate yield of the explosion;

(3) the type or types of rock in which the explosion will be carried out, including the degree of liquid saturation of the rock at the point of emplacement of each explosive; and

(4) a description of specific technological features of the project, of which the explosion is a part, that could influence the determination of its yield and confirmation of purpose; and

(b) not later than 60 days before the beginning of emplacement of the explosives the information specified in subparagraph 1(a) of this article to the full extent and with the precision indicated in that subparagraph.

2. For each explosion with a planned aggregate yield exceeding 50 kilotons, the Party carrying out the explosion shall provide the other Party, not later than 60 days before the beginning of emplacement of the explosives, with the following information:

(a) the number of explosives, the planned yield of each explosive, the location of each explosive to be used in a group explosion relative to all other explosives in the group with a precision of 100 or less meters, the depth of emplacement of each explosive with a precision of one meter and the time intervals between individual explosions in any group explosion with a precision of one-tenth second; and

(b) a description of specific features of geological structure or other local conditions that could influence the determination of the yield.

3. For each explosion with a planned aggregate yield exceeding 75 kilotons, the Party carrying out the explosion shall provide the other Party, not later than 60 days before the beginning of emplacement of the explosives, with a description of the geological and geophysical characteristics of the site of each explosion which could influence determination of the yield, which shall include: the depth of the water table; a stratigraphic column above each emplacement point; the position of each emplacement point relative to nearby geological and other features which influenced the design of the project of which the explosion is a part; and the physical parameters of the rock, including density, seismic velocity, porosity, degree of liquid saturation, and rock strength, within the sphere centered on each emplacement point and having a radius, in meters, equal to 30 times the cube root of the planned yield in kilotons of the explosive emplaced at that point.

4. For each explosion with a planned aggregate yield exceeding 100 kilotons, the Party carrying out the explosion shall provide the other Party, not later than 60 days before the beginning of emplacement of the explosives, with:

(a) information on locations and purposes of facilities and installations which are associated with the conduct of the explosion;

(b) information regarding the planned date of the beginning of emplacement of each explosive; and

(c) a topographic plan in local coordinates of the areas specified in paragraph 7 of Article IV, at a scale of 1 : 24,000 or 1 : 25,000 with a contour interval of 10 meters or less.

5. For application of an explosion to alleviate the consequences of an emergency situation involving an unforeseen combination of circumstances which calls for immediate action for which it would not be practicable to observe the timing requirements of paragraphs 1, 2 and 3 of this article, the following conditions shall be met:

(a) the Party deciding to carry out an explosion for such purposes shall inform the other Party of that decision immediately after it has been made and describe such circumstances;

(b) the planned aggregate yield of an explosion for such purpose shall not exceed 100 kilotons; and

(c) the Party carrying out an explosion for such purpose shall provide to the other Party the information specified in paragraph 1 of this article, and the information specified in paragraphs 2 and 3 of this article if applicable, after the decision to conduct the explosion is taken, but not later than 30 days before the beginning of emplacement of the explosives.

6. For each explosion, the Party carrying out the explosion shall inform the other Party, not later than two days before the explosion, of the planned time of detonation of each explosive with a precision of one second.

7. Prior to the explosion, the Party carrying out the explosion shall provide the other Party with timely notification of changes in the information provided in accordance with this article.

8. The explosion shall not be carried out earlier than 90 days after notification of any change in the information provided in accordance with this article which requires more extensive verification procedures than those required on the basis of the original information, unless an earlier time for carrying out the explosion is agreed between the Parties.

9. Not later than 90 days after each explosion the Party carrying out the explosion shall provide the other Party with the following information:

(a) the actual time of the explosion with a precision of one-tenth second and its aggregate yield;

(b) when the planned aggregate yield of a group explosion exceeds 50 kilotons, the actual time of the first individual explosion with a precision of one-tenth second, the time interval between individual explosions with a precision of one milli-second and the yield of each individual explosion; and

(c) confirmation of other information provided in accordance with paragraphs 1, 2, 3 and 4 of this article and explanation of any changes or corrections based on the results of the explosion.

10. At any time, but not later than one year after the explosion, the other Party may request the Party carrying out the explosion to clarify any item of the information provided in accordance with this article. Such clarification shall be provided as soon as practicable, but not later than 30 days after the request is made.

Article III

1. For the purposes of this Protocol:

(a) "designated personnel" means those nationals of the other Party identified to the Party carrying out an explosion as the persons who will exercise the rights and functions provided for in the Treaty and this Protocol; and

(b) "emplacement hole" means the entire interior of any drill-hole, shaft, adit or tunnel in which an explosive and associated cables and other equipment are to be installed.

2. For any explosion with a planned aggregate yield exceeding 100 kilotons but not exceeding 150 kilotons if the Parties, in consultation based on information provided in accordance with Article II and other information that may be introduced by either Party, deem it appropriate for the confirmation of the yield of the explosion, and for any explosion with a planned aggregate yield exceeding 150 kilotons, the Party carrying out the explosion shall allow designated personnel within the areas and at the locations described in Article V to exercise the following rights and functions:

(a) confirmation that the local circumstances, including facilities and installations associated with the project, are consistent with the stated peaceful purposes;

(b) confirmation of the validity of the geological and geophysical information provided in accordance with Article II through the following procedures:

(1) examination by designated personnel of research and measurement data of the Party carrying out the explosion and of rock core or rock fragments removed from each emplacement hole, and of any logs and drill core from existing exploratory holes which shall be provided to designated personnel upon their arrival at the site of the explosion;

(2) examination by designated personnel of rock core or rock fragments as they become available in accordance with the procedures specified in subparagraph 2(b)(3) of this article; and

(3) observation by designated personnel of implementation by the Party carrying out the explosion of one of the following four procedures, unless this right is waived by the other Party:

(i) construction of that portion of each emplacement hole starting from a point nearest the entrance of the emplacement hole which is at a distance, in meters, from the nearest emplacement point equal to 30 times the cube root of the planned yield in kilotons of the explosive to be emplaced at that point and continuing to the completion of the emplacement hole; or

(ii) construction of that portion of each emplacement hole starting from a point nearest the entrance of the emplacement hole which is at a distance, in meters, from the nearest emplacement point equal to six times the cube root of the planned yield in kilotons of the explosive to be emplaced at that point and continuing to the completion of the emplacement hole as well as the removal of rock core or rock fragments from the wall of an existing exploratory hole, which is substantially parallel with and at no point more than 100 meters from the emplacement hole, at locations specified by designated personnel which lie within a distance, in meters, from the same horizon as each emplacement point of 30 times the cube root of the planned yield in kilotons of the explosive to be emplaced at that point; or

(iii) removal of rock core or rock fragments from the wall of each emplacement hole at locations specified by designated personnel which lie within a distance, in meters, from each emplacement point of 30 times the cube root of the planned yield in kilotons of the explosive to be emplaced at each such point; or

(iv) construction of one or more new exploratory holes so that for each emplacement hole there will be a new exploratory hole to the same depth as that of the emplacement of the explosive, substantially parallel with and at no point more than 100 meters from each emplacement hole, from which rock cores would be removed at locations specified by designated personnel which lie within a distance, in meters, from the same horizon as each emplacement point of 30 times the cube root of the planned yield in kilotons of the explosive to be emplaced at each such point:

(c) observation of the emplacement of each explosive, confirmation of the depth of its emplacement and observation of the stemming of each emplacement hole;

(d) unobstructed visual observation of the area of the entrance to each emplacement hole at any time from the time of emplacement of each explosive until all personnel have been withdrawn from the site for the detonation of the explosion; and

(e) observation of each explosion.

3. Designated personnel, using equipment provided in accordance with paragraph 1 of Article IV, shall have the right, for any explosion with a planned aggregate yield exceeding 150 kilotons, to determine the yield of each individual explosion in a group explosion in accordance with the provisions of Article VI.

4. Designated personnel, when using their equipment in accordance with paragraph 1 of Article IV, shall have the right, for any explosion with planned aggregate yield exceeding 500 kilotons, to emplace, install and operate under the observation and with the assistance of personnel of the Party carrying out the explosion, if such assistance is requested by designated personnel, a local seismic network in accordance with the provisions of paragraph 7 of Article IV. Radio links may be used for the transmission of data and control signals between the seismic stations and the control center. Frequencies, maximum power output of radio transmitters, directivity of antennas and times of operation of the local seismic network radio transmitters before the explosion shall be agreed between the Parties in accordance with Article X and time of operation after the explosion shall conform to the time specified in paragraph 7 of Article IV.

5. Designated personnel shall have the right to:

(a) acquire photographs under the following conditions:

(1) the Party carrying out the explosion shall identify to the other Party those personnel of the Party carrying out the explosion who shall take photographs as requested by designated personnel;

(2) photographs shall be taken by personnel of the Party carrying out the explosion in the presence of designated personnel and at the time requested by designated personnel for taking such photographs. Designated personnel shall determine whether these photographs are in conformity with their requests and, if not, additional photographs shall be taken immediately;

(3) photographs shall be taken with cameras provided by the other Party having built-in, rapid developing capability and a copy of each photograph shall be provided at the completion of the development process to both Parties;

(4) cameras provided by designated personnel shall be kept in agreed secure storage when not in use; and

(5) the request for photographs can be made, at any time, of the following:

(i) exterior views of facilities and installations associated with the conduct of the explosion as described in subparagraph 4(a) of Article II;

(ii) geological samples used for confirmation of geological and geo-physical information, as provided for in subparagraph 2(b) of this article and the equipment utilized in the acquisition of such samples;

(iii) emplacement and installation of equipment and associated cables used by designated personnel for yield determination;

(iv) emplacement and installation of the local seismic network used by designated personnel;

(v) emplacement of the explosives and the stemming of the emplacement hole; and

(vi) containers, facilities and installations for storage and operation of equipment used by designated personnel;

(b) photographs of visual displays and records produced by the equipment used by designated personnel and photographs within the control centers taken by cameras which are component parts of such equipment; and

(c) receive at the request of designated personnel and with the agreement of the Party carrying out the explosion supplementary photographs taken by the Party carrying out the explosion.

Article IV

1. Designated personnel in exercising their rights and functions may choose to use the following equipment of either Party, of which choice the Party carrying out the explosion shall be informed not later than 150 days before the beginning of emplace-ment of the explosives:

(a) electrical equipment for yield determination and equipment for a local seismic network as described in paragraphs 3, 4 and 7 of this article; and

(b) geologist's field tools and kits and equipment for recording of field notes.

2. Designated personnel shall have the right in exercising their rights and functions to utilize the following additional equipment which shall be provided by the Party carrying out the explosion, under procedures to be established in accordance with Article X to ensure that the equipment meets the specifications of the other Party: portable short-range communication equipment, field glasses, optical equipment for

surveying and other items which may be specified by the other Party. A description of such equipment and operating instructions shall be provided to the other Party not later than 90 days before the beginning of emplacement of the explosives in connection with which such equipment is to be used.

3. A complete set of electrical equipment for yield determination shall consist of:

(a) sensing elements and associated cables for transmission of electrical power, control signals and data;

(b) equipment of the control center, electrical power supplies and cables for transmission of electrical power, control signals and data; and

(c) measuring and calibration instruments, maintenance equipment and spare parts necessary for ensuring the functioning of sensing elements, cables and equipment of the control center.

4. A complete set of equipment for the local seismic network shall consist of:

(a) seismic stations each of which contains a seismic instrument, electrical power supply and associated cables and radio equipment for receiving and transmission of control signals and data or equipment for recording control signals and data;

(b) equipment of the control center and electrical power supplies; and

(c) measuring and calibration instruments, maintenance equipment and spare parts necessary for ensuring the functioning of the complete network.

5. In case designated personnel, in accordance with paragraph 1 of this article, choose to use equipment of the Party carrying out the explosion for yield determination or for a local seismic network, a description of such equipment and installation and operating instructions shall be provided to the other Party not later than 90 days before the beginning of emplacement of the explosives in connection with which such equipment is to be used. Personnel of the Party carrying out the explosion shall emplace, install and operate the equipment in the presence of designated personnel. After the explosion, designated personnel shall receive duplicate copies of the recorded data. Equipment for yield determination shall be emplaced in accordance with Article VI. Equipment for a local seismic network shall be emplaced in accordance with paragraph 7 of this article.

6. In case designated personnel, in accordance with paragraph 1 of this article, choose to use their own equipment for yield determination and their own equipment for a local seismic network, the following procedures shall apply:

(a) the Party carrying out the explosion shall be provided by the other Party with the equipment and information specified in subparagraphs (a)(1) and (a)(2) of this paragraph not later than 150 days prior to the beginning of emplacement of the explosives in connection with which such equipment is to be used in order to permit the Party carrying out the explosion to familiarize itself with such equipment, if such equipment and information has not been previously provided, which equipment shall be returned to the other Party not later than 90 days before the beginning of emplacement of the explosives. The equipment and information to be provided are:

(1) one complete set of electrical equipment for yield determination as described in paragraph 3 of this aritcle, electrical and mechanical design information, specifications and installation and operating instructions concerning this equipment; and

(2) one complete set of equipment for the local seismic network described in paragraph 4 of this article, including one seismic station, electrical and mechanical design information, specifications and installation and operating instructions concerning this equipment;

(b) not later than 35 days prior to the beginning of emplacement of the explosives in connection with which the following equipment is to be used, two complete sets of electrical equipment for yield determination as described in paragraph 3 of this article and specific installation instructions for the emplacement of the sensing elements based on information provided in accordance with subparagraph 2(a) of Article VI and two complete sets of equipment for the local seismic network as described in paragraph 4 of this article, which sets of equipment shall have the same components and technical characteristics as the corresponding equipment specified in subparagraph 6(a) of this article, shall be delivered in sealed containers to the port of entry;

(c) The Party carrying out the explosion shall choose one of each of the two sets of equipment described above which shall be used by designated personnel in connection with the explosions;

(d) the set or sets of equipment not chosen for use in connection with the explosion shall be at the disposal of the Party carrying out the explosion for a period that may be as long as 30 days after the explosion at which time such equipment shall be returned to the other Party;

(e) the set or sets of equipment chosen for use shall be transported by the Party carrying out the explosion in the sealed containers in which this equipment arrived, after seals of the Party carrying out the explosion have been affixed to them, to the site of the explosion, so that this equipment is delivered to designated personnel for emplacement, installation and operation not later than 20 days before the beginning of emplacement of the explosives. This equipment shall remain in the custody of designated personnel in accordance with paragraph 7 of Article V or in agreed secure storage. Personnel of the Party carrying out the explosion shall have the right to observe the use of this equipment by designated personnel during the time the equipment is at the site of the explosion. Before the beginning of emplacement of the explosives, designated personnel shall demonstrate to personnel of the Party carrying out the explosion that this equipment is in working order;

(f) each set of equipment shall include two sets of components for recording data and associated calibration equipment. Both of these sets of components in the equipment chosen for use shall simultaneously record data. After the explosion, and after duplicate copies of all data have been obtained by designated personnel and the Party carrying out the explosion, one of each of the two sets of components for recording data and associated calibration equipment shall be selected, by an agreed process of chance, to be retained by designated personnel. Designated personnel shall pack and seal such components for recording data and associated calibration equipment which shall accompany them from the site of the explosion to the port of exit; and

(g) all remaining equipment may be retained by the Party carrying out the explosion for a period that may be as long as 30 days, after which time this equipment shall be returned to the other Party.

7. For any explosion with a planned aggregate yield exceeding 500 kilotons, a local seismic network, the number of stations of which shall be determined by designated personnel but shall not exceed the number of explosives in the group plus five, shall be emplaced, installed and operated at agreed sites of emplacement within an area circumscribed by circles of 15 kilometers in radius centered on points on the surface of the earth above the points of emplacement of the explosives during a period beginning not later than 20 days before the beginning of emplacement of the explosives and continuing after the explosion not later than three days unless otherwise agreed between the Parties.

8. The Party carrying out the explosion shall have the right to examine in the presence of designated personnel all equipment, instruments and tools of designated personnel specified in subparagraph 1(b) of this article.

9. The Joint Consultative Commission will consider proposals that either Party may put forward for the joint development of standardized equipment for verification purposes.

Article V

1. Except as limited by the provisions of paragraph 5 of this article, designated personnel in the exercise of their rights and functions shall have access along agreed routes:

(a) for an explosion with a planned aggregate yield exceeding 100 kilotons in accordance with paragraph 2 of Article III:

(1) to the locations of facilities and installations associated with the conduct of the explosion provided in accordance with subparagraph 4(a) of Article II; and

(2) to the locations of activities described in paragraph 2 of Article III; and

(b) for any explosion with a planned aggregate yield exceeding 150 kilotons, in addition to the access described in subparagraph 1(a) of this article:

(1) to other locations within the area circumscribed by circles of 10 kilometers in radius centered on points on the surface of the earth above the points of emplacement of the explosives in order to confirm that the local circumstances are consistent with the stated peaceful purposes;

(2) to the locations of the components of the electrical equipment for yield determination to be used for recording data when, by agreement between the Parties, such equipment is located outside the area described in subparagraph 1(b)(1) of this article; and

(3) to the sites of emplacement of the equipment of the local seismic network provided for in paragraph 7 of Article IV.

2. The Party carrying out the explosion shall notify the other Party of the procedure it has chosen from among those specified in subparagraph 2(b)(3) of Article III not later than 30 days before beginning the implementation of such procedure. Designated personnel shall have the right to be present at the site of the explosion to exercise their rights and functions in the areas and at the locations described in paragraph 1 of this article for a period of time beginning two days before the beginning of the implementation of the procedure and continuing for a period of three days after the completion of this procedure.

3. Except as specified in paragraph 5 of this article, designated personnel shall have the right to be present in the areas and at the locations described in paragraph 1 of this article:

(a) for an explosion with a planned aggregate yield exceeding 100 kilotons but not exceeding 150 kilotons, in accordance with paragraph 2 of Article III, at any time beginning five days before the beginning of emplacement of the explosives and continuing after the explosion and after safe access to evacuated areas has been established according to standards determined by the Party carrying out the explosion for a period of two days; and

(b) for any explosion with a planned aggregate yield exceeding 150 kilotons, at any time beginning 20 days before the beginning of emplacement of the explosives and continuing after the explosion and after safe access to evacuated areas has been established according to standards determined by the Party carrying out the explosion for a period of:

(1) five days in the case of an explosion with a planned aggregate yield exceeding 150 kilotons but not exceeding 500 kilotons; or

(2) eight days in the case of an explosion with a planned aggregate yield exceeding 500 kilotons.

4. Designated personnel shall not have the right to be present in those areas from which all personnel have been evacuated in connection with carrying out an explosion, but shall have the right to re-enter those areas at the same time as personnel of the Party carrying out the explosion.

5. Designated personnel shall not have or seek access by physical, visual or technical means to the interior of the canister containing an explosive, to documentary or other information descriptive of the design of an explosive nor to equipment for control and firing of explosives. The Party carrying out the explosion shall not locate documentary or other information descriptive of the design of an explosive in such ways as to impede the designated personnel in the exercise of their rights and functions.

6. The number of designated personnel present at the site of an explosion shall not exceed:

(a) for the exercise of their rights and functions in connection with the confirmation of the geological and geophysical information in accordance with the provisions of subparagraph 2(b) and applicable provisions of paragraph 5 of Article III—the number of emplacement holes plus three;

(b) for the exercise of their rights and functions in connection with confirming that the local circumstances are consistent with the information provided and with the stated peaceful purposes in accordance with the provisions in subparagraphs 2(a), 2(c), 2(d) and 2(e) and applicable provisions of paragraph 5 of Article III—the number of explosives plus two;

(c) for the exercise of their rights and functions in connection with confirming that the local circumstances are consistent with the information provided and with the stated peaceful purposes in accordance with the provisions in subparagraphs 2(a), 2(c), 2(d) and 2(e) and applicable provisions of paragraph 5 of Article III and in connection with the use of electrical equipment for determination of the yield in accordance with paragraph 3 of Article III—the number of explosives plus seven; and

(d) for the exercise of their rights and functions in connection with confirming that the local circumstances are consistent with the information provided and with the stated peaceful purposes in accordance with the provisions in subparagraph 2(a), 2(c), 2(d) and 2(e) and applicable provisions of paragraph 5 of Article III and in connection with the use of electrical equipment for determination of the yield in accordance with paragraph 3 of Article III and with the use of the local seismic network in accordance with paragraph 4 of Article III—the number of explosives plus 10.

7. The Party carrying out the explosion shall have the right to assign its personnel to accompany designated personnel while the latter exercise their rights and functions.

8. The Party carrying out an explosion shall assure for designated personnel telecommunications with their authorities, transportation and other services appropriate to their presence and to the exercise of their rights and functions at the site of the explosion.

9. The expenses incurred for the transportation of designated personnel and their equipment to and from the site of the explosion, telecommunications provided for in paragraph 8 of this article, their living and working quarters, subsistence and all other personal expenses shall be the responsibility of the Party other than the Party carrying out the explosion.

10. Designated personnel shall consult with the Party carrying out the explosion in order to coordinate the planned program and schedule of activities of designated personnel with the program of the Party carrying out the explosion for the conduct of the project so as to ensure that designated personnel are able to conduct their activities in an orderly and timely way that is compatible with the implementation of the project. Procedures for such consultations shall be established in accordance with Article X.

Article VI

For any explosion with a planned aggregate yield exceeding 150 kilotons, determination of the yield of each explosive used shall be carried out in accordance with the following provisions:

1. Determination of the yield of each individual explosion in the group shall be based on measurements of the velocity of propagation, as a function of time, of the hydrodynamic shock wave generated by the explosion, taken by means of electrical equipment described in paragraph 3 of Article IV.

2. The Party carrying out the explosion shall provide the other Party with the following information:

(a) not later than 60 days before the beginning of emplacement of the explosives, the length of each canister in which the explosive will be contained in the corresponding emplacement hole, the dimensions of the tube or other device used to emplace the canister and the cross-sectional dimensions of the emplacement hole to a distance, in meters, from the emplacement point of 10 times the cube root of its yield in kilotons;

(b) not later than 60 days before the beginning of emplacement of the explosives, a description of materials, including their densities, to be used to stem each emplacement hole; and

(c) not later than 30 days before the beginning of emplacement of the explosives, for each emplacement hole of a group explosion, the local coordinates of the point of emplacement of the explosive, the entrance of the emplacement hole, the point of the emplacement hole most distant from the entrance, the location of the emplacement hole at each 200 meters distance from the entrance and the configuration of any known voids larger than one cubic meter located within the distance, in meters, of 10 times the cube root of the planned yield in kilotons measured from the bottom of the canister containing the explosive. The error in these coordinates shall not exceed one percent of the distance between the emplacement hole and the nearest other emplacement hole or one percent of the distance between the point of measurement and the entrance of the emplacement hole, whichever is smaller, but in no case shall the error be required to be less than one meter.

3. The Party carrying out the explosion shall emplace for each explosive that portion of the electrical equipment for yield determination described in subparagraph 3(a) of Article IV, supplied in accordance with paragraph 1 of Article IV, in the same emplacement hole as the explosive in accordance with the installation instructions supplied under the provisions of paragraph 5 or 6 of Article IV. Such emplacement shall be carried out under the observation of designated personnel. Other equipment specified in subparagraph 3(b) of Article IV shall be emplaced and installed:

(a) by designated personnel under the observation and with the assistance of personnel of the Party carrying out the explosion, if such assistance is requested by designated personnel; or

(b) in accordance with paragraph 5 of Article IV.

4. That portion of the electrical equipment for yield determination described in subparagraph 3(a) of Article IV that is to be emplaced in each emplacement hole shall be located so that the end of the electrical equipment which is farthest from the entrance to the emplacement hole is at a distance, in meters, from the bottom of the canister containing the explosive equal to 3.5 times the cube root of the planned yield in kilotons of the explosive when the planned yield is less than 20 kilotons and three times the cube root of the planned yield in kilotons of the explosive when the planned yield is 20 kilotons or more. Canisters longer than 10 meters containing the explosive shall only be utilized if there is prior agreement between the Parties establishing provisions for their use. The Party carrying out the explosion shall provide the other Party with data on the distribution of density inside any other canister in the emplacement hole with a transverse cross-sectional area exceeding 10 square centimeters located within a distance, in meters, of 10 times the cube root of the planned yield in kilotons of the explosion from the bottom of the canister containing the explosive. The Party carrying out the explosion shall provide the other Party with access to confirm such data on density distribution within any such canister.

5. The Party carrying out an explosion shall fill each emplacement hole, including all pipes and tubes contained therein which have at any transverse section an aggregate cross-sectional area exceeding 10 square centimeters in the region containing the electrical equipment for yield determination and to a distance, in meters, of six times the cube root of the planned yield in kilotons of the explosive from the explosive emplacement point, with material having a density not less than seven-tenths of the average density of the surrounding rock, and from that point to a distance of not less than 60 meters from the explosive emplacement point with material having a density greater than one gram per cubic centimeter.

6. Designated personnel shall have the right to:

(a) confirm information provided in accordance with subparagraph 2(a) of this article;

(b) confirm information provided in accordance with subparagraph 2(b) of this article and be provided, upon request, with a sample of each batch of stemming material as that material is put into the emplacement hole; and

(c) confirm the information provided in accordance with subparagraph 2(c) of this article by having access to the data acquired and by observing, upon their request, the making of measurements.

7. For those explosives which are emplaced in separate holes, the emplacement shall be such that the distance D, in meters, between any explosive and any portion of the electrical equipment for determination of the yield of any other explosive in the group shall be not less than 10 times the cube root of the planned yield in kilotons of the larger explosive of such a pair of explosives. Individual explosions shall be separated by time intervals, in milliseconds, not greater than one-sixth the amount by which the distance D, in meters, exceeds 10 times the cube root of the planned yield in kilotons of the larger explosive of such a pair of explosives.

8. For those explosives in a group which are emplaced in a common emplacement hole, the distance, in meters, between each explosive and any other explosive in that emplacement hole shall be not less than 10 times the cube root of the planned yield in kilotons of the larger explosive of such a pair of explosives, and the explosives shall be detonated in sequential order, beginning with the explosive farthest from the entrance to the emplacement hole, with the individual detonations separated by time intervals, in milliseconds, of not less than one times the cube root of the planned yield in kilotons of the largest explosive in this emplacement hole.

Article VII

1. Designated personnel with their personal baggage and their equipment as provided in Article IV shall be permitted to enter the territory of the Party carrying out the explosion at an entry port to be agreed upon by the Parties, to remain in the territory of the Party carrying out the explosion for the purpose of fulfilling their rights and functions provided for in the Treaty and this Protocol, and to depart from an exit port to be agreed upon by the Parties.

2. At all times while designated personnel are in the territory of the Party carrying out the explosion, their persons, property, personal baggage, archives and documents as well as their temporary official and living quarters shall be accorded the same privileges and immunities as provided in Articles 22, 23, 24, 29, 30, 31, 34 and 36 of the Vienna Convention on Diplomatic Relations of 1961 to the persons, property, personal baggage, archives and documents of diplomatic agents as well as to the premises of diplomatic missions and private residences of diplomatic agents.

3. Without prejudice to their privileges and immunities it shall be the duty of designated personnel to respect the laws and regulations of the State in whose territory the explosion is to be carried out insofar as they do not impede in any way whatsoever the proper exercising of their rights and functions provided for by the Treaty and this Protocol.

Article VIII

The Party carrying out an explosion shall have sole and exclusive control over and full responsibility for the conduct of the explosion.

Article IX

1. Nothing in the Treaty and this Protocol shall affect proprietary rights in information made available under the Treaty and this Protocol and in information which may be disclosed in preparation for and carrying out of explosions; however, claims to such proprietary rights shall not impede implementation of the provisions of the Treaty and this Protocol.

2. Public release of the information provided in accordance with Article II or publication of material using such information, as well as public release of the results of observation and measurements obtained by designated personnel, may take place only by agreement with the Party carrying out an explosion; however, the other Party shall have the right to issue statements after the explosion that do not divulge information in which the Party carrying out the explosion has rights which are referred to in paragraph 1 of this article.

Article X

The Joint Consultative Commission shall establish procedures through which the Parties will, as appropriate, consult with each other for the purpose of ensuring efficient implementation of this Protocol.

DONE at Washington and Moscow, on May 28, 1976.

For the United States of America:

GERALD R. FORD,

The President of the United States of America.

For the Union of Soviet Socialist Republics:

L. BREZHNEV,

General Secretary of the Central Committee of the CPSU.

Agreed Statement

May 13, 1976

The Parties to the Treaty Between the United States of America and the Union of Soviet Socialist Republics on Underground Nuclear Explosions for Peaceful Purposes, hereinafter referred to as the Treaty, agree that under subparagraph 2(c) of Article III of the Treaty:

(a) Development testing of nuclear explosives does not constitute a "peaceful application" and any such development tests shall be carried out only within the boundaries of nuclear weapon test sites specified in accordance with the Treaty between the United States of America and the Union of Soviet Socialist Republics on the Limitation of Underground Nuclear Weapon Tests;

(b) Associating test facilities, instrumentation or procedures related only to testing of nuclear weapons or their effects with any explosion carried out in accordance with the Treaty does not constitute a "peaceful application."

Convention on the Prohibition of Military or Any Other Hostile Use of Environmental Modification Techniques

Use of environmental modification techniques for hostile purposes does not play a major role in military planning at the present time. Such techniques might be developed in the future, however, and would pose a threat of serious damage unless action is taken to prohibit their use. In July 1972, the U.S. Government renounced the use of climate modification techniques for hostile purposes, even if their development were proved to be feasible in the future.

Both the U.S. Senate and the House of Representatives held hearings, beginning in 1972, and the Senate adopted a resolution in 1973 calling for an international agreement "prohibiting the use of any environmental or geophysical modification activity as a weapon of war...." In response to this resolution, the President ordered the Department of Defense to undertake an in-depth review of the military aspects of weather and other environmental modification techniques. The results of this study and a subsequent interagency study led to the U.S. Government's decision to seek agreement with the Soviet Union to explore the possibilities of an international agreement.

During the summit meeting in Moscow in July 1974, President Nixon and General Secretary Brezhnev formally agreed to hold bilateral discussions on how to bring about "the most effective measures possible to overcome the dangers of the use of environmental modification techniques for military purposes." Three sets of discussions were held in 1974 and 1975, resulting in agreement on a common approach and common language.

In August 1975, the chief representatives of the U.S. and the Soviet delegations to the Conference of the Committee on Disarmament (CCD) tabled, in parallel, identical draft texts of a "Convention on the Prohibition of Military or any Other Hostile Use of Environmental Modification Techniques."

The convention defines environmental modification techniques as changing—through the deliberate manipulation of natural processes—the dynamics, composition or structure of the earth, including its biota, lithosphere, hydrosphere, and atmosphere, or of outer space. Changes in weather or climate patterns, in ocean currents, or in the state of the ozone layer or ionosphere, or an upset in the ecological balance of a region are some of the effects which might result from the use of environmental modification techniques.

Intensive negotiations held in the CCD during the spring and summer of 1976 resulted in a modified text and, in addition, to understandings regarding four of the treaty articles. These were transmitted to the U.N. General Assembly for consideration during the fall session.

Article I sets forth the basic commitment: "Each State Party to this convention undertakes not to engage in military or any other hostile use of environmental modification techniques having widespread, long-lasting or severe effects as the means of destruction, damage or injury to any other State Party." An understanding defines the terms "widespread, long-lasting or severe." "Widespread" is defined as "encompassing an area on the scale of several hundred square kilometers"; "long-lasting" is defined as "lasting for a period of months, or approximately a season"; and "severe" is defined as "involving serious or significant disruption or harm to human life, natural and economic resources or other assets."

With regard to peaceful uses of environmental modification techniques, the convention provides that the parties shall have the right to participate in the fullest possible exchange of scientific and technological information.

In addition to the provision for mutual consultation regarding complaints and for recourse to the Security Council, the revised draft establishes the framework for a Consultative Committee of Experts, which would meet on an *ad hoc* basis when so requested by a party, in order to clarify the nature of activities suspected to be in violation of the convention. Responding to the suggestion of many delegations, the revised text incorporates a provision for periodic conferences to review the convention's operation.

During the 1976 fall session, the U.N. General Assembly held extensive debate on the draft convention, including several resolutions relating thereto. On December 10, the General Assembly adopted a resolution by a vote of 96 to 8, with 30 abstentions, which referred the convention to all member nations for their consideration, signature, and ratification, and requested the U.N. Secretary-General to open the convention for signature.

The U.N. Secretary-General officiated at the signing ceremony in Geneva on May 18. The United States joined 33 other nations in signing the convention. The convention entered into force on October 5, 1978, when the 20th state to sign the convention deposited its instrument of ratification. President Carter transmitted the convention to the Senate on September 22, 1978. The Senate gave its advice and consent to ratification on November 28, 1979, by a vote of 98-0. The President ratified the convention December 13, 1979. The convention entered into force for the United States on January 17, 1980, when the United States instrument of ratification was deposited in New York.

Convention on the Prohibition of Military or Any Other Hostile Use of Environmental Modification Techniques

Signed in Geneva May 18, 1977
Entered into force October 5, 1978
Ratification advised by U.S. Senate November 28, 1979
Ratified by U.S. President December 13, 1979
U.S. ratification deposited at New York January 17, 1980

The States Parties to this Convention,

Guided by the interest of consolidating peace, and wishing to contribute to the cause of halting the arms race, and of bringing about general and complete disarmament under strict and effective international control, and of saving mankind from the danger of using new means of warfare,

Determined to continue negotiations with a view to achieving effective progress towards further measures in the field of disarmament,

Recognizing that scientific and technical advances may open new possibilities with respect to modification of the environment,

Recalling the Declaration of the United Nations Conference on the Human Environment adopted at Stockholm on 16 June 1972,

Realizing that the use of environmental modification techniques for peaceful purposes could improve the interrelationship of man and nature and contribute to the preservation and improvement of the environment for the benefit of present and future generations,

Recognizing, however, that military or any other hostile use of such techniques could have effects extremely harmful to human welfare,

Desiring to prohibit effectively military or any other hostile use of environmental modification techniques in order to eliminate the dangers to mankind from such use, and affirming their willingness to work towards the achievement of this objective,

Desiring also to contribute to the strengthening of trust among nations and to the further improvement of the international situation in accordance with the purposes and principles of the Charter of the United Nations,

Have agreed as follows:

Article I

1. Each State Party to this Convention undertakes not to engage in military or any other hostile use of environmental modification techniques having widespread, long-lasting or severe effects as the means of destruction, damage or injury to any other State Party.

2. Each State Party to this Convention undertakes not to assist, encourage or induce any State, group of States or international organization to engage in activities contrary to the provisions of paragraph 1 of this article.

Article II

As used in article I, the term "environmental modification techniques" refers to any technique for changing—through the deliberate manipulation of natural processes—the dynamics, composition or structure of the Earth, including its biota, lithosphere, hydrosphere and atmosphere, or of outer space.

Article III

1. The provisions of this Convention shall not hinder the use of environmental modification techniques for peaceful purposes and shall be without prejudice to the generally recognized principles and applicable rules of international law concerning such use.

2. The States Parties to this Convention undertake to facilitate, and have the right to participate in, the fullest possible exchange of scientific and technological information on the use of environmental modification techniques for peaceful purposes. States Parties in a position to do so shall contribute, alone or together with other States or international organizations, to international economic and scientific co-operation in the preservation, improvement, and peaceful utilization of the environment, with due consideration for the needs of the developing areas of the world.

Article IV

Each State Party to this Convention undertakes to take any measures it considers necessary in accordance with its constitutional processes to prohibit and prevent any activity in violation of the provisions of the Convention anywhere under its jurisdiction or control.

Article V

1. The States Parties to this Convention undertake to consult one another and to co-operate in solving any problems which may arise in relation to the objectives of, or in the application of the provisions of, the Convention. Consultation and co-operation pursuant to this article may also be undertaken through appropriate international procedures within the framework of the United Nations and in accordance with its Charter. These international procedures may include the services of appropriate international organizations, as well as of a Consultative Committee of Experts as provided for in paragraph 2 of this article.

2. For the purposes set forth in paragraph 1 of this article, the Depositary shall, within one month of the receipt of a request from any State Party to this convention, convene a Consultative Committee of Experts. Any State Party may appoint an expert to the Committee whose functions and rules of procedure are set out in the annex, which constitutes an integral part of this Convention. The Committee shall transmit to the Depositary a summary of its findings of fact, incorporating all views and information presented to the Committee during its proceedings. The Depositary shall distribute the summary to all States Parties.

3. Any State Party to this Convention which has reason to believe that any other State Party is acting in breach of obligations deriving from the provisions of the Convention may lodge a complaint with the Security Council of the United Nations. Such a complaint should include all relevant information as well as all possible evidence supporting its validity.

4. Each State Party to this Convention undertakes to co-operate in carrying out any investigation which the Security Council may initiate, in accordance with the provisions of the Charter of the United Nations, on the basis of the complaint received by the

Council. The Security Council shall inform the States Parties of the results of the investigation.

5. Each State Party to this Convention undertakes to provide or support assistance, in accordance with the provisions of the Charter of the United Nations, to any State Party which so requests, if the Security Council decides that such Party has been harmed or is likely to be harmed as a result of violation of the Convention.

Article VI

1. Any State Party to this Convention may propose amendments to the Convention. The text of any proposed amendment shall be submitted to the Depositary who shall promptly circulate it to all States Parties.

2. An amendment shall enter into force for all States Parties to this Convention which have accepted it, upon the deposit with the Depositary of instruments of acceptance by a majority of States Parties. Thereafter it shall enter into force for any remaining State Party on the date of deposit of its instrument of acceptance.

Article VII

This Convention shall be of unlimited duration.

Article VIII

1. Five years after the entry into force of this Convention, a conference of the States Parties to the Convention shall be convened by the Depositary at Geneva, Switzerland. The conference shall review the operation of the Convention with a view to ensuring that its purposes and provisions are being realized, and shall in particular examine the effectiveness of the provisions of paragraph 1 of Article I in eliminating the dangers of military or any other hostile use of environmental modification techniques.

2. At intervals of not less than five years thereafter, a majority of the States Parties to the Convention may obtain, by submitting a proposal to this effect to the Depositary, the convening of a conference with the same objectives.

3. If no conference has been convened pursuant to paragraph 2 of this article within ten years following the conclusion of a previous conference, the Depositary shall solicit the views of all States Parties to the Convention, concerning the convening of such a conference. If one third or ten of the States Parties, whichever number is less, respond affirmatively, the Depositary shall take immediate steps to convene the conference.

Article IX

1. This Convention shall be open to all States for signature. Any State which does not sign the Convention before its entry into force in accordance with paragraph 3 of this article may accede to it at any time.

2. This Convention shall be subject to ratification by signatory States. Instruments of ratification or accession shall be deposited with the Secretary-General of the United Nations.

3. This Convention shall enter into force upon the deposit of instruments of ratification by twenty Governments in accordance with paragraph 2 of this article.

4. For those States whose instruments of ratification or accession are deposited after the entry into force of this Convention, it shall enter into force on the date of the deposit of their instruments of ratification or accession.

5. The Depositary shall promptly inform all signatory and acceding States of the date of each signature, the date of deposit of each instrument of ratification or

accession and the date of the entry into force of this Convention and of any amendments thereto, as well as of the receipt of other notices.

6. This Convention shall be registered by the Depositary in accordance with Article 102 of the Charter of the United Nations.

Article X

This Convention, of which the English, Arabic, Chinese, French, Russian, and Spanish texts are equally authentic, shall be deposited with the Secretary-General of the United Nations, who shall send certified copies thereof to the Governments of the signatory and acceding States.

IN WITNESS WHEREOF, the undersigned, being duly authorized thereto by their respective governments, have signed this Convention, opened for signature at Geneva on the eighteenth day of May, one thousand nine hundred and seventy-seven.

DONE at Gevena on May 18, 1977.

Annex to the Convention
Consultative Committee of Experts

1. The Consultative Committee of Experts shall undertake to make appropriate findings of fact and provide expert views relevant to any problem raised pursuant to paragraph 1 of Article V of this Convention by the State Party requesting the convening of the Committee.

2. The work of the Consultative Committee of Experts shall be organized in such a way as to permit it to perform the functions set forth in paragraph 1 of this annex. The Committee shall decide procedural questions relative to the organization of its work, where possible by consensus, but otherwise by a majority of those present and voting. There shall be no voting on matters of substance.

3. The Depositary or his representative shall serve as the Chairman of the Committee.

4. Each expert may be assisted at meetings by one or more advisers.

5. Each expert shall have the right, through the Chairman, to request from States, and from international organizations, such information and assistance as the expert considers desirable for the accomplishment of the Committee's work.

Understandings Regarding the Convention[1]

Understanding Relating to Article I

It is the understanding of the Committee that, for the purposes of this Convention, the terms, "widespread", "long-lasting" and "severe" shall be interpreted as follows:

(a) "widespread": encompassing an area on the scale of several hundred square kilometres;

(b) "long-lasting": lasting for a period of months, or approximately a season;

(c) "severe": involving serious or significant disruption or harm to human life, natural and economic resources or other assets.

It is further understood that the interpretation set forth above is intended exclusively for this Convention and is not intended to prejudice the interpretation of the same or similar terms if used in connexion with any other international agreement.

Understanding Relating to Article II

It is the understanding of the Committee that the following examples are illustrative of phenomena that could be caused by the use of environmental modification techniques as defined in Article II of the Convention: earthquakes; tsunamis; an upset in the ecological balance of a region; changes in weather patterns (clouds, precipitation, cyclones of various types and tornadic storms); changes in climate patterns; changes in ocean currents; changes in the state of the ozone layer; and changes in the state of the ionosphere.

It is further understood that all the phenomena listed above, when produced by military or any other hostile use of environmental modification techniques, would result, or could reasonably be expected to result, in widespread, long-lasting or severe destruction, damage or injury. Thus, military or any other hostile use of environmental modification techniques as defined in Article II, so as to cause those phenomena as a means of destruction, damage or injury to another State Party, would be prohibited.

It is recognized, moreover, that the list of examples set out above is not exhaustive. Other phenomena which could result from the use of environmental modification techniques as defined in Article II could also be appropriately included. The absence of such phenomena from the list does not in any way imply that the undertaking contained in Article I would not be applicable to those phenomena, provided the criteria set out in that article were met.

Understanding Relating to Article III

It is the understanding of the Committee that this Convention does not deal with the question whether or not a given use of environmental modification techniques for peaceful purposes is in accordance with generally recognized principles and applicable rules of international law.

---

[1]These are not incorporated into the Convention but are part of the negotiating record and were included in the report transmitted by the CCD to the U.N. General Assembly in September 1976.

Understanding Relating to Article VIII

It is the understanding of the Committee that a proposal to amend the Convention may also be considered at any conference of Parties held pursuant to Article VIII. It is further understood that any proposed amendment that is intended for such consideration should, if possible, be submitted to the Depositary no less than 90 days before the commencement of the conference.

Environmental Modification Convention

Country	Date of[1] Signature	Date of Deposit[1] of Ratification	Date of Deposit[1] of Accession
Australia	5/31/78		
Bangladesh			10/ 3/79
Belgium	5/18/77		
Benin	6/10/77		
Bolivia	5/18/77		
Brazil	11/ 9/77		
Bulgaria	5/18/77	5/31/78	
Byelorussian S.S.R.[2]	5/18/77	6/ 7/78	
Canada	5/18/77	6/11/81	
Cape Verde			10/ 3/79
Cuba	9/23/77	4/10/78	
Cyprus	10/ 7/77	4/12/78	
Czechoslovakia	5/18/77	5/12/78	
Denmark	5/18/77	4/19/78	
Ethiopia	5/18/77		
Finland	5/18/77	5/12/78	
German Democratic Republic	5/18/77	5/25/78	
Germany, Federal Republic of	5/18/77		
Ghana	3/21/78	6/22/78	
Holy See	5/27/77		
Hungary	5/18/77	4/19/78	
Iceland	5/18/77		
India	12/10/77	12/15/78	
Iran	5/18/77		
Iraq	8/15/77		
Ireland	5/18/77		
Italy	5/18/77	11/27/81	
Kuwait			1/ 2/80
Laos	4/13/78	10/ 5/78	
Lebanon	5/18/77		
Liberia	5/18/77		
Luxembourg	5/18/77		
Malawi			10/ 5/78
Mongolia	5/18/77	5/19/78	

See footnotes on page 290.

Environmental Modification Convention

Country	Date of[1] Signature	Date of Deposit[1] of Ratification	Date of Deposit[1] of Accession
Morocco	5/18/77		
Netherlands	5/18/77		
Nicaragua	8/11/77		
Norway	5/18/77	2/15/79	
Papua New Guinea			10/28/80
Poland	5/18/77	6/8/78	
Portugal	5/18/77		
Romania	5/18/77		
São Tomé and Principe			10/5/79
Sierra Leone	4/12/78		
Solomon Islands			6/18/81
Spain	5/18/77	7/19/78	
Sri Lanka	6/8/77	4/25/78	
Syrian Arab Republic	8/4/77		
Tunisia	5/11/78	5/11/78	
Turkey	5/18/77		
Uganda	5/18/77		
Ukrainian S.S.R.[2]	5/18/77	6/13/78	
Union of Soviet Socialist Republics	5/18/77	5/30/78	
United Kingdom	5/18/77	5/16/78	
United States	5/18/77	1/17/80	
Vietnam			8/26/80
Yemen Arab Republic (Sana)	5/18/77	7/20/77	
Yemen, People's Democratic Republic of (Aden)			6/12/79
Zaire	2/28/78		
Totals[3]	48	23	9

See footnotes on page 290.

Agreement Between the United States of America and the International Atomic Energy Agency for the Application of Safeguards in the United States (and Protocol Thereto)

The United States-IAEA agreement for the application by IAEA of safeguards in designated facilities in the United States originated in the ENDC negotiation of the Treaty on the Non-Proliferation of Nuclear Weapons (NPT). During those negotiations, particularly in 1967, Japan and the nonnuclear-weapon states of the European Community opposed the NPT provision (article III.1) that requires only nonnuclear-weapon states party to the treaty to accept IAEA[1] safeguards in all of their peaceful nuclear activities.

It was argued that the absence of any requirement for IAEA safeguards in nuclear-weapon states would place the industries of nonnuclear-weapon states at a commercial disadvantage, because of interference by these safeguards with efficient operation of their commercial activities and by compromise, through IAEA personnel, of their industrial and trade secrets. Efforts to devise acceptable treaty provisions for IAEA safeguards in nuclear-weapon states were unsuccessful, and by late 1967, the safeguards issue had become a serious obstacle to acceptance of the NPT by major industrialized nonnuclear-weapon states.

In an effort to break that impasse, President Johnson, on December 2, 1967, stated that the United States was not asking any country to accept safeguards that the United States was unwilling to accept and that ". . . when such safeguards are applied under the treaty, the United States will permit the International Atomic Energy Agency to apply its safeguards to all nuclear activities in the United States—excluding only those with direct national security significance." The United Kingdom announced a similar offer on December 4, 1967. These offers were instrumental in gaining acceptance of the NPT by key industrialized countries, and their importance was emphasized in public statements by the Federal Republic of Germany, Japan, and others. In the course of hearings by the Senate Foreign Relations Committee in July 1968, the

---

[1] International Atomic Energy Agency, a U.N.-affiliated organization headquartered in Vienna, Austria.

Administration explained that the U.S. offer would be fulfilled by the conclusion of a formal agreement with the IAEA.

Shortly after the NPT entered into force in March 1970, a Safeguards Committee established by the IAEA Board of Governors undertook to advise the Board concerning the form and content of the safeguards agreements to be concluded with the nonnuclear-weapon states parties to the NPT. Nearly 50 governments participated in the Committee's work, which continued until early 1971.

Among the most difficult issues the Committee addressed was that of financing the increase in IAEA's safeguards activities that would result from the NPT. Only in that context did the Committee address the manner in which the offers by the United States and the United Kingdom might be implemented. It was recognized that the number of facilities in those two countries that would come within the terms of their offers would equal the total number of facilities in all nonnuclear-weapon states. Thus, if the IAEA were to apply its safeguards in all the facilities under the offers, the IAEA's budget for its safeguards activities would be doubled. Accordingly, a number of nonnuclear-weapon states led by Australia proposed that the purpose of the offers could be achieved at reasonable cost to the IAEA by its carrying out full inspection of only those facilities in the United States and the United Kingdom that were of advanced design or were sensitive in terms of international competition. Under the proposal, which was endorsed by Italy, Japan, and the Federal Republic of Germany, the IAEA would apply something less than the full regime of inspections to all other eligible facilities in the two offering countries. Australia's proposal succeeded in demonstrating to the Committee that the costs of implementing the offers could be kept within reasonable bounds while achieving their purpose.

By March 1971, the Safeguards Committee completed its formulation of detailed provisions for the individual safeguards agreements. The Board approved the document, and shortly thereafter Austria and Finland negotiated safeguards agreements with the IAEA which became the models for future such agreements. They were also used in the development of the voluntary offer agreements with the United States and the United Kingdom.

In order for the U.S. offer to achieve its purpose, it was essential that the IAEA, in applying its safeguards in a particular type of U.S. facility, use the same procedures it follows in similar facilities in nonnuclear-weapon states. Many of the model provisions could therefore be incorporated into the U.S.-IAEA agreement without change.

Other provisions required adaptation in light of fundamental differences between the terms of the U.S. offer and the obligations of a nonnuclear-weapon state party to the NPT. The provisions which differ are identified and explained in detail in the report of the Senate Foreign Relations Committee recommending Senate advice and consent to ratification of the U.S.-IAEA Safeguards Agreement. These differences reflect several facts. The U.S. offer excludes activities of direct national security significance and does not contain any limitations on use of nuclear material by the United States. (Thus, the agreement provides that at any time the United States can remove a facility from the list of those eligible for safeguards should the facility become associated with activities of direct national security significance, and the United States can transfer nuclear material from eligible facilities to any location including noneligible facilities.) The United States has sole authority to decide which U.S. facilities are eligible for safeguards. The IAEA has sole authority to decide which eligible facilities will be selected for safeguards (although the IAEA is obliged to take into account the requirement that the U.S. Government avoid discriminatory treatment between U.S. commercial firms similarly situated). Lastly, the United States had made separate commitments to provide to the IAEA, for safeguards purposes, information on imports and exports of nuclear material.

The U.S.-IAEA agreement proper addresses only the selection of facilities for the application of the full regime of safeguards procedures, including routine inspections. Australia and several other key nonnuclear-weapon states had also proposed in the Safeguards Committee that all of the eligible facilities should bear some burden of safeguards. In further consultations it appeared that a satisfactory arrangement would be for the facilities not selected for the application of safeguards to submit design information, permit IAEA inspectors to verify such information in the facility, maintain accounting records, and provide accounting reports to the IAEA. The IAEA, however, was concerned lest the negotiation of the individual arrangements and the wholesale submission of such information overwhelm its staff. Consequently, the concept of a secondary selection was introduced, whereby complete flexibility was provided to the IAEA, so that any or all of the eligible facilities could be required to submit the specified information, maintain records, etc. For ease of drafting, and to maintain the distinction between "safeguards," which includes routine inspections by the IAEA, and only the submission of information and maintenance of records, the provisions dealing with the secondary category of selected facilities are grouped into a protocol to the agreement. The technical provisions in the protocol follow closely the comparable provisions in the agreement proper.

In September 1976, when negotiation of the safeguards agreements between the IAEA and the nonnuclear-weapon states members of the European Community had been completed and negotiations with Japan appeared to be approaching completion, the U.S.-IAEA agreement was submitted to the IAEA Board of Governors for its approval. The Board at that time included the Federal Republic of Germany, Italy, and Japan. The Director General informed the Board that, in selecting facilities in which the IAEA would apply the full regime of safeguards, including inspections, the IAEA would take into account the need to avoid discrimination among commercial firms in the United States. The IAEA, he stated, would also observe the criteria for selection that had been proposed by Australia and others—facilities of advanced design and those sensitive in terms of international competition. The Board, acting by consensus, authorized the Director General to conclude the agreement.

The agreement was submitted to the U.S. Senate on February 9, 1978. Its advice and consent to ratification was given unanimously, with understandings, on July 2, 1980. The agreement was brought into force on December 9 of that year. At that time the United States submitted to the IAEA a list of more than 200 eligible facilities, including more than 100 commercial power reactors in operation or under construction, about 80 research and test reactors and critical assemblies, and 13 fuel fabrication plants.

In early 1981, the IAEA made its initial selection of facilities in which the full regime of safeguards, including inspection, was to be applied, pursuant to the agreement proper. Two operating commercial power reactors and one commercial fuel fabrication plant were selected. The facilities submitted design information, and negotiations were begun regarding each of the detailed "facility attachments." While those negotiations proceeded, the IAEA carried out *ad hoc* inspections in the facilities as permitted by the agreement. In August 1981, the IAEA also selected for full safeguards a decommissioned government-owned research reactor in which a quantity of plutonium was stored. The facility attachments for this research reactor and for the fuel fabrication plant entered into force in February 1982.

Also in February 1982, the IAEA made its first selection under the protocol of two commercial fuel fabrication plants and identified two additional such plants that it intended to select soon thereafter.

Agreement Between the United States of America and the International Atomic Energy Agency for the Application of Safeguards in the United States

Signed at Vienna November 18, 1977
Ratification advised by U.S. Senate July 2, 1980
Ratified by U.S. President July 31, 1980
Entered into force December 9, 1980
Proclaimed by U.S. President December 31, 1980

Whereas the United States of America (hereinafter referred to as the "United States") is a Party to the Treaty on the Non-Proliferation of Nuclear Weapons (hereinafter referred to as the "Treaty") which was opened for signature at London, Moscow and Washington on 1 July 1968 and which entered into force on 5 March 1970;[1]

Whereas States Parties to the Treaty undertake to co-operate in facilitating the application of International Atomic Energy Agency (hereinafter referred to as the "Agency") safeguards on peaceful nuclear activities;

Whereas non-nuclear-weapon States Parties to the Treaty undertake to accept safeguards, as set forth in an agreement to be negotiated and concluded with the Agency, on all source or special fissionable material in all their peaceful nuclear activities for the exclusive purpose of verification of the fulfilment of their obligations under the Treaty with a view to preventing diversion of nuclear energy from peaceful uses to nuclear weapons or other nuclear explosive devices;

Whereas the United States, a nuclear-weapon State as defined by the Treaty, has indicated that at such time as safeguards are being generally applied in accordance with paragraph 1 of Article III of the Treaty, the United States will permit the Agency to apply its safeguards to all nuclear activities in the United States—excluding only those with direct national security significance—by concluding a safeguards agreement with the Agency for that purpose;

Whereas the United States has made this offer and has entered into this agreement for the purpose of encouraging widespread adherence to the Treaty by demonstrating to non-nuclear-weapon States that they would not be placed at a commercial disadvantage by reason of the application of safeguards pursuant to the Treaty;

Whereas the purpose of a safeguards agreement giving effect to this offer by the United States would thus differ necessarily from the purposes of safeguards agreements concluded between the Agency and non-nuclear-weapon States Party to the Treaty;

Whereas it is in the interest of Members of the Agency, that, without prejudice to the principles and integrity of the Agency's safeguards system, the expenditure of the Agency's financial and other resources for implementation of such an agreement not exceed that necessary to accomplish the purpose of the Agreement;

Whereas the Agency is authorized, pursuant to Article III of the Statute of the International Atomic Energy Agency[2] (hereinafter referred to as the "Statute"), to conclude such a safeguards agreement;

Now, therefore, the United States and the Agency have agreed as follows:

---

[1] TIAS 6839; 21 UST 483.

[2] Done Oct. 26, 1956. TIAS 3873, 5284, 7668; 8 UST 1095; 14 UST 135; 24 UST 1637.

PART I

Article 1

(a) The United States undertakes to permit the Agency to apply safeguards, in accordance with the terms of this Agreement, on all source or special fissionable material in all facilities within the United States, excluding only those facilities associated with activities with direct national security significance to the United States, with a view to enabling the Agency to verify that such material is not withdrawn, except as provided for in this Agreement, from activities in facilities while such material is being safeguarded under this Agreement.

(b) The United States shall, upon entry in force of this Agreement, provide the Agency with a list of facilities within the United States not associated with activities with direct national security significance to the United States and may, in accordance with the procedures set forth in Part II of this Agreement, add facilities to or remove facilities from that list as it deems appropriate.

(c) The United States may, in accordance with the procedures set forth in this Agreement, withdraw nuclear material from activities in facilities included in the list referred to in Article 1(b).

Article 2

(a) The Agency shall have the right to apply safeguards, in accordance with the terms of this Agreement, on all source or special fissionable material in all facilities within the United States, excluding only those facilities associated with activities with direct national security significance to the United States, with a view to enabling the Agency to verify that such material is not withdrawn, except as provided for in this Agreement, from activities in facilities while such material is being safeguarded under this Agreement.

(b) The Agency shall, from time to time, identify to the United States those facilities, selected from the then current list provided by the United States in accordance with Article 1(b), in which the Agency wishes to apply safeguards, in accordance with the terms of this Agreement.

(c) In identifying facilities and in applying safeguards thereafter on source or special fissionable material in such facilities, the Agency shall proceed in a manner which the Agency and the United States mutually agree takes into account the requirement on the United States to avoid discriminatory treatment as between United States commercial firms similarly situated.

Article 3

(a) The United States and the Agency shall co-operate to facilitate the implementation of the safeguards provided for in this Agreement.

(b) The source or special fissionable material subject to safeguards under this Agreement shall be that material in those facilities which shall have been identified by the Agency at any given time pursuant to Article 2(b).

(c) The safeguards to be applied by the Agency under this Agreement on source or special fissionable material in facilities in the United States shall be implemented by the same procedures followed by the Agency in applying its safeguards on similar material in similar facilities in non-nuclear-weapon States under agreements pursuant to paragraph 1 of Article III of the Treaty.

Article 4

The safeguards provided for in this Agreement shall be implemented in a manner designed:

(a) To avoid hampering the economic and technological development of the United States or international co-operation in the field of peaceful nuclear activities, including international exchange of nuclear material;

(b) To avoid undue interference in peaceful nuclear activities of the United States and in particular in the operation of facilities; and

(c) To be consistent with prudent management practices required for the economic and safe conduct of nuclear activities.

Article 5

(a) The agency shall take every precaution to protect commercial and industrial secrets and other confidential information coming to its knowledge in the implementation of this Agreement.

(b) (i) The Agency shall not publish or communicate to any State, organization or person any information obtained by it in connection with the implementation of this Agreement, except that specific information relating to the implementation thereof may be given to the Board of Governors of the Agency (hereinafter referred to as "the Board") and to such Agency staff members as require such knowledge by reason of their official duties in connection with safeguards, but only to the extent necessary for the Agency to fulfill its responsibilities in implementing this Agreement.

   (ii) Summarized information on nuclear material subject to safeguards under this Agreement may be published upon the decision of the Board if the United States agrees thereto.

Article 6

(a) The Agency shall, in implementing safeguards pursuant to this Agreement, take full account of technological developments in the field of safeguards, and shall make every effort to ensure optimum cost-effectiveness and the application of the principle of safeguarding effectively the flow of nuclear material subject to safeguards under this Agreement by use of instruments and other techniques at certain strategic points to the extent that present or future technology permits.

(b) In order to ensure optimum cost-effectiveness, use shall be made, for example, of such means as:

   (i) Containment as a means of defining material balance areas for accounting purposes;

   (ii) Statistical techniques and random sampling in evaluating the flow of nuclear material; and

   (iii) Concentration of verification procedures on those stages in the nuclear fuel cycle involving the production, processing, use or storage of nuclear material from which nuclear weapons or other nuclear explosive devices could readily be made, and minimization of verification procedures in respect of other nuclear material, on condition that this does not hamper the Agency in applying safeguards under this Agreement.

Article 7

(a)   The United States shall establish and maintain a system of accounting for and control of all nuclear material subject to safeguards under this Agreement.

(b)   The Agency shall apply safeguards in accordance with Article 3(c) in such a manner as to enable the Agency to verify, in ascertaining that there has been no withdrawal of nuclear material, except as provided for in this Agreement, from activities in facilities while such material is being safeguarded under this Agreement, findings of the accounting and control system of the United States. The Agency's verification shall include, inter alia, independent measurements and observations conducted by the Agency in accordance with the procedures specified in Part II. The Agency, in its verification, shall take due account of the technical effectiveness of the system of the United States.

Article 8

(a)   In order to ensure the effective implementation of safeguards under this Agreement, the United States shall, in accordance with the provisions set out in Part II, provide the Agency with information concerning nuclear material subject to safeguards under this Agreement and the features of facilities relevant to safeguarding such material.

(b)   (i)   The Agency shall require only the minimum amount of information and data consistent with carrying out its responsibilities under this Agreement.

      (ii) Information pertaining to facilities shall be the minimum necessary for safeguarding nuclear material subject to safeguards under this Agreement.

(c)   If the United States so requests, the Agency shall be prepared to examine on premises of the United States design information which the United States regards as being of particular sensitivity. Such information need not be physicially transmitted to the Agency provided that it remains readily available for further examination by the Agency on premises of the United States.

Article 9

(a)   (i)   The Agency shall secure the consent of the United States to the designation of Agency inspectors to the United States.

      (ii) If the United States, either upon proposal of a designation or at any other time after designation has been made, objects to the designation, the Agency shall propose to the United States an alternative designation or designations.

      (iii) If, as a result of the repeated refusal of the United States to accept the designation of Agency inspectors, inspections to be conducted under this Agreement would be impeded, such refusal shall be considered by the Board, upon referral by the Director General of the Agency (hereinafter referred to as "the Director General") with a view to its taking appropriate action.

(b)   The United States shall take the necessary steps to ensure that Agency inspectors can effectively discharge their functions under this Agreement.

(c)   The visits and activities of Agency inspectors shall be so arranged as:

      (i)   To reduce to a minimum the possible inconvenience and disturbance to the United States and to the peaceful nuclear activities inspected; and

(ii)   To ensure protection of industrial secrets or any other confidential information coming to the inspectors' knowledge.

Article 10

The provisions of the International Organizations Immunities Act of the United States of America[3] shall apply to Agency inspectors performing functions in the United States under this Agreement and to any property of the Agency used by them.

Article 11

Safeguards shall terminate on nuclear material upon determination by the Agency that the material has been consumed, or has been diluted in such a way that it is no longer usable for any nuclear activity relevant from the point of view of safeguards, or has become practicably irrecoverable.

Article 12

(a)   If the United States intends to exercise its right to withdraw nuclear material from activities in facilities identified by the Agency pursuant to Articles 2(b) and 39(b) other than those facilities removed, pursuant to Article 34(b)(i) from the list provided for by Article 1(b) and to transfer such material to a destination in the United States other than to a facility included in the list established and maintained pursuant to Articles 1(b) and 34, the United States shall notify the Agency in advance of such withdrawal. Nuclear material in respect of which such notification has been given shall cease to be subject to safeguards under this Agreement as from the time of its withdrawal.

(b)   Nothing in this Agreement shall effect the right of the United States to transfer material subject to safeguards under this Agreement to destinations not within or under the jurisdiction of the United States. The United States shall provide the Agency with information with respect to such transfers in accordance with Article 89. The Agency shall keep records of each such transfer and, where applicable, of the reapplication of safeguards to the transferred nuclear material.

Article 13

Where nuclear material subject to safeguards under this Agreement is to be used in non-nuclear activities, such as the production of alloys or ceramics, the United States shall agree with the Agency, before the material is so used, on the circumstances under which the safeguards on such material may be terminated.

Article 14

The United States and the Agency will bear the expenses incurred by them in implementing their respective responsibilities under this Agreement. However, if the United States or persons under its jurisdiction incur extraordinary expenses as a result of a specific request by the Agency, the Agency shall reimburse such expenses provided that it has agreed in advance to do so. In any case the Agency shall bear the cost of any additional measuring or sampling which inspectors may request.

---

[3] 59 Stat. 669; 22 U.S.C. § 288 note.

Article 15

In carrying out its functions under this Agreement within the United States, the Agency and its personnel shall be covered to the same extent as nationals of the United States by any protection against third-party liability provided under the Price-Anderson Act,[4] including insurance or other indemnity coverage that may be required by the Price-Anderson Act with respect to nuclear incidents.

Article 16

Any claim by the United States against the Agency or by the Agency against the United States in respect of any damage resulting from the implementation of safeguards under this Agreement, other than damage arising out of a nuclear incident, shall be settled in accordance with international law.

Article 17

If the Board, upon report of the Director General, decides that an action by the United States is essential and urgent in order to ensure compliance with this Agreement, the Board may call upon the United States to take the required action without delay, irrespective of whether procedures have been invoked pursuant to Article 21 for the settlement of a dispute.

Article 18

If the Board, upon examination of relevant information reported to it by the Director General, determines there has been any non-compliance with this Agreement, the Board may call upon the United States to remedy forthwith such non-compliance. In the event there is a failure to take fully corrective action within a reasonable time, the Board may make the reports provided for in paragraph C of Article XII of the Statute and may also take, where applicable, the other measures provided for in that paragraph. In taking such action the Board shall take account of the degree of assurance provided by the safeguards measures that have been applied and shall afford the United States every reasonable opportunity to furnish the Board with any necessary reassurance.

Article 19

The United States and the Agency shall, at the request of either, consult about any question arising out of the interpretation or application of this Agreement.

Article 20

The United States shall have the right to request that any question arising out of the interpretation or application of this Agreement be considered by the Board. The Board shall invite the United States to participate in the discussion of any such question by the Board.

---

[4] 71 Stat. 576; 42 U.S.C. § 2210.

Article 21

Any dispute arising out of the interpretation or application of this Agreement, except a dispute with regard to a determination by the Board under Article 18 or an action taken by the Board pursuant to such a determination which is not settled by negotiation or another procedure agreed to by the United States and the Agency shall, at the request of either, be submitted to an arbitral tribunal composed as follows: The United States and the Agency shall each designate one arbitrator, and the two arbitrators so designated shall elect a third, who shall be the Chairman. If, within thirty days of the request for arbitration, either the United States or the Agency has not designated an arbitrator, either the United States or the Agency may request the President of the International Court of Justice to appoint an arbitrator. The same procedure shall apply if, within thirty days of the designation or appointment of the second arbitrator, the third arbitrator has not been elected. A majority of the members of the arbitral tribunal shall constitute a quorum, and all decisions shall require the concurrence of two arbitrators. The arbitral procedure shall be fixed by the tribunal. The decisions of the tribunal shall be binding on the United States and the Agency.

Article 22

The Parties shall institute steps to suspend the application of Agency safeguards in the United States under other safeguards agreements with the Agency while this Agreement is in force. However, the United States and the Agency shall ensure that nuclear material being safeguarded under this Agreement shall be at all times at least equivalent in amount and composition to that which would be subject to safeguards in the United States under the agreements in question. The detailed arrangements for the implementation of this provision shall be specified in the subsidiary arrangements provided for in Article 39, and shall reflect the nature of any undertaking given under such other safeguards agreements.

Article 23

(a)   The United States and the Agency shall, at the request of either, consult each other on amendments to this Agreement.

(b)   All amendments shall require the agreement of the United States and the Agency.

Article 24

This Agreement or any amendments thereto shall enter into force on the date on which the Agency receives from the United States written notification that statutory and constitutional requirements of the United States for entry into force have been met.[5]

Article 25

The Director General shall promptly inform all Member States of the Agency of the entry into force of this Agreement, or of any amendments thereto.

Article 26

The Agreement shall remain in force as long as the United States is a party to the Treaty except that the Parties to this Agreement shall, upon the request of either of them,

---

[5] Dec. 9, 1980.

consult and, to the extent mutually agreed, modify this Agreement in order to ensure
that it continues to serve the purpose for which it was originally intended. If the Parties
are unable after such consultation to agree upon necessary modifications, either Party
may, upon six months' notice, terminate this Agreement.

PART II

Article 27

The purpose of this part of the Agreement is to specify the procedures to be applied
in the implementation of the safeguards provisions of Part I.

Article 28

The objective of the safeguards procedures set forth in this part of the Agreement is
the timely detection of withdrawal, other than in accordance with the terms of this Agreement, of significant quantities of nuclear material from activities in facilities while such
material is being safeguarded under this Agreement.

Article 29

For the purpose of achieving the objective set forth in Article 28, material accountancy
shall be used as a safeguards measure of fundamental importance, with containment and
surveillance as important complementary measures.

Article 30

The technical conclusion of the Agency's verification activities shall be a statement, in
respect of each material balance area, of the amount of material unaccounted for over a
specific period, and giving the limits of accuracy of the amounts stated.

Article 31

Pursuant to Article 7, the Agency, in carrying out its verification activities, shall make
full use of the United States' system of accounting for and control of all nuclear material
subject to safeguards under this Agreement and shall avoid unnecessary duplication of the
United States' accounting and control activities.

Article 32

The United States' system of accounting for and control of all nuclear material subject
to safeguards under this Agreement shall be based on a structure of material balance areas,
and shall make provision, as appropriate and specified in the Subsidiary Arrangements,
for the establishment of such measures as:

(a)   A measurement system for the determination of the quantities of nuclear material
      received, produced, shipped, lost or otherwise removed from inventory, and the
      quantities on inventory.
(b)   The evaluation of precision and accuracy of measurements and the estimation of
      measurement uncertainty;
(c)   Procedures for identifying, reviewing and evaluating differences in shipper/
      receiver measurements;

(d)   Procedures for taking a physical inventory;

(e)   Procedures for the evaluation of accumulations of unmeasured inventory and unmeasured losses;

(f)   A system of records and reports showing, for each material balance area, the inventory of nuclear material and the changes in that inventory including receipts into and transfers out of the material balance area;

(g)   Provisions to ensure that the accounting procedures and arrangements are being operated correctly; and

(h)   Procedures for the provision of reports to the Agency in accordance with Articles 57 through 63 and 65 through 67.

Article 33

Safeguards under this Agreement shall not apply to material in mining or ore processing activities.

Article 34

The United States may, at any time, notify the Agency of any facility or facilities to be added to or removed from the list provided for in Article 1(b):

(a)   In case of addition to the list, the notification shall specify the facility or facilities to be added to the list and the date upon which the addition is to take effect;

(b)   In the case of removal from the list of a facility or facilities then currently identified pursuant to Articles 2(b) or 39(b):

     (i)   The Agency shall be notified in advance and the notification shall specify: the facility or facilities being removed, the date of removal, and the quantity and composition of the nuclear material contained therein at the time of notification. In exceptional circumstances, the United States may remove facilities without giving advance notification;

     (ii)   Any facility in respect of which notification has been given in accordance with sub-paragraph (i) shall be removed from the list and the nuclear material contained therein shall cease to be subject to safeguards under this Agreement in accordance with and at the time specified in the notification by the United States.

(c)   In the case of removal from the list of a facility or facilities not then currently identified pursuant to Articles 2(b) or 39(b), the notification shall specify the facility or facilities being removed and the date of removal. Such facility or facilities shall be removed from the list at the time specified in the notification by the United States.

Article 35

(a)   Safeguards shall terminate on nuclear material subject to safeguards under this Agreement, under the conditions set forth in Article 11. Where the conditions of that Article are not met, but the United States considers that the recovery of safeguarded nuclear material from residues is not for the time being practicable or desirable, the United States and the Agency shall consult on the appropriate safeguards measures to be applied.

(b) Safeguards shall terminate on nuclear material subject to safeguards under this Agreement, under the conditions set forth in Article 13, provided that the United States and the Agency agree that such nuclear material is practicably irrecoverable.

Article 36

At the request of the United States, the Agency shall exempt from safeguards nuclear material, which would otherwise be subject to safeguards under this Agreement, as follows:

(a) Special fissionable material, when it is used in gram quantities or less as a sensing component in instruments;

(b) Nuclear material, when it is used in non-nuclear activities in accordance with Article 13, if such nuclear material is recoverable; and

(c) Plutonium with an isotopic concentration of plutonium-238 exceeding 80%.

Article 37

At the request of the United States, the Agency shall exempt from safeguards nuclear material that would otherwise be subject to safeguards under this Agreement, provided that the total quantity of nuclear material which has been exempted in the United States in accordance with this Article may not at any time exceed:

(a) One kilogram in total of special fissionable material, which may consist of one or more of the following:

    (i) Plutonium;

    (ii) Uranium with an enrichment of 0.2 (20%) and above, taken account of by multiplying its weight by its enrichment; and

    (iii) Uranium with an enrichment below 0.2 (20%) and above that of natural uranium, taken account of by multiplying its weight by five times the square of its enrichment;

(b) Ten metric tons in total of natural uranium and depleted uranium with an enrichment above 0.005 (0.5%);

(c) Twenty metric tons of depleted uranium with an enrichment of 0.005 (0.5%) or below; and

(d) Twenty metric tons of thorium;

or such greater amounts as may be specified by the Board for uniform application.

Article 38

If exempted nuclear material is to be processed or stored together with nuclear material subject to safeguards under this Agreement, provision shall be made for the re-application of safeguards thereto.

Article 39

(a)   The United States and the Agency shall make Subsidiary Arrangements which shall:

   (i)   contain a current listing of those facilities identified by the Agency pursuant to Article 2(b) and thus containing nuclear material subject to safeguards under this Agreement; and
   (ii)   specify in detail, to the extent necessary to permit the Agency to fulfil its responsibilities under this Agreement in an effective and efficient manner, how the procedures laid down in this Agreement are to be applied.

(b)   (i)   After entry into force of this Agreement, the Agency shall identify to the United States, from the list provided in accordance with Article 1(b), those facilities to be included in the initial Subsidiary Arrangements listing;
       (ii)   The Agency may thereafter identify for inclusion in the Subsidiary Arrangements listing additional facilities from the list provided in accordance with Article 1(b) as that list may have been modified in accordance with Article 34.

(c)   The Agency shall also designate to the United States those facilities to be removed from the Subsidiary Arrangements listing which have not otherwise been removed pursuant to notification by the United States in accordance with Article 34. Such facility or facilities shall be removed from the Subsidiary Arrangements listing upon such designation to the United States.

(d)   The Subsidiary Arrangements may be extended or changed by agreement between the Agency and the United States without amendment to this Agreement.

Article 40

(a)   With respect to those facilities which shall have been identified by the Agency in accordance with Article 39(b)(i), such Subsidiary Arrangements shall enter into force at the same time as, or as soon as possible after, entry into force of this Agreement. The United States and the Agency shall make every effort to achieve their entry into force within 90 days after entry into force of this Agreement; an extension of that period shall require agreement between the United States and the Agency.

(b)   With respect to facilities which, after the entry into force of this Agreement, have been identified by the Agency in accordance with Article 39(b)(ii) for inclusion in the Subsidiary Arrangements listing, the United States and the Agency shall make every effort to achieve the entry into force of such Subsidiary Arrangements within ninety days following such identification to the United States; an extension of that period shall require agreement between the Agency and the United States.

(c)   Upon identification of a facility by the Agency in accordance with Article 39(b), the United States shall provide the Agency promptly with the information required for completing the Subsidiary Arrangements, and the Agency shall have the right to apply the procedures set forth in this Agreement to the nuclear material listed in the inventory provided for in Article 41, even if the Subsidiary Arrangements have not yet entered into force.

Article 41

   The Agency shall establish, on the basis of the initial reports referred to in Article 60(a) below, a unified inventory of all nuclear material in the United States subject to safeguards under this Agreement, irrespective of its origin, and shall maintain this inventory on the basis of subsequent reports concerning those facilities, of the initial reports referred to in Article 60(b), of subsequent reports concerning the facilities listed pursuant to Article 39(b)(ii), and of the results of its verification activities. Copies of the inventory shall be made available to the United States at intervals to be agreed.

Article 42

Pursuant to Article 8, design information in respect of facilities identified by the Agency in accordance with Article 39(b)(i) shall be provided to the Agency during the discussion of the Subsidiary Arrangements. The time limits for the provision of design information in respect of any facility which is identified by the Agency in accordance with Article 39(b)(ii) shall be specified in the Subsidiary Arrangements and such information shall be provided as early as possible after such identification.

Article 43

The design information to be provided to the Agency shall include, in respect of each facility identified by the Agency in accordance with Article 39(b), when applicable:

(a) The identification of the facility, stating its general character, purpose, nominal capacity and geographic location, and the name and address to be used for routine business purposes;

(b) A description of the general arrangement of the facility with reference, to the extent feasible, to the form, location and flow of nuclear material and to the general layout of important items of equipment which use, produce or process nuclear material;

(c) A description of features of the facility relating to material accountancy, containment and surveillance; and

(d) A description of the existing and proposed procedures at the facility for nuclear material accountancy and control, with special reference to material balance areas established by the operator, measurements of flow and procedures for physical inventory taking.

Article 44

Other information relevant to the application of safeguards shall also be provided to the Agency in respect of each facility identified by the Agency in accordance with Article 39(b), in particular on organizational responsibility for material accountancy and control. The United States shall provide the Agency with supplementary information on the health and safety procedures which the Agency shall observe and with which the inspectors shall comply at the facility.

Article 45

The Agency shall be provided with design information in respect of a modification relevant for safeguards purposes, for examination, and shall be informed of any change in the information provided to it under Article 44, sufficiently in advance for the safeguards procedures to be adjusted when necessary.

Article 46

The design information provided to the Agency shall be used for the following purposes:

(a) To identify the features of facilities and nuclear material relevant to the application of safeguards to nuclear material in sufficient detail to facilitate verification;

(b) To determine material balance areas to be used for Agency accounting purposes and to select those strategic points which are key measurement points and which will be used to determine flow and inventory of nuclear material; in determining such material balance areas the Agency shall, inter alia, use the following criteria:

(i)   The size of the material balance area shall be related to the accuracy with which the material balance can be established;

(ii) In determining the material balance area, advantage shall be taken of any opportunity to use containment and surveillance to help ensure the completeness of flow measurements and thereby to simplify the application of safeguards and to concentrate measurement efforts at key measurement points;

(iii) A number of material balance areas in use at a facility or at distinct sites may be combined in one material balance area to be used for Agency accounting purposes when the Agency determines that this is consistent with its verification requirements; and

(iv) A special material balance area may be established at the request of the United States around a process step involving commercially sensitive information;

(c) To establish the nominal timing and procedures for taking of physical inventory of nuclear material for Agency accounting purposes;

(d) To establish the records and reports requirements and records evaluation procedures;

(e) To establish requirements and procedures for verification of the quantity and location of nuclear material; and

(f) To select appropriate combinations of containment and surveillance methods and techniques at the strategic points at which they are to be applied.

The results of the examination of the design information shall be included in the Subsidiary Arrangements.

Article 47

Design information shall be re-examined in the light of changes in operating conditions, of developments in safeguards technology or of experience in the application of verification procedures, with a view to modifying the action the Agency has taken pursuant to Article 46.

Article 48

The Agency, in co-operation with the United States, may send inspectors to facilities to verify the design information provided to the Agency pursuant to Article 42 through 45, for the purposes stated in Article 46.

Article 49

In establishing a national system of materials control as referred to in Article 7, the United States shall arrange that records are kept in respect of each material balance area determined in accordance with Article 46(b). The records to be kept shall be described in the Subsidiary Arrangements.

Article 50

The United States shall make arrangements to facilitate the examination of records referred to in Article 49 by inspectors.

Article 51

Records referred to in Article 49 shall be retained for at least five years.

Article 52

Records referred to in Article 49 shall consist, as appropriate, of:

(a) Accounting records of all nuclear material subject to safeguards under this Agreement; and
(b) Operating records for facilities containing such nuclear material.

Article 53

The system of measurements on which the records used for the preparation of reports are based shall either conform to the latest international standards or be equivalent in quality to such standards.

Article 54

The accounting records referred to in Article 52(a) shall set forth the following in respect of each material balance area determined in accordance with Article 46(b):

(a) All inventory changes, so as to permit a determination of the book inventory at any time;
(b) All measurement results that are used for determination of the physical inventory; and
(c) All adjustments and corrections that have been made in respect of inventory changes, book inventories and physical inventories.

Article 55

For all inventory changes and physical inventories the records referred to in Article 52(a) shall show, in respect of each batch of nuclear material: material identification, batch data and source data. The records shall account for uranium, thorium and plutonium separately in each batch of nuclear material. For each inventory change, the date of the inventory change and, when appropriate, the originating material balance area and the receiving material balance area or the recipient shall be indicated.

Article 56

The operating records referred to in Article 52(b) shall set forth, as appropriate, in respect of each material balance area determined in accordance with Article 46(b):

(a) Those operating data which are used to establish changes in the quantities and composition of nuclear material;

(b) The data obtained from the calibration of tanks and instruments and from sampling and analyses, the procedures to control the quality of measurements and the derived estimates of random and systematic error;

(c) A description of the sequence of the actions taken in preparing for, and in taking, a physical inventory, in order to ensure that it is correct and complete; and

(d) A description of the actions taken in order to ascertain the cause and magnitude of any accidental or unmeasured loss that might occur.

Article 57

The United States shall provide the Agency with reports as detailed in Articles 58 through 67 in respect of nuclear material subject to safeguards under this Agreement.

Article 58

Reports shall be made in English.

Article 59

Reports shall be based on the records kept in accordance with Articles 49 through 56 and shall consist, as appropriate, of accounting reports and special reports.

Article 60

The United States shall provide the Agency with an initial report on all nuclear material contained in each facility which becomes listed in the Subsidiary Arrangements in accordance with Article 39(b):

(a) With respect to those facilities listed pursuant to Article 39(b)(i), such reports shall be dispatched to the Agency within thirty days of the last day of the calendar month in which this Agreement enters into force, and shall reflect the situation as of the last day of that month.

(b) With respect to each facility listed pursuant to Article 39(b)(ii), an initial report shall be dispatched to the Agency within thirty days of the last day of the calendar month in which the Agency identifies the facility to the United States and shall reflect the situation as of the last day of that month.

Article 61

The United States shall provide the Agency with the following accounting reports for each material balance area determined in accordance with Article 46(b):

(a) Inventory change reports showing all changes in the inventory of nuclear material. The reports shall be dispatched as soon as possible and in any event within thirty days after the end of the month in which the inventory changes occurred or were established; and

(b) Material balance reports showing the material balance based on a physical inventory of nuclear material actually present in the material balance area. The reports shall be dispatched as soon as possible and in any event within thirty days after the physical inventory has been taken.

The reports shall be based on data available as of the date of reporting and may be corrected at a later date, as required.

Article 62

Inventory change reports submitted in accordance with Article 61(a) shall specify identification and batch data for each batch of nuclear material, the date of the inventory change, and, as appropriate, the originating material balance area and the receiving material balance area or the recipient. These reports shall be accompanied by concise notes:

(a) Explaining the inventory changes, on the basis of the operating data contained in the operating records provided for under Article 56(a); and

(b) Describing, as specified in the Subsidiary Arrangements, the anticipated operational programme, particularly the taking of a physical inventory.

Article 63

The United States shall report each inventory change, adjustment and correction, either periodically in a consolidated list or individually. Inventory changes shall be reported in terms of batches. As specified in the Subsidiary Arrangements, small changes in inventory of nuclear materials, such as transfers of analytical samples, may be combined in one batch and reported as one inventory change.

Article 64

The Agency shall provide the United States with semi-annual statements of book inventory of nuclear material subject to safeguards under this Agreement, for each material balance area, as based on the inventory change reports for the period covered by each such statement.

Article 65

Material balance reports submitted in accordance with Article 61(b) shall include the following entries, unless otherwise agreed by the United States and the Agency:

(a) Beginning physical inventory;
(b) Inventory changes (first increases, then decreases);
(c) Ending book inventory;
(d) Shipper/receiver differences;
(e) Adjusted ending book inventory;
(f) Ending physical inventory; and
(g) Material unaccounted for.

A statement of the physical inventory, listing all batches separately and specifying material identification and batch data for each batch, shall be attached to each material balance report.

Article 66

The United States shall make special reports without delay:

(a) If any unusual incident or circumstances lead the United States to believe that there is or may have been loss of nuclear material subject to safeguards under this Agreement that exceeds the limits specified for this purpose in the Subsidiary Arrangements; or

(b) If the containment has unexpectedly changed from that specified in the Subsidiary Arrangements to the extent that unauthorized removal of nuclear material subject to safeguards under this Agreement has become possible.

Article 67

If the Agency so requests, the United States shall provide it with amplifications or clarifications of any report submitted in accordance with Articles 57 through 63, 65 and 66, in so far as relevant for the purpose of safeguards.

Article 68

The Agency shall have the right to make inspections as provided for in Articles 69 through 82.

Article 69

The Agency may make ad hoc inspections in order to:

(a) Verify the information contained in the initial reports submitted in accordance with Article 60;

(b) Identify and verify changes in the situation which have occurred since the date of the relevant initial report; and

(c) Identify and if possible verify the quantity and composition of the nuclear material subject to safeguards under this Agreement in respect of which the information referred to in Article 89(a) has been provided to the Agency.

Article 70

The Agency may make routine inspections in order to:

(a) Verify that reports submitted pursuant to Articles 57 through 63, 65 and 66 are consistent with records kept pursuant to Articles 49 through 56;

(b) Verify the location, identity, quantity and composition of all nuclear material subject to safeguards under this Agreement; and

(c) Verify information on the possible causes of material unaccounted for, shipper/receiver differences and uncertainties in the book inventory.

Article 71

Subject to the procedures laid down in Article 75, the Agency may make special inspections:

(a) In order to verify the information contained in special reports submitted in accordance with Article 66; or

(b) If the Agency considers that information made available by the United States, including explanations from the United States and information obtained from routine inspections, is not adequate for the Agency to fulfil its responsibilities under this Agreement.

An inspection shall be deemed to be special when it is either additional to the routine inspection effort provided for in Articles 76 through 80, or involves access to information or locations in addition to the access specified in Article 74 for ad hoc and routine inspections, or both.

Article 72

For the purposes specified in Articles 69 through 71, the Agency may:

(a) Examine the records kept pursuant to Articles 49 through 56;

(b) Make independent measurements of all nuclear material subject to safeguards under this Agreement;

(c) Verify the functioning and calibration of instruments and other measuring and control equipment;

(d) Apply and make use of surveillance and containment measures; and

(e) Use other objective methods which have been demonstrated to be technically feasible.

Article 73

Within the scope of Article 72, the Agency shall be enabled:

(a) To observe that samples at key measurement points for material balance accountancy are taken in accordance with procedures which produce representative samples, to observe the treatment and analysis of the samples and to obtain duplicates of such samples;

(b) To observe that the measurements of nuclear material at key measurement points for material balance accountancy are representative, and to observe the calibration of the instruments and equipment involved;

(c) To make arrangements with the United States that, if necessary:

(i) Additional measurements are made and additional samples taken for the Agency's use;

(ii) The Agency's standard analytical samples are analysed;

(iii) Appropriate absolute standards are used in calibrating instruments and other equipment; and

(v) Other calibrations are carried out;

(d) To arrange to use its own equipment for independent measurement and surveillance, and if so agreed and specified in the Subsidiary Arrangements to arrange to install such equipment;

(e) To apply its seals and other identifying and tamper-indicating devices to contain-
     ments, if so agreed and specified in the Subsidiary Arrangements; and

(f) To make arrangements with the United States for the shipping of samples taken
     for the Agency's use.

Article 74

(a) For the purposes specified in Article 69 (a) and (b) and until such time as the
     strategic points have been specified in the Subsidiary Arrangements, Agency
     inspectors shall have access to any location where the initial report or any inspec-
     tions carried out therewith indicate that nuclear material subject to safeguards
     under this Agreement is present.

(b) For the purposes specified in Article 69(c), the inspectors shall have access to
     any facility identified pursuant to Articles 2(b) or 39(b) in which nuclear material
     referred to in Article 69(c) is located.

(c) For the purposes specified in Article 70 the inspectors shall have access only to
     the strategic points specified in the Subsidiary Arrangements and to the records
     maintained pursuant to Articles 49 through 56; and

(d) In the event of the United States concluding that any unusual circumstances
     require extended limitations on access by the Agency, the United States and the
     Agency shall promptly make arrangements with a view to enabling the Agency
     to discharge its safeguards responsibilities in the light of these limitations. The
     Director General shall report each such arrangement to the Board.

Article 75

In circumstances which may lead to special inspections for the purposes specified in
Article 71 the United States and the Agency shall consult forthwith. As a result of such
consultations the Agency may:

(a) Make inspections in addition to the routine inspection effort provided for in
     Articles 76 through 80; and

(b) Obtain access, in agreement with the United States, to information or locations
     in addition to those specified in Article 74. Any disagreement concerning the
     need for additional access shall be resolved in accordance with Articles 20 and
     21; in case action by the United States is essential and urgent, Article 17 shall
     apply.

Article 76

The Agency shall keep the number, intensity and duration of routine inspections,
applying optimum timing, to the minimum consistent with the effective implementation
of the safeguards procedures set forth in this Agreement, and shall make the optimum and
most economical use of inspection resources available to it.

Article 77

The Agency may carry out one routine inspection per year in respect of facilities listed
in the Subsidiary Arrangements pursuant to Article 39 with a content or annual throughput, whichever is greater, of nuclear material not exceeding five effective kilograms.

Article 78

The number, intensity, duration, timing and mode of routine inspections in respect of facilities listed in the Subsidiary Arrangements pursuant to Article 39 with a content or annual throughput of nuclear material exceeding five effective kilograms shall be determined on the basis that in the maximum or limiting case the inspection regime shall be no more intensive than is necessary and sufficient to maintain continuity of knowledge of the flow and inventory of nuclear material, and the maximum routine inspection effort in respect of such facilities shall be determined as follows:

(a) For reactors and sealed storage installations the maximum total of routine inspection per year shall be determined by allowing one sixth of a man-year of inspection for each such facility;

(b) For facilities, other than reactors or sealed storage installations, involving plutonium or uranium enriched to more than 5%, the maximum total of routine inspection per year shall be determined by allowing for each such facility $30 \times \sqrt{E}$ man-days of inspection per year, where E is the inventory or annual throughput of nuclear material, whichever is greater, expressed in effective kilograms. The maximum established for any such facility shall not, however, be less than 1.5 man-years of inspection; and

(c) For facilities not covered by paragraphs (a) or (b), the maximum total of routine inspection per year shall be determined by allowing for each such facility one third of a man-year of inspection plus $0.4 \times E$ man-days of inspection per year, where E is the inventory or annual throughput of nuclear material, whichever is greater, expressed in effective kilograms.

The United States and the Agency may agree to amend the figures for the maximum inspection effort specified in this Article, upon determination by the Board that such amendment is reasonable.

Article 79

Subject to Articles 76 through 78 the criteria to be used for determining the actual number, intensity, duration, timing and mode of routine inspections in respect of any facility listed in the Subsidiary Arrangements pursuant to Article 39 shall include:

(a) The form of the nuclear material, in particular, whether the nuclear material is in bulk form or contained in a number of separate items; its chemical composition and, in the case of uranium, whether it is of low or high enrichment; and its accessibility;

(b) The effectiveness of the United States' accounting and control system, including the extent to which the operators of facilities are functionally independent of the United States' accounting and control system; the extent to which the measures specified in Article 32 have been implemented by the United States; the promptness of reports provided to the Agency; their consistency with the Agency's independent verification; and the amount and accuracy of the material unaccounted for, as verified by the Agency;

(c) Characteristics of that part of the United States fuel cycle in which safeguards are applied under this Agreement, in particular, the number and types of facilities containing nuclear material subject to safeguards under this Agreement, the characteristics of such facilities relevant to safeguards, notably the degree of containment; the extent to which the design of such facilities facilitates verification of the flow and inventory of nuclear material; and the extent to which information from different material balance areas can be correlated;

(d)   International interdependence, in particular the extent to which nuclear material, safeguarded under this Agreement, is received from or sent to other States for use or processing; any verification activities by the Agency in connection therewith; and the extent to which activities in facilities in which safeguards are applied under this Agreement are interrelated with those of other States; and

(e)   Technical developments in the field of safeguards, including the use of statistical techniques and random sampling in evaluating the flow of nuclear material.

Article 80

The United States and the Agency shall consult if the United States considers that the inspection effort is being deployed with undue concentration on particular facilities.

Article 81

The Agency shall give advance notice to the United States of the arrival of inspectors at facilities listed in the Subsidiary Arrangements pursuant to Article 39, as follows:

(a)   For ad hoc inspections pursuant to Article 69(c), at least 24 hours; for those pursuant to Article 69(a) and (b), as well as the activities provided for in Article 48, at least one week;

(b)   For special inspections pursuant to Article 71, as promptly as possible after the United States and the Agency have consulted as provided for in Article 75, it being understood that notification of arrival normally will constitute part of the consultations; and

(c)   For routine inspections pursuant to Article 70 at least twenty-four hours in respect of the facilities referred to in Article 78(b) and sealed storage installations containing plutonium or uranium enriched to more than 5% and one week in all other cases.

Such notice of inspections shall include the names of the inspectors and shall indicate the facilities to be visited and the periods during which they will be visited. If the inspectors are to arrive from outside the United States the Agency shall also give advance notice of place and time of their arrival in the United States.

Article 82

Notwithstanding the provisions of Article 81, the Agency may, as a supplementary measure, carry out without advance notification a portion of the routine inspections pursuant to Article 78 in accordance with the principle of random sampling. In performing any unannounced inspections, the Agency shall fully take into account any operational programme provided by the United States pursuant to Article 62(b). Moreover, whenever practicable, and on the basis of the operational programme, it shall advise the United States periodically of its general programme of announced and unannounced inspections, specifying the general periods when inspections are foreseen. In carrying out any unannounced inspections, the Agency shall make every effort to minimize any practical difficulties for the United States and facility operators bearing in mind the relevant provisions of Articles 44 and 87. Similarly the United States shall make every effort to facilitate the task of the inspectors.

Article 83

The following procedures shall apply to the designation of inspectors:

(a) The Director General shall inform the United States in writing of the name, qualifications, nationality, grade and such other particulars as may be relevant, of each Agency official he proposes for designation as an inspector for the United States;

(b) The United States shall inform the Director General within thirty days of the receipt of such a proposal whether it accepts the proposal;

(c) The Director General may designate each official who has been accepted by the United States as one of the inspectors for the United States, and shall inform the United States of such designations; and

(d) The Director General, acting in response to a request by the United States or on his own initiative, shall immediately inform the United States of the withdrawal of the designation of any official as an inspector for the United States.

However, in respect of inspectors needed for the activities provided for in Article 48 and to carry out ad hoc inspections pursuant to Article 69(a) and (b) the designation procedures shall be completed if possible within thirty days after the entry into force of this Agreement. If such designation appears impossible within this time limit, inspectors for such purposes shall be designated on a temporary basis.

Article 84

The United States shall grant or renew as quickly as possible appropriate visas, where required, for each inspector designated for United States.

Article 85

Inspectors, in exercising their functions under Article 48 and 69 to 73, shall carry out their activities in a manner designed to avoid hampering or delaying the construction, commissioning or operation of facilities, or affecting their safety. In particular inspectors shall not operate any facility themselves or direct the staff of a facility to carry out any operation. If inspectors consider that in pursuance of paragraphs 72 and 73, particular operations in a facility should be carried out by the operator, they shall make a request therefor.

Article 86

When inspectors require services available in the United States, including the use of equipment, in connection with the performance of inspections, the United States shall facilitate the procurement of such services and the use of such equipment by inspectors.

Article 87

The United States shall have the right to have inspectors accompanied during their inspections by its representatives, provided that inspectors shall not thereby be delayed or otherwise impeded in the exercise of their functions.

Article 88

The Agency shall inform the United States of:

(a) The results of inspections, at intervals to be specified in the Subsidiary Arrangements; and

(b) The conclusions it has drawn from its verification activities in the United States, in particular by means of statements in respect of each material balance area determined in accordance with Article 46(b) which shall be made as soon as possible after a physical inventory has been taken and verified by the Agency and a material balance has been struck.

Article 89

(a) Information concerning nuclear material exported from and imported into the United States shall be provided to the Agency in accordance with arrangements made with the Agency as, for example, those set forth in INFCIRC/207.

(b) In the case of international transfers to or from facilities identified by the Agency pursuant to Articles 2(b) and 39(b) with respect to which information has been provided to the Agency in accordance with arrangements referred to in paragraph (a), a special report, as envisaged in Article 66, shall be made if any unusual incident or circumstances lead the United States to believe that there is or may have been loss of nuclear material, including the occurrence of significant delay, during the transfer.

DEFINITIONS

Article 90

For the purposes of this Agreement:

A   Adjustment means an entry into an accounting record or a report showing a shipper/receiver difference or material unaccounted for.

B   Annual throughput means, for the purposes of Articles 77 and 78, the amount of nuclear material transferred annually out of a facility working at nominal capacity.

C   Batch means a portion of nuclear material handled as a unit for accounting purposes at a key measurement point and for which the composition and quantity are defined by a single set of specifications or measurements. The nuclear material may be in bulk form or contained in a number of separate items.

D   Batch data means the total weight of each element of nuclear material and, in the case of plutonium and uranium, the isotopic composition when appropriate. The units of account shall be as follows:

(a) Grams of contained plutonium;

(b) Grams of total uranium and grams of contained uranium-235 plus uranium-233 for uranium enriched in these isotopes; and

(c) Kilograms of contained thorium, natural uranium or depleted uranium.

For reporting purposes the weights of individual items in the batch shall be added together before rounding to the nearest unit.

E   Book inventory of a material balance area means the algebraic sum of the most recent physical inventory of that material balance area and of all inventory changes that have occurred since that physical inventory was taken.

F   Correction means an entry into an accounting record or a report to rectify an identified mistake or to reflect an improved measurement of a quantity previously entered into the record or report. Each correction must identify the entry to which it pertains.

G   Effective kilogram means a special unit used in safeguarding nuclear material. The quantity in effective kilograms is obtained by taking:

  (a) For plutonium, its weight in kilograms;
  (b) For uranium with an enrichment of 0.01 (1%) and above, its weight in kilograms multiplied by the square of its enrichment;
  (c) For uranium with an enrichment below 0.01 (1%) and above 0.005 (0.5%), its weight in kilograms multiplied by 0.0001; and
  (d) For depleted uranium with an enrichment of 0.005 (0.5%) or below, and for thorium, its weight in kilograms multiplied by 0.00005.

H   Enrichment means the ratio of the combined weight of the isotopes uranium-233 and uranium-235 to that of the total uranium in question.

I   Facility means:

  (a) A reactor, a critical facility, a conversion plant, a fabrication plant, a reprocessing plant, an isotope separation plant or a separate storage installation; or
  (b) Any location where nuclear material in amounts greater than one effective kilogram is customarily used.

J   Inventory change means an increase or decrease, in terms of batches, of nuclear material in a material balance area; such a change shall involve one of the following:

  (a) Increases:

    (i) Import;
    (ii) Domestic receipt: receipts from other material balance areas, receipts from a non-safeguarded activity or receipts at the starting point of safeguards;
    (iii) Nuclear production: production of special fissionable material in a reactor; and
    (iv) De-exemption: reapplication of safeguards on nuclear material previously exempted therefrom on account of its use or quantity.

  (b) Decreases:

    (i) Export;
    (ii) Domestic shipment: shipments to other material balance areas or shipments for a non-safeguarded activity;
    (iii) Nuclear loss: loss of nuclear material due to its transformation into other element(s) or isotope(s) as a result of nuclear reactions;
    (iv) Measured discard: nuclear material which has been measured, or estimated on the basis of measurements, and disposed of in such a way that it is not suitable for further nuclear use;

    (v) Retained waste: nuclear material generated from processing or from an operational accident, which is deemed to be unrecoverable for the time being but which is stored;

    (vi) Exemption: exemption of nuclear material from safeguards on account of its use or quantity; and

    (vii) Other loss: for example, accidental loss (that is, irretrievable and inadvertent loss of nuclear material as the result of an operational accident) or theft.

K   Key measurement point means a location where nuclear material appears in such a form that it may be measured to determine material flow or inventory. Key measurement points thus include, but are not limited to, the inputs and outputs (including measured discards) and storages in material balance areas.

L   Man-year of inspection means, for the purposes of Article 78, 300 man-days of inspection, a man-day being a day during which a single inspector has access to a facility at any time for a total of not more than eight hours.

M   Material balance area means an area in or outside of a facility such that:

    (a) The quantity of nuclear material in each transfer into or out of each material balance area can be determined; and

    (b) The physical inventory of nuclear material in each material balance area can be determined when necessary in accordance with specified procedures,

in order that the material balance for Agency safeguards purposes can be established.

N   Material unaccounted for means the difference between book inventory and physical inventory.

O   Nuclear material means any source or any special fissionable material as defined in Article XX of the Statute. The term source material shall not be interpreted as applying to ore or ore residue. Any determination by the Board under Article XX of the Statute after the entry into force of this Agreement which adds to the materials considered to be source material or special fissionable material shall have effect under this Agreement only upon acceptance by the United States.

P   Physical inventory means the sum of all the measured or derived estimates of batch quantities of nuclear material on hand at a given time within a material balance area, obtained in accordance with specified procedures.

Q   Shipper/receiver difference means the difference between the quantity of nuclear material in a batch as stated by the shipping material balance area and as measured at the receiving material balance area.

R   Source data means those data, recorded during measurement or calibration or used to derive empirical relationships, which identify nuclear material and provide batch data. Source data may include, for example, weight of compounds, conversion factors to determine weight of element, specific gravity, element concentration, isotopic ratios, relationship between volume and manometer readings and relationship between plutonium produced and power generated.

S   Strategic point means a location selected during examination of design information where, under normal conditions and when combined with the information from all strategic points taken together, the information necessary and sufficient for the implementation of safeguards measures is obtained and verified; a strategic point may include any location where key measurements related to material balance accountancy are made and where containment and surveillance measures are executed.

For the United States
of America:

For the International
Atomic Energy Agency:

G.S.

D.A.V.F.

Protocol to the Agreement Between the United States of America and the International Atomic Energy Agency for the Application of Safeguards in the United States

Article 1

This Protocol specifies the procedures to be followed with respect to facilities identified by the Agency pursuant to Article 2 of this Protocol.

Article 2

(a) The Agency may from time to time identify to the United States those facilities included in the list, established and maintained pursuant to Articles 1(b) and 34 of the Agreement, of facilities not associated with activities having direct national security significance to the United States, other than those which are then currently identified by the Agency pursuant to Articles 2(b) and 39(b) of the Agreement, to which the provisions of this Protocol shall apply.

(b) The Agency may also include among the facilities identified to the United States pursuant to the foregoing paragraph, any facility which had previously been identified by the Agency pursuant to Articles 2(b) and 39(b) of the Agreement but which had subsequently been designated by the Agency pursuant to Article 39(c) of the Agreement for removal from the Subsidiary Arrangements listing.

(c) In identifying facilities pursuant to the foregoing paragraphs and in the preparation of Transitional Subsidiary Arrangements pursuant to Article 3 of this Protocol, the Agency shall proceed in a manner which the Agency and the United States mutually agree takes into account the requirement on the United States to avoid discriminatory treatment as between United States commercial firms similarly situated.

Article 3

The United States and the Agency shall make Transitional Subsidiary Arrangements which shall:

(a) contain a current listing of those facilities identified by the Agency pursuant to Article 2 of this Protocol;

(b) specify in detail how the procedures set forth in this Protocol are to be applied.

Article 4

(a) The United States and the Agency shall make every effort to complete the Transitional Subsidiary Arrangements with respect to each facility identified by the Agency pursuant to Article 2 of this Protocol within ninety days following such identification to the United States.

(b) With respect to any facility identified pursuant to Article 2(b) of this Protocol, the information previously submitted to the Agency in accordance with Articles 42 through 45 of the Agreement, the results of the examination of the design information and other provisions of the Subsidiary Arrangements relative to such facility, to the extent that such information, results and provisions satisfy the provisions of this Protocol relating to the submission and examination of information and the preparation of Transitional Subsidiary Arrangements, shall constitute the Transitional

Subsidiary Arrangements for such facility, until and unless the United States and the Agency shall otherwise complete Transitional Subsidiary Arrangements for such facility in accordance with the provisions of this Protocol.

Article 5

In the event that a facility currently identified by the Agency pursuant to Article 2(a) of this Protocol is identified by the Agency pursuant to Articles 2(b) and 39(b) of the Agreement, the Transitional Subsidiary Arrangements relevant to such facility shall, to the extent that such Transitional Subsidiary Arrangements satisfy the provisions of the Agreement, be deemed to have been made part of the Subsidiary Arrangements to the Agreement.

Article 6

Design information in respect of each facility identified by the Agency pursuant to Article 2 of this Protocol shall be provided to the Agency during the discussion of the relevant Transitional Subsidiary Arrangements. The information shall include, when applicable:

(a) The identification of the facility, stating its general character, purpose, nominal capacity and geographic location, and the name and address to be used for routine business purpose;

(b) A description of the general arrangement of the facility with reference, to the extent feasible, to the form, location and flow of nuclear material and to the general layout of important items of equipment which use, produce or process nuclear material;

(c) A description of features of the facility relating to material accountancy, containment and surveillance; and

(d) A description of the existing and proposed procedures at the facility for nuclear material accountancy and control, with special reference to material balance areas established by the operator, measurements of flow and procedures for physical inventory taking.

Article 7

Other information relevant to the application of the provisions of this Protocol shall also be provided to the Agency in respect of each facility identified by the Agency in accordance with Article 2 of this Protocol, in particular on organizational responsibility for material accountancy and control. The United States shall provide the Agency with supplementary information on the health and safety procedures which the Agency shall observe and with which inspectors shall comply when visiting the facility in accordance with Article 11 of this Protocol.

Article 8

The Agency shall be provided with design information in respect of a modification relevant to the application of the provisions of this Protocol, for examination, and shall be informed of any change in the information provided to it under Article 7 of this Protocol, sufficiently in advance for the procedures under this Protocol to be adjusted when necessary.

Article 9

The design information provided to the Agency in accordance with the provisions of this Protocol, in anticipation of the application of safeguards under the Agreement, shall be used for the following purposes:

(a) To identify the features of facilities and nuclear material relevant to the application of safeguards to nuclear material in sufficient detail to facilitate verification;

(b) To determine material balance areas to be used for Agency accounting purposes and to select those strategic points which are key measurement points and which will be used to determine flow and inventory of nuclear material; in determining such material balance areas the Agency shall, inter alia, use the following criteria;

    (i) The size of the material balance area shall be related to the accuracy with which the material balance can be established;

    (ii) In determining the material balance area, advantage shall be taken of any opportunity to use containment and surveillance to help ensure the completeness of flow measurements and thereby to simplify the application of safeguards and to concentrate measurement efforts at key measurement points;

    (iii) A number of material balance areas in use at a facility or at distinct sites may be combined in one material balance area to be used for Agency accounting purposes when the Agency determines that this is consistent with its verification requirements; and

    (iv) A special material balance area may be established at the request of the United States around a process step involving commercially sensitive information;

(c) To establish the nominal timing and procedures for taking of physical inventory of nuclear material for Agency accounting purposes;

(d) To establish the records and reports requirements and records evaluation procedures;

(e) To establish requirements and procedures for verification of the quantity and location of nuclear material; and

(f) To select appropriate combinations of containment and surveillance methods and techniques and the strategic points at which they are to be applied.

The results of the examination of the design information shall be included in the relevant Transitional Subsidiary Arrangements.

Article 10

Design information provided in accordance with the provisions of this Protocol shall be re-examined in the light of changes in operating conditions, of developments in safeguards technology or of experience in the application of verification procedures, with a view to modifying the action taken pursuant to Article 9 of this Protocol.

Article 11

(a) The Agency, in co-operation with the United States, may send inspectors to facilities identified by the Agency pursuant to Article 2 of this Protocol to verify the design information provided to the Agency in accordance with the provisions of this

Protocol, for the purposes stated in Article 9 of this Protocol or for such other purposes as may be agreed between the United States and the Agency.

(b)   The Agency shall give notice to the United States with respect to each such visit at least one week prior to the arrival of inspectors at the facility to be visited.

Article 12

In establishing a national system of materials control as referred to in Article 7(a) of the Agreement, the United States shall arrange that records are kept in respect of each material balance area determined in accordance with Article 9(b) of this Protocol. The records to be kept shall be described in the relevant Transitional Subsidiary Arrangements.

Article 13

Records referred to in Article 12 of this Protocol shall be retained for at least five years.

Article 14

Records referred to in Article 12 of this Protocol shall consist, as appropriate, of:

(a)   Accounting records of all nuclear material stored, processed, used or produced in each facility; and

(b)   Operating records for activities within each facility.

Article 15

The system of measurements on which the records used for the preparation of reports are based shall either conform to the latest international standards or be equivalent in quality to such standards.

Article 16

The accounting records referred to in Article 14(a) of this Protocol shall set forth the following in respect of each material balance area determined in accordance with Article 9(b) of this Protocol:

(a)   All inventory changes, so as to permit a determination of the book inventory at any time;

(b)   All measurement results that are used for determination of the physical inventory; and

(c)   All adjustments and corrections that have been made in respect of inventory changes, book inventories and physical inventories.

Article 17

For all inventory changes and physical inventories the records referred to in Article 14(a) of this Protocol shall show, in respect of each batch of nuclear material: material identification, batch data and source data. The records shall account for uranium, thorium and plutonium separately in each batch of nuclear material. For each inventory change, the date of the inventory change and, when appropriate, the originating material balance area and the receiving material balance area or the recipient, shall be indicated.

Article 18

The operating records referred to in Article 14(b) of this Protocol shall set forth, as appropriate, in respect of each material balance area determined in accordance with Article 9(b) of this Protocol:

(a) Those operating data which are used to establish changes in the quantities and composition of nuclear material;

(b) The data obtained from the calibration of tanks and instruments and from sampling and analyses, the procedures to control the quality of measurements and the derived estimates of random and systematic error;

(c) A description of the sequence of the actions taken in preparing for, and in taking, a physical inventory, in order to ensure that it is correct and complete; and

(d) A description of the actions taken in order to ascertain the cause and magnitude of any accidental or unmeasured loss that might occur.

Article 19

The United States shall provide the Agency with accounting reports as detailed in Articles 20 through 25 of this Protocol in respect of nuclear material in each facility identified by the Agency pursuant to Article 2 of this Protocol.

Article 20

The accounting reports shall be based on the records kept in accordance with Articles 12 to 18 to this Protocol. They shall be made in English.

Article 21

The United States shall provide the Agency with an initial report on all nuclear material in each facility identified by the Agency pursuant to Article 2 of this Protocol. Such report shall be dispatched to the Agency within thirty days of the last day of the calendar month in which the facility is identified by the Agency and shall reflect the situation as of the last day of that month.

Article 22

The United States shall provide the Agency with the following accounting reports for each material balance area determined in accordance with Article 9(b) of this Protocol:

(a) Inventory change reports showing all changes in the inventory of nuclear material. The reports shall be dispatched as soon as possible and in any event within thirty days after the end of the month in which the inventory changes occurred or were established; and

(b) Material balance reports showing the material balance based on a physical inventory of nuclear material actually present in the material balance area. The reports shall be dispatched as soon as possible and in any event within thirty days after the physical inventory has been taken.

The reports shall be based on data available as of the date of reporting and may be corrected at a later date, as required.

Article 23

Inventory change reports submitted in accordance with Article 22(a) of this Protocol shall specify identification and batch data for each batch of nuclear material, the date of the inventory change, and, as appropriate, the originating material balance area and the receiving material balance area or the recipient. These reports shall be accompanied by concise notes:

(a) Explaining the inventory changes, on the basis of the operating data contained in the operating records provided for in Article 18(a) of this Protocol; and

(b) Describing, as specified in the relevant Transitional Subsidiary Arrangements, the anticipated operational programme, particularly the taking of a physical inventory.

Article 24

The United States shall report each inventory change, adjustment and correction, either periodically in a consolidated list or individually. Inventory changes shall be reported in terms of batches. As specified in the relevant Transitional Subsidiary Arrangements, small changes in inventory of nuclear material, such as transfers of analytical samples, may be combined in one batch and reported as one inventory change.

Article 25

Material balance reports submitted in accordance with Article 22(b) of this Protocol shall include the following entries, unless otherwise agreed by the United States and the Agency:

(a) Beginning physical inventory;

(b) Inventory changes (first increases, then decreases);

(c) Ending book inventory;

(d) Shipper/receiver differences;

(e) Adjusted ending book inventory;

(f) Ending physical inventory; and

(g) Material unaccounted for.

A statement of the physical inventory, listing all batches separately and specifying material identification and batch data for each batch, shall be attached to each material balance report.

Article 26

The Agency shall provide the United States with semi-annual statements of book inventory of nuclear material in facilities identified pursuant to Article 2 of this Protocol, for each material balance area, as based on the inventory change reports for the period covered by each such statement.

Article 27

(a) If the Agency so requests, the United States shall provide it with amplifications or clarifications of any report submitted in accordance with Article 19 of this Protocol, in so far as consistent with the purpose of the Protocol.

(b) The Agency shall inform the United States of any significant observations resulting from its examination of reports received pursuant to Article 19 of this Protocol and from visits of inspectors made pursuant to Article 11 of this Protocol.

(c) The United States and the Agency shall, at the request of either, consult about any question arising out of the interpretation or application of this Protocol, including corrective action which, in the opinion of the Agency, should be taken by the United States to ensure compliance with its terms, as indicated by the Agency in its observations pursuant to paragraph (b) of this Article.

Article 28

The definitions set forth in Article 90 of the Agreement shall apply, to the extent relevant, to this Protocol.

DONE in Vienna on the eighteenth day of November 1977, in duplicate, in the English language.

FOR THE UNITED STATES OF AMERICA:

G.S. *18 November 1977*

FOR THE INTERNATIONAL ATOMIC ENERGY AGENCY:

D.A.V.F. *18 November 1977*

Strategic Arms Limitation Talks (SALT II)

In accordance with Article VII of the Interim Agreement in which the sides committed themselves to continue active negotiations on strategic offensive arms, the SALT II negotiations began in November 1972. The primary goal of SALT II was to replace the Interim Agreement with a long-term comprehensive treaty providing broad limits on strategic offensive weapons systems. The principal U.S. objectives as the SALT II negotiations began were to provide for equal numbers of strategic nuclear delivery vehicles for the sides, to begin the process of reduction of these delivery vehicles, and to impose restraints on qualitative developments which could threaten future stability.

Early discussion between the sides focused on the weapon systems to be included, factors involved in providing for equality in numbers of strategic nuclear delivery vehicles, taking into account the important differences between the forces of the two sides, bans on new systems, qualitative limits, and a Soviet proposal to include U.S. forward-based systems. The positions of the sides differed widely on many of these issues.

A major breakthrough occurred at the Vladivostok meeting in November 1974, between President Ford and General Secretary Brezhnev. At this meeting, the sides agreed to a basic framework for the SALT II agreement. Basic elements of the Aide-Memoire, which recorded this agreement, included:

- 2,400 equal aggregate limit on strategic nuclear delivery vehicles (ICBMs, SLBMs, and heavy bombers) of the sides;
- 1,320 equal aggregate limit on MIRV systems;
- ban on construction of new land-based ICBM launchers;
- limits on deployment of new types of strategic offensive arms; and
- important elements of the Interim Agreement (e.g., relating to verification) would be incorporated in the new agreement.

In addition, the Aide-Memoire stated that the duration of the new agreement would be through 1985.

In early 1975, the delegations in Geneva resumed negotiations, working toward an agreement based on this general framework. It was during this time that a Joint Draft Text was first prepared and many limitations were agreed. During the negotiations, however, it became clear that there was fundamental disagreement between the two sides on two major issues: how cruise missiles were to be addressed, and whether the new Soviet bomber known to the United States as Backfire would be considered a heavy bomber and therefore counted in the 2,400 aggregate. While there was disagreement on other issues such as MIRV verification provisions, restrictions on new systems, and missile throw-weight ceilings, progress was made in these areas. However, the issues of cruise missiles and Backfire remained unresolved.

When the new Administration took office in 1977, renewed emphasis was placed on the Strategic Arms Limitation Talks. A comprehensive interagency review of SALT was undertaken. Building on the work of the previous Administration, particularly the Vladivostok accord and the subsequent agreement on many issues in Geneva, the United States made a comprehensive proposal which was presented to the Soviets by Secretary of State Vance in March 1977. This proposal would have added significant reductions and qualitative constraints to the ceilings which were agreed to at Vladivostok. At the same time, the United States also presented an alternative proposal for a SALT II agreement similar to the framework agreed to at Vladivostok, with the Backfire and cruise missile issues deferred until SALT III.

Both proposals were rejected by the Soviets as inconsistent with their understandings of the Vladivostok accord.

In subsequent negotiations, the sides agreed on a general framework for SALT II which accommodated both the Soviet desire to retain the Vladivostok framework for an agreement, and the U.S. desire for more comprehensive limitations in SALT II.

The agreement would consist of three parts:

• A Treaty which would be in force through 1985 based on the Vladivostok accord;

• A Protocol of about 3-years' duration which would cover certain issues such as cruise missile constraints, mobile ICBM limits, and qualitative constraints on ICBMs, while deferring further negotiations on these issues to SALT III;

• A Joint Statement of Principles which would be an agreed set of guidelines for future negotiations.

Within this framework, negotiations to resolve the remaining differences continued on several levels. President Carter, Secretary Vance, and Soviet Foreign Minister Gromyko met in Washington in September 1977. Further high-level meetings were held in Washington, Moscow, and Geneva during 1978 and 1979. In addition, the SALT delegations of the United States and Soviet Union in Geneva were in session nearly continuously since the 1974 Vladivostok meeting to work out agreed Treaty language on those issues where agreement in principle had been reached at the ministerial level.

The completed SALT II agreement was signed by President Carter and General Secretary Brezhnev in Vienna on June 18, 1979. President Carter transmitted it to the Senate on June 22 for its advice and consent to ratification.

Although Senate consent has not been given, both President Carter and President Reagan have declared that they would do nothing to jeopardize the treaty as long as the Soviet Union abided by it, and President Brezhnev has made a similar statement regarding Soviet intentions.

Treaty Between the United States of America and the Union of Soviet Socialist Republics on the Limitation of Strategic Offensive Arms

The SALT II Treaty would have provided for:

- an equal aggregate limit on the number of strategic nuclear delivery vehicles—ICBM and SLBM launchers, heavy bombers, and air-to-surface ballistic missiles (ASBMs). Initially, this ceiling would have been 2,400, as agreed at Vladivostok. The ceiling would have been lowered to 2,250 at the end of 1981;
- an equal aggregate limit of 1,320 on the total number of launchers of MIRVed ballistic missiles and heavy bombers with long-range cruise missiles;
- an equal aggregate limit of 1,200 on the total number of launchers of MIRVed ballistic missiles; and
- an equal aggregate limit of 820 on launchers of MIRVed ICBMs.

In addition to these numerical limits, the agreement would have included:

- A ban on construction of additional fixed ICBM launchers, and on increases in the number of fixed heavy ICBM launchers;
- a ban on heavy mobile ICBM launchers, and on launchers of heavy SLBMs and ASBMs;
- a ban on flight-testing or deployment of new types of ICBMs, with an exception of one new type of light ICBM for each side;
- a ban on increasing the numbers of warheads on existing types of ICBMs, and a limit of 10 warheads on the one new type of ICBM permitted to each Party, a limit of 14 warheads on SLBMs, and 10 warheads on ASBMs. The number of long-range cruise missiles per heavy bomber would have been limited to an average of 28; and the number of long-range cruise missiles per heavy bomber of existing types would have been limited to 20;
- ceilings on the launch weight and throw weight of strategic ballistic missiles and a ban on the conversion of light ICBM launchers to launchers of heavy ICBMs;
- a ban on the Soviet SS-16 ICBM;

- a ban on rapid reload ICBM systems;
- a ban on certain new types of strategic offensive systems which were technologically feasible, but which had not yet been deployed. Such systems included long-range ballistic missiles on surface ships, and ballistic and cruise missile launchers on the seabeds;
- advance notification of certain ICBM test launches; and
- an agreed data base for systems included in various SALT-limited categories.

The Treaty also included detailed definitions of limited systems, provisions to enhance verification, a ban on circumvention of the provisions of the agreement, and a provision outlining the duties of the SCC in connection with the SALT II Treaty. The duration of the Treaty was to have been through 1985.

Verification of the SALT II agreement would have been by national technical means (NTM), including photo-reconnaissance satellites. The sides had agreed not to interfere with each others' national technical means of verification, and not to use deliberate concealment measures which would have impeded verification by NTM of compliance with the provisions of the agreement. Because specific characteristics of some SALT-limited systems become apparent during the testing phase, monitoring of testing programs was an important aspect of SALT verification. Such monitoring might have involved collection of electronic signals known as telemetry which are used during tests to transmit information about systems while they are being tested. Therefore, the sides had agreed not to engage in deliberate denial of telemetric information whenever such denial would have impeded verification of compliance with the provisions of the agreement.

In addition to these provisions of the agreement which directly addressed the question of verification, counting and distinguishability rules, as well as some constraints on specific systems, were incorporated into the agreement specifically for verification purposes.

To facilitate verification of the MIRV limits, the sides agreed that once a missile had been tested with MIRVs, then all missiles of that type were to be considered to have been equipped with MIRVs, even if that missile type had also been tested with a non-MIRV payload. Additionally, the sides agreed that once a launcher contained or launched a MIRVed missile, then all launchers of that type would be considered to be launchers of MIRVed missiles and included in the 1,320 limit. Similar counting rules were adopted for cruise missiles and for heavy bombers.

A constraint included for verification purposes was a ban on production, testing, and deployment of the Soviet SS-16 ICBM. The missile appeared to share a number of components with the Soviet SS-20, an intermediate range ballistic missile (IRBM). As the Parties had agreed that land-based launchers of ballistic missiles which are not ICBMs should not be converted into launchers of ICBMs, the U.S. sought this ban on the SS-16 in order to prevent verification problems which might have arisen if the SS-16 program had gone forward, since in that case distinguishing between SS-16 and SS-20 deployments would have been very difficult.

Pursuant to a Memorandum of Understanding, the sides exchanged data on the numbers of weapons in SALT-limited categories, and agreed to maintain this agreed data base through regular updates at each session of the Standing Consultative Commission. Although the United States did not require (and did not rely upon) this data for verification purposes, maintenance of the agreed data base would have insured that both parties applied the provisions of the Treaty in a consistent manner.

The Protocol to the Treaty was to have remained in force until December 31, 1981. In the Protocol the sides agreed to ban deployment of mobile ICBM launchers and flight-testing of ICBMs from such launchers. Development of such systems short of flight-testing would have been permitted. (After the Protocol period, the Treaty specifically permitted the deployment of mobile ICBM launchers.)

Additionally, the Protocol banned deployment, but not testing, of cruise missiles capable of ranges in excess of 600 kilometers on ground- and sea-based launchers. (The Protocol would not have limited deployment of such systems after its expiration in 1981.)

Finally, the Protocol included a ban on flight testing and deployment of air-to-surface ballistic missiles (ASBMs).

The Joint Statement of Principles, the third element of the SALT II agreement, would have established a basic framework for the next stage of SALT negotiations, SALT III. The sides agreed on the following general goals to be achieved in the next round of talks:

• significant and substantial reductions in the number of strategic offensive arms;

- further qualitative limitations on strategic offensive arms; and
- resolution of the issues included in the Protocol.

The sides would also have considered other steps to enhance strategic stability, and either side could have brought up any other topic relevant to the limitation of strategic arms.

The Joint Statement of Principles also established the principle that cooperative measures might be used to ensure adequate verification of a SALT III agreement, raising the possibility of thus going beyond reliance on national technical means alone.

Treaty Between the United States of America and the Union of Soviet Socialist Republics on the Limitation of Strategic Offensive Arms*

Signed at Vienna June 18, 1979

The United States of America and the Union of Soviet Socialist Republics, hereinafter referred to as the Parties,

Conscious that nuclear war would have devastating consequences for all mankind,

Proceeding from the Basic Principles of Relations Between the United States of America and the Union of Soviet Socialist Republics of May 29, 1972,

Attaching particular significance to the limitation of strategic arms and determined to continue their efforts begun with the Treaty on the Limitation of Anti-Ballistic Missile Systems and the Interim Agreement on Certain Measures with Respect to the Limitation of Strategic Offensive Arms, of May 26, 1972,

Convinced that the additional measures limiting strategic offensive arms provided for in this Treaty will contribute to the improvement of relations between the Parties, help to reduce the risk of outbreak of nuclear war and strengthen international peace and security,

Mindful of their obligations under Article VI of the Treaty on the Non-Proliferation of Nuclear Weapons,

Guided by the principle of equality and equal security,

Recognizing that the strengthening of strategic stability meets the interests of the Parties and the interests of international security,

Reaffirming their desire to take measures for the further limitation and for the further reduction of strategic arms, having in mind the goal of achieving general and complete disarmament,

Declaring their intention to undertake in the near future negotiations further to limit and further to reduce strategic offensive arms,

Have agreed as follows:

---

*The text of the SALT II Treaty and Protocol, as signed in Vienna, is accompanied by a set of Agreed Statements and Common Understandings, also signed by Presidents Carter and Brezhnev, which is prefaced as follows:

In connection with the Treaty Between the United States of America and the Union of Soviet Socialist Republics on the Limitation of Strategic Offensive Arms, the Parties have agreed on the following Agreed Statements and Common Understandings undertaken on behalf of the Government of the United States and the Government of the Union of Soviet Socialist Republics.

As an aid to the reader, the texts of the Agreed Statements and Common Understandings are beneath the articles of the Treaty or Protocol to which they pertain.

Article I

Each Party undertakes, in accordance with the provisions of this Treaty, to limit strategic offensive arms quantitatively and qualitatively, to exercise restraint in the development of new types of strategic offensive arms, and to adopt other measures provided for in this Treaty.

Article II

For the purposes of this Treaty:

1. Intercontinental ballistic missile (ICBM) launchers are land-based launchers of ballistic missiles capable of a range in excess of the shortest distance between the northeastern border of the continental part of the territory of the United States of America and the northwestern border of the continental part of the territory of the Union of Soviet Socialist Republics, that is, a range in excess of 5,500 kilometers.

First Agreed Statement. The term "intercontinental ballistic missile launchers," as defined in paragraph 1 of Article II of the Treaty, includes all launchers which have been developed and tested for launching ICBMs. If a launcher has been developed and tested for launching an ICBM, all launchers of that type shall be considered to have been developed and tested for launching ICBMs.

First Common Understanding. If a launcher contains or launches an ICBM, that launcher shall be considered to have been developed and tested for launching ICBMs.

Second Common Understanding. If a launcher has been developed and tested for launching an ICBM, all launchers of that type, except for ICBM test and training launchers, shall be included in the aggregate numbers of strategic offensive arms provided for in Article III of the Treaty, pursuant to the provisions of Article VI of the Treaty.

Third Common Understanding. The one hundred and seventy-seven former Atlas and Titan I ICBM launchers of the United States of America, which are no longer operational and are partially dismantled, shall not be considered as subject to the limitations provided for in the Treaty.

Second Agreed Statement. After the date on which the Protocol ceases to be in force, mobile ICBM launchers shall be subject to the relevant limitations provided for in the Treaty which are applicable to ICBM launchers, unless the Parties agree that mobile ICBM launchers shall not be deployed after that date.

---

2. Submarine-launched ballistic missile (SLBM) launchers are launchers of ballistic missiles installed on any nuclear-powered submarine or launchers of modern ballistic missiles installed on any submarine, regardless of its type.

Agreed Statement. Modern submarine-launched ballistic missiles are: for the United States of America, missiles installed in all nuclear-powered submarines; for the Union of Soviet Socialist Republics, missiles of the type installed in nuclear-powered submarines made operational since 1965; and for both Parties, submarine-launched ballistic missiles first flight-tested since 1965 and installed in any submarine, regardless of its type.

---

3. Heavy bombers are considered to be:

(a) currently, for the United States of America, bombers of the B-52 and B-1 types, and for the Union of Soviet Socialist Republics, bombers of the Tupolev-95 and Myasishchev types;

(b) in the future, types of bombers which can carry out the mission of a heavy bomber in a manner similar or superior to that of bombers listed in subparagraph (a) above;

(c) types of bombers equipped for cruise missiles capable of a range in excess of 600 kilometers; and

(d) types of bombers equipped for ASBMs.

First Agreed Statement. The term "bombers," as used in paragraph 3 of Article II and other provisions of the Treaty, means airplanes of types initially constructed to be equipped for bombs or missiles.

Second Agreed Statement. The Parties shall notify each other on a case-by-case basis in the Standing Consultative Commission of inclusion of types of bombers as heavy bombers pursuant to the provisions of paragraph 3 of Article II of the Treaty; in this connection the Parties shall hold consultations, as appropriate, consistent with the provisions of paragraph 2 of Article XVII of the Treaty.

Third Agreed Statement. The criteria the Parties shall use to make case-by-case determinations of which types of bombers in the future can carry out the mission of a heavy bomber in a manner similar or superior to that of current heavy bombers, as referred to in subparagraph 3(b) of Article II of the Treaty, shall be agreed upon in the Standing Consultative Commission.

Fourth Agreed Statement. Having agreed that every bomber of a type included in paragraph 3 of Article II of the Treaty is to be considered a heavy bomber, the Parties further agree that:

(a) airplanes which otherwise would be bombers of a heavy bomber type shall not be considered to be bombers of a heavy bomber type if they have functionally related observable differences which indicate that they cannot perform the mission of a heavy bomber;

(b) airplanes which otherwise would be bombers of a type equipped for cruise missiles capable of a range in excess of 600 kilometers shall not be considered to be bombers of a type equipped for cruise missiles capable of a range in excess of 600 kilometers if they have functionally related observable differences which indicate that they cannot perform the mission of a bomber equipped for cruise missiles capable of a range in excess of 600 kilometers, except that heavy bombers of current types, as designated in subparagraph 3(a) of Article II of the Treaty, which otherwise would be of a type equipped for cruise missiles capable of a range in excess of 600 kilometers shall not be considered to be heavy bombers of a type equipped for cruise missiles capable of a range in excess of 600 kilometers if they are distinguishable on the basis of externally observable differences from heavy bombers of a type equipped for cruise missiles capable of a range in excess of 600 kilometers; and

(c) airplanes which otherwise would be bombers of a type equipped for ASBMs shall not be considered to be bombers of a type equipped for ASBMs if they have functionally related observable differences which indicate that they cannot perform the mission of a bomber equipped for ASBMs, except that heavy bombers of current types, as designated in subparagraph 3(a) of Article II of the Treaty, which otherwise would be of a type equipped for ASBMs shall not be considered to be heavy bombers of a type equipped for ASBMs if they are distinguishable on the basis of externally observable differences from heavy bombers of a type equipped for ASBMs.

First Common Understanding. Functionally related observable differences are differences in the observable features of airplanes which indicate whether or not these airplanes can perform the mission of a heavy bomber, or whether or not they can perform the mission of a bomber equipped for cruise missiles capable of a range in excess of 600 kilometers or whether or not they can perform the mission of a bomber equipped for ASBMs. Functionally related observable differences shall be verifiable by national technical means. To this end, the Parties may take, as appropriate, cooperative measures contributing to the effectiveness of verification by national technical means.

Fifth Agreed Statement. Tupolev-142 airplanes in their current configuration, that is, in the configuration for anti-submarine warfare, are considered to be airplanes of a type different from types of heavy bombers referred to in subparagraph 3(a) of Article II of the Treaty and not subject to the Fourth Agreed Statement to paragraph 3 of Article II of the Treaty. This Agreed Statement does not preclude improvement of Tupolev-142 airplanes as an anti-submarine system, and does not prejudice or set a precedent for designation in the future of types of airplanes as heavy bombers pursuant to subparagraph 3(b) of Article II of the Treaty or for application of the Fourth Agreed Statement to paragraph 3 of Article II of the Treaty to such airplanes.

Second Common Understanding. Not later than six months after entry into force of the Treaty the Union of Soviet Socialist Republics will give its thirty-one Myasishchev airplanes used as tankers in existence as of the date of signature of the Treaty functionally related observable differences which indicate that they cannot perform the mission of a heavy bomber.

Third Common Understanding. The designations by the United States of America and by the Union of Soviet Socialist Republics for heavy bombers referred to in subparagraph 3(a) of Article II of the Treaty correspond in the following manner:

Heavy bombers of the types designated by the United States of America as the B-52 and the B-1 are known to the Union of Soviet Socialist Republics by the same designations;

Heavy bombers of the type designated by the Union of Socialist Republics as the Tupolev-95 are known to the United States of America as heavy bombers of the Bear type; and

Heavy bombers of the type designated by the Union of Soviet Socialist Republics as the Myasishchev are known to the United States of America as heavy bombers of the Bison type.

---

4. Air-to-surface ballistic missiles (ASBMs) are any such missiles capable of a range in excess of 600 kilometers and installed in an aircraft or on its external mountings.

5. Launchers of ICBMs and SLBMs equipped with multiple independently targetable reentry vehicles (MIRVs) are launchers of the types developed and tested for launching ICBMs or SLBMs equipped with MIRVs.

First Agreed Statement. If a launcher has been developed and tested for launching an ICBM or an SLBM equipped with MIRVs, all launchers of that type shall be considered to have been developed and tested for launching ICBMs or SLBMs equipped with MIRVs.

First Common Understanding. If a launcher contains or launches an ICBM or an SLBM equipped with MIRVs, that launcher shall be considered to have been developed and tested for launching ICBMs or SLBMs equipped with MIRVs.

Second Common Understanding. If a launcher has been developed and tested for launching an ICBM or an SLBM equipped with MIRVs, all launchers of that type, except for ICBM and SLBM test and training launchers, shall be included in the corresponding aggregate numbers provided for in Article V of the Treaty, pursuant to the provisions of Article VI of the Treaty.

Second Agreed Statement. ICBMs and SLBMs equipped with MIRVs are ICBMs and SLBMs of the types which have been flight-tested with two or more independently targetable reentry vehicles, regardless of whether or not they have also been flight-tested with a single reentry vehicle or with multiple reentry vehicles which are not independently targetable. As of the date of signature of the Treaty, such ICBMs and SLBMS are: for the United States of America, Minuteman III ICBMs, Poseidon C-3 SLBMs, and Trident C-4 SLBMs; and for the Union of Soviet Socialist Republics, RS-16, RS-18, RS-20 ICBMs and RSM-50 SLBMs.

Each Party will notify the other Party in the Standing Consultative Commission on a case-by-case basis of the designation of the one new type of light ICBM, if equipped with MIRVs, permitted pursuant to paragraph 9 of Article IV of the Treaty when first flight-tested; of designations of additional types of SLBMs equipped with MIRVs when first installed on a submarine; and of designations of types of ASBMs equipped with MIRVs when first flight-tested.

Third Common Understanding. The designations by the United States of America and by the Union of Soviet Socialist Republics for ICBMs and SLBMs equipped with MIRVs correspond in the following manner:

Missiles of the type designated by the United States of America as the Minuteman III and known to the Union of Soviet Socialist Republics by the same designation, a light ICBM that has been flight-tested with multiple independently targetable reentry vehicles;

Missiles of the type designated by the United States of America as the Poseiden C-3 and known to the Union of Soviet Socialist Republics by the same designation, an SLBM that was first flight-tested in 1968 and that has been flight-tested with multiple independently targetable reentry vehicles;

Missiles of the type designated by the United States of America as the Trident C-4 and known to the Union of Soviet Socialist Republics by the same designation, an SLBM that was first flight-tested in 1977 and that has been flight-tested with multiple independently targetable reentry vehicles;

Missiles of the type designated by the Union of Soviet Socialist Republics as the RS-16 and known to the United States of America as the SS-17, a light ICBM that has been flight-tested with a single reentry vehicle and with multiple independently targetable reentry vehicles;

Missiles of the type designated by the Union of Soviet Socialist Republics as the RS-18 and known to the United States of America as the SS-19, the heaviest in terms of launch-weight and throw-weight of light ICBMs, which has been flight-tested with a single reentry vehicle and with multiple independently targetable reentry vehicles;

Missiles of the type designated by the Union of Soviet Socialist Republics as the RS-20 and known to the United States of America as the SS-18, the heaviest in terms of launch-weight and throw-weight of heavy ICBMs, which has been flight-tested with a single reentry vehicle and with multiple independently targetable reentry vehicles;

Missiles of the type designated by the Union of Soviet Socialist Republics as the RSM-50 and known to the United States of America as the SS-N-18, an SLBM that has been flight-tested with a single reentry vehicle and with multiple independently targetable reentry vehicles.

Third Agreed Statement. Reentry vehicles are independently targetable:

(a) if, after separation from the booster, maneuvering and targeting of the reentry vehicles to separate aim points along trajectories which are unrelated to each other are accomplished by means of devices which are installed in a self-contained dispensing mechanism or on the reentry vehicles, and which are based on the use of electronic or other computers in combination with devices using jet engines, including rocket engines, or aerodynamic systems;

(b) if maneuvering and targeting of the reentry vehicles to separate aim points along trajectories which are unrelated to each other are accomplished by means of other devices which may be developed in the future.

Fourth Common Understanding. For the purposes of this Treaty, all ICBM launchers in the Derazhnya and Pervomaysk areas in the Union of Soviet Socialist Republics are included in the aggregate numbers provided for in Article V of the Treaty.

Fifth Common Understanding. If ICBM or SLBM launchers are converted, constructed or undergo significant changes to their principal observable structural design features after entry into force of the Treaty, any such launchers which are launchers of missiles equipped with MIRVs shall be distinguishable from launchers of missiles not equipped with MIRVs, and any such launchers which are launchers of missiles not equipped with MIRVs shall be distinguishable from launchers of missiles equipped with MIRVs, on the basis of externally observable design features of the launchers. Submarines with launchers of SLBMs equipped with MIRVs shall be distinguishable from submarines with launchers of SLBMs not equipped with MIRVs on the basis of externally observable design features of the submarines.

This Common Understanding does not require changes to launcher conversion or construction programs, or to programs including significant changes to the principal observable structural design features of launchers, underway as of the date of signature of the Treaty.

---

6. ASBMs equipped with MIRVs are ASBMs of the types which have been flight-tested with MIRVs.

First Agreed Statement. ASBMs of the types which have been flight-tested with MIRVs are all ASBMs of the types which have been flight-tested with two or more independently targetable reentry vehicles, regardless of whether or not they have also been flight-tested with a single reentry vehicle or with multiple reentry vehicles which are not independently targetable.

Second Agreed Statement. Reentry vehicles are independently targetable:

(a) if, after separation from the booster, maneuvering and targeting of the reentry vehicles to separate aim points along trajectories which are unrelated to each other are accomplished by means of devices which are installed in a self-contained dispensing mechanism or on the reentry vehicles, and which are based on the use of electronic or other computers in combination with devices using jet engines, including rocket engines, or aerodynamic systems;

(b) if maneuvering and targeting of the reentry vehicles to separate aim points along trajectories which are unrelated to each other are accomplished by means of other devices which may be developed in the future.

---

7. Heavy ICBMs are ICBMs which have a launch-weight greater or a throw-weight greater than that of the heaviest, in terms of either launch-weight or throw-weight, respectively, of the light ICBMs deployed by either Party as of the date of signature of this Treaty.

First Agreed Statement. The launch-weight of an ICBM is the weight of the fully loaded missile itself at the time of launch.

Second Agreed Statement. The throw-weight of an ICBM is the sum of the weight of:

(a) its reentry vehicle or reentry vehicles;
(b) any self-contained dispensing mechanisms or other appropriate devices for targeting one reentry vehicle, or for releasing or for dispensing and targeting two or more reentry vehicles; and
(c) its penetration aids, including devices for their release.

Common Understanding. The term "other appropriate devices," as used in the definition of the throw-weight of an ICBM in the Second Agreed Statement to paragraph 7 of Article II of the Treaty, means any devices for dispensing and targeting two or more reentry vehicles; and any devices for releasing two or more reentry vehicles or for targeting one reentry vehicle, which cannot provide their reentry vehicles or reentry vehicle with additional velocity of more than 1,000 meters per second.

---

8. Cruise missiles are unmanned, self-propelled, guided, weapon-delivery vehicles which sustain flight through the use of aerodynamic lift over most of their flight path and which are flight-tested from or deployed on aircraft, that is, air-launched cruise missiles, or such vehicles which are referred to as cruise missiles in subparagraph 1(b) of Article IX.

First Agreed Statement. If a cruise missile is capable of a range in excess of 600 kilometers, all cruise missiles of that type shall be considered to be cruise missiles capable of a range in excess of 600 kilometers.

First Common Understanding. If a cruise missile has been flight-tested to a range in excess of 600 kilometers, it shall be considered to be a cruise missile capable of a range in excess of 600 kilometers.

Second Common Understanding. Cruise missiles not capable of a range in excess of 600 kilometers shall not be considered to be of a type capable of a range in excess of 600 kilometers if they are distinguishable on the basis of externally observable design features from cruise missiles of types capable of a range in excess of 600 kilometers.

Second Agreed Statement. The range of which a cruise missile is capable is the maximum distance which can be covered by the missile in its standard design mode flying until fuel exhaustion, determined by projecting its flight path onto the Earth's sphere from the point of launch to the point of impact.

Third Agreed Statement. If an unmanned, self-propelled, guided vehicle which sustains flight through the use of aerodynamic lift over most of its flight path has been flight-tested or deployed for weapon delivery, all vehicles of that type shall be considered to be weapon-delivery vehicles.

Third Common Understanding. Unmanned, self-propelled, guided vehicles which sustain flight through the use of aerodynamic lift over most of their flight path and are not weapon-delivery vehicles, that is, unarmed, pilotless, guided vehicles, shall not be considered to be cruise missiles if such vehicles are distinguishable from cruise missiles on the basis of externally observable design features.

Fourth Common Understanding. Neither Party shall convert unarmed, pilotless, guided vehicles into cruise missiles capable of a range in excess of 600 kilometers, nor shall either Party convert cruise missiles capable of a range in excess of 600 kilometers into unarmed, pilotless, guided vehicles.

Fifth Common Understanding. Neither Party has plans during the term of the Treaty to flight-test from or deploy on aircraft unarmed, pilotless, guided vehicles which are capable of a range in excess of 600 kilometers. In the future, should a Party have such plans, that Party will provide notification thereof to the other Party well in advance of such flight-testing or deployment. This Common Understanding does not apply to target drones.

Article III

1. Upon entry into force of this Treaty, each Party undertakes to limit ICBM launchers, SLBM launchers, heavy bombers, and ASBMs to an aggregate number not to exceed 2,400.

2. Each Party undertakes to limit, from January 1, 1981, strategic offensive arms referred to in paragraph 1 of this Article to an aggregate number not to exceed 2,250, and to initiate reductions of those arms which as of that date would be in excess of this aggregate number.

3. Within the aggregate numbers provided for in paragraphs 1 and 2 of this Article and subject to the provisions of this Treaty, each Party has the right to determine the composition of these aggregates.

4. For each bomber of a type equipped for ASBMs, the aggregate numbers provided for in paragraphs 1 and 2 of this Article shall include the maximum number of such missiles for which a bomber of that type is equipped for one operational mission.

5. A heavy bomber equipped only for ASBMs shall not itself be included in the aggregate numbers provided for in paragraphs 1 and 2 of this Article.

6. Reductions of the numbers of strategic offensive arms required to comply with the provisions of paragraphs 1 and 2 of this Article shall be carried out as provided for in Article XI.

Article IV

1. Each Party undertakes not to start construction of additional fixed ICBM launchers.

2. Each Party undertakes not to relocate fixed ICBM launchers.

3. Each Party undertakes not to convert launchers of light ICBMs, or of ICBMs of older types deployed prior to 1964, into launchers of heavy ICBMs of types deployed after that time.

4. Each Party undertakes in the process of modernization and replacement of ICBM silo launchers not to increase the original internal volume of an ICBM silo launcher by

more than thirty-two percent. Within this limit each Party has the right to determine whether such an increase will be made through an increase in the original diameter or in the original depth of an ICBM silo launcher, or in both of these dimensions.

Agreed Statement. The word "original" in paragraph 4 of Article IV of the Treaty refers to the internal dimensions of an ICBM silo launcher, including its internal volume, as of May 26, 1972, or as of the date on which such launcher becomes operational, whichever is later.

Common Understanding. The obligations provided for in paragraph 4 of Article IV of the Treaty and in the Agreed Statement thereto mean that the original diameter or the original depth of an ICBM silo launcher may not be increased by an amount greater than that which would result in an increase in the original internal volume of the ICBM silo launcher by thirty-two percent solely through an increase in one of these dimensions.

5. Each Party undertakes:

   (a) not to supply ICBM launcher deployment areas with intercontinental ballistic missiles in excess of a number consistent with normal deployment, maintenance, training, and replacement requirements;
   (b) not to provide storage facilities for or to store ICBMs in excess of normal deployment requirements at launch sites of ICBM launchers;
   (c) not to develop, test, or deploy systems for rapid reload of ICBM launchers.

Agreed Statement. The term "normal deployment requirements," as used in paragraph 5 of Article IV of the Treaty, means the deployment of one missile at each ICBM launcher.

6. Subject to the provisions of this Treaty, each Party undertakes not to have under construction at any time strategic offensive arms referred to in paragraph 1 of Article III in excess of numbers consistent with a normal construction schedule.

Common Understanding. A normal construction schedule, in paragraph 6 of Article IV of the Treaty, is understood to be one consistent with the past or present construction practices of each Party.

7. Each Party undertakes not to develop, test, or deploy ICBMs which have a launch-weight greater or a throw-weight greater than that of the heaviest, in terms of either launch-weight or throw-weight, respectively, of the heavy ICBMs, deployed by either Party as of the date of signature of this Treaty.

First Agreed Statement. The launch-weight of an ICBM is the weight of the fully loaded missile itself at the time of launch.

Second Agreed Statement. The throw-weight of an ICBM is the sum of the weight of:

   (a) its reentry vehicle or reentry vehicles;

(b) any self-contained dispensing mechanisms or other appropriate devices for targeting one reentry vehicle, or for releasing or for dispensing and targeting two or more reentry vehicles; and

(c) its penetration aids, including devices for their release.

Common Understanding. The term "other appropriate devices," as used in the definition of the throw-weight of an ICBM in the Second Agreed Statement to paragraph 7 of Article IV of the Treaty, means any devices for dispensing and targeting two or more reentry vehicles; and any devices for releasing two or more reentry vehicles or for targeting one reentry vehicle, which cannot provide their reentry vehicles or reentry vehicle with additional velocity of more than 1,000 meters per second.

---

8. Each Party undertakes not to convert land-based launchers of ballistic missiles which are not ICBMs into launchers for launching ICBMs, and not to test them for this purpose.

Common Understanding. During the term of the Treaty, the Union of Soviet Socialist Republics will not produce, test, or deploy ICBMs of the type designated by the Union of Soviet Socialist Republics as the RS-14 and known to the United States of America as the SS-16, a light ICBM first flight-tested after 1970 and flight-tested only with a single reentry vehicle; this Common Understanding also means that the Union of Soviet Socialist Republics will not produce the third stage of that missile, the reentry vehicle of that missile, or the appropriate device for targeting the reentry vehicle of that missile.

---

9. Each Party undertakes not to flight-test or deploy new types of ICBMs, that is, types of ICBMs not flight-tested as of May 1, 1979, except that each Party may flight-test and deploy one new type of light ICBM.

First Agreed Statement. The term "new types of ICBMs," as used in paragraph 9 of Article IV of the Treaty, refers to any ICBM which is different from those ICBMs flight-tested as of May 1, 1979 in any one or more of the following respects:

(a) the number of stages, the length, the largest diameter, the launch-weight, or the throw-weight, of the missile;

(b) the type of propellant (that is, liquid or solid) of any of its stages.

First Common Understanding. As used in the First Agreed Statement to paragraph 9 of Article IV of the Treaty, the term "different," referring to the length, the diameter, the launch-weight, and the throw-weight, of the missile, means a difference in excess of five percent.

Second Agreed Statement. Every ICBM of the one new type of light ICBM permitted to each Party pursuant to paragraph 9 of Article IV of the Treaty shall have the same number of stages and the same type of propellant (that is, liquid or solid) of each stage as the first ICBM of the one new type of light ICBM launched by that Party. In addition, after the twenty-fifth launch of an ICBM of that type, or after the last launch before deployment begins of ICBMs of that type, whichever occurs earlier, ICBMs of the one new type of light ICBM permitted to that Party shall not be different in any one or more of the following respects: the length, the largest diameter, the launch-weight, or the throw-weight, of the missile.

A Party which launches ICBMs of the one new type of light ICBM permitted pursuant to paragraph 9 of Article IV of the Treaty shall promptly notify the other Party of the date of the first launch and of the date of either the twenty-fifth or the last launch before deployment begins of ICBMs of that type, whichever occurs earlier.

Second Common Understanding. As used in the Second Agreed Statement to paragraph 9 of Article IV of the Treaty, the term "different," referring to the length, the diameter, the launch-weight, and the throw-weight, of the missile, means a difference in excess of five percent from the value established for each of the above parameters as of the twenty-fifth launch or as of the last launch before deployment begins, whichever occurs earlier. The values demonstrated in each of the above parameters during the last twelve of the twenty-five launches or during the last twelve launches before deployment begins, whichever twelve launches occur earlier, shall not vary by more than ten percent from any other of the corresponding values demonstrated during those twelve launches.

Third Common Understanding. The limitations with respect to launch-weight and throw-weight, provided for in the First Agreed Statement and the First Common Understanding to paragraph 9 of Article IV of the Treaty, do not preclude the flight-testing or the deployment of ICBMs with fewer reentry vehicles, or fewer penetration aids, or both, than the maximum number of reentry vehicles and the maximum number of penetration aids with which ICBMs of that type have been flight-tested as of May 1, 1979, even if this results in a decrease in launch-weight or in throw-weight in excess of five percent.

In addition to the aforementioned cases, those limitations do not preclude a decrease in launch-weight or in throw-weight in excess of five percent, in the case of the flight-testing or the deployment of ICBMs with a lesser quantity of propellant, including the propellant of a self-contained dispensing mechanism or other appropriate device, than the maximum quantity of propellant, including the propellant of a self-contained dispensing mechanism or other appropriate device, with which ICBMs of that type have been flight-tested as of May 1, 1979, provided that such an ICBM is at the same time flight-tested or deployed with fewer reentry vehicles, or fewer penetration aids, or both, than the maximum number of reentry vehicles and the maximum number of penetration aids with which ICBMs of that type have been flight-tested as of May 1, 1979, and the decrease in launch-weight and throw-weight in such cases results only from the reduction in the number of reentry vehicles, or penetration aids, or both, and the reduction in the quantity of propellant.

Fourth Common Understanding. The limitations with respect to launch-weight and throw-weight, provided for in the Second Agreed Statement and the Second Common Understanding to paragraph 9 of Article IV of the Treaty, do not preclude the flight-testing or the deployment of ICBMs of the one new type of light ICBM permitted to each Party pursuant to paragraph 9 of Article IV of the Treaty with fewer reentry vehicles, or fewer penetration aids, or both, than the maximum number of reentry vehicles and the maximum number of penetration aids with which ICBMs of that type have been flight-tested, even if this results in a decrease in launch-weight or in throw-weight in excess of five percent.

In addition to the aforementioned cases, those limitations do not preclude a decrease in launch-weight or in throw-weight in excess of five percent, in the case of the flight-testing or the deployment of ICBMs of that type with a lesser quantity of propellant, including the propellant of a self-contained dispensing mechanism or other appropriate device, than the maximum quantity of propellant, including the propellant of a self-contained dispensing mechanism or other appropriate device, with which ICBMs of that type have been flight-tested, provided that such an ICBM is at the same time flight-tested or deployed with fewer reentry vehicles, or fewer penetration aids, or both, than the maximum number of reentry vehicles and the maximum number of penetration aids with which ICBMs of that type have been flight-tested, and the decrease in launch-weight and throw-weight in such cases results only from the reduction in the number of reentry vehicles, or penetration aids, or both, and the reduction in the quantity of propellant.

---

10. Each Party undertakes not to flight-test or deploy ICBMs of a type flight-tested as of May 1, 1979 with a number of reentry vehicles greater than the maximum number of reentry vehicles with which an ICBM of that type has been flight-tested as of that date.

First Agreed Statement. The following types of ICBMs and SLBMs equipped with MIRVs have been flight-tested with the maximum number of reentry vehicles set forth below:

For the United States of America

ICBMs of the Minuteman III type—seven reentry vehicles;
SLBMs of the Poseidon C-3 type—fourteen reentry vehicles;
SLBMs of the Trident C-4 type—seven reentry vehicles.

For the Union of Soviet Socialist Republics

ICBMs of the RS-16 type—four reentry vehicles;
ICBMs of the RS-18 type—six reentry vehicles;
ICBMs of the RS-20 type—ten reentry vehicles;
SLBMs of the RSM-50 type—seven reentry vehicles.

Common Understanding. Minuteman III ICBMs of the United States of America have been deployed with no more than three reentry vehicles. During the term of the Treaty, the United States of America has no plans to and will not flight-test or deploy missiles of this type with more than three reentry vehicles.

Second Agreed Statement. During the flight-testing of any ICBM, SLBM, or ASBM after May 1, 1979, the number of procedures for releasing or for dispensing may not exceed the maximum number of reentry vehicles established for missiles of corresponding types as provided for in paragraphs 10, 11, 12, and 13 of Article IV of the Treaty. In this Agreed Statement "procedures for releasing or for dispensing" are understood to mean maneuvers of a missile associated with targeting and releasing or dispensing its reentry vehicles to aim points, whether or not a reentry vehicle is actually released or dispensed. Procedures for releasing anti-missile defense penetration aids will not be considered to be procedures for releasing or for dispensing a reentry vehicle so long as the procedures for releasing anti-missile defense penetration aids differ from those for releasing or for dispensing reentry vehicles.

Third Agreed Statement. Each Party undertakes:

(a) not to flight-test or deploy ICBMs equipped with multiple reentry vehicles, of a type flight-tested as of May 1, 1979, with reentry vehicles the weight of any of which is less than the weight of the lightest of those reentry vehicles with which an ICBM of that type has been flight-tested as of that date;
(b) not to flight-test or deploy ICBMs equipped with a single reentry vehicle and without an appropriate device for targeting a reentry vehicle, of a type flight-tested as of May 1, 1979, with a reentry vehicle the weight of which is less than the weight of the

lightest reentry vehicle on an ICBM of a type equipped with MIRVs and flight-tested by that Party as of May 1, 1979; and

(c) not to flight-test or deploy ICBMs equipped with a single reentry vehicle and with an appropriate device for targeting a reentry vehicle, of a type flight-tested as of May 1, 1979, with a reentry vehicle the weight of which is less than fifty percent of the throw-weight of that ICBM.

---

11. Each Party undertakes not to flight-test or deploy ICBMs of the one new type permitted pursuant to paragraph 9 of this Article with a number of reentry vehicles greater than the maximum number of reentry vehicles with which an ICBM of either Party has been flight-tested as of May 1, 1979, that is, ten.

First Agreed Statement. Each Party undertakes not to flight-test or deploy the one new type of light ICBM permitted to each Party pursuant to paragraph 9 of Article IV of the Treaty with a number of reentry vehicles greater than the maximum number of reentry vehicles with which an ICBM of that type has been flight-tested as of the twenty-fifth launch or the last launch before deployment begins of ICBMs of that type, whichever occurs earlier.

Second Agreed Statement. During the flight-testing of any ICBM, SLBM, or ASBM after May 1, 1979 the number of procedures for releasing or for dispensing may not exceed the maximum number of reentry vehicles established for missiles of corresponding types as provided for in paragraphs 10, 11, 12, and 13 of Article IV of the Treaty. In this Agreed Statement "procedures for releasing or for dispensing" are understood to mean maneuvers of a missile associated with targeting and releasing or dispensing its reentry vehicles to aim points, whether or not a reentry vehicle is actually released or dispensed. Procedures for releasing anti-missile defense penetration aids will not be considered to be procedures for releasing or for dispensing a reentry vehicle so long as the procedures for releasing anti-missile defense penetration aids differ from those for releasing or for dispensing reentry vehicles.

---

12. Each Party undertakes not to flight-test or deploy SLBMs with a number of reentry vehicles greater than the maximum number of reentry vehicles with which an SLBM of either Party has been flight-tested as of May 1, 1979, that is, fourteen.

First Agreed Statement. The following types of ICBMs and SLBMs equipped with MIRVs have been flight-tested with the maximum number of reentry vehicles set forth below:

For the United States of America

ICBMs of the Minuteman III type—seven reentry vehicles;
SLBMs of the Poseidon C-3 type—fourteen reentry vehicles;
SLBMs of the Trident C-4 type—seven reentry vehicles.

For the Union of Soviet Socialist Republics

ICBMs of the RS-16 type—four reentry vehicles;
ICBMs of the RS-18 type—six reentry vehicles;
ICBMs of the RS-20 type—ten reentry vehicles;
SLBMs of the RSM-50 type—seven reentry vehicles.

Second Agreed Statement. During the flight-testing of any ICBM, SLBM, or ASBM after May 1, 1979 the number of procedures for releasing or for dispensing may not exceed the maximum number of reentry vehicles established for missiles of corresponding types as provided for in paragraphs 10, 11, 12, and 13 of Article IV of the Treaty. In this Agreed Statement "procedures for releasing or dispensing" are understood to mean maneuvers of a missile associated with targeting and releasing or dispensing its reentry vehicles to aim points, whether or not a reentry vehicle is actually released or dispensed. Procedures for releasing anti-missile defense penetration aids will not be considered to be procedures for releasing or for dispensing a reentry vehicle so long as the procedures for releasing anti-missile defense penetration aids differ from those for releasing or for dispensing reentry vehicles.

---

13. Each Party undertakes not to flight-test or deploy ASBMs with a number of reentry vehicles greater than the maximum number of reentry vehicles with which an ICBM of either Party has been flight-tested as of May 1, 1979, that is, ten.

Agreed Statement. During the flight-testing of any ICBM, SLBM, or ASBM after May 1, 1979 the number of procedures for releasing or for dispensing may not exceed the maximum number of reentry vehicles established for missiles of corresponding types as provided for in paragraphs 10, 11, 12, and 13 of Article IV of the Treaty. In this Agreed Statement "procedures for releasing or for dispensing" are understood to mean maneuvers of a missile associated with targeting and releasing or dispensing its reentry vehicles to aim points, whether or not a reentry vehicle is actually released or dispensed. Procedures for releasing anti-missile defense penetration aids will not be considered to be procedures for releasing or for dispensing a reentry vehicle so long as the procedures for releasing anti-missile defense penetration aids differ from those for releasing or for dispensing reentry vehicles.

---

14. Each Party undertakes not to deploy at any one time on heavy bombers equipped for cruise missiles capable of a range in excess of 600 kilometers a number of such cruise missiles which exceeds the product of 28 and the number of such heavy bombers.

First Agreed Statement. For the purposes of the limitation provided for in paragraph 14 of Article IV of the Treaty, there shall be considered to be deployed on each heavy bomber of a type equipped for cruise missiles capable of a range in excess of 600 kilometers the maximum number of such missiles for which any bomber of that type is equipped for one operational mission.

Second Agreed Statement. During the term of the Treaty no bomber of the B-52 or B-1 types of the United States of America and no bomber of the Tupolev-95 or Myasishchev types of the Union of Soviet Socialist Republics will be equipped for more than twenty cruise missiles capable of a range in excess of 600 kilometers.

Article V

1. Within the aggregate numbers provided for in paragraphs 1 and 2 of Article III, each Party undertakes to limit launchers of ICBMs and SLBMs equipped with MIRVs, ASBMs equipped with MIRVs, and heavy bombers equipped for cruise missiles

capable of a range in excess of 600 kilometers to an aggregate number not to exceed 1,320.

2. Within the aggregate number provided for in paragraph 1 of this Article, each Party undertakes to limit launchers of ICBMs and SLBMs equipped with MIRVs, and ASBMs equipped with MIRVs to an aggregate number not to exceed 1,200.

3. Within the aggregate number provided for in paragraph 2 of this Article, each Party undertakes to limit launchers of ICBMs equipped with MIRVs to an aggregate number not to exceed 820.

4. For each bomber of a type equipped for ASBMs equipped with MIRVs, the aggregate numbers provided for in paragraphs 1 and 2 of this Article shall include the maximum number of ASBMs for which a bomber of that type is equipped for one operational mission.

Agreed Statement. If a bomber is equipped for ASBMs equipped with MIRVs, all bombers of that type shall be considered to be equipped for ASBMs equipped with MIRVs.

---

5. Within the aggregate numbers provided for in paragraphs 1, 2, and 3 of this Article and subject to the provisions of this Treaty, each Party has the right to determine the composition of these aggregates.

Article VI

1. The limitations provided for in this Treaty shall apply to those arms which are:

(a) operational;

(b) in the final stage of construction;

(c) in reserve, in storage, or mothballed;

(d) undergoing overhaul, repair, modernization, or conversion.

2. Those arms in the final stage of construction are:

(a) SLBM launchers on submarines which have begun sea trials;

(b) ASBMs after a bomber of a type equipped for such missiles has been brought out of the shop, plant, or other facility where its final assembly or conversion for the purpose of equipping it for such missiles has been performed;

(c) other strategic offensive arms which are finally assembled in a shop, plant, or other facility after they have been brought out of the shop, plant, or other facility where their final assembly has been performed.

3. ICBM and SLBM launchers of a type not subject to the limitation provided for in Article V, which undergo conversion into launchers of a type subject to that limitation, shall become subject to that limitation as follows:

(a) fixed ICBM launchers when work on their conversion reaches the stage which first definitely indicates that they are being so converted;

(b) SLBM launchers on a submarine when that submarine first goes to sea after their conversion has been performed.

Agreed Statement. The procedures referred to in paragraph 7 of Article VI of the Treaty shall include procedures determining the manner in which mobile ICBM launchers of a type not subject to the limitation provided for in Article V of the Treaty, which undergo conversion into launchers of a type subject to that limitation, shall become subject to that limitation, unless the Parties agree that mobile ICBM launchers shall not be deployed after the date on which the Protocol ceases to be in force.

4. ASBMs on a bomber which undergoes conversion from a bomber of a type equipped for ASBMs which are not subject to the limitation provided for in Article V into a bomber of a type equipped for ASBMs which are subject to that limitation shall become subject to that limitation when the bomber is brought out of the shop, plant, or other facility where such conversion has been performed.

5. A heavy bomber of a type not subject to the limitation provided for in paragraph 1 of Article V shall become subject to that limitation when it is brought out of the shop, plant, or other facility where it has been converted into a heavy bomber of a type equipped for cruise missiles capable of a range in excess of 600 kilometers. A bomber of a type not subject to the limitation provided for in paragraph 1 or 2 of Article III shall become subject to that limitation and to the limitation provided for in paragraph 1 of Article V when it is brought out of the shop, plant, or other facility where it has been converted into a bomber of a type equipped for cruise missiles capable of a range in excess of 600 kilometers.

6. The arms subject to the limitations provided for in this Treaty shall continue to be subject to these limitations until they are dismantled, are destroyed, or otherwise cease to be subject to these limitations under procedures to be agreed upon.

Agreed Statement. The procedures for removal of strategic offensive arms from the aggregate numbers provided for in the Treaty, which are referred to in paragraph 6 of Article VI of the Treaty, and which are to be agreed upon in the Standing Consultative Commission, shall include:

(a) procedures for removal from the aggregate numbers, provided for in Article V of the Treaty, of ICBM and SLBM launchers which are being converted from launchers of a type subject to the limitation provided for in Article V of the Treaty, into launchers of a type not subject to that limitation;

(b) procedures for removal from the aggregate numbers, provided for in Articles III and V of the Treaty, of bombers which are being converted from bombers of a type subject to the limitations provided for in Article III of the Treaty or in Articles III and V of the Treaty into airplanes or bombers of a type not so subject.

Common Understanding. The procedures referred to in subparagraph (b) of the Agreed Statement to paragraph 6 of Article VI of the Treaty for removal of bombers from the aggregate numbers provided for in Articles III and V of the Treaty shall be based upon the existence of functionally related observable differences which indicate whether or not they can perform the mission of a heavy bomber, or whether or not they can perform the mission of a bomber equipped for cruise missiles capable of a range in excess of 600 kilometers.

7. In accordance with the provisions of Article XVII, the Parties will agree in the Standing Consultative Commission upon procedures to implement the provisions of this Article.

Article VII

1. The limitations provided for in Article III shall not apply to ICBM and SLBM test and training launchers or to space vehicle launchers for exploration and use of outer

space. ICBM and SLBM test and training launchers are ICBM and SLBM launchers used only for testing or training.

Common Understanding. The term "testing," as used in Article VII of the Treaty, includes research and development.

---

2. The Parties agree that:

(a) there shall be no significant increase in the number of ICBM or SLBM test and training launchers or in the number of such launchers of heavy ICBMs;

(b) construction or conversion of ICBM launchers at test ranges shall be undertaken only for purposes of testing and training;

(c) there shall be no conversion of ICBM test and training launchers or of space vehicle launchers into ICBM launchers subject to the limitations provided for in Article III.

First Agreed Statement. The term "significant increase," as used in subparagraph 2(a) of Article VII of the Treaty, means an increase of fifteen percent or more. Any new ICBM test and training launchers which replace ICBM test and training launchers at test ranges will be located only at test ranges.

Second Agreed Statement. Current test ranges where ICBMs are tested are located: for the United States of America, near Santa Maria, California, and at Cape Canaveral, Florida; and for the Union of Soviet Socialist Republics, in the areas of Tyura-Tam and Plesetskaya. In the future, each Party shall provide notification in the Standing Consultative Commission of the location of any other test range used by that Party to test ICBMs.

First Common Understanding. At test ranges where ICBMs are tested, other arms, including those not limited by the Treaty, may also be tested.

Second Common Understanding. Of the eighteen launchers of fractional orbital missiles at the test range where ICBMs are tested in the area of Tyura-Tam, twelve launchers shall be dismantled or destroyed and six launchers may be converted to launchers for testing missiles undergoing modernization.

Dismantling or destruction of the twelve launchers shall begin upon entry into force of the Treaty and shall be completed within eight months, under procedures for dismantling or destruction of these launchers to be agreed upon in the Standing Consultative Commission. These twelve launchers shall not be replaced.

Conversion of the six launchers may be carried out after entry into force of the Treaty. After entry into force of the Treaty, fractional orbital missiles shall be removed and shall be destroyed pursuant to the provisions of subparagraph 1(c) of Article IX and of Article XI of the Treaty and shall not be replaced by other missiles, except in the case of conversion of these six launchers for testing missiles undergoing modernization. After removal of the fractional orbital missiles, and prior to such conversion, any activities associated with these launchers shall be limited to normal maintenance requirements for launchers in which missiles are not deployed. These six launchers shall be subject to the provisions of Article VII of the Treaty and, if converted, to the provisions of the Fifth Common Understanding to paragraph 5 of Article II of the Treaty.

Article VIII

1. Each Party undertakes not to flight-test cruise missiles capable of a range in excess of 600 kilometers or ASBMs from aircraft other than bombers or to convert such aircraft into aircraft equipped for such missiles.

Agreed Statement. For purposes of testing only, each Party has the right, through initial construction or, as an exception to the provisions of paragraph 1 of Article VIII of the Treaty, by conversion, to equip for cruise missiles capable of a range in excess of 600 kilometers or for ASBMs no more than sixteen airplanes, including airplanes which are prototypes of bombers equipped for such missiles. Each Party also has the right, as an exception to the provisions of paragraph 1 of Article VIII of the Treaty, to flight-test from such airplanes cruise missiles capable of a range in excess of 600 kilometers and, after the date on which the Protocol ceases to be in force, to flight-test ASBMs from such airplanes as well, unless the Parties agree that they will not flight-test ASBMs after that date. The limitations provided for in Article III of the Treaty shall not apply to such airplanes.

The aforementioned airplanes may include only:

(a) airplanes other than bombers which, as an exception to the provisions of paragraph 1 of Article VIII of the Treaty, have been converted into airplanes equipped for cruise missiles capable of a range in excess of 600 kilometers or for ASBMs;

(b) airplanes considered to be heavy bombers pursuant to subparagraph 3(c) or 3(d) of Article II of the Treaty; and

(c) airplanes other than heavy bombers which, prior to March 7, 1979, were used for testing cruise missiles capable of a range in excess of 600 kilometers.

The airplanes referred to in subparagraphs (a) and (b) of this Agreed Statement shall be distinguishable on the basis of functionally related observable differences from airplanes which otherwise would be of the same type but cannot perform the mission of a bomber equipped for cruise missiles capable of a range in excess of 600 kilometers or for ASBMs.

The airplanes referred to in subparagraph (c) of this Agreed Statement shall not be used for testing cruise missiles capable of a range in excess of 600 kilometers after the expiration of a six-month period from the date of entry into force of the Treaty, unless by the expiration of that period they are distinguishable on the basis of functionally related observable differences from airplanes which otherwise would be of the same type but cannot perform the mission of a bomber equipped for cruise missiles capable of a range in excess of 600 kilometers.

First Common Understanding. The term "testing," as used in the Agreed Statement to paragraph 1 of Article VIII of the Treaty, includes research and development.

Second Common Understanding. The Parties shall notify each other in the Standing Consultative Commission of the number of airplanes, according to type, used for testing pursuant to the Agreed Statement to paragraph 1 of Article VIII of the Treaty. Such notification shall be provided at the first regular session of the Standing Consultative Commission held after an airplane has been used for such testing.

Third Common Understanding. None of the sixteen airplanes referred to in the Agreed Statement to paragraph 1 of Article VIII of the Treaty may be replaced, except in the event of the involuntary destruction of any such airplane or in the case of the dismantling or destruction of any such airplane. The procedures for such replacement and for removal of any such airplane from that number, in case of its conversion, shall be agreed upon in the Standing Consultative Commission.

2. Each Party undertakes not to convert aircraft other than bombers into aircraft which can carry out the mission of a heavy bomber as referred to in subparagraph 3(b) of Article II.

Article IX

1. Each Party undertakes not to develop, test, or deploy:

(a) ballistic missiles capable of a range in excess of 600 kilometers for installation on waterborne vehicles other than submarines, or launchers of such missiles;

Common Understanding to subparagraph (a). The obligations provided for in subparagraph 1(a) of Article IX of the Treaty do not affect current practices for transporting ballistic missiles.

(b) fixed ballistic or cruise missile launchers for emplacement on the ocean floor, on the seabed, or on the beds of internal waters and inland waters, or in the subsoil thereof, or mobile launchers of such missiles, which move only in contact with the ocean floor, the seabed, or the beds of internal waters and inland waters, or missiles for such launchers;

Agreed Statement to subparagraph (b). The obligations provided for in subparagraph 1(b) of Article IX of the Treaty shall apply to all areas of the ocean floor and the seabed, including the seabed zone referred to in Articles I and II of the 1971 Treaty on the Prohibition of the Emplacement of Nuclear Weapons and Other Weapons of Mass Destruction on the Seabed and the Ocean Floor and in the Subsoil Thereof.

(c) systems for placing into Earth orbit nuclear weapons or any other kind of weapons of mass destruction, including fractional orbital missiles;

Common Understanding to subparagraph (c). The provisions of subparagraph 1(c) of Article IX of the Treaty do not require the dismantling or destruction of any existing launchers of either Party.

(d) mobile launchers of heavy ICBMs;
(e) SLBMs which have a launch-weight greater or a throw-weight greater than that of the heaviest, in terms of either launch-weight or throw-weight, respectively, of the light ICBMs deployed by either Party as of the date of signature of this Treaty, or launchers of such SLBMs; or
(f) ASBMs which have a launch-weight greater or a throw-weight greater than that of the heaviest, in terms of either launch-weight or throw-weight, respectively, of the light ICBMs deployed by either Party as of the date of signature of this Treaty.

First Agreed Statement to subparagraphs (e) and (f). The launch-weight of an SLBM or of an ASBM is the weight of the fully loaded missile itself at the time of launch.

Second Agreed Statement to subparagraphs (e) and (f). The throw-weight of an SLBM or of an ASBM is the sum of the weight of:

(a) its reentry vehicle or reentry vehicles;
(b) any self-contained dispensing mechanisms or other appropriate devices for targeting one reentry vehicle, or for releasing or for dispensing and targeting two or more reentry vehicles; and
(c) its penetration aids, including devices for their release.

Common Understanding to subparagraphs (e) and (f). The term "other appropriate devices," as used in the definition of the throw-weight of an SLBM or of an ASBM in the Second Agreed Statement to subparagraphs 1(e) and 1(f) of Article IX of the Treaty, means any devices for dispensing and targeting two or more reentry vehicles; and any devices for releasing two or more reentry vehicles or for targeting one reentry vehicle, which cannot provide their reentry vehicles or reentry vehicle with additional velocity of more than 1,000 meters per second.

---

2. Each Party undertakes not to flight-test from aircraft cruise missiles capable of a range in excess of 600 kilometers which are equipped with multiple independently targetable warheads and not to deploy such cruise missiles on aircraft.

Agreed Statement. Warheads of a cruise missile are independently targetable if maneuvering or targeting of the warheads to separate aim points along ballistic trajectories or any other flight paths, which are unrelated to each other, is accomplished during a flight of a cruise missile.

Article X

Subject to the provisions of this Treaty, modernization and replacement of strategic offensive arms may be carried out.

Article XI

1. Strategic offensive arms which would be in excess of the aggregate numbers provided for in this Treaty as well as strategic offensive arms prohibited by this Treaty shall be dismantled or destroyed under procedures to be agreed upon in the Standing Consultative Commission.
2. Dismantling or destruction of strategic offensive arms which would be in excess of the aggregate number provided for in paragraph 1 of Article III shall begin on the date of the entry into force of this Treaty and shall be completed within the following periods from that date: four months for ICBM launchers; six months for SLBM launchers; and three months for heavy bombers.
3. Dismantling or destruction of strategic offensive arms which would be in excess of the aggregate number provided for in paragraph 2 of Article III shall be initiated no later than January 1, 1981, shall be carried out throughout the ensuing twelve-month period, and shall be completed no later than December 31, 1981.
4. Dismantling or destruction of strategic offensive arms prohibited by this Treaty shall be completed within the shortest possible agreed period of time, but not later than six months after the entry into force of this Treaty.

Article XII

1. In order to ensure the viability and effectiveness of this Treaty, each Party undertakes not to circumvent the provisions of this Treaty, through any other state or states, or in any other manner.

Article XIII

1. Each Party undertakes not to assume any international obligations which would conflict with this Treaty.

Article XIV

The Parties undertake to begin, promptly after the entry into force of this Treaty, active negotiations with the objective of achieving, as soon as possible, agreement on further measures for the limitation and reduction of strategic arms. It is also the objective of the Parties to conclude well in advance of 1985 an agreement limiting strategic offensive arms to replace this Treaty upon its expiration.

Article XV

1. For the purpose of providing assurance of compliance with the provisions of this Treaty, each Party shall use national technical means of verification at its disposal in a manner consistent with generally recognized principles of international law.

2. Each party undertakes not to interfere with the national technical means of verification of the other Party operating in accordance with paragraph 1 of this Article.

3. Each Party undertakes not to use deliberate concealment measures which impede verification by national technical means of compliance with the provisions of this Treaty. This obligation shall not require changes in current construction, assembly, conversion, or overhaul practices.

First Agreed Statement. Deliberate concealment measures, as referred to in paragraph 3 of Article XV of the Treaty, are measures carried out deliberately to hinder or deliberately to impede verification by national technical means of compliance with the provisions of the Treaty.

Second Agreed Statement. The obligation not to use deliberate concealment measures, provided for in paragraph 3 of Article XV of the Treaty, does not preclude the testing of anti-missile defense penetration aids.

First Common Understanding. The provisions of paragraph 3 of Article XV of the Treaty and the First Agreed Statement thereto apply to all provisions of the Treaty, including provisions associated with testing. In this connection, the obligation not to use deliberate concealment measures includes the obligation not to use deliberate concealment measures associated with testing, including those measures aimed at concealing the association between ICBMs and launchers during testing.

Second Common Understanding. Each Party is free to use various methods of transmitting telemetric information during testing, including its encryption, except that, in accordance with the provisions of paragraph 3 of Article XV of the Treaty, neither Party shall engage in deliberate denial of telemetric information, such as through the use of telemetry encryption, whenever such denial impedes verfication of compliance with the provisions of the Treaty.

Third Common Understanding. In addition to the obligations provided for in paragraph 3 of Article XV of the Treaty, no shelters which impede verification by national technical means of compliance with the provisions of the Treaty shall be used over ICBM silo launchers.

Article XVI

1. Each Party undertakes, before conducting each planned ICBM launch, to notify the other Party well in advance on a case-by-case basis that such a launch will occur, except for single ICBM launches from test ranges or from ICBM launcher deployment areas, which are not planned to extend beyond its national territory.

First Common Understanding. ICBM launches to which the obligations provided for in Article XVI of the Treaty apply, include, among others, those ICBM launches for which advance notification is required pursuant to the provisions of the Agreement on Measures to Reduce the Risk of Outbreak of Nuclear War Between the United States of America and the Union of Soviet Socialist Republics, signed September 30, 1971, and the Agreement Between the Government of the United States of America and the Government of the Union of Soviet Socialist Republics on the Prevention of Incidents On and Over the High Seas, signed May 25, 1972. Nothing in Article XVI of the Treaty is intended to inhibit advance notification, on a voluntary basis, of any ICBM launches not subject to its provisions, the advance notification of which would enhance confidence between the Parties.

Second Common Understanding. A multiple ICBM launch conducted by a Party, as distinct from single ICBM launches referred to in Article XVI of the Treaty, is a launch which would result in two or more of its ICBMs being in flight at the same time.

Third Common Understanding. The test ranges referred to in Article XVI of the Treaty are those covered by the Second Agreed Statement to paragraph 2 of Article VII of the Treaty.

2. The Parties shall agree in the Standing Consultative Commission upon procedures to implement the provisions of this Article.

Article XVII

1. To promote the objectives and implementation of the provisions of this Treaty, the Parties shall use the Standing Consultative Commission established by the Memorandum of Understanding Between the Government of the United States of America and the Government of the Union of Soviet Socialist Republics Regarding the Establishment of a Standing Consultative Commission of December 21, 1972.

2. Within the framework of the Standing Consultative Commission, with respect to this Treaty, the Parties will:

(a) consider questions concerning compliance with the obligations assumed and related situations which may be considered ambiguous;

(b) provide on a voluntary basis such information as either Party considers necessary to assure confidence in compliance with the obligations assumed;

(c) consider questions involving unintended interference with national technical means of verification, and questions involving unintended impeding of verification by national technical means of compliance with the provisions of this Treaty;

(d) consider possible changes in the strategic situation which have a bearing on the provisions of this Treaty;

(e) agree upon procedures for replacement, conversion, and dismantling or destruction, of strategic offensive arms in cases provided for in the provisions of this Treaty and upon procedures for removal of such arms from the aggregate numbers when they otherwise cease to be subject to the limitations provided for in this Treaty, and at regular sessions of the Standing Consultative Commission, notify each other in accordance with the aforementioned procedures, at least twice annually, of actions completed and those in process;

(f) consider, as appropriate, possible proposals for further increasing the viability of this Treaty, including proposals for amendments in accordance with the provisions of this Treaty;

(g) consider, as appropriate, proposals for further measures limiting strategic offensive arms.

3. In the Standing Consultative Commission the Parties shall maintain by category the agreed data base on the numbers of strategic offensive arms established by the Memorandum of Understanding Between the United States of America and the Union of Soviet Socialist Republics Regarding the Establishment of a Data Base on the Numbers of Strategic Offensive Arms of June 18, 1979.

Agreed Statement. In order to maintain the agreed data base on the numbers of strategic offensive arms subject to the limitations provided for in the Treaty in accordance with paragraph 3 of Article XVII of the Treaty, at each regular session of the Standing Consultative Commission the Parties will notify each other of and consider changes in those numbers in the following categories: launchers of ICBMs; fixed launchers of ICBMs; launchers of ICBMs equipped with MIRVs; launchers of SLBMs; launchers of SLBMs equipped with MIRVs; heavy bombers; heavy bombers equipped for cruise missiles capable of a range in excess of 600 kilometers; heavy bombers equipped only for ASBMs; ASBMs; and ASBMs equipped with MIRVs.

Article XVIII

Each Party may propose amendments to this Treaty. Agreed amendments shall enter into force in accordance with the procedures governing the entry into force of this Treaty.

Article XIX

1. This Treaty shall be subject to ratification in accordance with the constitutional procedures of each Party. This Treaty shall enter into force on the day of the exchange of instruments of ratification and shall remain in force through December 31, 1985, unless replaced earlier by an agreement further limiting strategic offensive arms.

2. This Treaty shall be registered pursuant to Article 102 of the Charter of the United Nations.

3. Each Party shall, in exercising its national sovereignty, have the right to withdraw from this Treaty if it decides that extraordinary events related to the subject matter of this Treaty have jeopardized its supreme interests. It shall give notice of its decision to the other Party six months prior to withdrawal from the Treaty. Such notice shall

include a statement of the extraordinary events the notifying Party regards as having jeopardized its supreme interests.

DONE at Vienna on June 18, 1979, in two copies, each in the English and Russian languages, both texts being equally authentic.

For the United States of America:

JIMMY CARTER

President of the United States of America

For the Union of Soviet Socialist Republics:

L. BREZHNEV,

General Secretary of the CPSU, Chairman of the Presidium of the Supreme Soviet of the U.S.S.R.

Protocol to the Treaty Between the United States of America and the Union of Soviet Socialist Republics on the Limitation of Strategic Offensive Arms

The United States of America and the Union of Soviet Socialist Republics, hereinafter referred to as the Parties,
Having agreed on limitations on strategic offensive arms in the Treaty,
Have agreed on additional limitations for the period during which this Protocol remains in force, as follows:

Article I

Each Party undertakes not to deploy mobile ICBM launchers or to flight-test ICBMs from such launchers.

Article II

1. Each Party undertakes not to deploy cruise missiles capable of a range in excess of 600 kilometers on sea-based launchers or on land-based launchers.
2. Each Party undertakes not to flight-test cruise missiles capable of a range in excess of 600 kilometers which are equipped with multiple independently targetable warheads from sea-based launchers or from land-based launchers.

Agreed Statement. Warheads of a cruise missile are independently targetable if maneuvering or targeting of the warheads to separate aim points along ballistic trajectories or any other flight paths, which are unrelated to each other, is accomplished during a flight of a cruise missile.

---

3. For the purposes of this Protocol, cruise missiles are unmanned, self-propelled, guided, weapon-delivery vehicles which sustain flight through the use of aerodynamic lift over most of their flight path and which are flight-tested from or deployed on sea-based or land-based launchers, that is, sea-launched cruise missiles and ground-launched cruise missiles, respectively.

First Agreed Statement. If a cruise missile is capable of a range in excess of 600 kilometers, all cruise missiles of that type shall be considered to be cruise missiles capable of a range in excess of 600 kilometers.

First Common Understanding. If a cruise missile has been flight-tested to a range in excess of 600 kilometers, it shall be considered to be a cruise missile capable of a range in excess of 600 kilometers.

Second Common Understanding. Cruise missiles not capable of a range in excess of 600 kilometers shall not be considered to be of a type capable of a range in excess of 600 kilometers if they are distinguishable on the basis of externally observable design features from cruise missiles of types capable of a range in excess of 600 kilometers.

270

Second Agreed Statement. The range of which a cruise missile is capable is the maximum distance which can be covered by the missile in its standard design mode flying until fuel exhaustion, determined by projecting its flight path onto the Earth's sphere from the point of launch to the point of impact.

Third Agreed Statement. If an unmanned, self-propelled, guided vehicle which sustains flight through the use of aerodynamic lift over most of its flight path has been flight-tested or deployed for weapon delivery, all vehicles of that type shall be considered to be weapon-delivery vehicles.

Third Common Understanding. Unmanned, self-propelled, guided vehicles which sustain flight through the use of aerodynamic lift over most of their flight path and are not weapon-delivery vehicles, that is, unarmed, pilotless, guided vehicles, shall not be considered to be cruise missiles if such vehicles are distinguishable from cruise missiles on the basis of externally observable design features.

Fourth Common Understanding. Neither Party shall convert unarmed, pilotless, guided vehicles into cruise missiles capable of a range in excess of 600 kilometers, nor shall either Party convert cruise missiles capable of a range in excess of 600 kilometers into unarmed, pilotless, guided vehicles.

Fifth Common Understanding. Neither Party has plans during the term of the Protocol to flight-test from or deploy on sea-based or land-based launchers unarmed, pilotless, guided vehicles which are capable of a range in excess of 600 kilometers. In the future, should a Party have such plans, that Party will provide notification thereof to the other Party well in advance of such flight-testing or deployment. This Common Understanding does not apply to target drones.

Article III

Each Party undertakes not to flight-test or deploy ASBMs.

Article IV

This Protocol shall be considered an integral part of the Treaty. It shall enter into force on the day of the entry into force of the Treaty and shall remain in force through December 31, 1981, unless replaced earlier by an agreement on further measures limiting strategic offensive arms.

DONE at Vienna on June 18, 1979, in two copies, each in the English and Russian languages, both texts being equally authentic.

For the United States of America:

JIMMY CARTER

President of the United States of America

For the Union of Soviet Socialist Republics:

L. BREZHNEV

General Secretary of the CPSU, Chairman of the Presidium of the Supreme Soviet of the U.S.S.R.

Memorandum of Understanding Between the United States of America and the Union of Soviet Socialist Republics Regarding the Establishment of a Data Base on the Numbers of Strategic Offensive Arms

For the purposes of the Treaty Between the United States of America and the Union of Soviet Socialist Republics on the Limitation of Strategic Offensive Arms, the Parties have considered data on numbers of strategic offensive arms and agree that as of November 1, 1978 there existed the following numbers of strategic offensive arms subject to the limitations provided for in the Treaty which is being signed today.

	U.S.A.	U.S.S.R.
Launchers of ICBMs	1,054	1,398
Fixed launchers of ICBMs	1,054	1,398
Launchers of ICBMs equipped with MIRVs	550	576
Launchers of SLBMs	656	950
Launchers of SLBMs equipped with MIRVs	496	128
Heavy bombers	574	156
Heavy bombers equipped for cruise missiles capable of a range in excess of 600 kilometers	0	0
Heavy bombers equipped only for ASBMs	0	0
ASBMs	0	0
ASBMs equipped with MIRVs	0	0

At the time of entry into force of the Treaty the Parties will update the above agreed data in the categories listed in this Memorandum.

DONE at Vienna on June 18, 1979, in two copies, each in the English and Russian languages, both texts being equally authentic.

For the United States of America

RALPH EARLE II

Chief of the United States Delegation to the Strategic Arms Limitation Talks

For the Union of Soviet Socialist Republics

V. KARPOV

Chief of the U.S.S.R. Delegation to the Strategic Arms Limitation Talks

Statement of Data on the Numbers of Strategic Offensive Arms as of the Date of Signature of the Treaty

The United States of America declares that as of June 18, 1979 it possesses the following numbers of strategic offensive arms subject to the limitations provided for in the Treaty which is being signed today:

Launchers of ICBMs	1,054
Fixed launchers of ICBMs	1,054
Launchers of ICBMs equipped with MIRVs	550
Launchers of SLBMs	656
Launchers of SLBMs equipped with MIRVs	496
Heavy bombers	573
Heavy bombers equipped for cruise missiles capable of a range in excess of 600 kilometers	3
Heavy bombers equipped only for ASBMs	0
ASBMs	0
ASBMs equipped with MIRVs	0

June 18, 1979

RALPH EARLE II

Chief of the United States Delegation to the Strategic Arms Limitation Talks

I certify that this is a true copy of the document signed by Ambassador Ralph Earle II entiled "Statement of Data on the Numbers of Strategic Offensive Arms as of the Date of Signature of the Treaty" and given to Ambassador V. Karpov on June 18, 1979 in Vienna, Austria.

THOMAS GRAHAM, JR.

General Counsel
United States Arms Control and Disarmament Agency

Statement of Data on the Numbers of Strategic Offensive Arms as of the Date of Signature of the Treaty

The Union of Soviet Socialist Republics declares that as of June 18, 1979, it possesses the following numbers of strategic offensive arms subject to the limitations provided for in the Treaty which is being signed today·

Launchers of ICBMs	1,398
Fixed launchers of ICBMs	1,398

Launchers of ICBMs equipped with MIRVs	608
Launchers of SLBMs	950
Launchers of SLBMs equipped with MIRVs	144
Heavy bombers	156
Heavy bombers equipped for cruise missiles capable of a range in excess of 600 kilometers	0
Heavy bombers equipped only for ASBMs	0
ASBMs	0
ASBMs equipped with MIRVs	0

June 18, 1979

V. KARPOV

Chief of the U.S.S.R. Delegation to the Strategic Arms Limitation Talks

Translation certified by:
W.D. Krimer,
Senior Language Officer,
Division of Language Services, U.S. Department of State

WILLIAM D. KRIMER

Joint Statement of Principles and Basic Guidelines for Subsequent Negotiations on the Limitation of Strategic Arms

The United States of America and the Union of Soviet Socialist Republics, hereinafter referred to as the Parties,

Having concluded the Treaty on the Limitation of Strategic Offensive Arms,

Reaffirming that the strengthening of strategic stability meets the interests of the Parties and the interests of international security,

Convinced that early agreement on the further limitation and further reduction of strategic arms would serve to strengthen international peace and security and to reduce the risk of outbreak of nuclear war,

Have agreed as follows:

First, The Parties will continue to pursue negotiations, in accordance with the principle of equality and equal security, on measures for the further limitation and reduction in the numbers of strategic arms, as well as for their further qualitative limitation.

In furtherance of existing agreements between the Parties on the limitation and reduction of strategic arms, the Parties will continue, for the purposes of reducing and averting the risk of outbreak of nuclear war, to seek measures to strengthen strategic stability by, among other things, limitations on strategic offensive arms most destabilizing to the strategic balance and by measures to reduce and to avert the risk of surprise attack.

Second. Further limitations and reductions of strategic arms must be subject to adequate verification by national technical means, using additionally, as appropriate, cooperative measures contributing to the effectiveness of verification by national technical means. The Parties will seek to strengthen verification and to perfect the operation of the Standing Consultative Commission in order to promote assurance of compliance with the obligations assumed by the Parties.

Third. The Parties shall pursue in the course of these negotiations, taking into consideration factors that determine the strategic situation, the following objectives:

1) significant and substantial reductions in the numbers of strategic offensive arms;

2) qualitative limitations on strategic offensive arms, including restrictions on the development, testing, and deployment of new types of strategic offensive arms and on the modernization of existing strategic offensive arms;

3) resolution of the issues included in the Protocol to the Treaty Between the United States of America and the Union of Soviet Socialist Republics on the Limitation of Strategic Offensive Arms in the context of the negotiations relating to the implementation of the principles and objectives set out herein.

Fourth. The Parties will consider other steps to ensure and enhance strategic stability, to ensure the equality and equal security of the Parties, and to implement the above principles and objectives. Each Party will be free to raise any issue relative to the further limitation of strategic arms. The Parties will also consider further joint measures, as appropriate, to strengthen international peace and security and to reduce the risk of outbreak of nuclear war.

Vienna, June 18, 1979

For the United States of America

JIMMY CARTER

President of the United States of America

For the Union of Soviet Socialist Republics

L. BREZHNEV

General Secretary of the CPSU, Chairman of the Presidium of the Supreme Soviet of the U.S.S.R.

Soviet Backfire Statement

On June 16, 1979, President Brezhnev handed President Carter the following written statement [original Russian text was attached]:

"The Soviet side informs the US side that the Soviet 'Tu-22M' airplane, called 'Backfire' in the USA, is a medium-range bomber, and that it does not intend to give this airplane the capability of operating at intercontinental distances. In this connection, the Soviet side states that it will not increase the radius of action of this airplane in such a way as to enable it to strike targets on the territory of the USA. Nor does it intend to give it such a capability in any other manner, including by in-flight refueling. At the same time, the Soviet side states that it will not increase the production rate of this airplane as compared to the present rate."

President Brezhnev confirmed that the Soviet Backfire production rate would not exceed 30 per year.

President Carter stated that the United States enters into the SALT II Agreement on the basis of the commitments contained in the Soviet statement and that it considers the carrying out of these commitments to be essential to the obligations assumed under the Treaty.

CYRUS VANCE

Convention on the Physical Protection of Nuclear Material

The Convention on the Physical Protection of Nuclear Material provides for certain levels of physical protection during international shipment of nuclear material. It also establishes a general framework for cooperation among states in the recovery and return of stolen nuclear material. Further, the Convention defines certain serious offenses involving nuclear material which state parties are to make punishable and for which offenders will be subject to a system of extradition or submission for prosecution.

This Convention resulted from a U.S. initiative in 1974, which was subsequently endorsed at the 1975 Non-Proliferation Treaty review conference. Two provisions of the Nuclear Non-Proliferation Act of 1978 call for negotiation of such a convention. Negotiation of the Convention was begun in 1977.

The Convention was adopted at a meeting of government representatives in Vienna on October 26, 1979, and signed by the United States on March 3, 1980. The U.S. Senate provided its advice and consent for the ratification of the Convention on July 30, 1981, by a vote of 98-0.

Legislation to implement the Convention is currently pending in the Congress.

Convention on the Physical Protection of Nuclear Material

Signed at New York March 3, 1980
Ratification advised by U.S. Senate July 30, 1981
Ratified by U.S. President September 4, 1981

The States Parties to This Convention,

Recognizing the right of all States to develop and apply nuclear energy for peaceful purposes and their legitimate interests in the potential benefits to be derived from the peaceful application of nuclear energy,

Convinced of the need for facilitating international co-operation in the peaceful application of nuclear energy,

Desiring to avert the potential dangers posed by the unlawful taking and use of nuclear material,

Convinced that offenses relating to nuclear material are a matter of grave concern and that there is an urgent need to adopt appropriate and effective measures to ensure the prevention, detection and punishment of such offenses,

Aware of the Need for international co-operation to establish, in conformity with the national law of each State Party and with this Convention, effective measures for the physical protection of nuclear material,

Convinced that this Convention should facilitate the safe transfer of nuclear material,

Stressing also the importance of the physical protection of nuclear material in domestic use, storage and transport,

Recognizing the importance of effective physical protection of nuclear material used for military purposes, and understanding that such material is and will continue to be accorded stringent physical protection,

Have Agreed as follows:

Article 1

For the purposes of this Convention:

(*a*) "nuclear material" means plutonium except that with isotopic concentration exceeding 80% in plutonium-238; uranium-233; uranium enriched in the isotopes 235 or 233; uranium containing the mixture of isotopes as occurring in nature other than in the form of ore or ore-residue; any material containing one or more of the foregoing;

(*b*) "uranium enriched in the 235 or 233" means uranium containing the isotopes 235 or 233 or both in an amount such that the abundance ratio of the sum of these isotopes to the isotope 238 is greater than the ratio of the isotope 235 to the isotope 238 occurring in nature;

(*c*) "international nuclear transport" means the carriage of a consignment of nuclear material by any means of transportation intended to go beyond the territory of the State where the shipment originates beginning with the departure from a facility of the shipper in that State and ending with the arrival at a facility of the receiver within the State of ultimate destination.

Article 2

1. The Convention shall apply to nuclear material used for peaceful purposes while in international nuclear transport.

279

2. With the exception of articles 3 and 4 and paragraph 3 of article 5, this Convention shall also apply to nuclear material used for peaceful purposes while in domestic use, storage and transport.

3. Apart from the commitments expressly undertaken by States Parties in the articles covered by paragraph 2 with respect to nuclear material used for peaceful purposes while in domestic use, storage and transport, nothing in this Convention shall be interpreted as affecting the sovereign rights of a State regarding the domestic use, storage and transport of such nuclear material.

Article 3

Each State Party shall take appropriate steps within the framework of its national law and consistent with international law to ensure as far as practicable that, during international nuclear transport, nuclear material within its territory, or on board a ship or aircraft under its jurisdiction insofar as such ship or aircraft is engaged in the transport to or from that State, is protected at the levels described in Annex I.

Article 4

1. Each State Party shall not export or authorize the export of nuclear material unless the State Party has received assurances that such material will be protected during the international nuclear transport at the levels described in Annex I.

2. Each State Party shall not import or authorize the import of nuclear material from a State not party to this Convention unless the State Party has received assurances that such material will during the international nuclear transport be protected at the levels described in Annex I.

3. A State Party shall not allow the transit of its territory by land or internal waterways or through its airports or seaports of nuclear material between States that are not parties to this Convention unless the State Party has received assurances as far as practicable that this nuclear material will be protected during international nuclear transport at the levels described in Annex I.

4. Each State Party shall apply within the framework of its national law the levels of physical protection described in Annex I to nuclear material being transported from a part of that State to another part of the same State through international waters or airspace.

5. The State Party responsible for receiving assurances that the nuclear material will be protected at the levels described in Annex I according to paragraphs 1 to 3 shall identify and inform in advance States which the nuclear material is expected to transit by land or internal waterways, or whose airports or seaports it is expected to enter.

6. The responsibility for obtaining assurances referred to in paragraph 1 may be transferred, by mutual agreement, to the State Party involved in the transport as the importing State.

7. Nothing in this article shall be interpreted as in any way affecting the territorial sovereignty and jurisdiction of a State, including that over its airspace and territorial sea.

Article 5

1. States Parties shall identify and make known to each other directly or through the International Atomic Energy Agency their central authority and point of contact having responsibility for physical protection of nuclear material and for co-ordinating recovery and response operations in the event of any unauthorized removal, use or alteration of nuclear material or in the event of credible threat thereof.

2. In the case of theft, robbery or any other unlawful taking of nuclear material or of credible threat thereof, States Parties shall, in accordance with their national law, provide co-operation and assistance to the maximum feasible extent in the recovery and protection of such material to any State that so requests. In particular:

(a) a State Party shall take appropriate steps to inform as soon as possible other States, which appear to it to be concerned, of any theft, robbery or other unlawful taking of nuclear material or credible threat thereof and to inform, where appropriate, international organizations;

(b) as appropriate, the States Parties concerned shall exchange information with each other or international organizations with a view to protecting threatened nuclear material, verifying the integrity of the shipping container, or recovering unlawfully taken nuclear material and shall:

(i) co-ordinate their efforts through diplomatic and other agreed channels;

(ii) render assistance, if requested;

(iii) ensure the return of nuclear material stolen or missing as a consequence of the above-mentioned events.

The means of implementation of this co-operation shall be determined by the States Parties concerned.

3. States Parties shall co-operate and consult as appropriate, with each other directly or through international organizations, with a view to obtaining guidance on the design, maintenance and improvement of systems of physical protection of nuclear material in international transport.

Article 6

1. States Parties shall take appropriate measures consistent with their national law to protect the confidentiality of any information which they receive in confidence by virtue of the provisions of this Convention from another State Party or through participation in an activity carried out for the implementation of this Convention. If States Parties provide information to international organizations in confidence, steps shall be taken to ensure that the confidentiality of such information is protected.

2. States Parties shall not be required by this Convention to provide any information which they are not permitted to communicate pursuant to national law or which would jeopardize the security of the State concerned or the physical protection of nuclear material.

Article 7

1. The intentional commission of:

(a) an act without lawful authority which constitutes the receipt, possession, use, transfer, alteration, disposal or dispersal of nuclear material and which causes or is likely to cause death or serious injury to any person or substantial damage to property;

(b) a theft or robbery of nuclear material;

(c) an embezzlement or fraudulent obtaining of nuclear material;

(d) an act constituting a demand for nuclear material by threat or use of force or by any other form of intimidation;

(e)   a threat:

(i)   to use nuclear material to cause death or serious injury to any person or substantial property damage, or

(ii)   to commit an offense described in subparagraph (b) in order to compel a natural or legal person, international organization or State to do or to refrain from doing any act;

(f)   an attempt to commit any offense described in paragraphs (a), (b) or (c); and

(g)   an act which constitutes participation in any offense described in paragraphs (a) to (f) shall be made a punishable offense by each State Party under its national law.

2. Each State Party shall make the offenses described in this article punishable by appropriate penalties which take into account their grave nature.

Article 8

1. Each State Party shall take such measures as may be necessary to establish its jurisdiction over the offenses set forth in article 7 in the following cases:

(a)   when the offense is committed in the territory of that State or on board a ship or aircraft registered in that State;

(b)   when the alleged offender is a national of that State.

2. Each State Party shall likewise take such measures as may be necessary to establish its jurisdiction over these offenses in cases where the alleged offender is present in its territory and it does not extradite him pursuant to article 11 to any of the States mentioned in paragraph 1.

3. This Convention does not exclude any criminal jurisdiction exercised in accordance with national law.

4. In addition to the State Parties mentioned in paragraphs 1 and 2, each State Party may, consistent with international law, establish its jurisdiction over the offenses set forth in article 7 when it is involved in international nuclear transport as the exporting or importing State.

Article 9

Upon being satisfied that the circumstances so warrant, the State Party in whose territory the alleged offender is present shall take appropriate measures, including detention, under its national law to ensure his presence for the purpose of prosecution or extradition. Measures taken according to this article shall be notified without delay to the States required to establish jurisdiction pursuant to article 8 and, where appropriate, all other States concerned.

Article 10

The State Party in whose territory the alleged offender is present shall, if it does not extradite him, submit, without exception whatsoever and without undue delay, the case to its competent authorities for the purpose of prosecution, through proceedings in accordance with the laws of that State.

Article 11

1. The offenses in article 7 shall be deemed to be included as extraditable offenses in any extradition treaty existing between States Parties. States Parties undertake to include those offenses as extraditable offenses in every future extradition treaty to be concluded between them.

2. If a State Party which makes extradition conditional on the existence of a treaty receives a request for extradition from another State Party with which it has no extradition treaty, it may at its option consider this Convention as the legal basis for extradition in respect of those offenses. Extradition shall be subject to the other conditions provided by the law of the requested State.

3. States Parties which do not make extradition conditional on the existence of a treaty shall recognize those offenses as extraditable offenses between themselves subject to the conditions provided by the law of the requested State.

4. Each of the offenses shall be treated, for the purpose of extradition between States Parties, as if it had been committed not only in the place in which it occurred but also in the territories of the States Parties required to establish their jurisdiction in accordance with paragraph 1 of article 8.

Article 12

Any person regarding whom proceedings are being carried out in connection with any of the offenses set forth in article 7 shall be guaranteed fair treatment at all stages of the proceedings.

Article 13

1. States Parties shall afford one another the greatest measure of assistance in connection with criminal proceedings brought in respect of the offenses set forth in article 7, including the supply of evidence at their disposal necessary for the proceedings. The law of the State requested shall apply in all cases.

2. The provisions of paragraph 1 shall not affect obligations under any other treaty, bilateral or multilateral, which governs or will govern, in whole or in part, mutual assistance in criminal matters.

Article 14

1. Each State Party shall inform the depositary of its laws and regulations which give effect to this Convention. The depositary shall communicate such information periodically to all States Parties.

2. The State Party where an alleged offender is prosecuted shall, wherever practicable, first communicate the final outcome of the proceedings to the States directly concerned. The State Party shall also communicate the final outcome to the depositary who shall inform all States.

3. Where an offense involves nuclear material used for peaceful purposes in domestic use, storage or transport, and both the alleged offender and the nuclear material remain in the territory of the State Party in which the offense was committed, nothing in this Convention shall be interpreted as requiring that State Party to provide information concerning criminal proceedings arising out of such an offense.

Article 15

The Annexes constitute an integral part of this Convention.

Article 16

1. A conference of States Parties shall be convened by the depositary five years after the entry into force of this Convention to review the implementation of the Convention and its adequacy as concerns the preamble, the whole of the operative part and the annexes in the light of the then prevailing situation.

2. At intervals of not less than five years thereafter, the majority of States Parties may obtain, by submitting a proposal to this effect to the depositary, the convening of further conferences with the same objective.

Article 17

1. In the event of a dispute between two or more States Parties concerning the interpretation or application of this Convention, such States Parties shall consult with a view to the settlement of the dispute by negotiation, or by any other peaceful means of settling disputes acceptable to all parties to the dispute.

2. Any dispute of this character which cannot be settled in the manner prescribed in paragraph 1 shall, at the request of any party to such dispute, be submitted to arbitration or referred to the International Court of Justice for decision. Where a dispute is submitted to arbitration, if, within six months from the date of the request, the parties to the dispute are unable to agree on the organization of the arbitration, a party may request the President of the International Court of Justice or the Secretary-General of the United Nations to appoint one or more arbitrators. In case of conflicting requests by the parties to the dispute, the request to the Secretary-General of the United Nations shall have priority.

3. Each State Party may at the time of signature, ratification, acceptance or approval of this Convention or accession thereto declare that it does not consider itself bound by either or both of the dispute settlement procedures provided for in paragraph 2. The other States Parties shall not be bound by a dispute settlement procedure provided for in paragraph 2, with respect to a State Party which has made a reservation to that procedure.

4. Any State Party which has made a reservation in accordance with paragraph 3 may at any time withdraw that reservation by notification to the depositary.

Article 18

1. This Convention shall be open for signature by all States at the Headquarters of the International Atomic Energy Agency in Vienna and at the Headquarters of the United Nations in New York from 3 March 1980 until its entry into force.

2. This Convention is subject to ratification, acceptance or approval by the signatory States.

3. After its entry into force, this Convention will be open for accession by all States.

4. (a) This Convention shall be open for signature or accession by international organizations and regional organizations of an integration or other nature, provided that any such organization is constituted by sovereign States and has competence in respect of the negotiation, conclusion and application of international agreements in matters covered by this Convention.

   (b) In matters within their competence, such organizations shall, on their own behalf, exercise the rights and fulfill the responsibilities which this Convention attributes to States Parties.

(c) When becoming party to this Convention such an organization shall communicate to the depositary a declaration indicating which States are members thereof and which articles of this Convention do not apply to it.

(d) Such an organization shall not hold any vote additional to those of its Member States.

5. Instruments of ratification, acceptance, approval or accession shall be deposited with the depositary.

Article 19

1. This Convention shall enter into force on the thirtieth day following the date of deposit of the twenty first instrument of ratification, acceptance or approval with the depositary.

2. For each State ratifying, accepting, approving or acceding to the Convention after the date of deposit of the twenty first instrument of ratification, acceptance or approval, the Convention shall enter into force on the thirtieth day after the deposit by such State of its instrument of ratification, acceptance, approval or accession.

Article 20

1. Without prejudice to article 16 a State Party may propose amendments to this Convention. The proposed amendment shall be submitted to the depositary who shall circulate it immediately to all States Parties. If a majority of States Parties request the depositary to convene a conference to consider the proposed amendments, the depositary shall invite all States Parties to attend such a conference to begin not sooner than thirty days after the invitations are issued. Any amendment adopted at the conference by a two-thirds majority of all States Parties shall be promptly circulated by the depositary to all States Parties.

2. The amendment shall enter into force for each State Party that deposits its instrument of ratification, acceptance or approval of the amendment on the thirtieth day after the date on which two thirds of the States Parties have deposited their instruments of ratification, acceptance or approval with the depositary. Thereafter, the amendment shall enter into force for any other State Party on the day on which that State Party deposits its instrument of ratification, acceptance or approval of the amendment.

Article 21

1. Any State Party may denounce this Convention by written notification to the depositary.

2. Denunciation shall take effect one hundred and eighty days following the date on which notification is received by the depositary.

Article 22

The depositary shall promptly notify all States of:

(a) each signature of this Convention;

(b) each deposit of an instrument of ratification, acceptance, approval or accession;

(c) any reservation or withdrawal in accordance with article 17;

(d) any communication made by an organization in accordance with paragraph 4(c) of article 18;

(e) the entry into force of this Convention;

(f) the entry into force of any amendment to this Convention; and

(g) any denunciation made under article 21.

Article 23

The original of this Convention, of which the Arabic, Chinese, English, French, Russian and Spanish texts are equally authentic, shall be deposited with the Director General of the International Atomic Energy Agency who shall send certified copies thereof to all States.

Annex I

Levels of Physical Protection To Be Applied in International Transport of Nuclear Material as Categorized in Annex II

1. Levels of physical protection for nuclear material during storage incidental to international nuclear transport include:

(*a*) For Category III materials, storage within an area to which access is controlled;

(*b*) For Category II materials, storage within an area under constant surveillance by guards or electronic devices, surrounded by a physical barrier with a limited number of points of entry under appropriate control or any area with an equivalent level of physical protection;

(*c*) For Category I material, storage within a protected area as defined for Category II above, to which, in addition, access is restricted to persons whose trustworthiness has been determined, and which is under surveillance by guards who are in close communication with appropriate response forces. Specific measures taken in this context should have as their object the detection and prevention of any assault, unauthorized access or unauthorized removal of material.

2. Levels of physical protection for nuclear material during international transport include:

(*a*) For Category II and III materials, transportation shall take place under special precautions including prior arrangements among sender, receiver, and carrier, and prior agreement between natural or legal persons subject to the jurisdiction and regulation of exporting and importing States, specifying time, place and procedures for transferring transport responsibility;

(*b*) For Category I materials, transportation shall take place under special precautions identified above for transportation of Category II and III materials, and in addition, under constant surveillance by escorts and under conditions which assure close communication with appropriate response forces;

(*c*) For natural uranium other than in the form of ore or ore-residue, transportation protection for quantities exceeding 500 kilograms U shall include advance notification of shipment specifying mode of transport, expected time of arrival and confirmation of receipt of shipment.

IN WITNESS WHEREOF, the undersigned, being duly authorized, have signed this Convention, opened for signature at Vienna and at New York on 3 March 1980.

Annex II

Table: Categorization of Nuclear Material

Material	Form	Category I	II	III[3]
1. Plutonium[1]	Unirradiated[2]	2 kg or more	Less than 2 kg but more than 500 g.	500 g or less but more than 15 g.
2. Uranium-235	Unirradiated[2] :			
	— uranium enriched to 20% U^{235} or more	5 kg or more	Less than 5 kg but more than 1 kg.	1 kg or less but more than 15 g.
	— uranium enriched to 10% U^{235} but less than 20%		10 kg or more	Less than 10 kg but more than 1 kg.
	— uranium enriched above natural, but less than 10% U^{235}.			10 kg or more.
3. Uranium-233	Unirradiated[2]	2 kg or more	Less than 2 kg but more than 500 g.	500 g or less but more than 15 g.
4. Irradiated fuel			Depleted or natural uranium, thorium or low-enriched fuel (less than 10% fissile content).[4,5]	

[1] All plutonium except that with isotopic concentration exceeding 80% in plutonium-238.

[2] Material not irradiated in a reactor or material irradiated in a reactor but with a radiation level equal to or less than 100 rads/hour at one metre unshielded.

[3] Quantities not falling in Category III and natural uranium should be protected in accordance with prudent management practice.

[4] Although this level of protection is recommended, it would be open to States, upon evaluation of the specific circumstances, to assign a different category of physical protection.

[5] Other fuel which by virtue of its original fissile material content is classified as Category I and II before irradiation may be reduced one category level while the radiation level from the fuel exceeds 100 rads/hour at one metre unshielded.

Convention on the Physical Protection of Nuclear Material

Country	Date of Signature	Date of Deposit of Ratification
USA	3/3/80	
Austria	3/3/80	
Greece	3/3/80	
Dominican Republic	3/3/80	
Guatemala	3/12/80	
Panama	3/18/80	
Haiti	4/10/80	
Philippines	5/19/80	9/21/81
GDR	5/21/80	2/5/81
Paraguay	5/21/80	
USSR	5/22/80	
Belgium	6/13/80	
Denmark	6/13/80	
France	6/13/80	
FRG	6/13/80	
Ireland	6/13/80	
Italy	6/13/80	
Luxembourg	6/13/80	
Netherlands	6/13/80	
UK	6/13/80	
EURATOM	6/13/80	
Hungary	6/17/80	
Sweden	7/2/80	8/1/80
Yugoslavia	7/15/80	
Morocco	7/25/80	
Poland	8/6/80	
Canada	9/23/80	
Romania	1/15/81	
Brazil	5/15/81	
South Africa	5/18/81	
Bulgaria	6/23/81	
Finland	6/25/81	
Czechoslovakia	9/14/81	
Korea, Republic of	12/29/81	
Total	34	3

Footnotes

1. Dates given are the earliest dates on which countries signed the agreements or deposited their ratifications or accessions—whether in Washington, London, Moscow, or New York. In the case of a country that was a dependent territory which became a party through succession, the date given is the date on which the country gave notice that it would continue to be bound by the terms of the agreement.
2. The United States regards the signature and ratification by the Byelorussian S.S.R. and the Ukrainian S.S.R. as already included under the signature and ratification of the Union of Soviet Socialist Republics.
3. This total does not include actions by the Byelorussian S.S.R. and the Ukrainian S.S.R. (See footnote 2.)

86